FAIRY TAIL

55

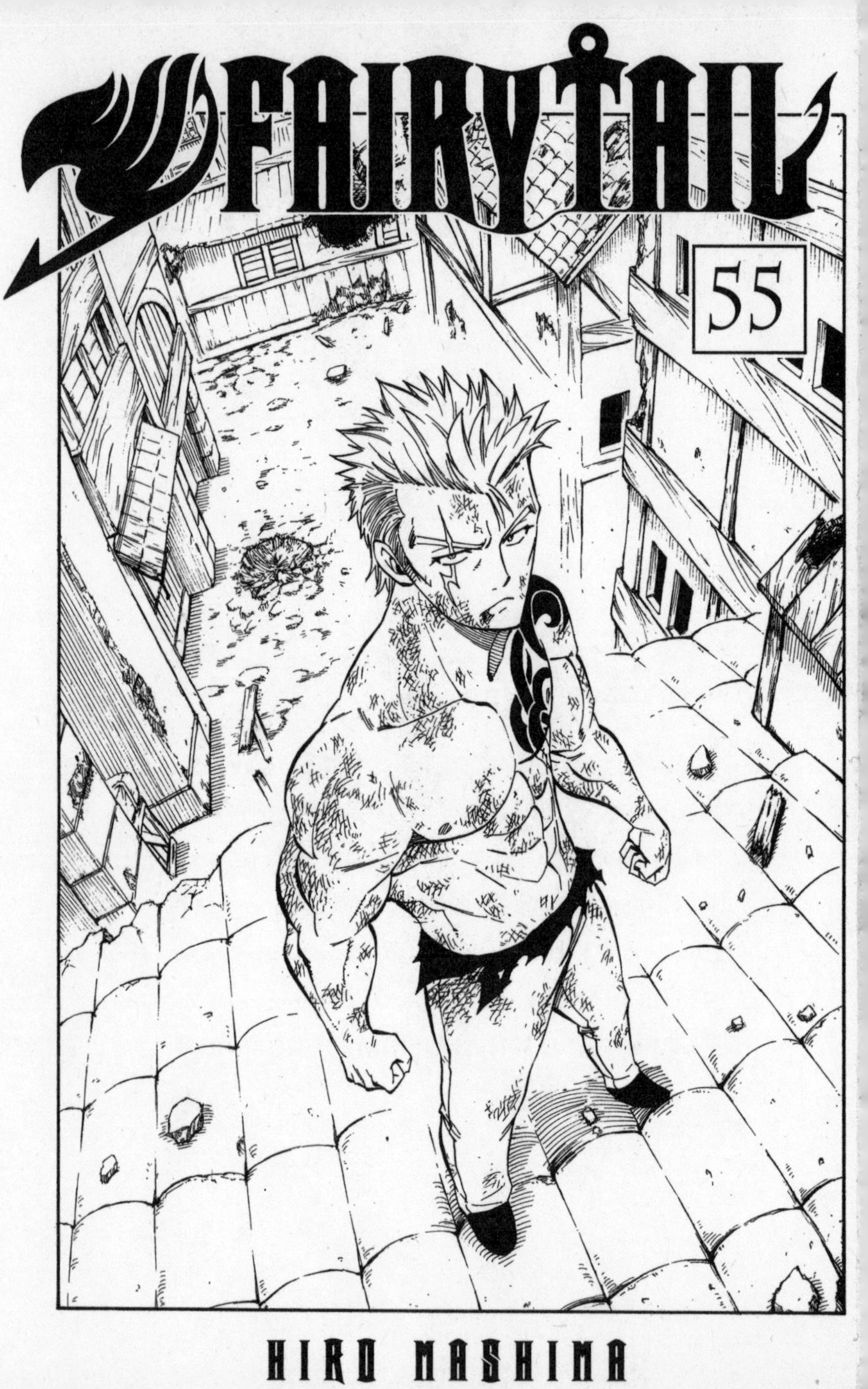

HIRO MASHIMA

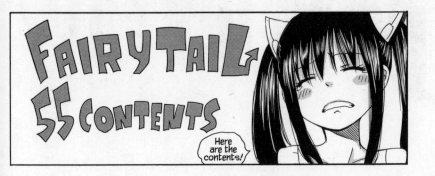

FAIRY TAIL 55 CONTENTS

Here are the contents!

FAIRY TAIL

フェアリーテイル

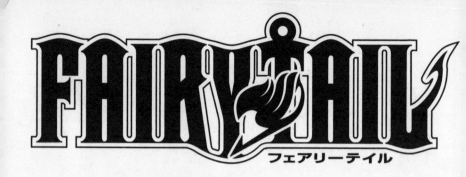

Chapter 465: 400 Years

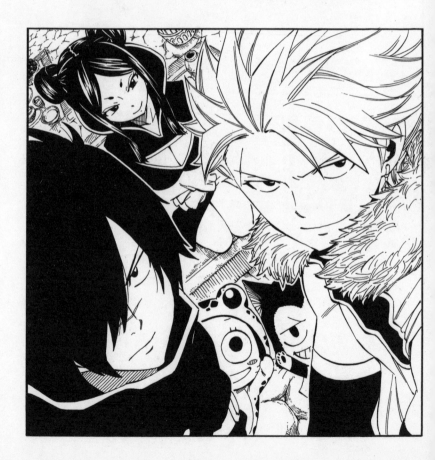

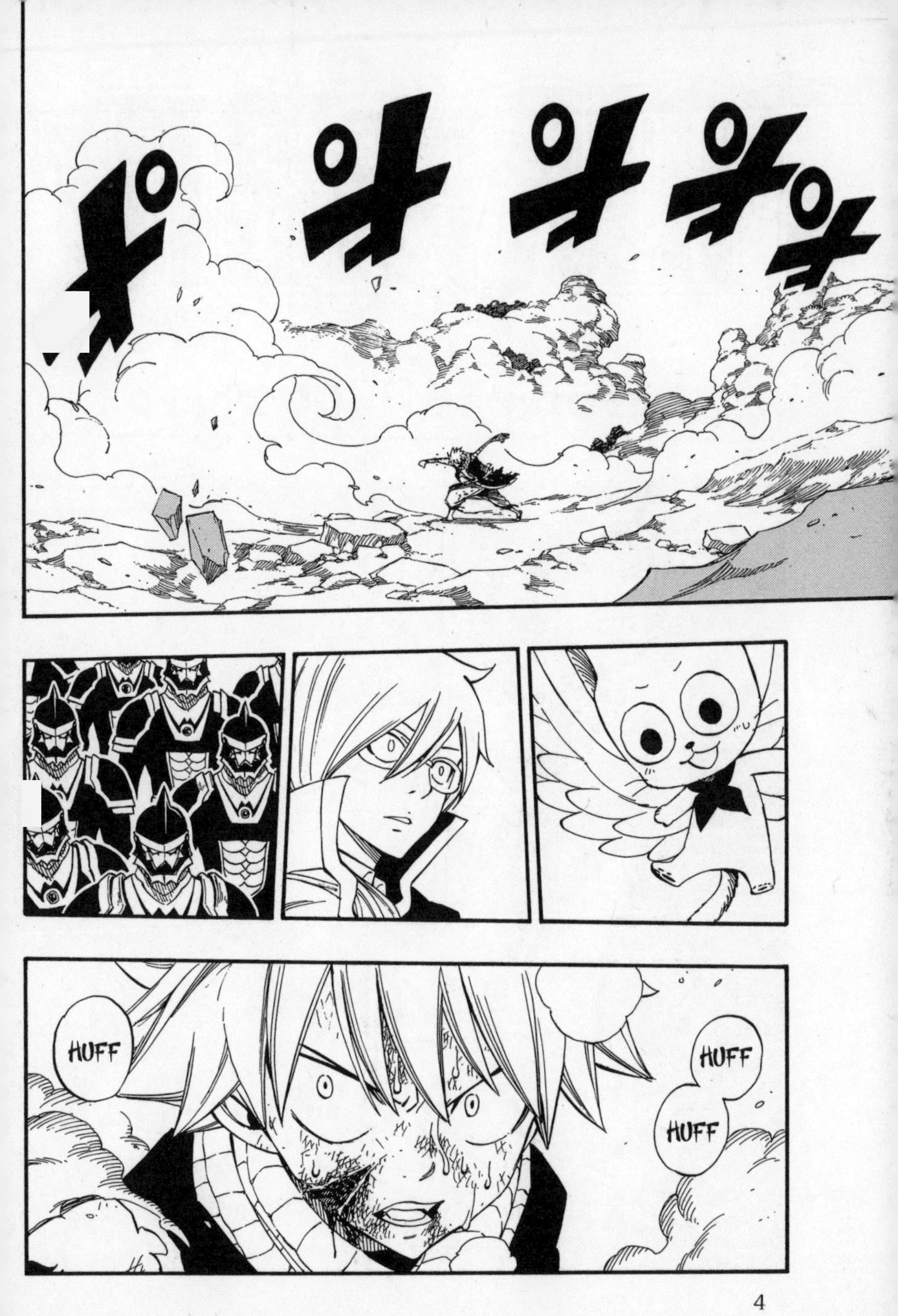
HUFF
HUFF
HUFF

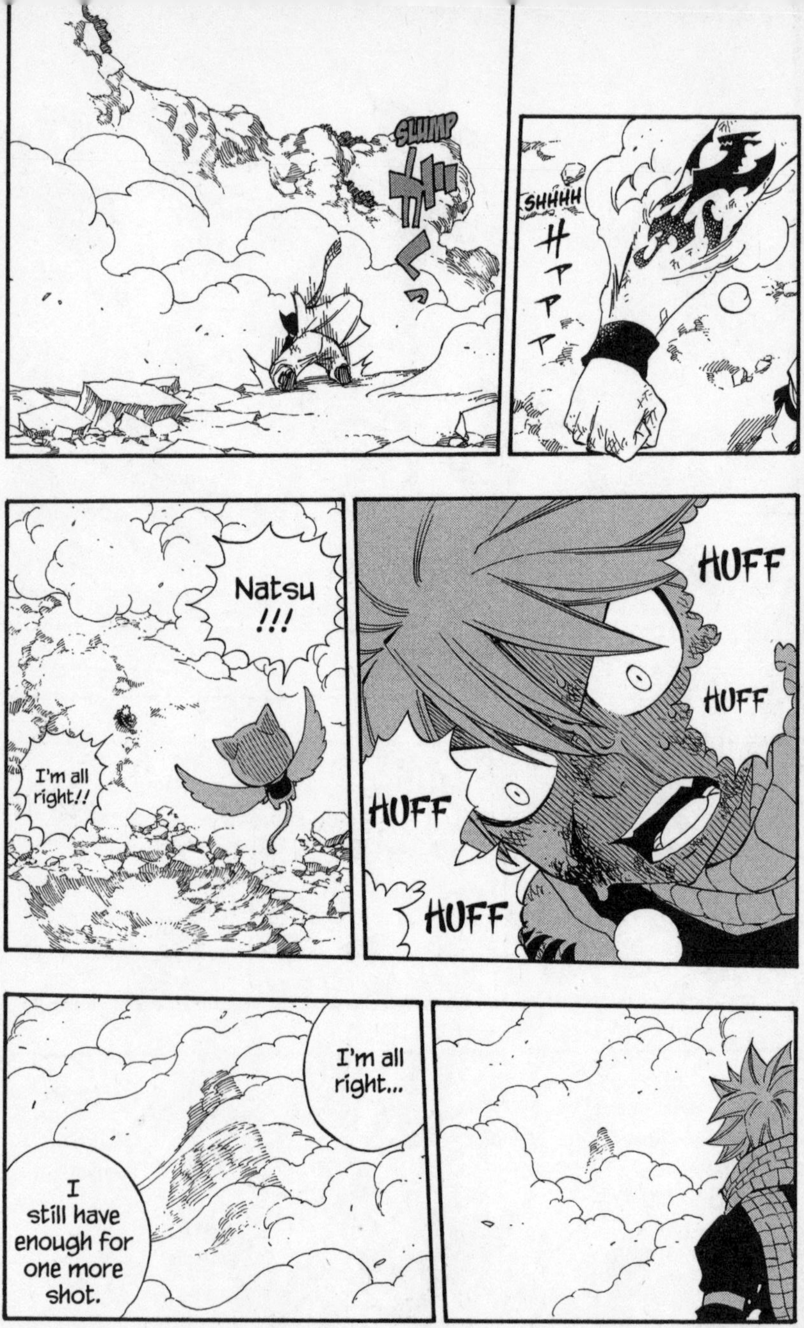
SHHHH
SLUMP
HUFF
HUFF
HUFF
HUFF
Natsu !!!
I'm all right!!
I'm all right...
I still have enough for one more shot.

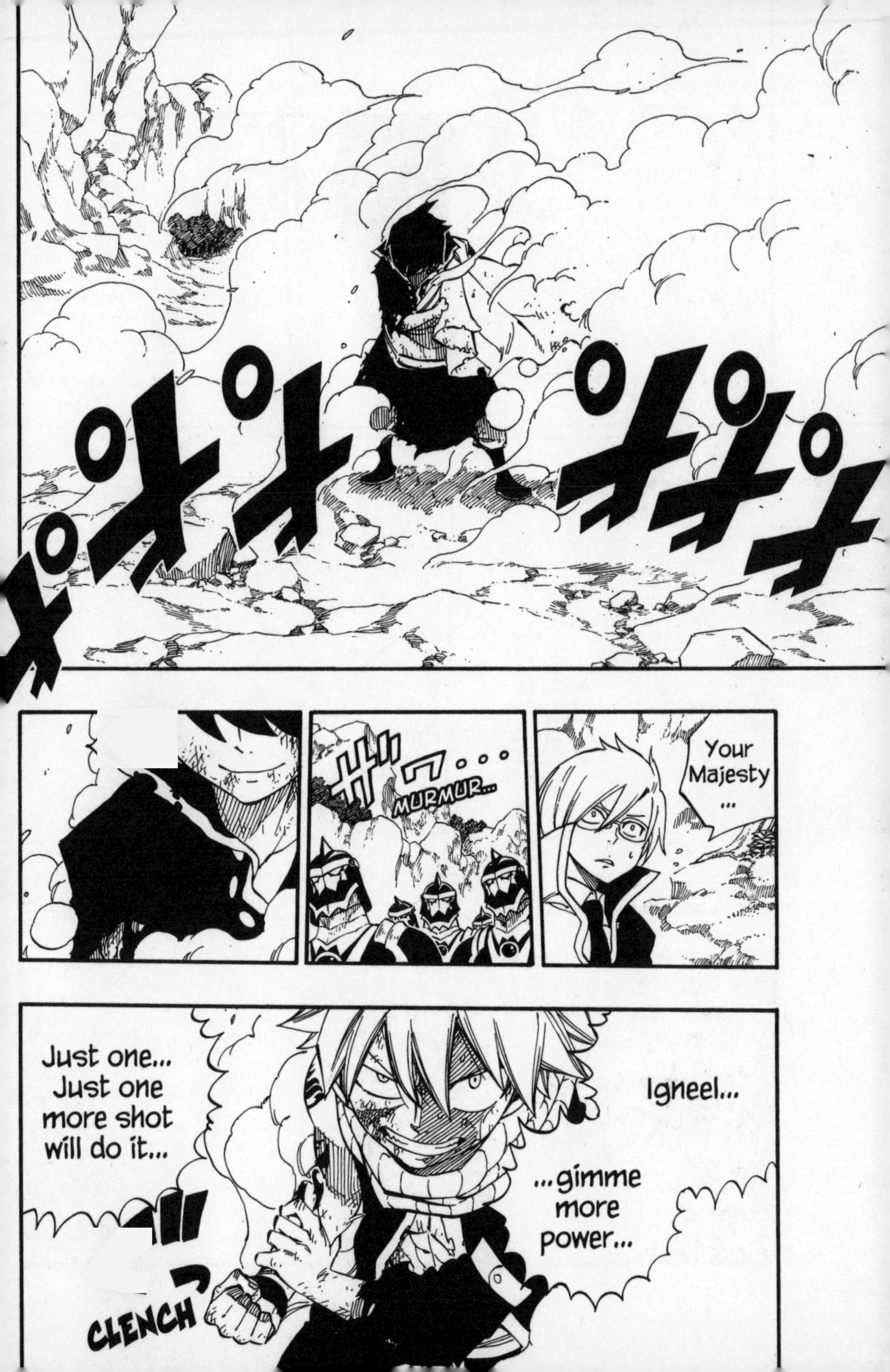
Your Majesty ...
ザワ…
MURMUR...
Igneel...
...gimme more power...
Just one... Just one more shot will do it...
CLENCH

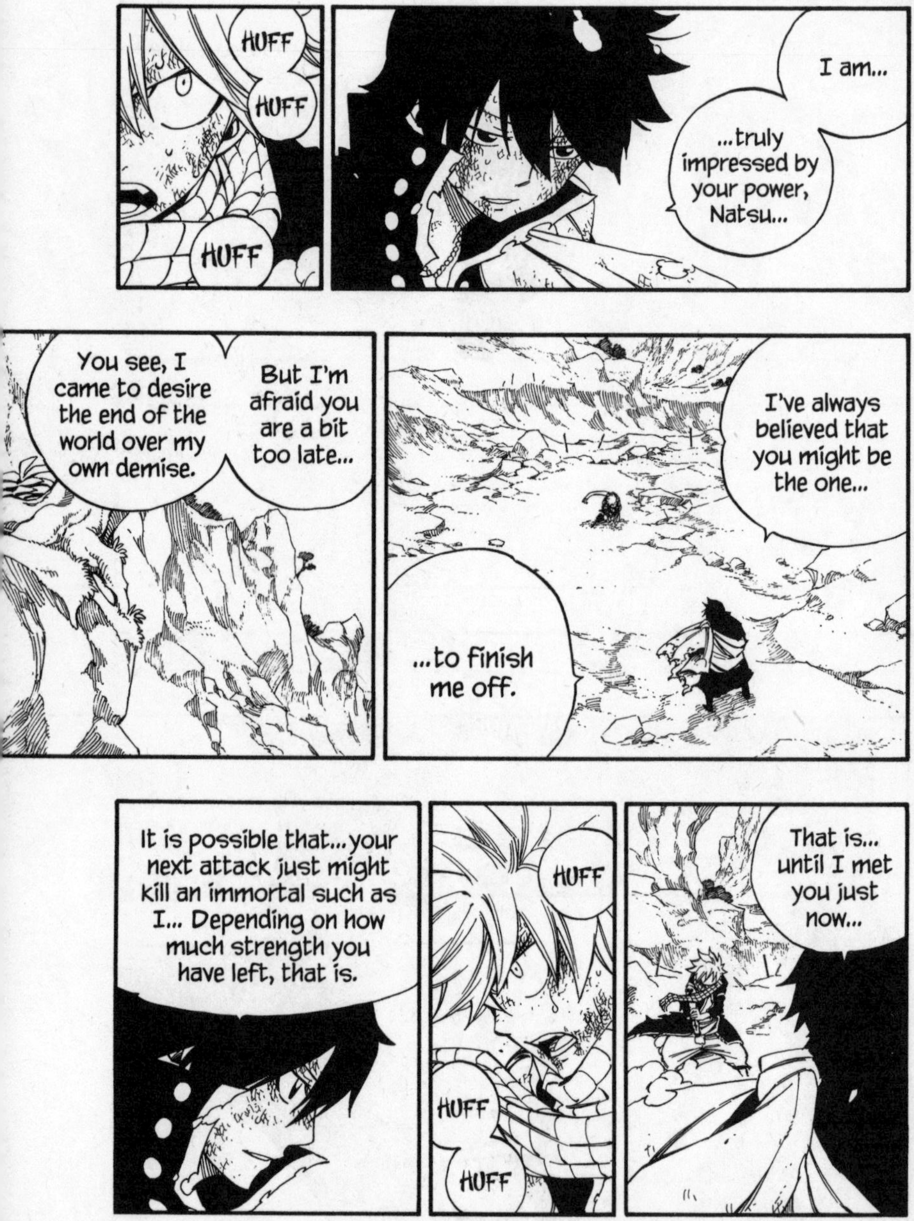
I am...
...truly impressed by your power, Natsu...
HUFF
HUFF
HUFF
I've always believed that you might be the one...
...to finish me off.
But I'm afraid you are a bit too late...
You see, I came to desire the end of the world over my own demise.
That is... until I met you just now...
HUFF
HUFF
HUFF
It is possible that...your next attack just might kill an immortal such as I... Depending on how much strength you have left, that is.

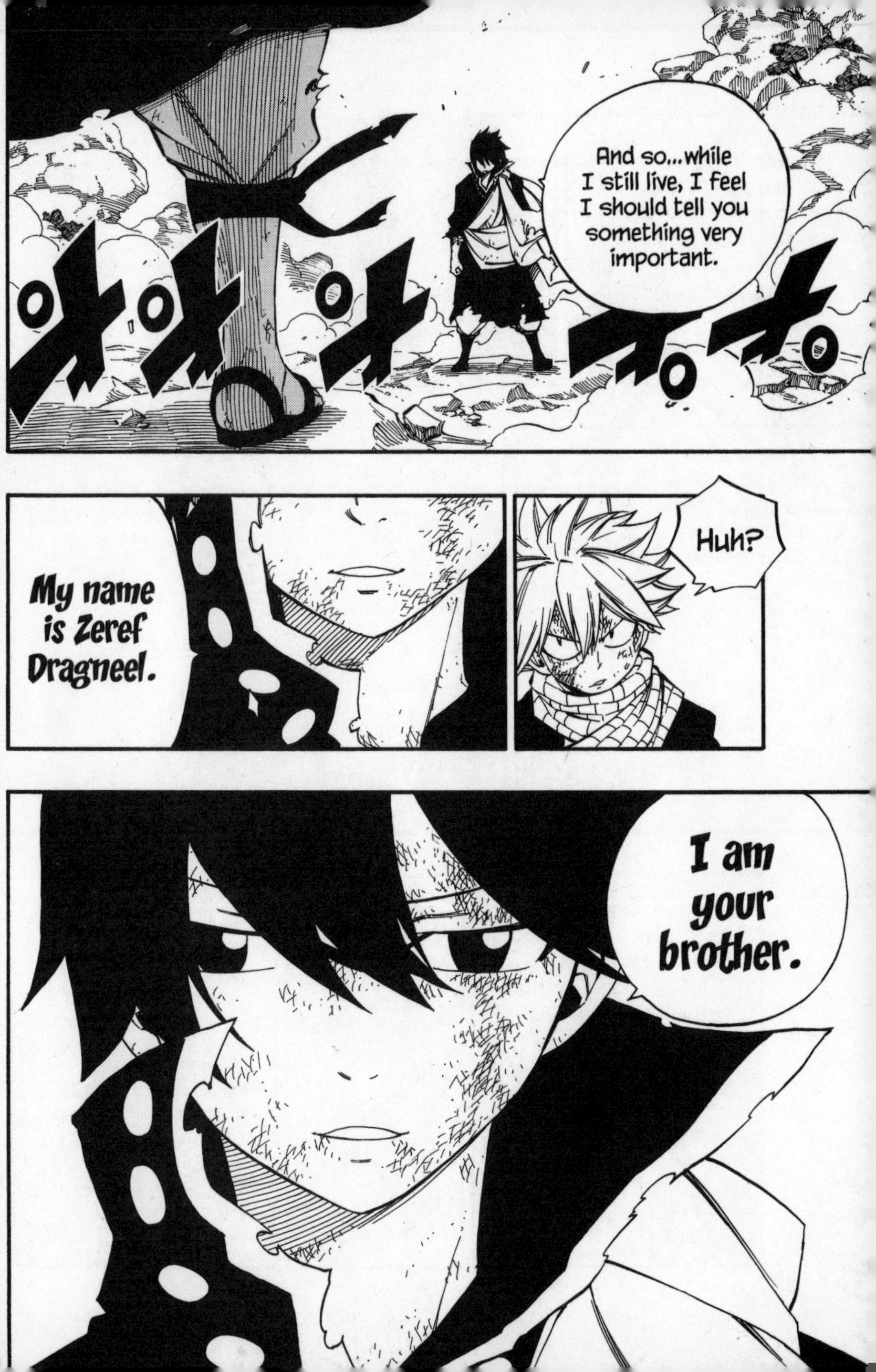
And so...while I still live, I feel I should tell you something very important.
Huh?
My name is Zeref Dragneel.
I am your brother.

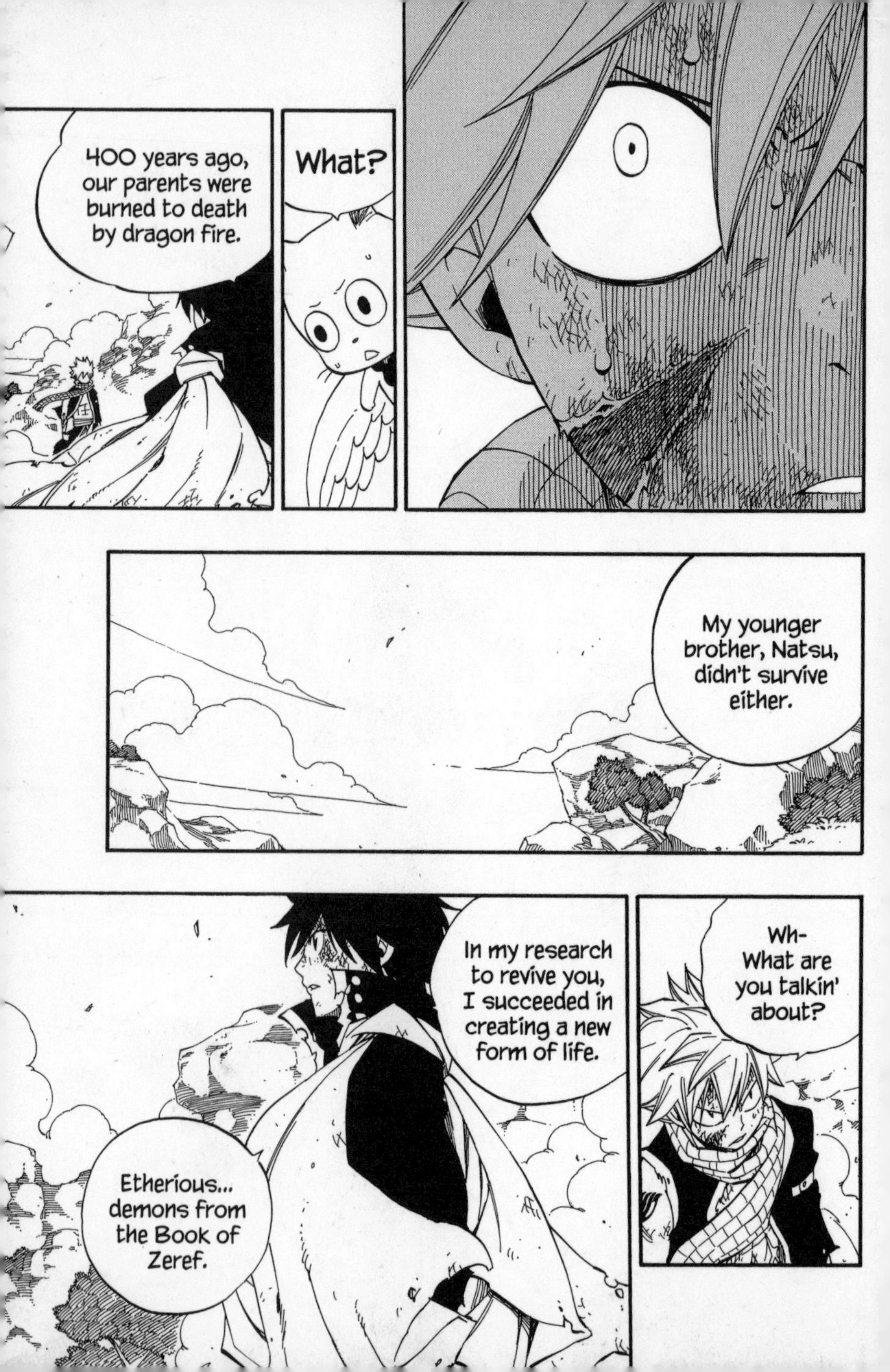
What?
400 years ago, our parents were burned to death by dragon fire.
My younger brother, Natsu, didn't survive either.
Wh- What are you talkin' about?
In my research to revive you, I succeeded in creating a new form of life.
Etherious... demons from the Book of Zeref.

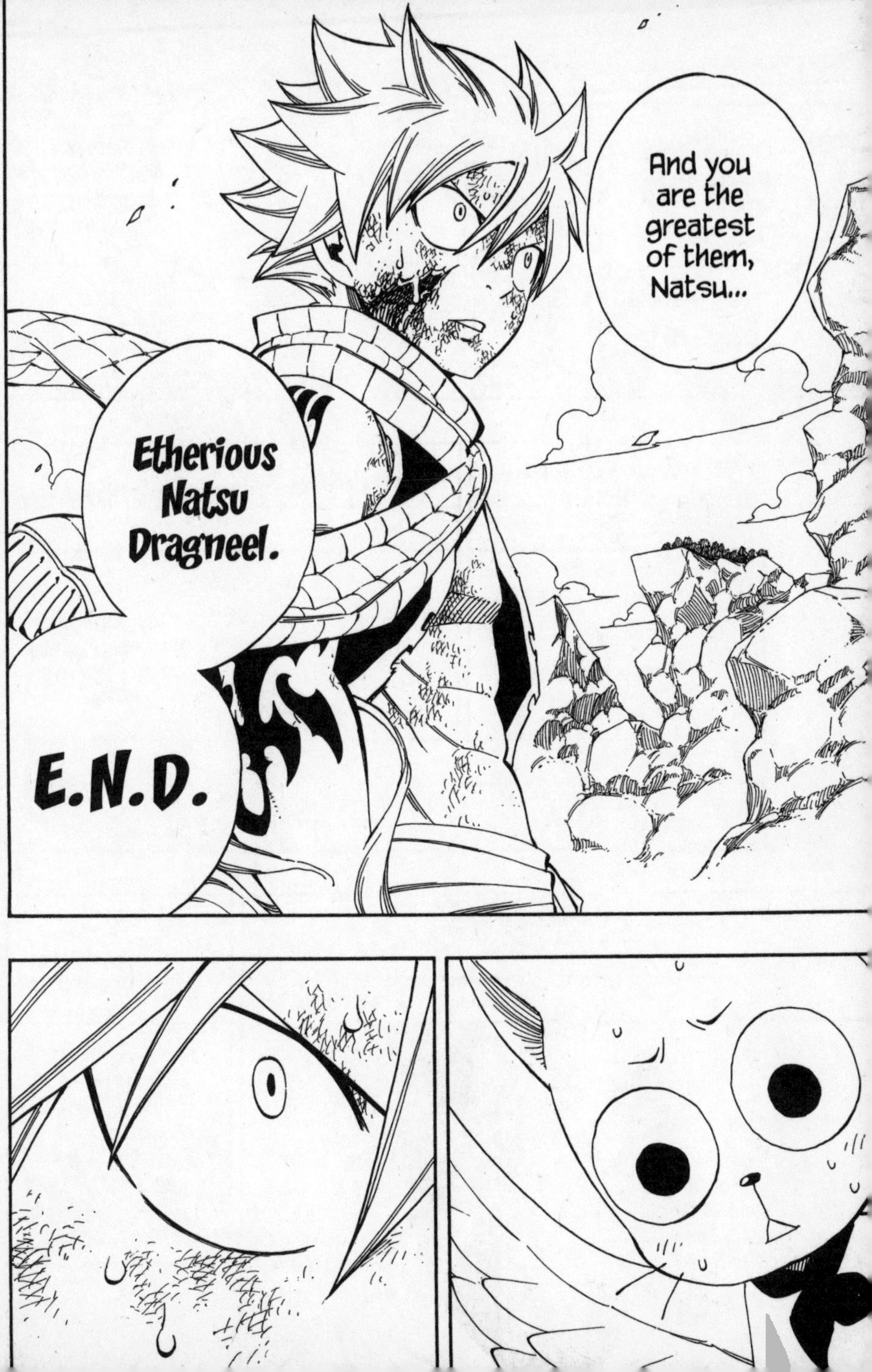
And you are the greatest of them, Natsu...
Etherious Natsu Dragneel.
E.N.D.

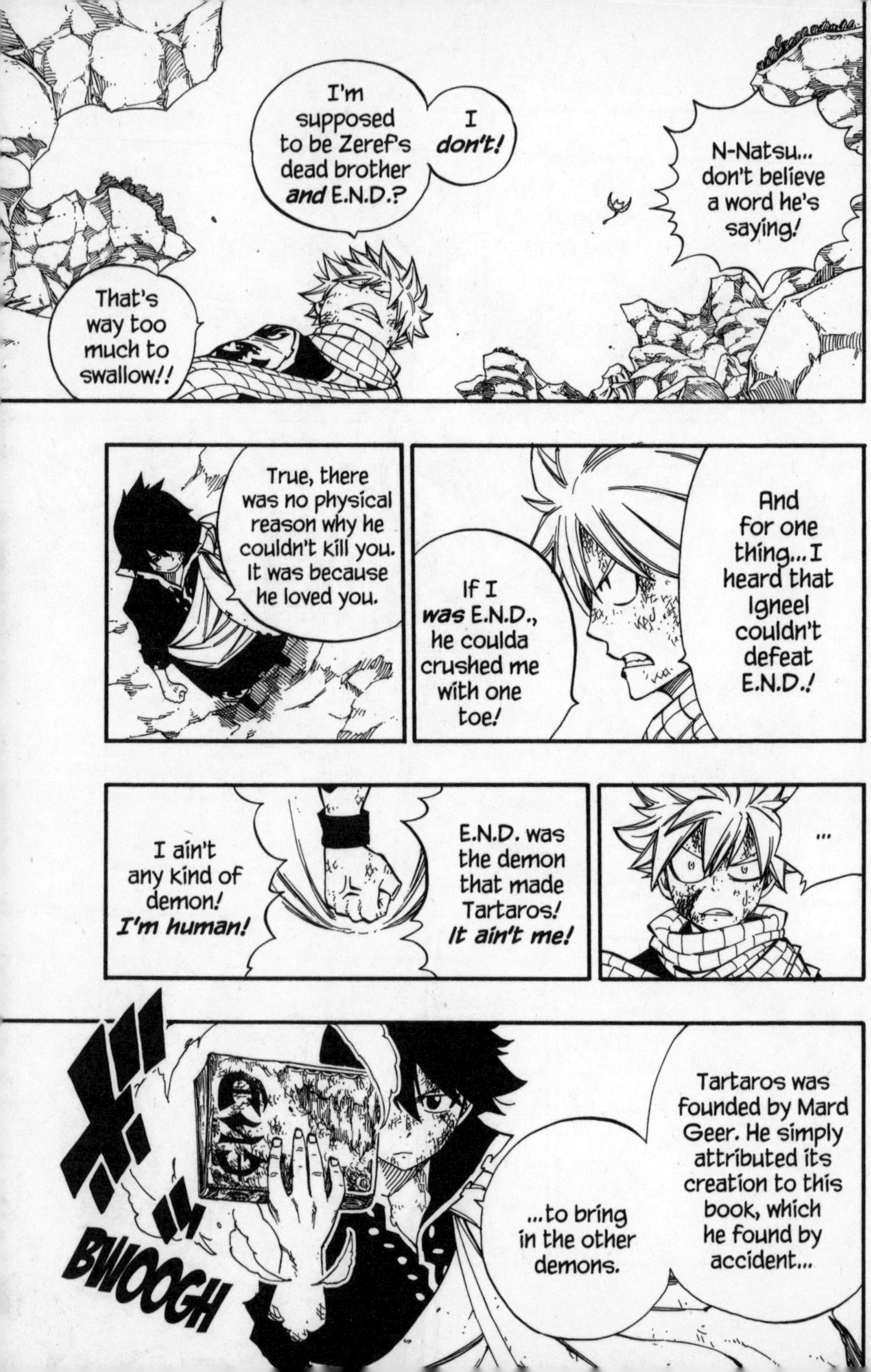
N-Natsu... don't believe a word he's saying!
I don't!
I'm supposed to be Zeref's dead brother and E.N.D.?
That's way too much to swallow!!
And for one thing... I heard that Igneel couldn't defeat E.N.D.!
If I was E.N.D., he coulda crushed me with one toe!
True, there was no physical reason why he couldn't kill you. It was because he loved you.
...
E.N.D. was the demon that made Tartaros! It ain't me!
I ain't any kind of demon! I'm human!
Tartaros was founded by Mard Geer. He simply attributed its creation to this book, which he found by accident...
...to bring in the other demons.
BWOOGH

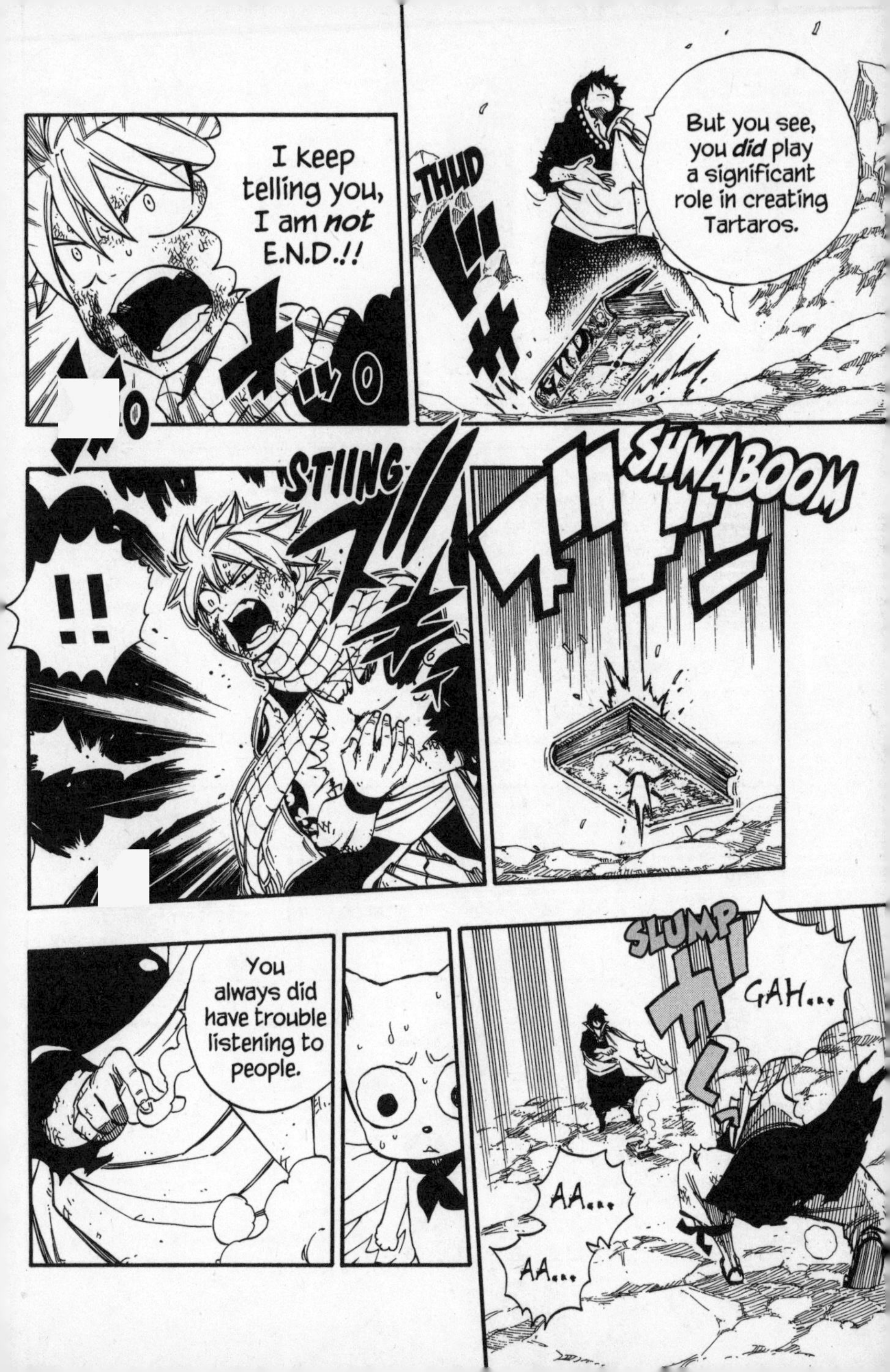
THUD
But you see, you *did* play a significant role in creating Tartaros.
I keep telling you, I am *not* E.N.D.!!
SHWABOOM
STIING
!!
SLUMP
GAH...
AA...
AA...
You always did have trouble listening to people.

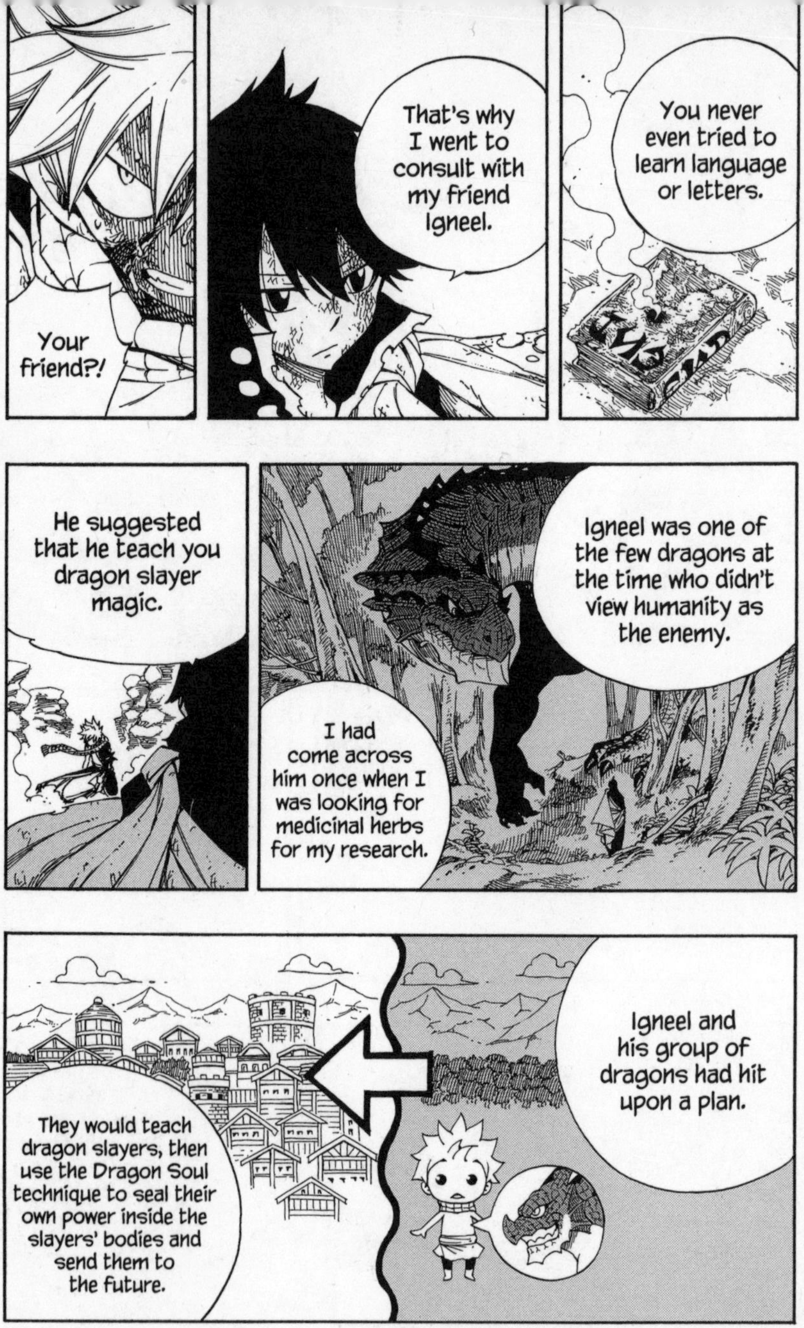
You never even tried to learn language or letters.
That's why I went to consult with my friend Igneel.
Your friend?!
Igneel was one of the few dragons at the time who didn't view humanity as the enemy.
I had come across him once when I was looking for medicinal herbs for my research.
He suggested that he teach you dragon slayer magic.
Igneel and his group of dragons had hit upon a plan.
They would teach dragon slayers, then use the Dragon Soul technique to seal their own power inside the slayers' bodies and send them to the future.

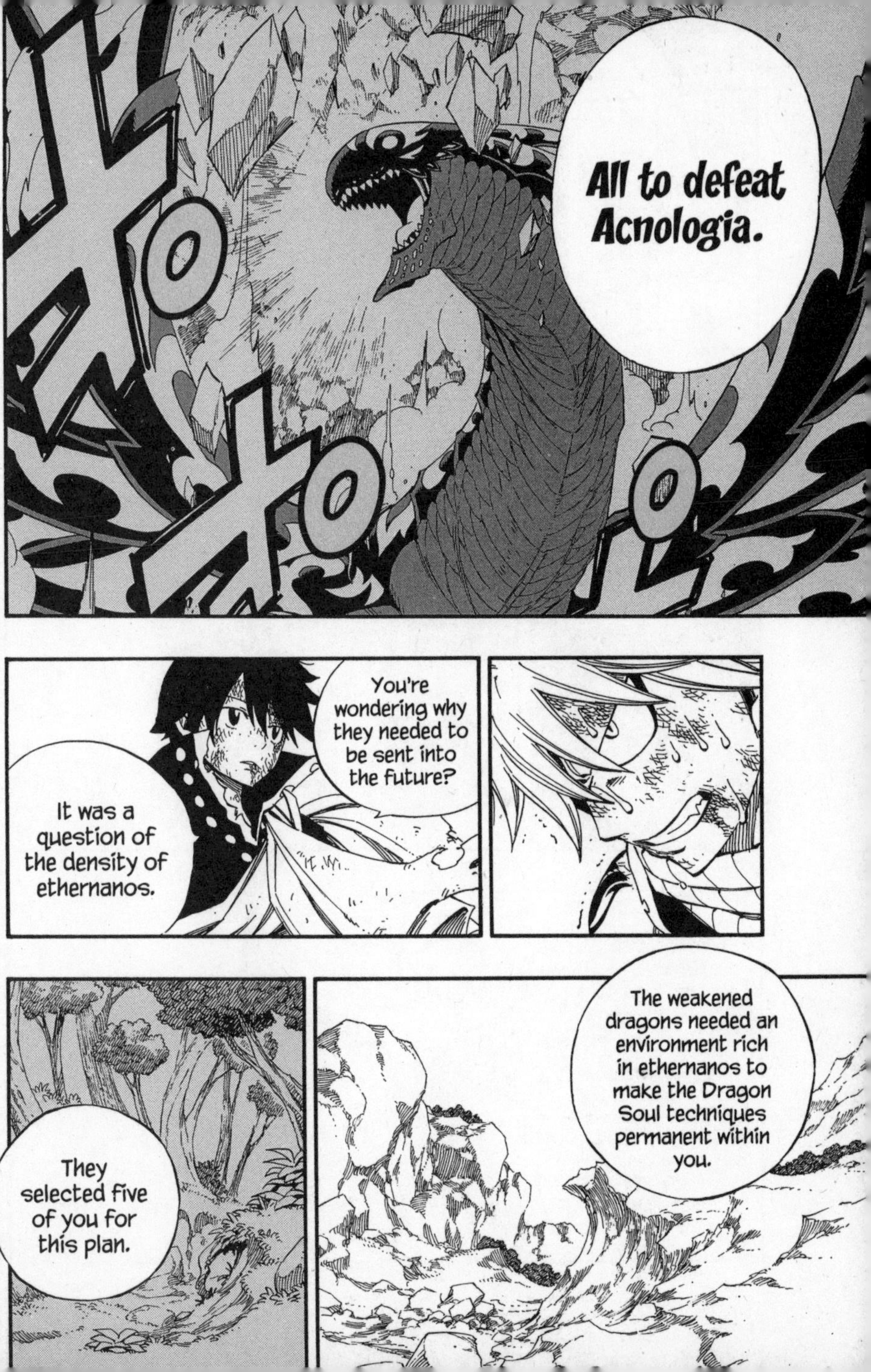
All to defeat Acnologia.
You're wondering why they needed to be sent into the future?
It was a question of the density of ethernanos.
The weakened dragons needed an environment rich in ethernanos to make the Dragon Soul techniques permanent within you.
They selected five of you for this plan.

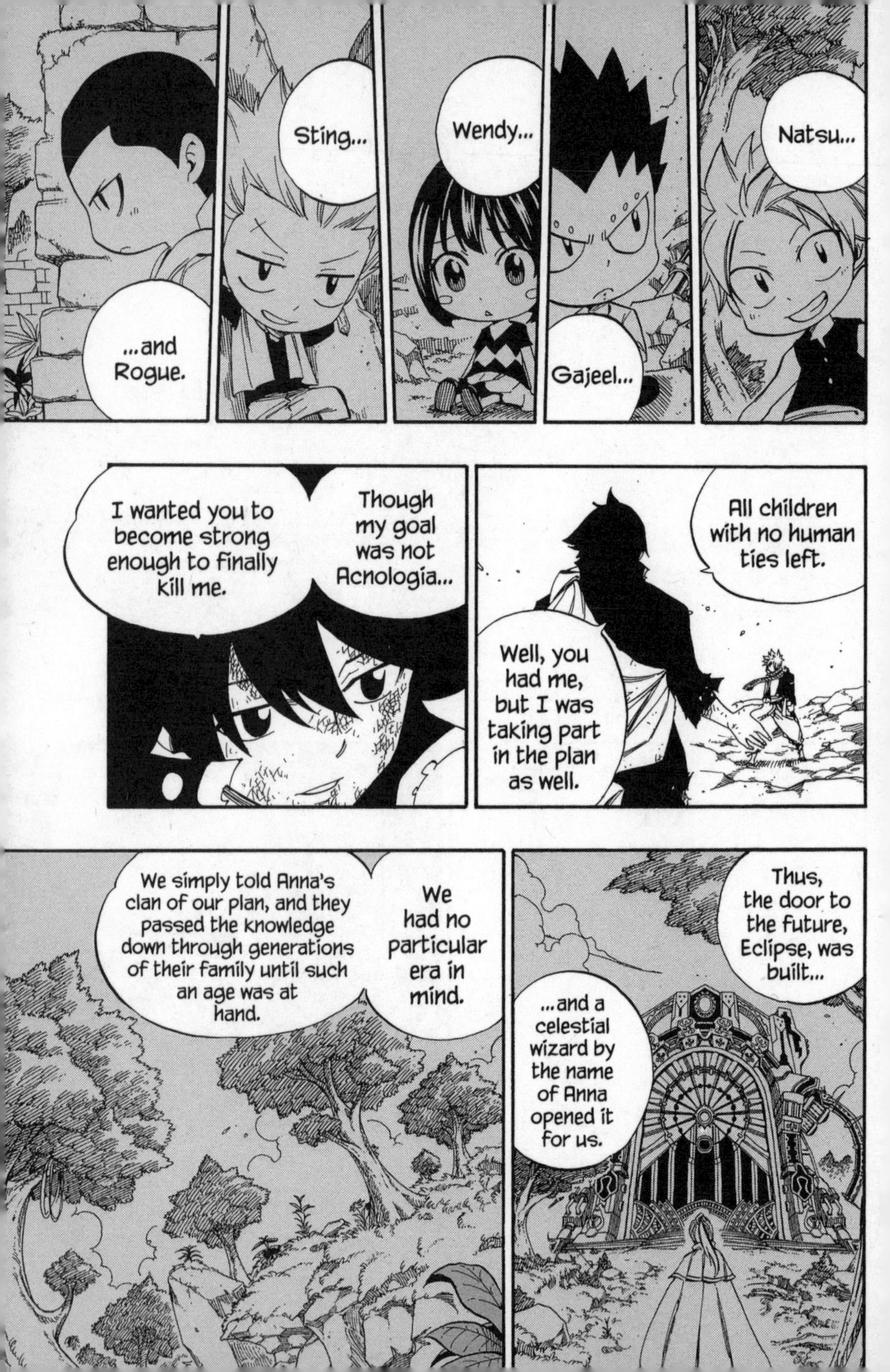
Natsu...
Gajeel...
Wendy...
Sting...
...and Rogue.
All children with no human ties left.
Well, you had me, but I was taking part in the plan as well.
Though my goal was not Acnologia...
I wanted you to become strong enough to finally kill me.
Thus, the door to the future, Eclipse, was built...
...and a celestial wizard by the name of Anna opened it for us.
We had no particular era in mind.
We simply told Anna's clan of our plan, and they passed the knowledge down through generations of their family until such an age was at hand.

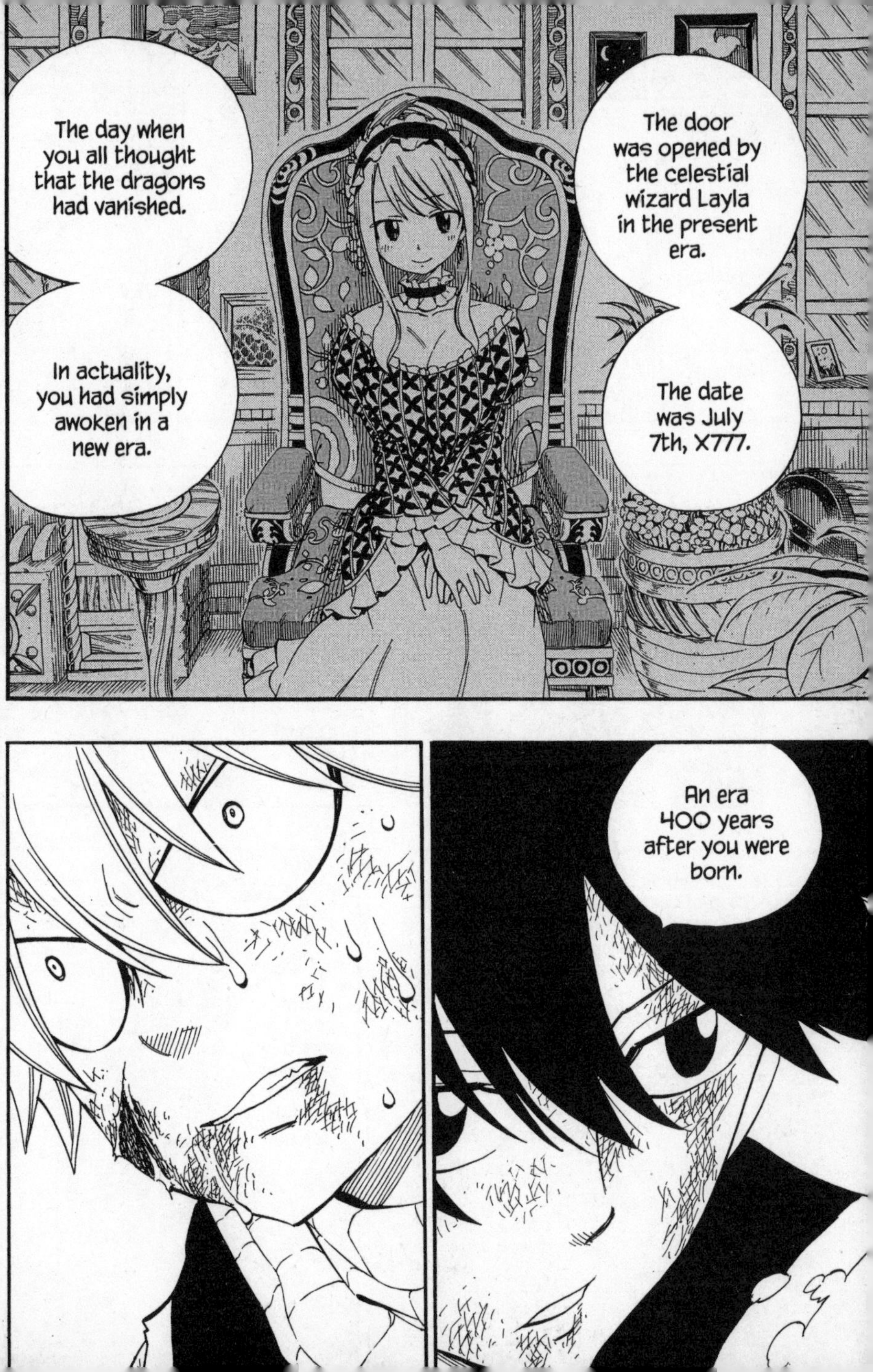
The door was opened by the celestial wizard Layla in the present era.
The date was July 7th, X777.
The day when you all thought that the dragons had vanished.
In actuality, you had simply awoken in a new era.
An era 400 years after you were born.

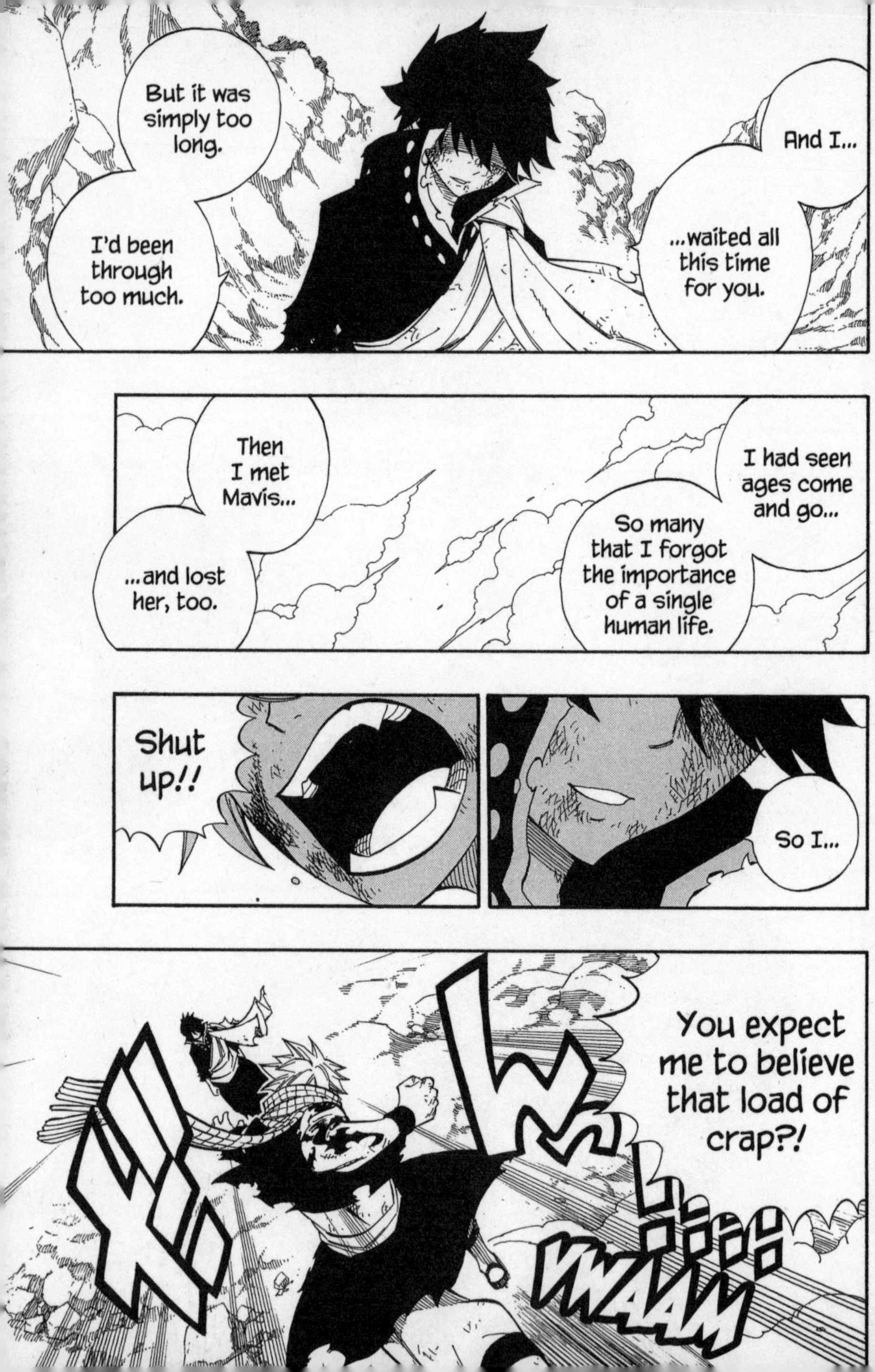
And I...
...waited all this time for you.
But it was simply too long.
I'd been through too much.
I had seen ages come and go...
So many that I forgot the importance of a single human life.
Then I met Mavis...
...and lost her, too.
So I...
Shut up!!
You expect me to believe that load of crap?!
VWAAM

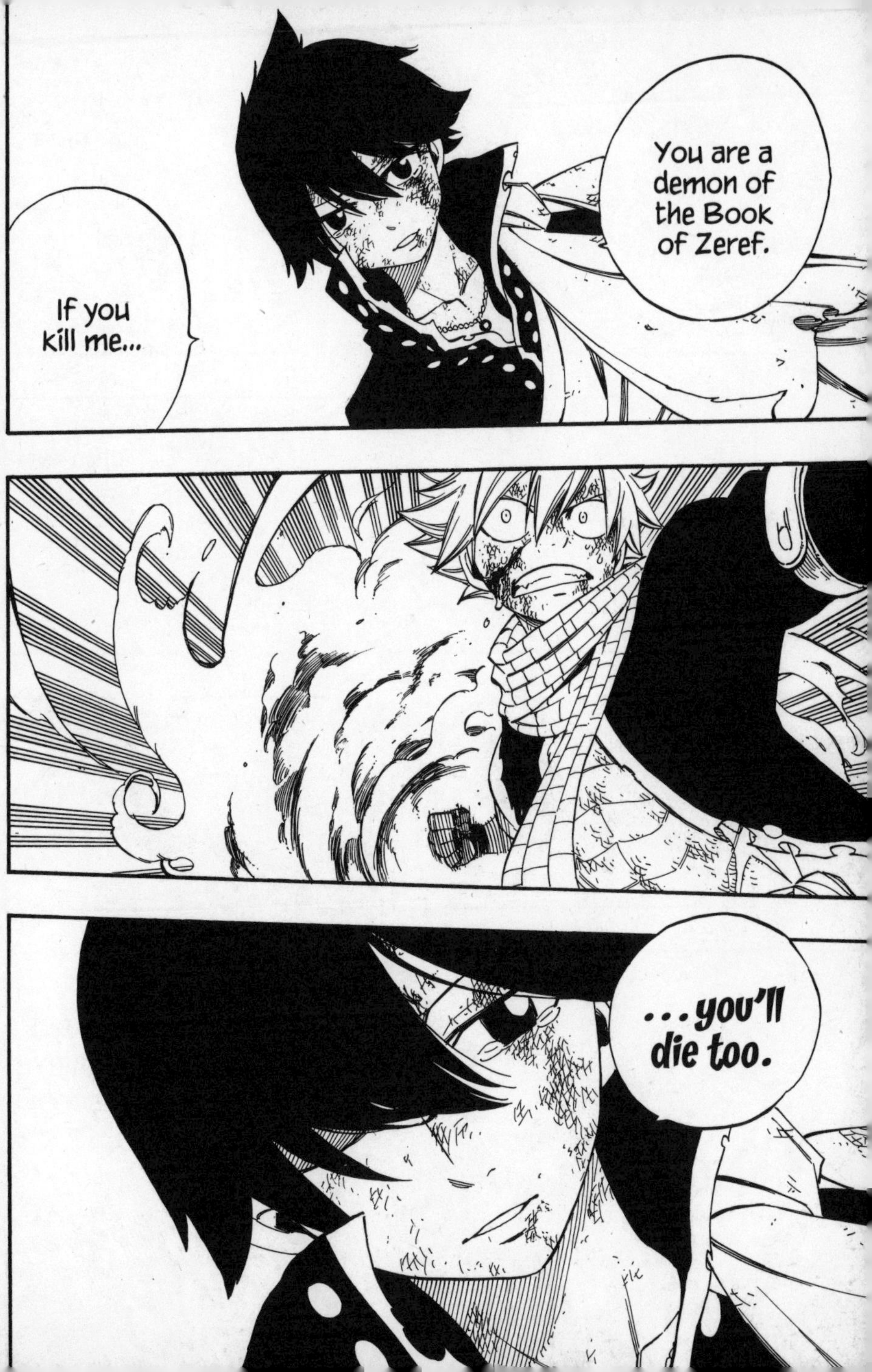
You are a demon of the Book of Zeref.
If you kill me...
...you'll die too.

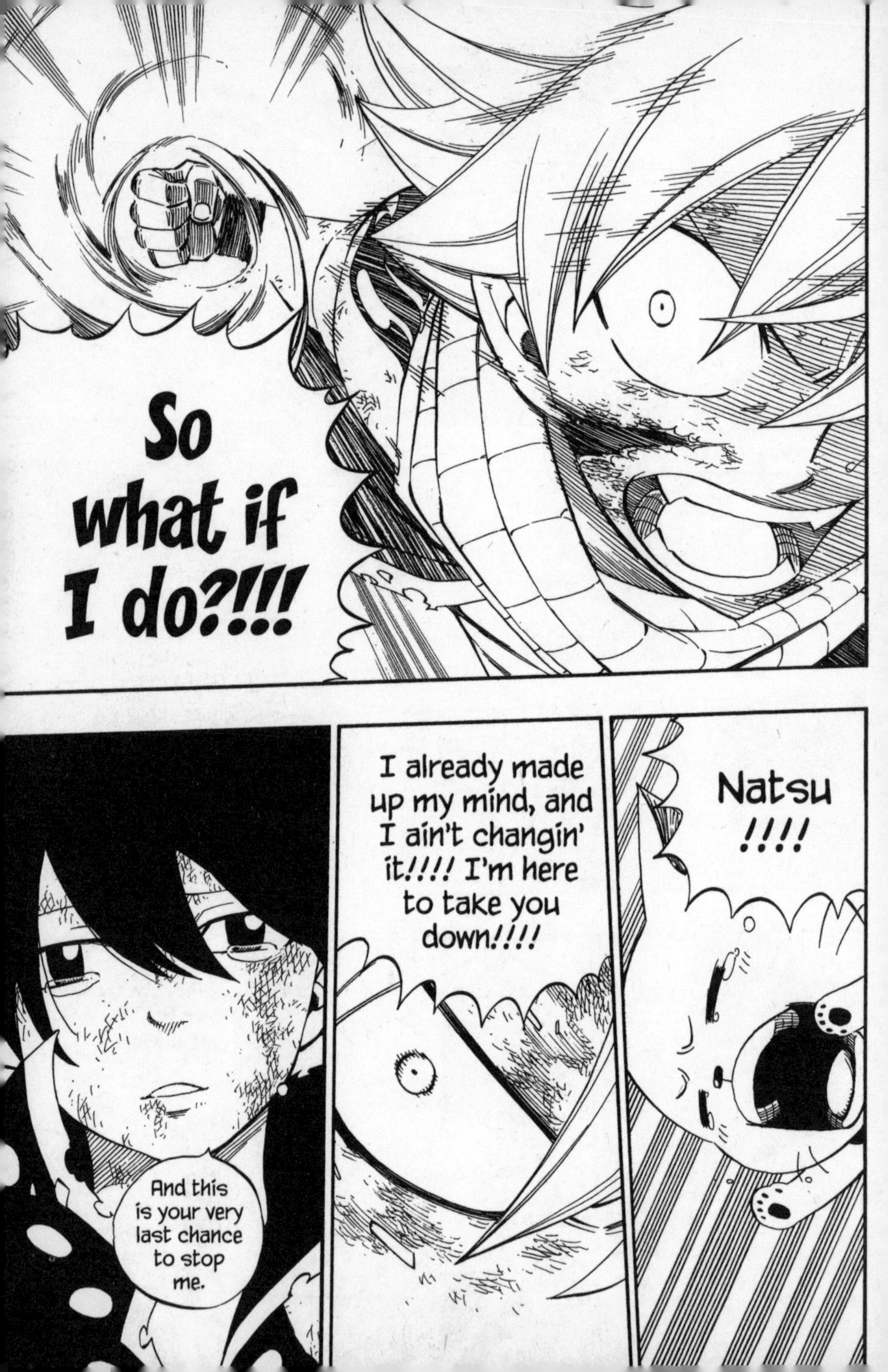
So what if I do?!!!
Natsu !!!!
I already made up my mind, and I ain't changin' it!!!! I'm here to take you down!!!!
And this is your very last chance to stop me.

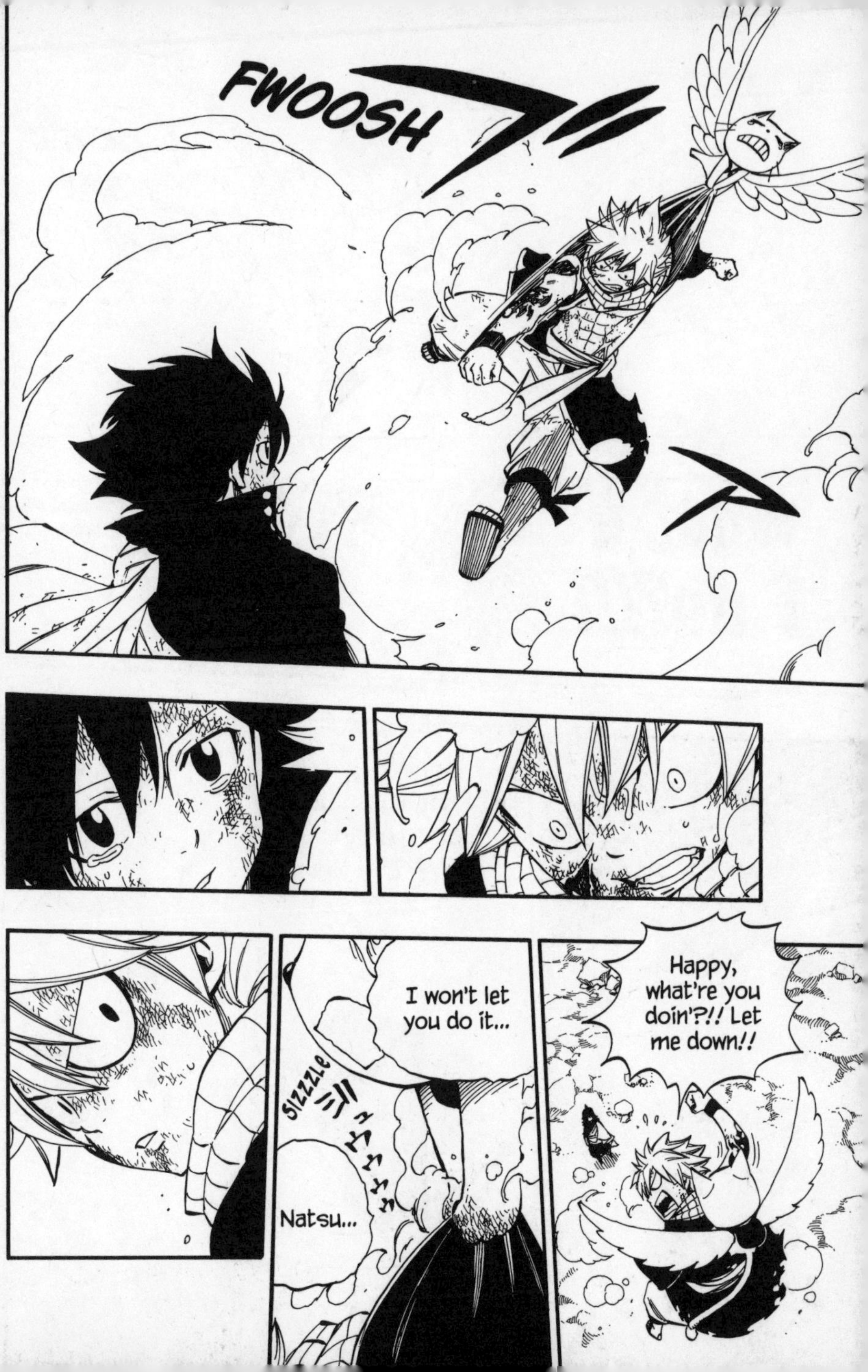
FWOOSH
Happy, what're you doin'?!! Let me down!!
I won't let you do it...
SIZZZLE
Natsu...

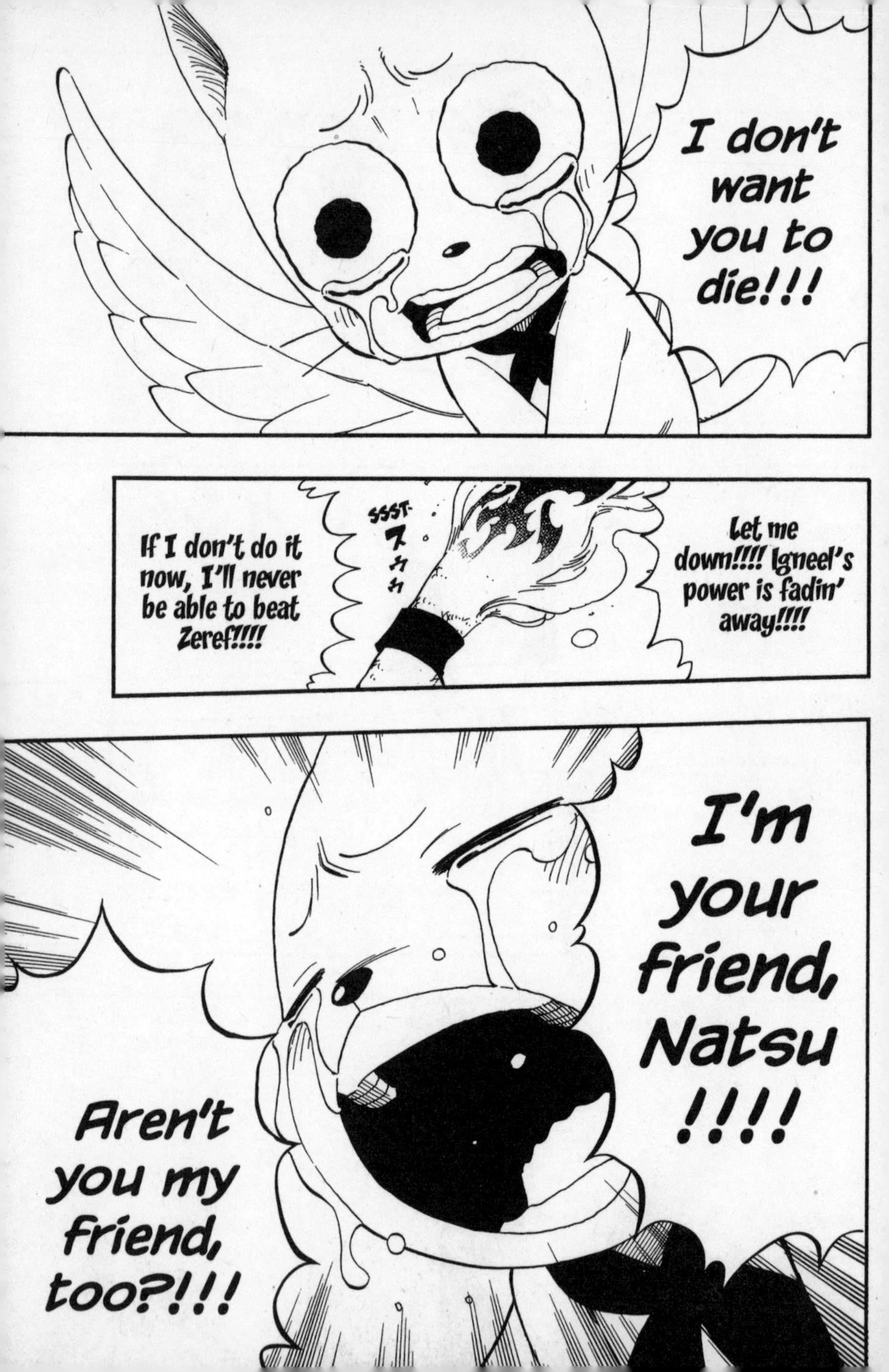
I don't want you to die!!!
Let me down!!!! Igneel's power is fadin' away!!!!
SSST-
If I don't do it now, I'll never be able to beat Zeref!!!!
I'm your friend, Natsu!!!!
Aren't you my friend, too?!!!

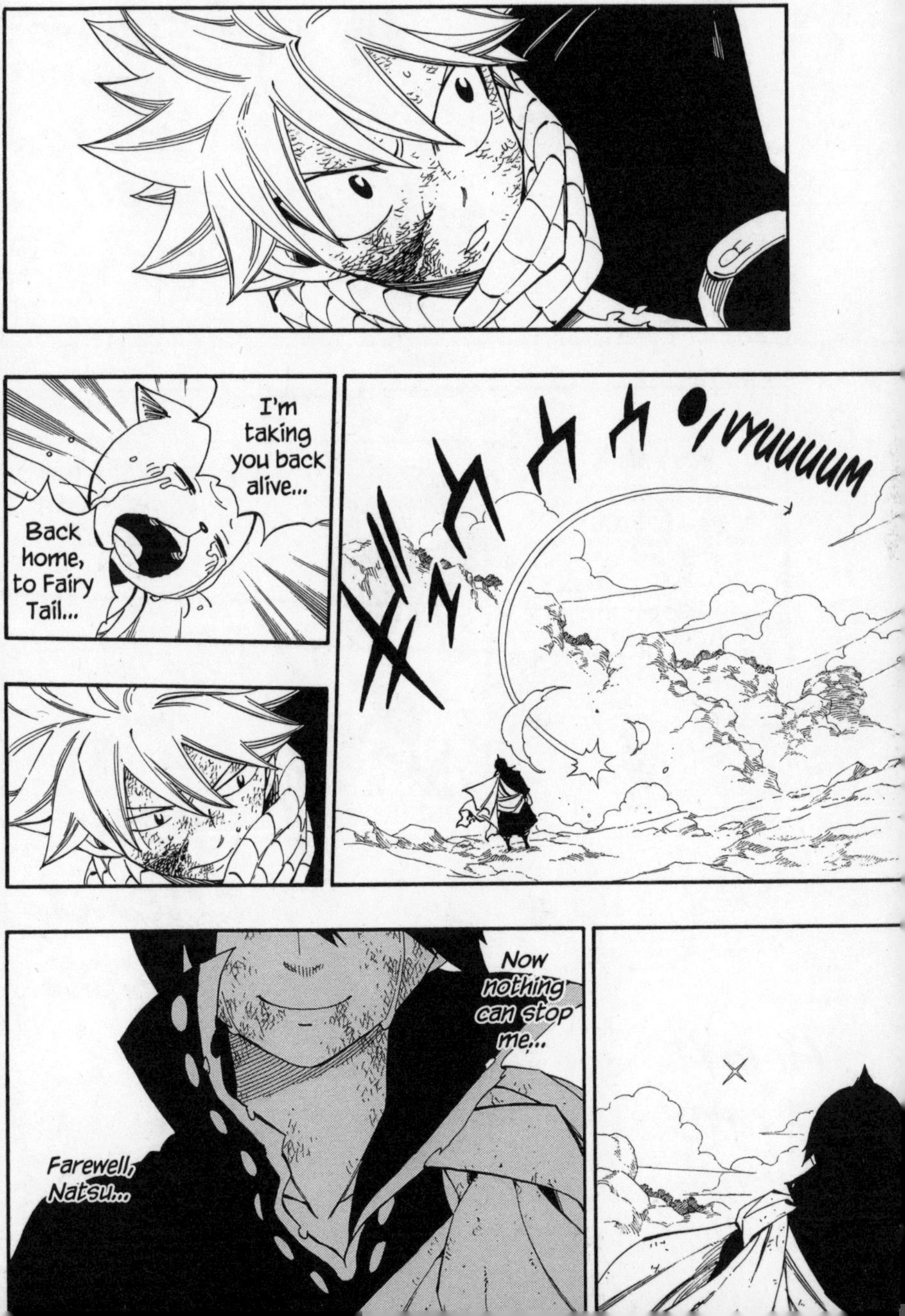
VYUUUUUM
I'm taking you back alive...
Back home, to Fairy Tail...
Now nothing can stop me...
Farewell, Natsu...

FAIRY TAIL

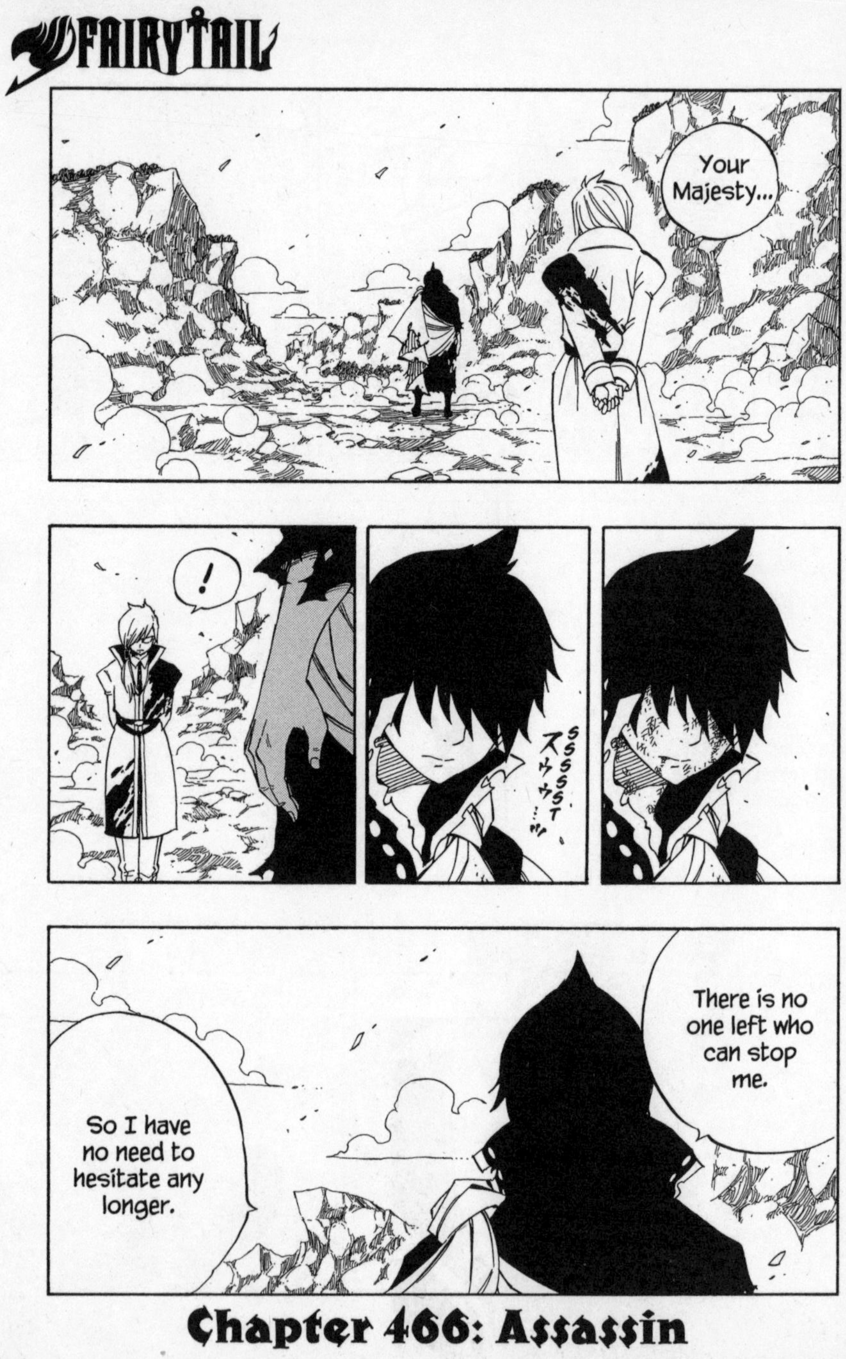
Your Majesty...
SSSSST
!
There is no one left who can stop me.
So I have no need to hesitate any longer.

Chapter 466: Assassin

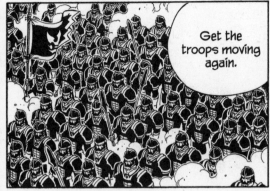

Get the troops moving again.

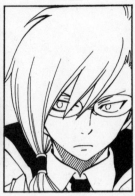

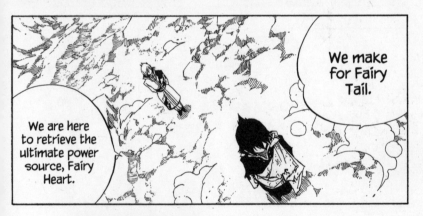

We make for Fairy Tail.

We are here to retrieve the ultimate power source, Fairy Heart.

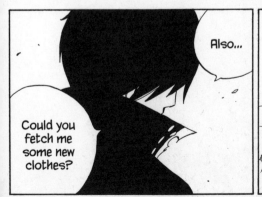

Also...

Could you fetch me some new clothes?

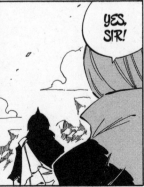

YES, SIR!

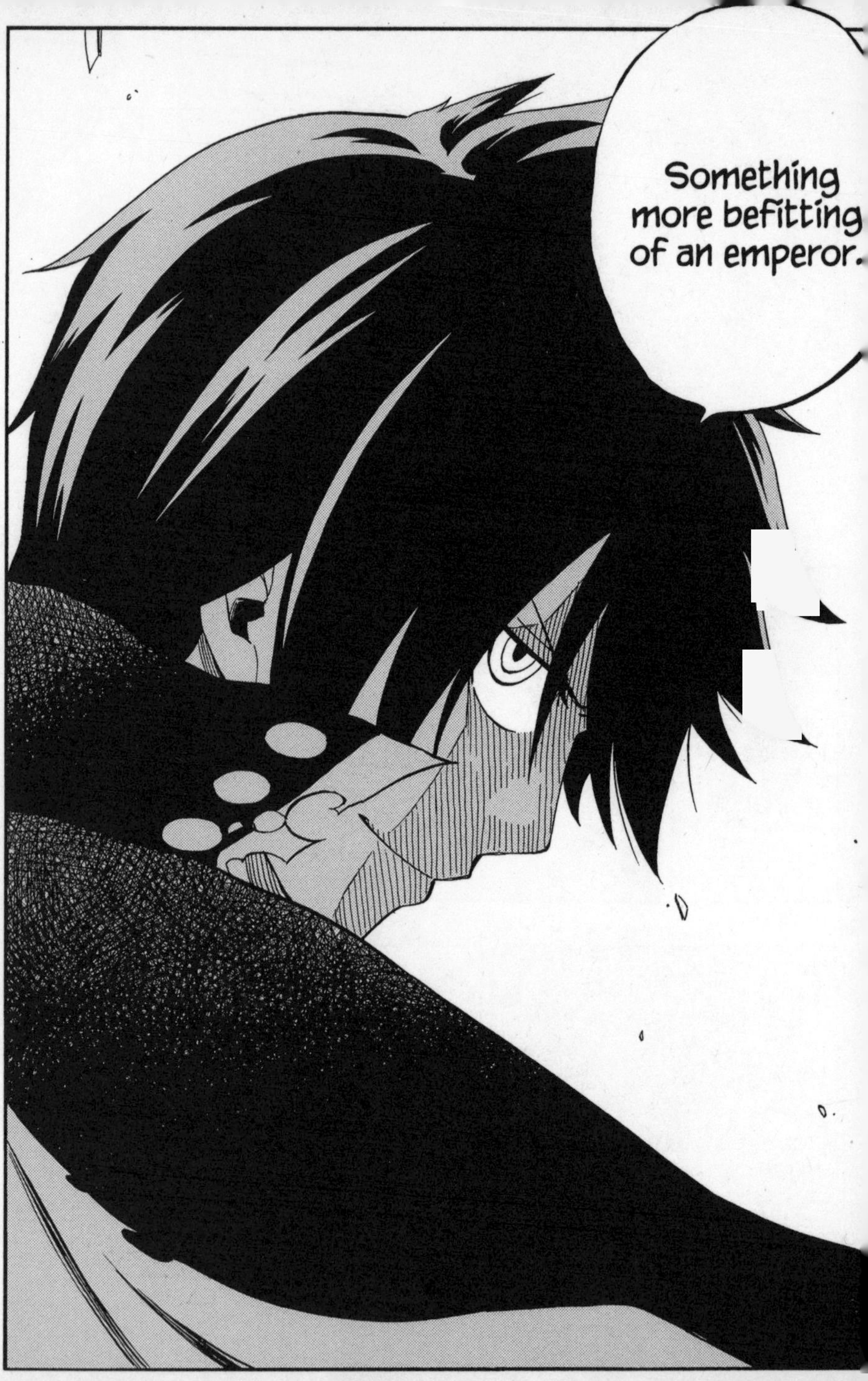
Something more befitting of an emperor.

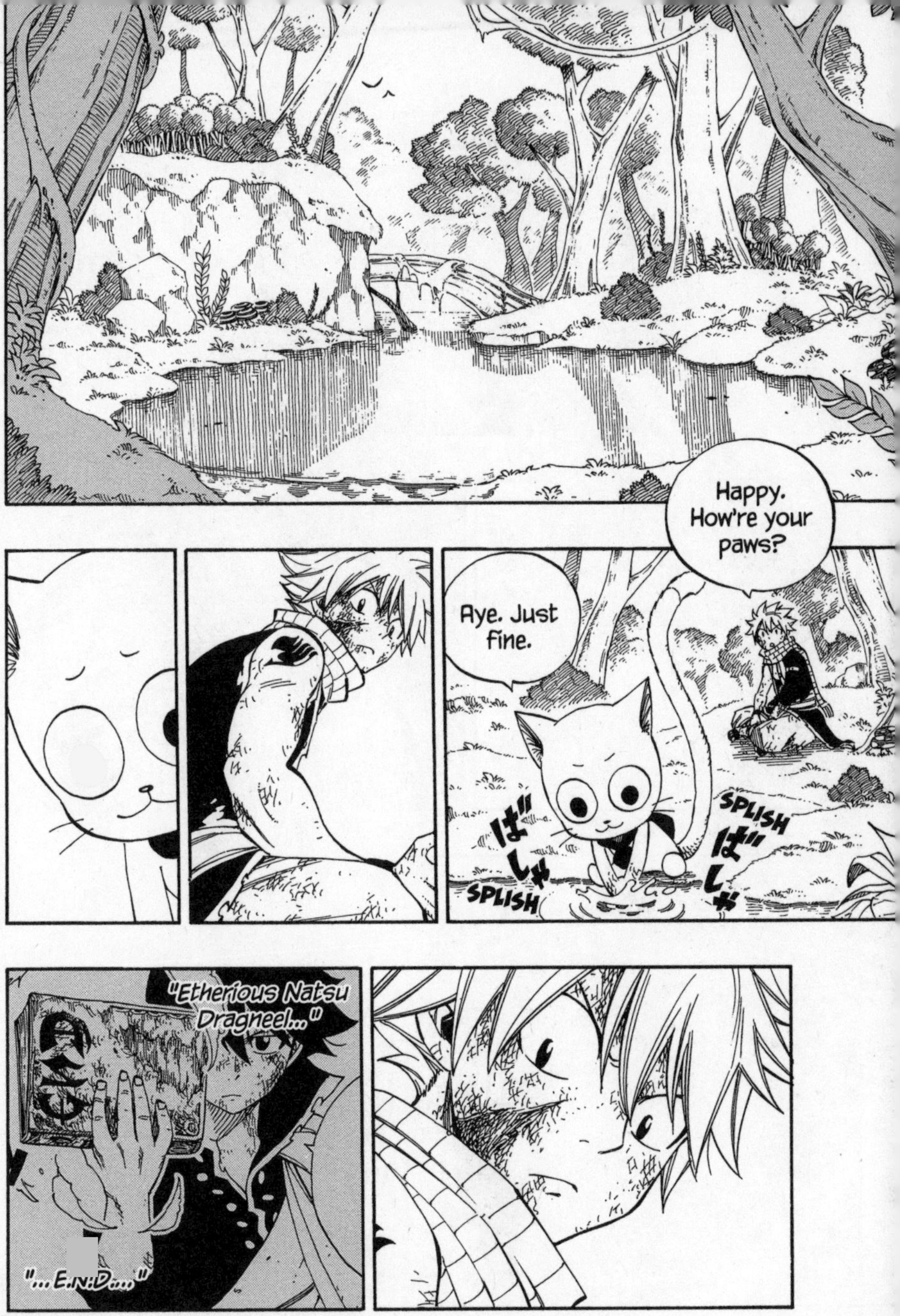
Happy. How're your paws?
Aye. Just fine.
SPLISH
ばしゃ
ばしゃ
SPLISH
"Etherious Natsu Dragneel..."
"...E.N.D..."

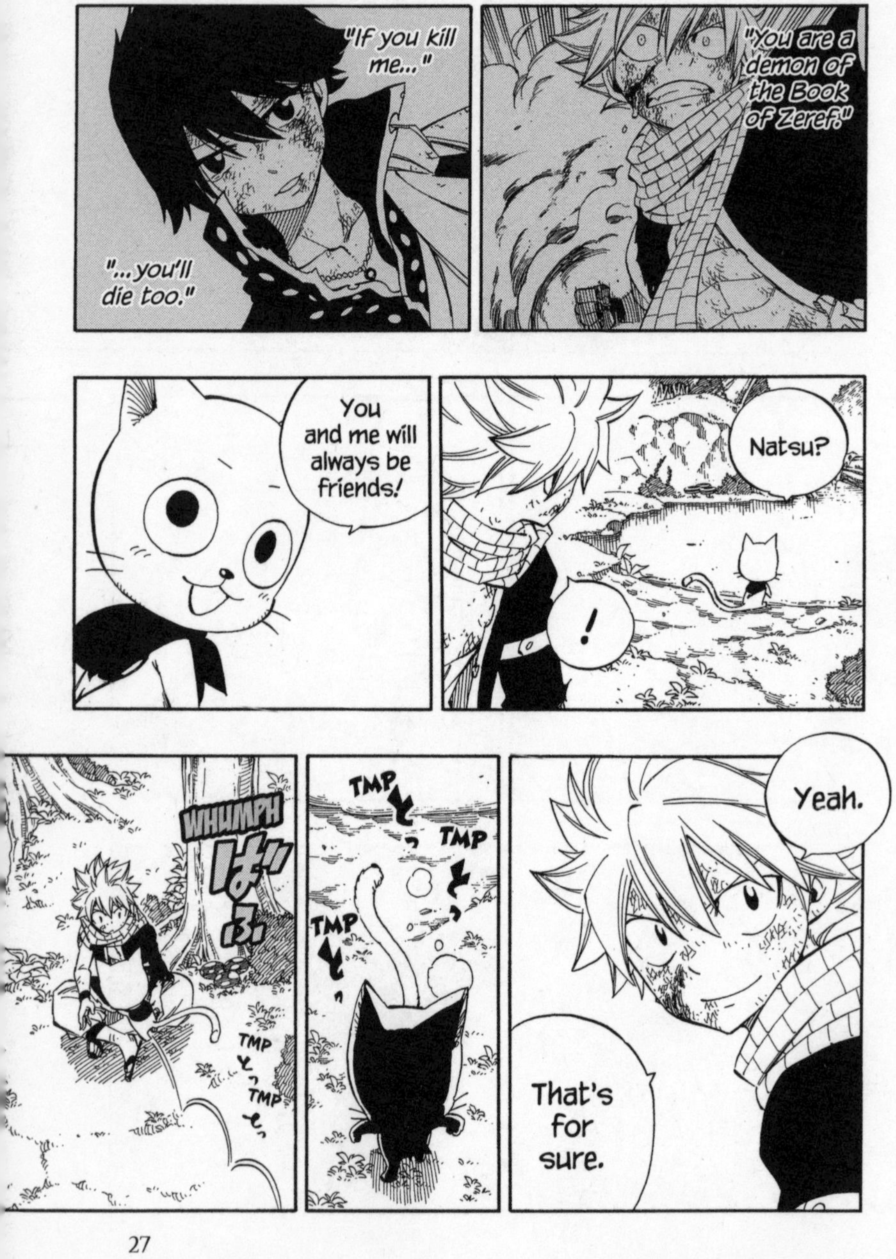
"You are a demon of the Book of Zeref."
"If you kill me..."
"...you'll die too."
Natsu?
!
You and me will always be friends!
Yeah.
That's for sure.
TMP
TMP
TMP
WHUMPH
ばふ
TMP
TMP

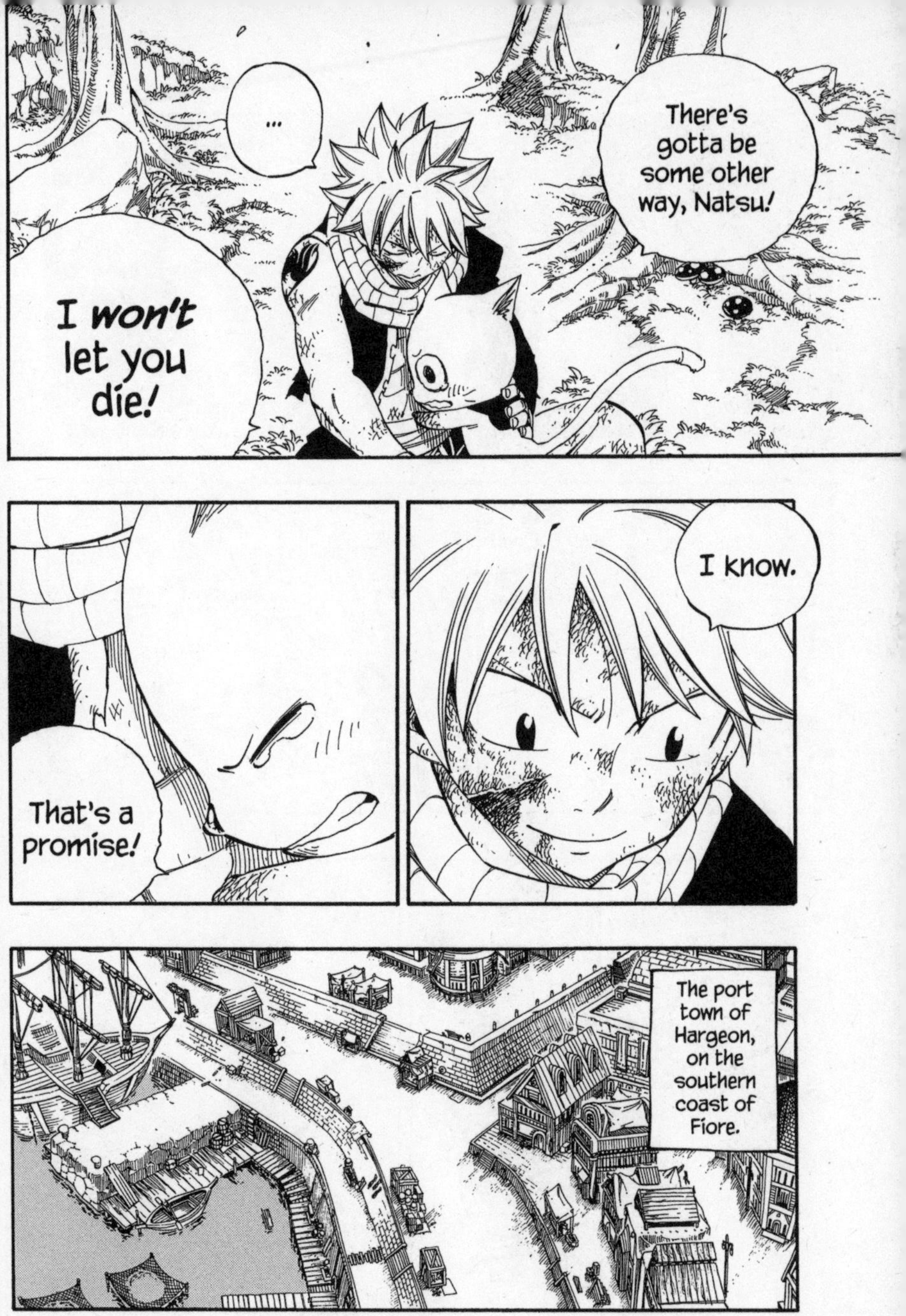
There's gotta be some other way, Natsu!
...
I *won't* let you die!
I know.
That's a promise!
The port town of Hargeon, on the southern coast of Fiore.

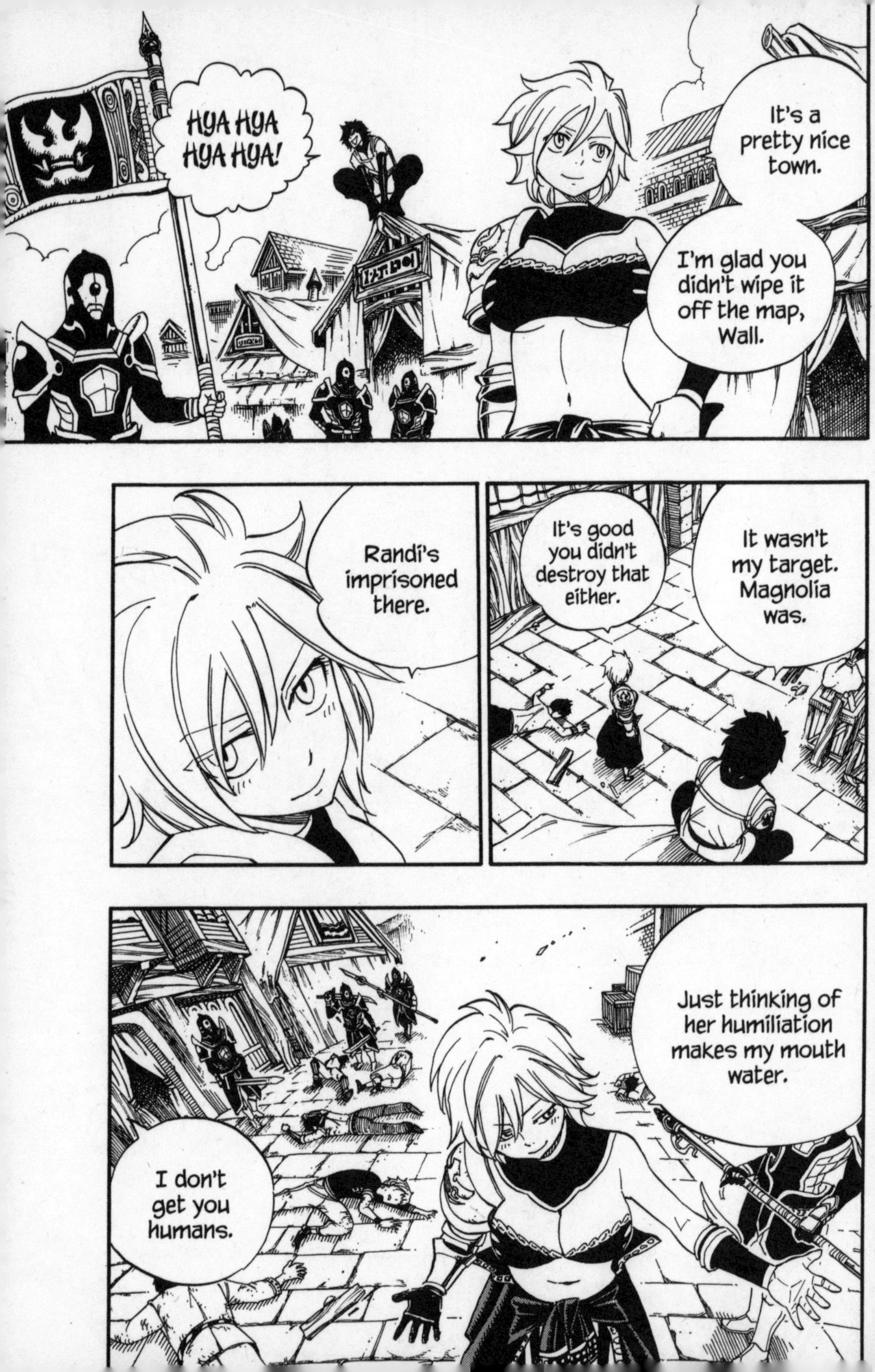
It's a pretty nice town.
I'm glad you didn't wipe it off the map, Wall.
HYA HYA HYA HYA!
It wasn't my target. Magnolia was.
It's good you didn't destroy that either.
Randi's imprisoned there.
Just thinking of her humiliation makes my mouth water.
I don't get you humans.

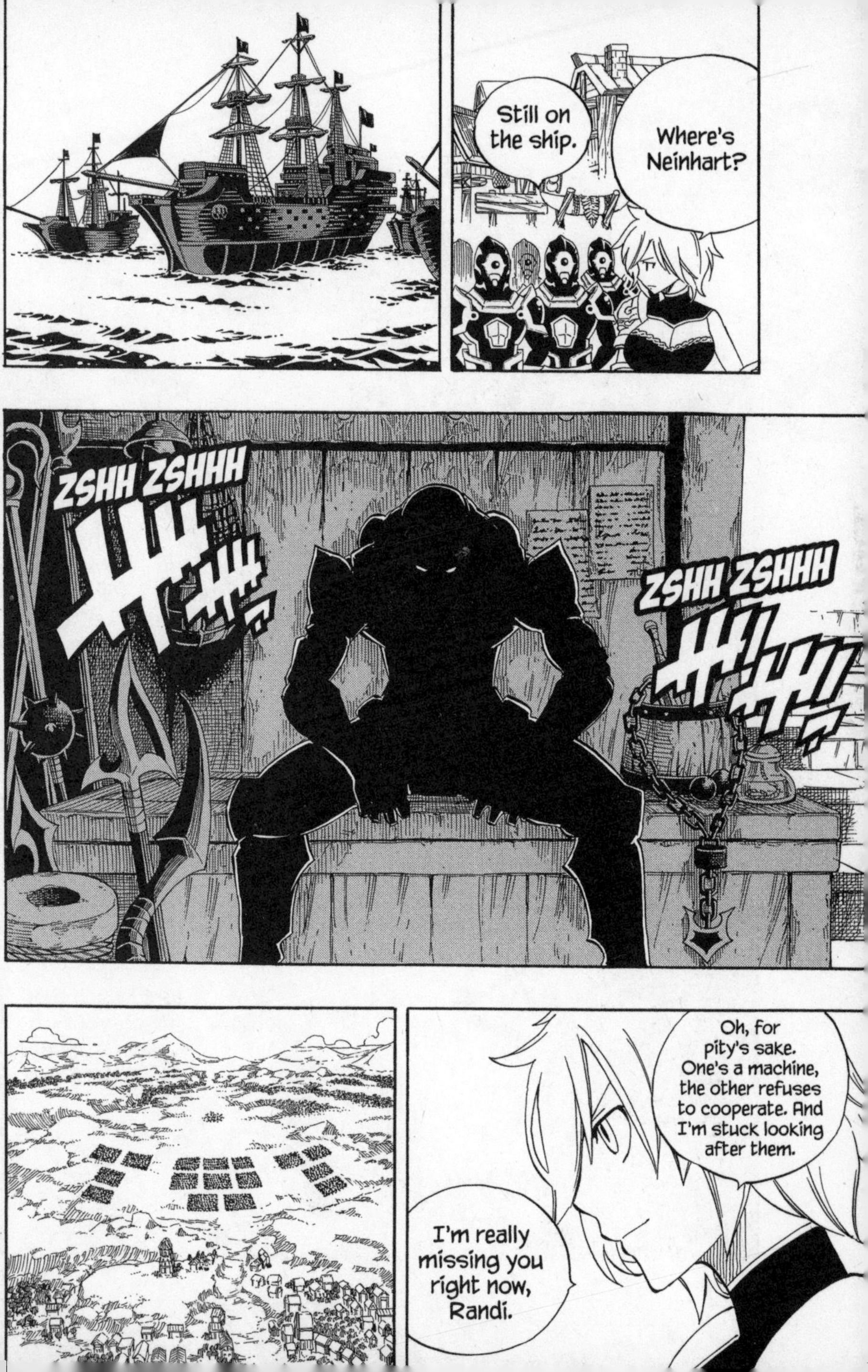
Where's Neinhart?
Still on the ship.
ZSHH ZSHHH
ZSHH ZSHHH
Oh, for pity's sake. One's a machine, the other refuses to cooperate. And I'm stuck looking after them.
I'm really missing you right now, Randi.

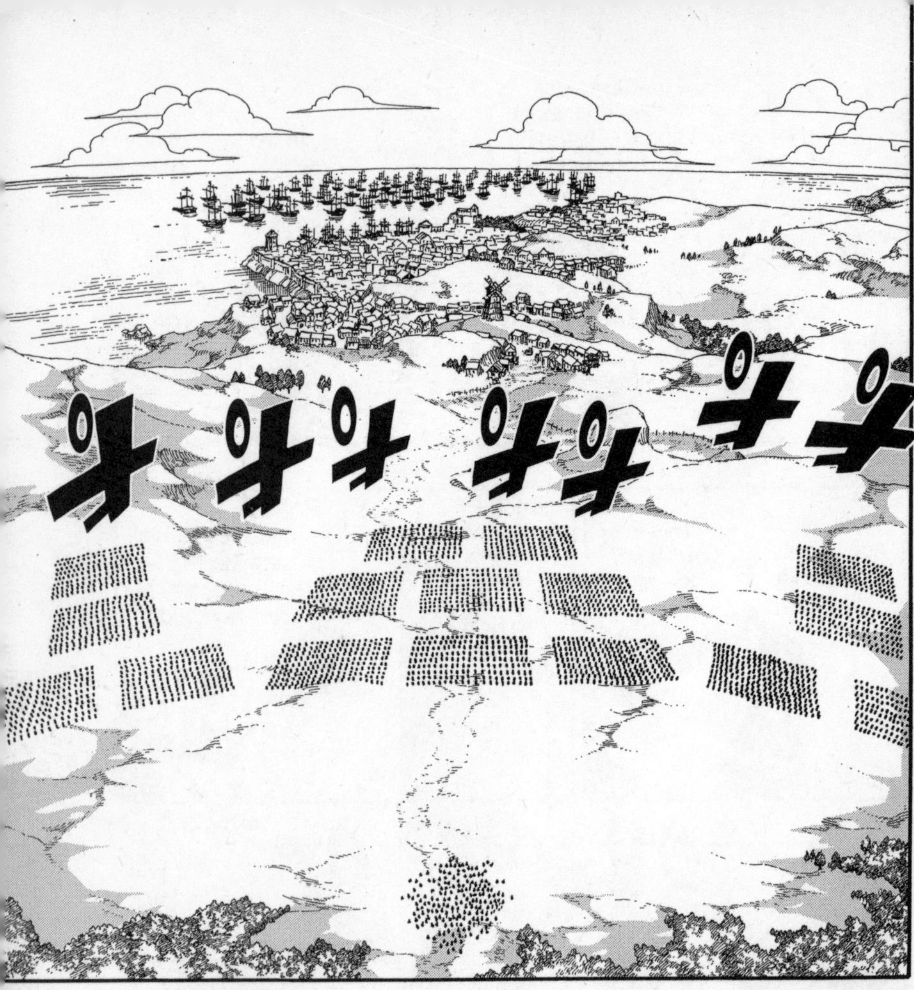

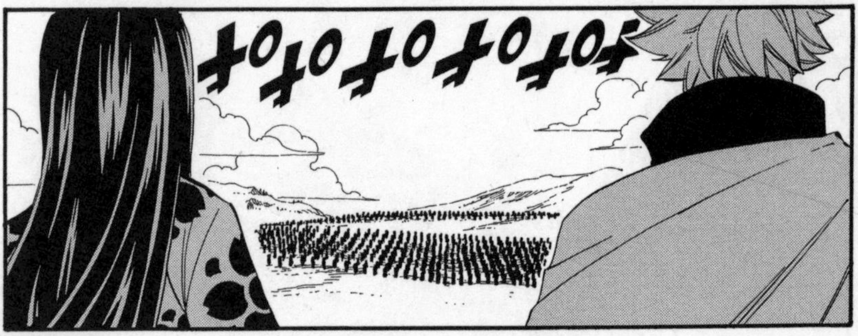

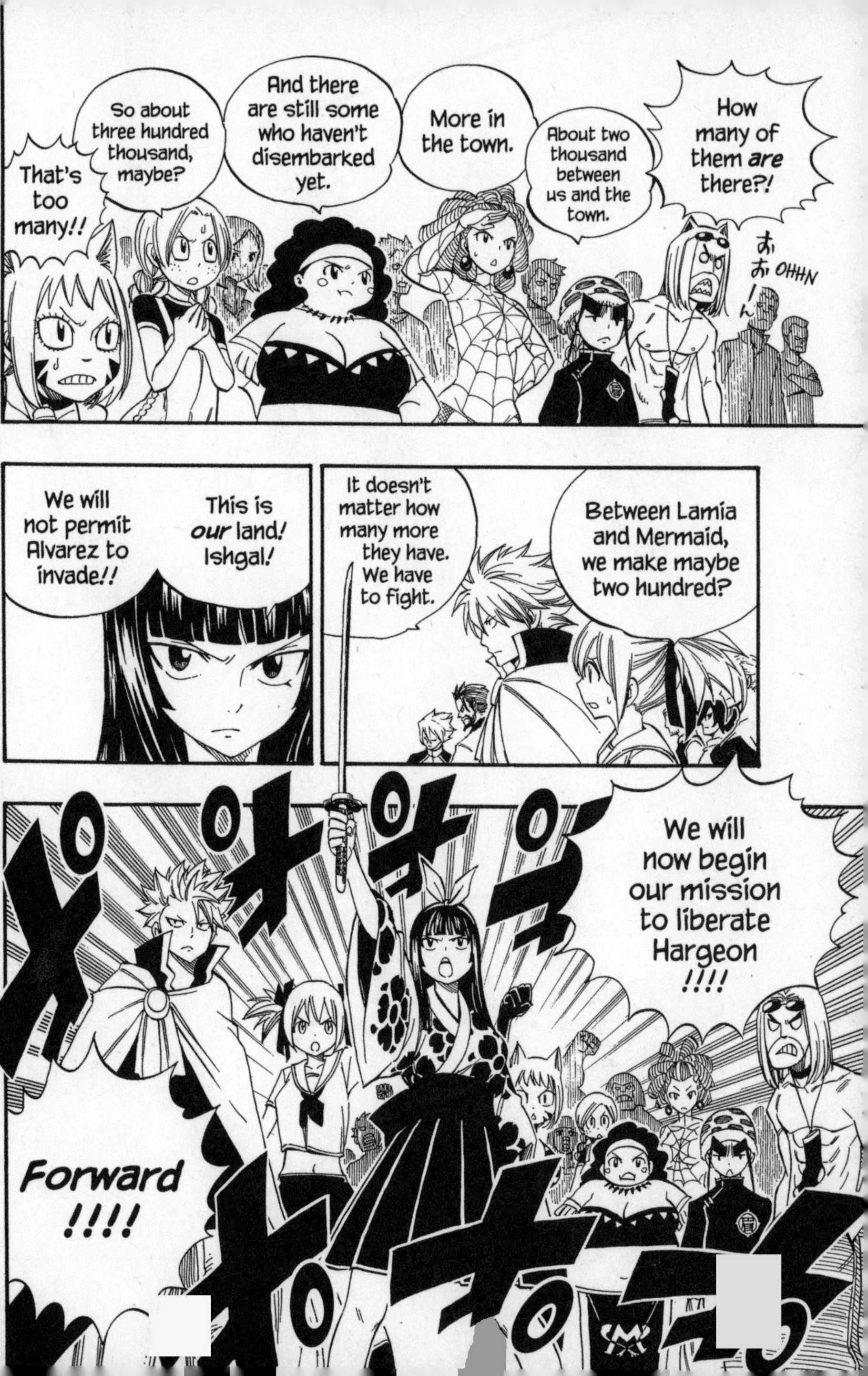
How many of them *are* there?!
About two thousand between us and the town.
More in the town.
And there are still some who haven't disembarked yet.
So about three hundred thousand, maybe?
That's too many!!
おおーん OHHN
Between Lamia and Mermaid, we make maybe two hundred?
It doesn't matter how many more they have. We have to fight.
This is *our* land! Ishgal!
We will not permit Alvarez to invade!!
We will now begin our mission to liberate Hargeon!!!!
Forward!!!!

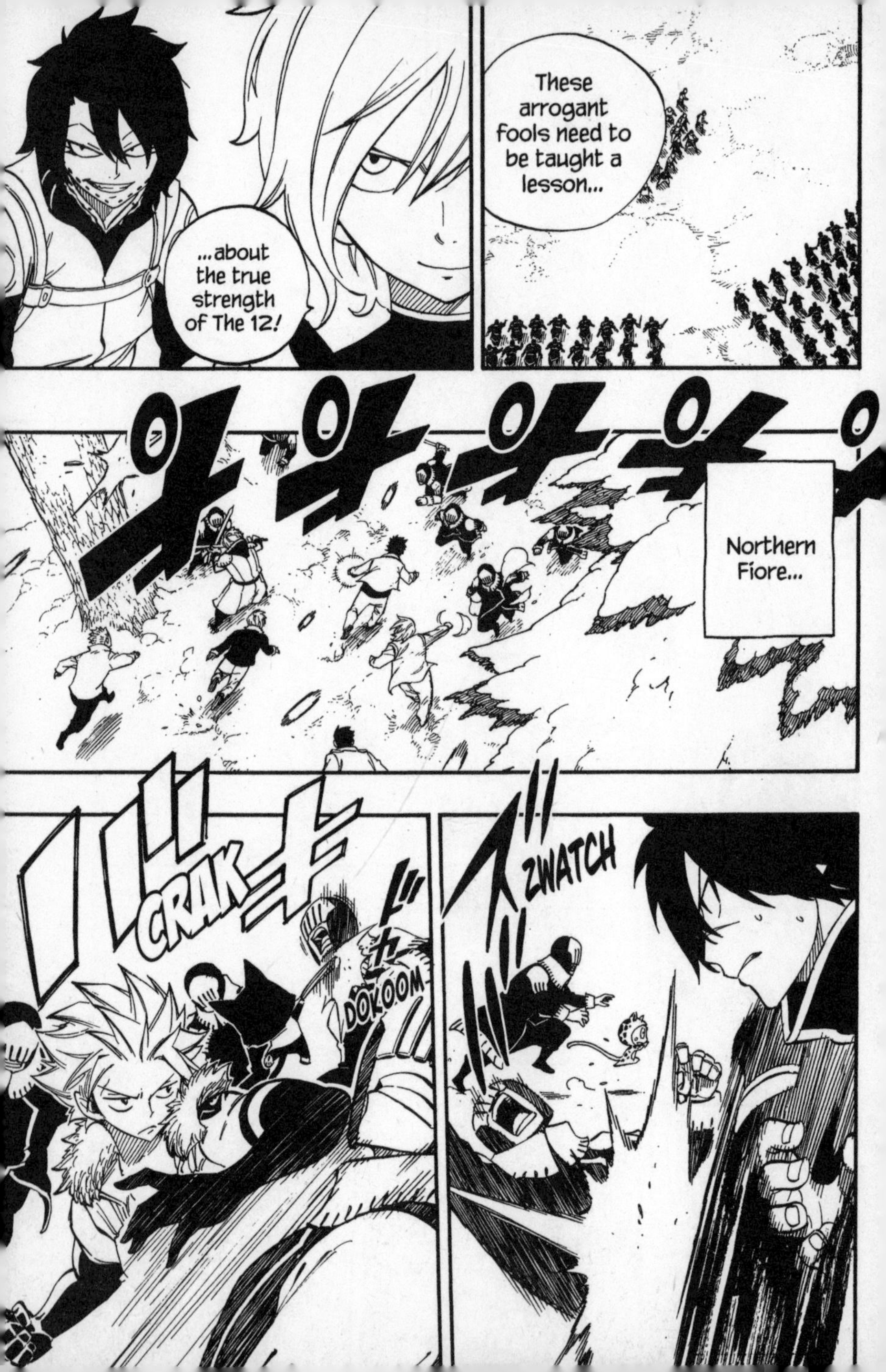
These arrogant fools need to be taught a lesson...
...about the true strength of The 12!
Northern Fiore...
ZWATCH
CRAK
DOKOOM

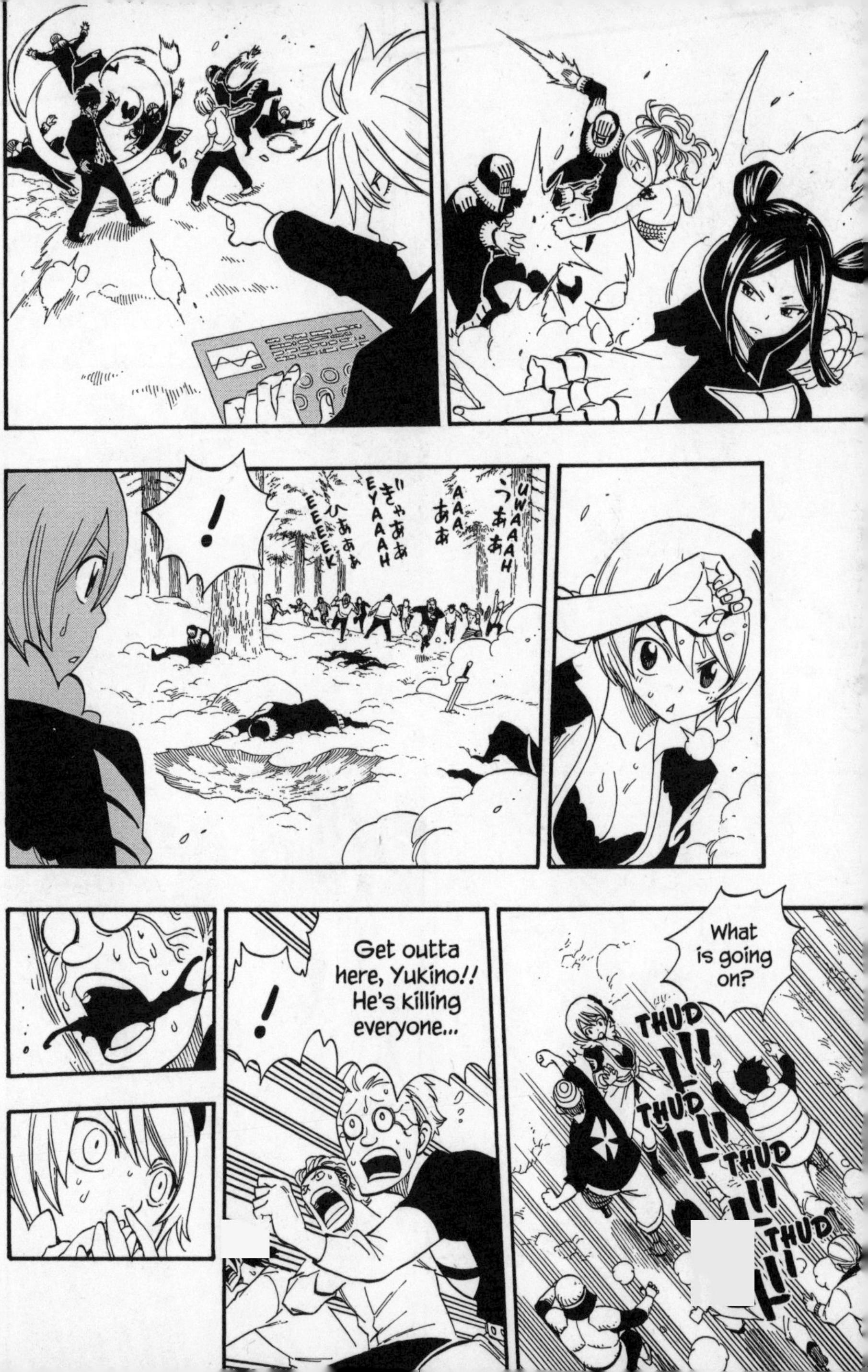
!
UWAAAAH
うあああ
AAAA
ああ
EYAAAH
きゃああ
EEEEK
ひあああ
What is going on?
THUD
THUD
THUD
THUD
Get outta here, Yukino!! He's killing everyone...
!

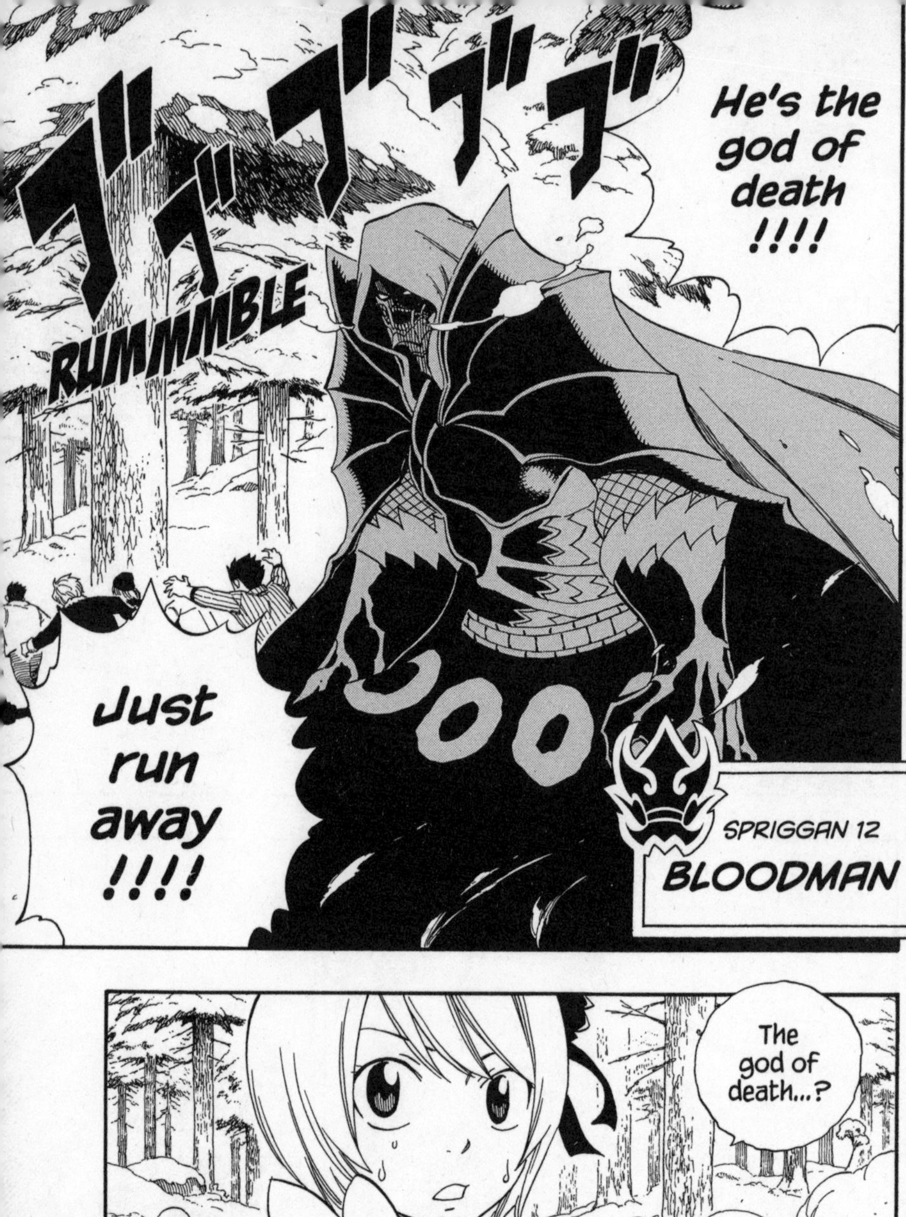
He's the god of death !!!!
RUMMMBLE
SPRIGGAN 12
BLOODMAN
Just run away !!!!
The god of death...?

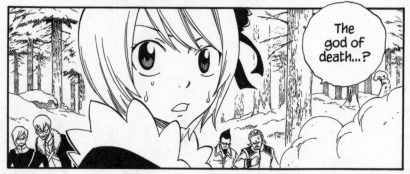

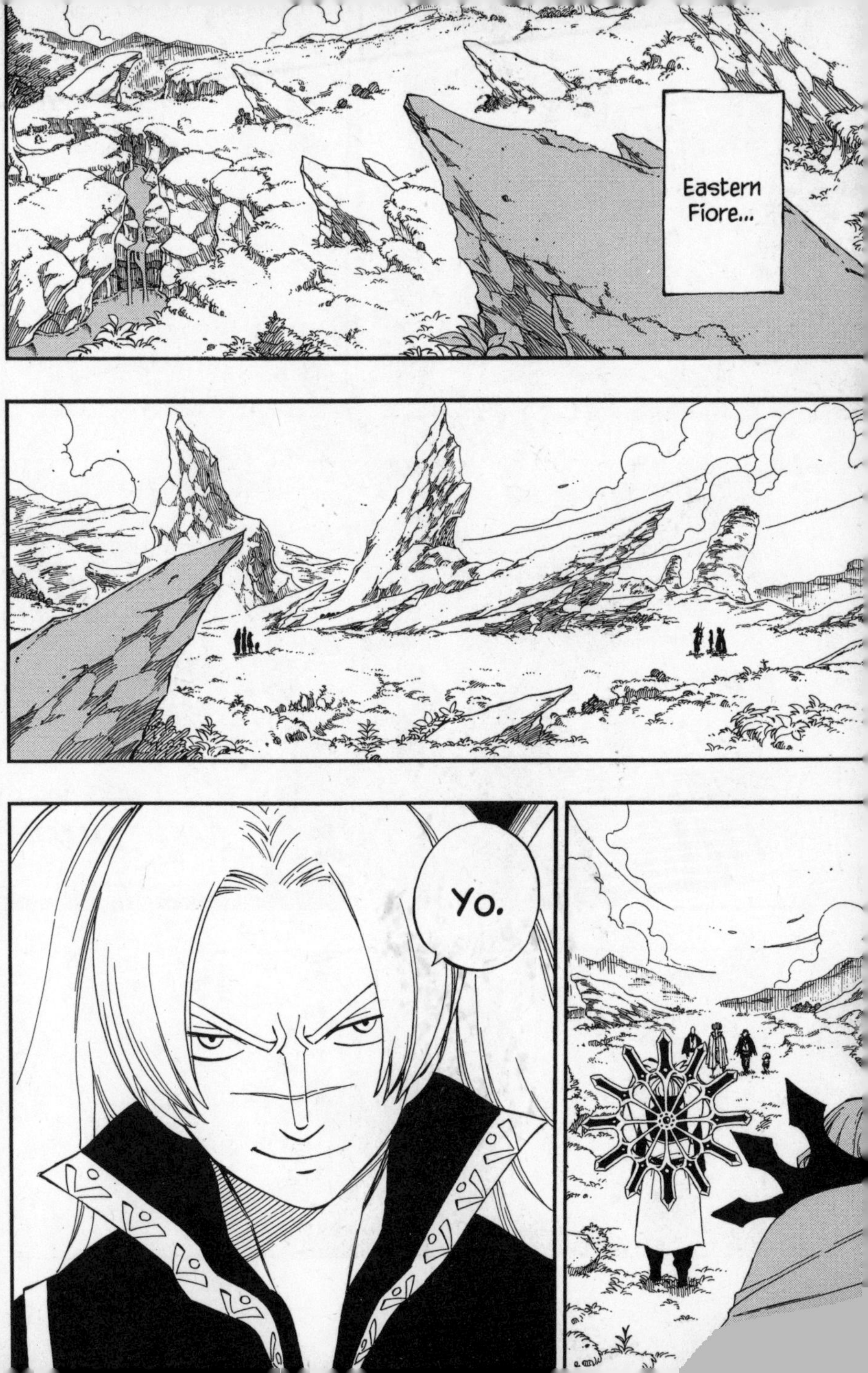
Eastern Fiore...
Yo.

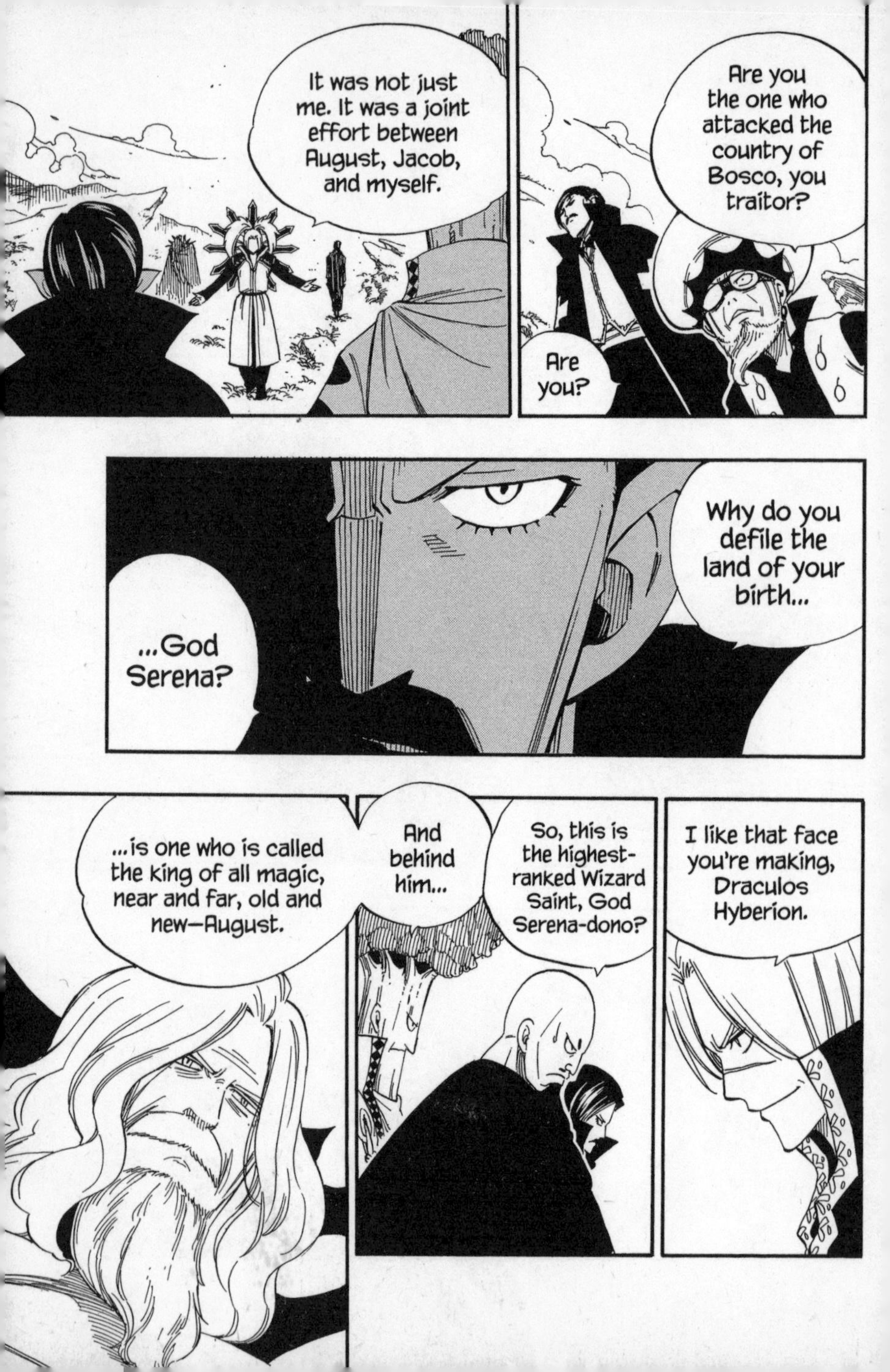
Are you the one who attacked the country of Bosco, you traitor?
Are you?
It was not just me. It was a joint effort between August, Jacob, and myself.
Why do you defile the land of your birth...
...God Serena?
I like that face you're making, Draculos Hyberion.
So, this is the highest-ranked Wizard Saint, God Serena-dono?
And behind him...
...is one who is called the king of all magic, near and far, old and new—August.

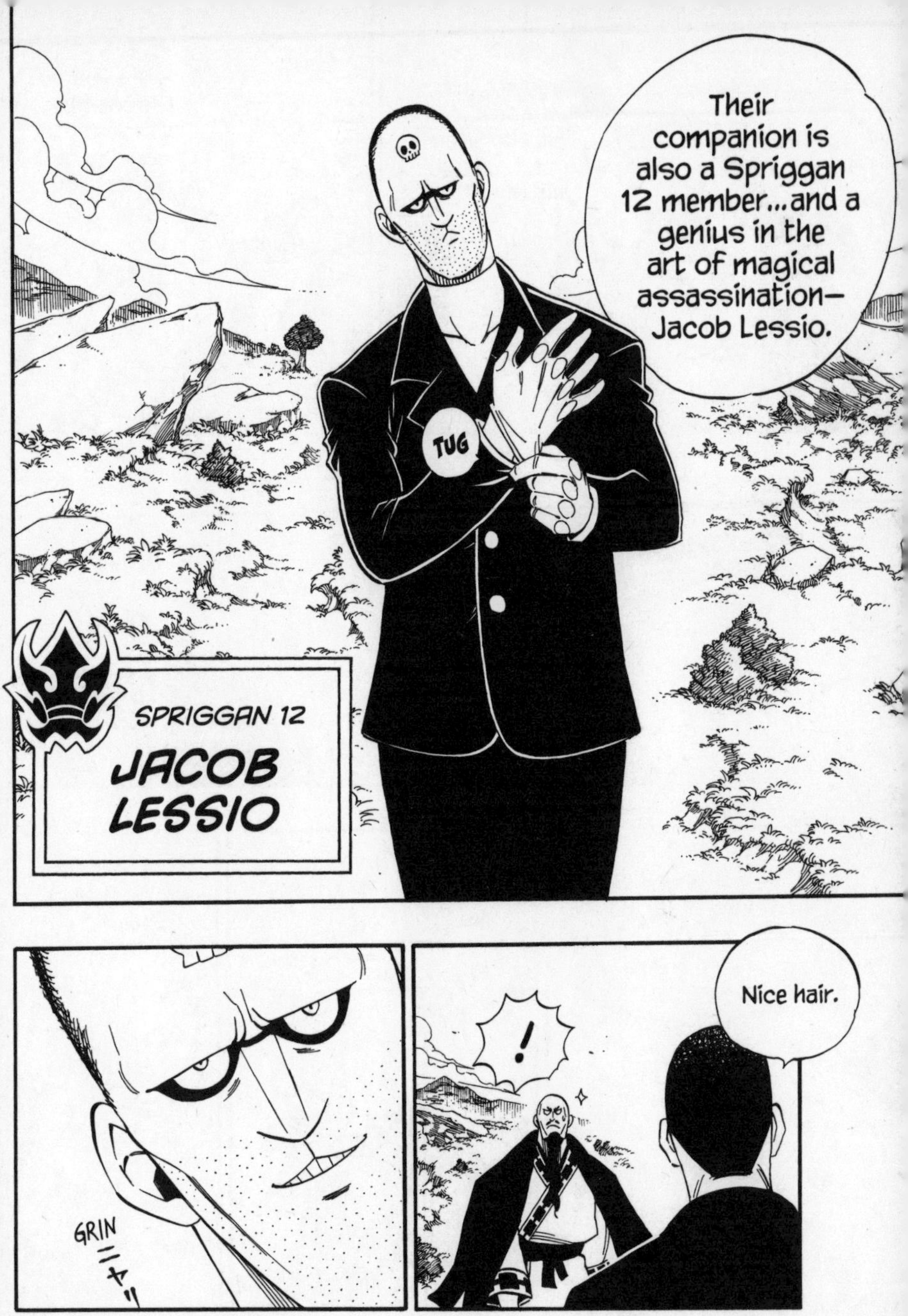

Their companion is also a Spriggan 12 member...and a genius in the art of magical assassination—Jacob Lessio.
TUG
SPRIGGAN 12
JACOB LESSIO
Nice hair.
!
GRIN
ニヤリ

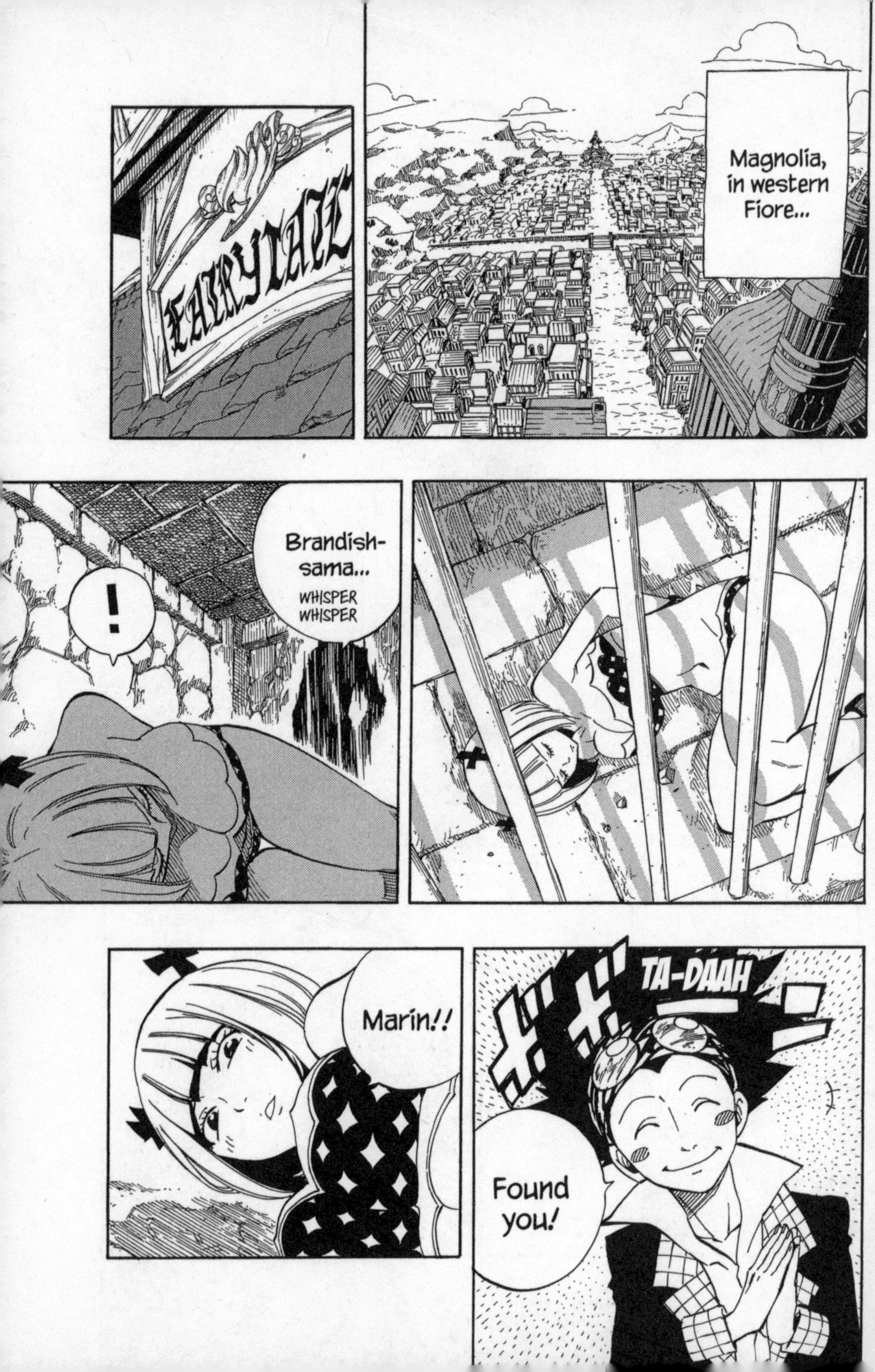
Magnolia, in western Fiore...
FAIRY TAIL
!
Brandish-sama...
WHISPER WHISPER
TA-DAAH
Found you!
Marin!!

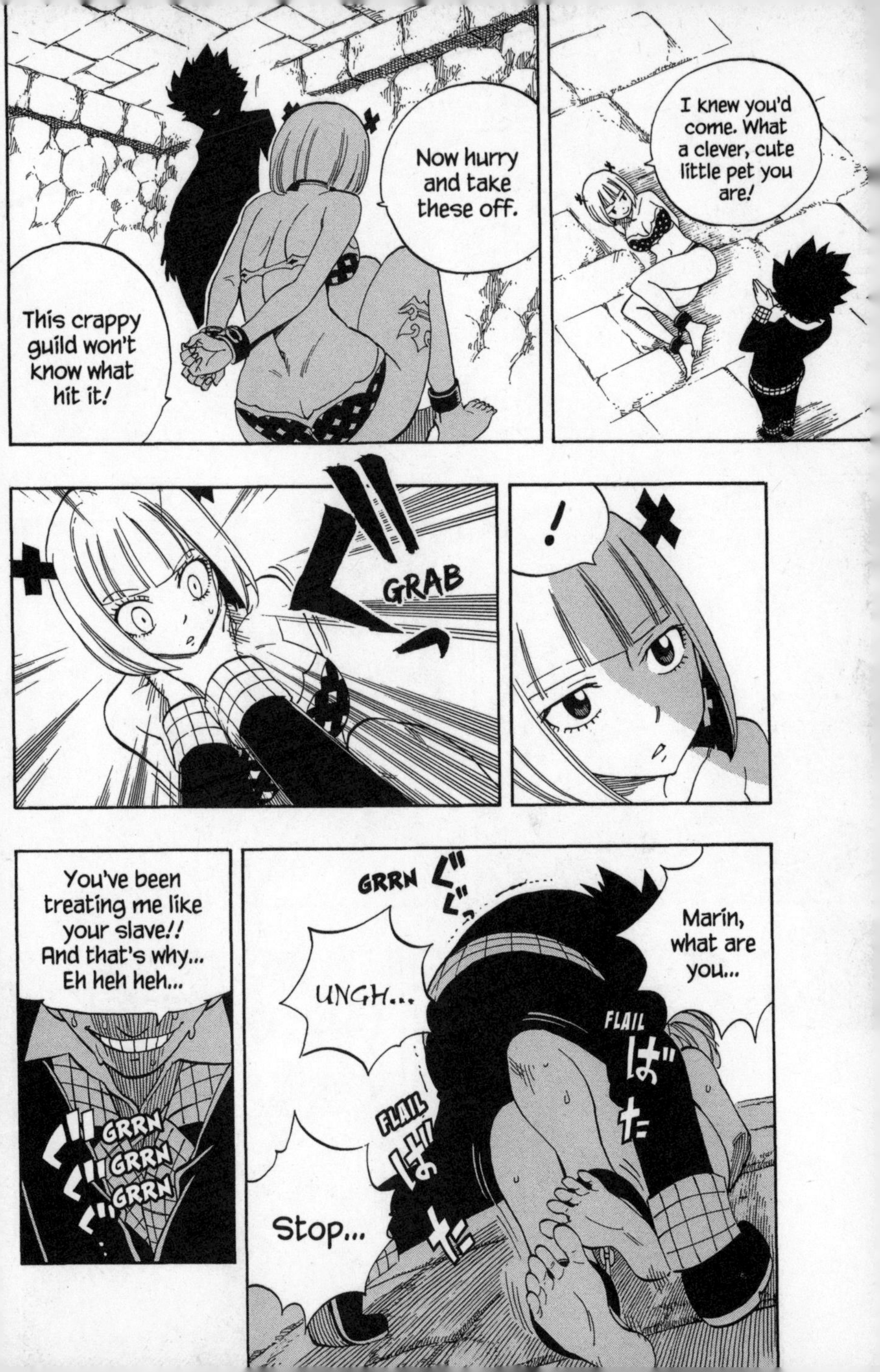

I knew you'd come. What a clever, cute little pet you are!
Now hurry and take these off.
This crappy guild won't know what hit it!
!
GRAB
Marin, what are you...
GRRN
UNGH...
FLAIL
ばた
FLAIL
ばた
Stop...
You've been treating me like your slave!! And that's why... Eh heh heh...
GRRN
GRRN
GRRN

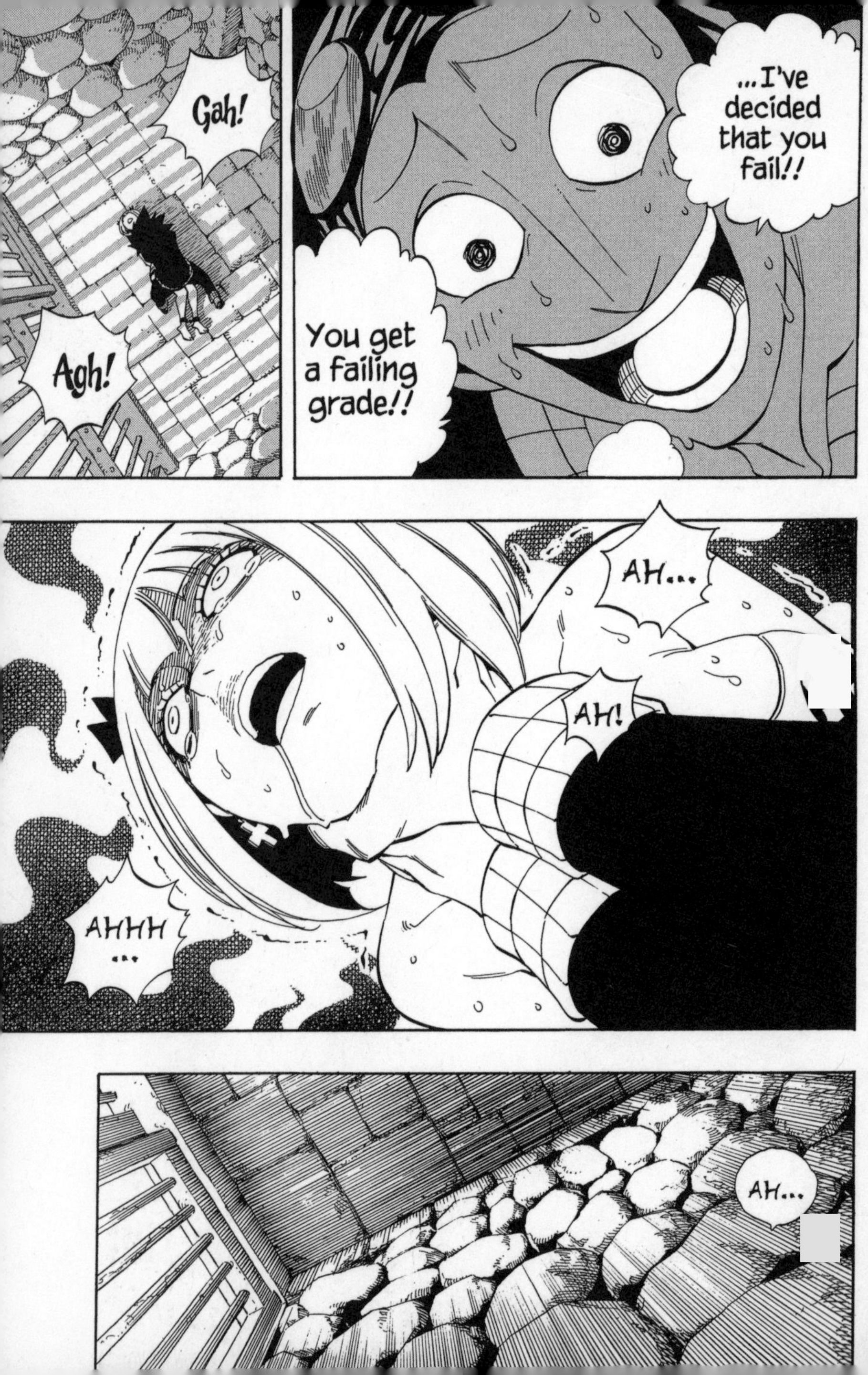
...I've decided that you fail!!
You get a failing grade!!
Gah!
Agh!
AH...
AH!
AHHH ...
AH...

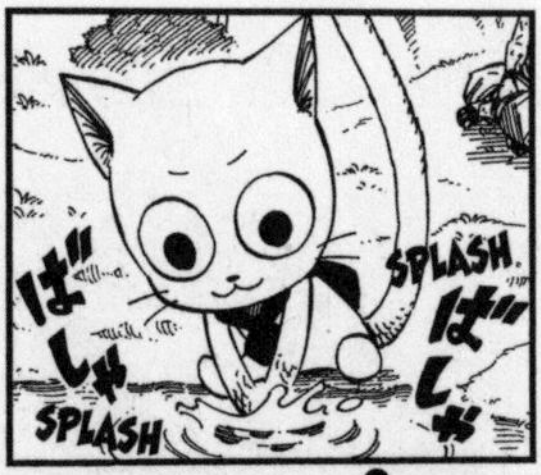
SPLASH.
ばしゃ
ばしゃ
SPLASH

FAIRY TAIL

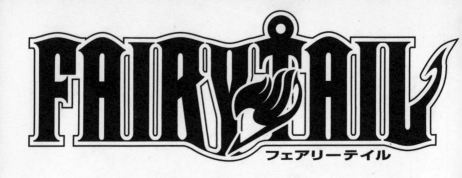

フェアリーテイル

Chapter 467: Mother's Key

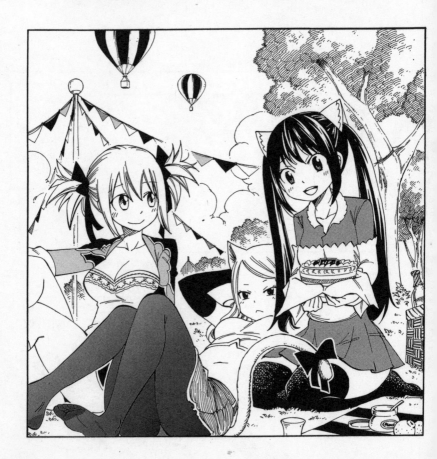

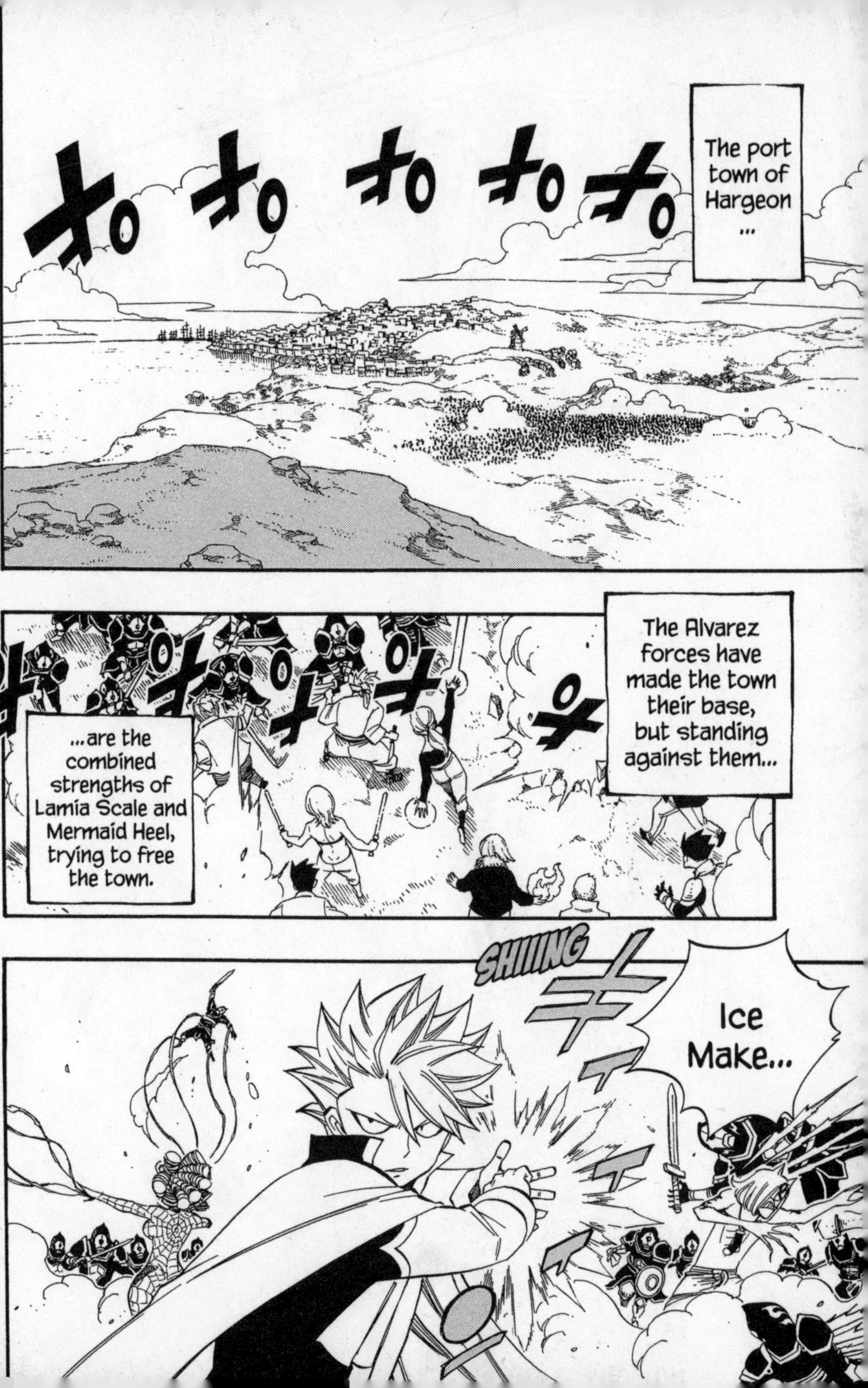
The port town of Hargeon ...
The Alvarez forces have made the town their base, but standing against them...
...are the combined strengths of Lamia Scale and Mermaid Heel, trying to free the town.
SHIIING
Ice Make...

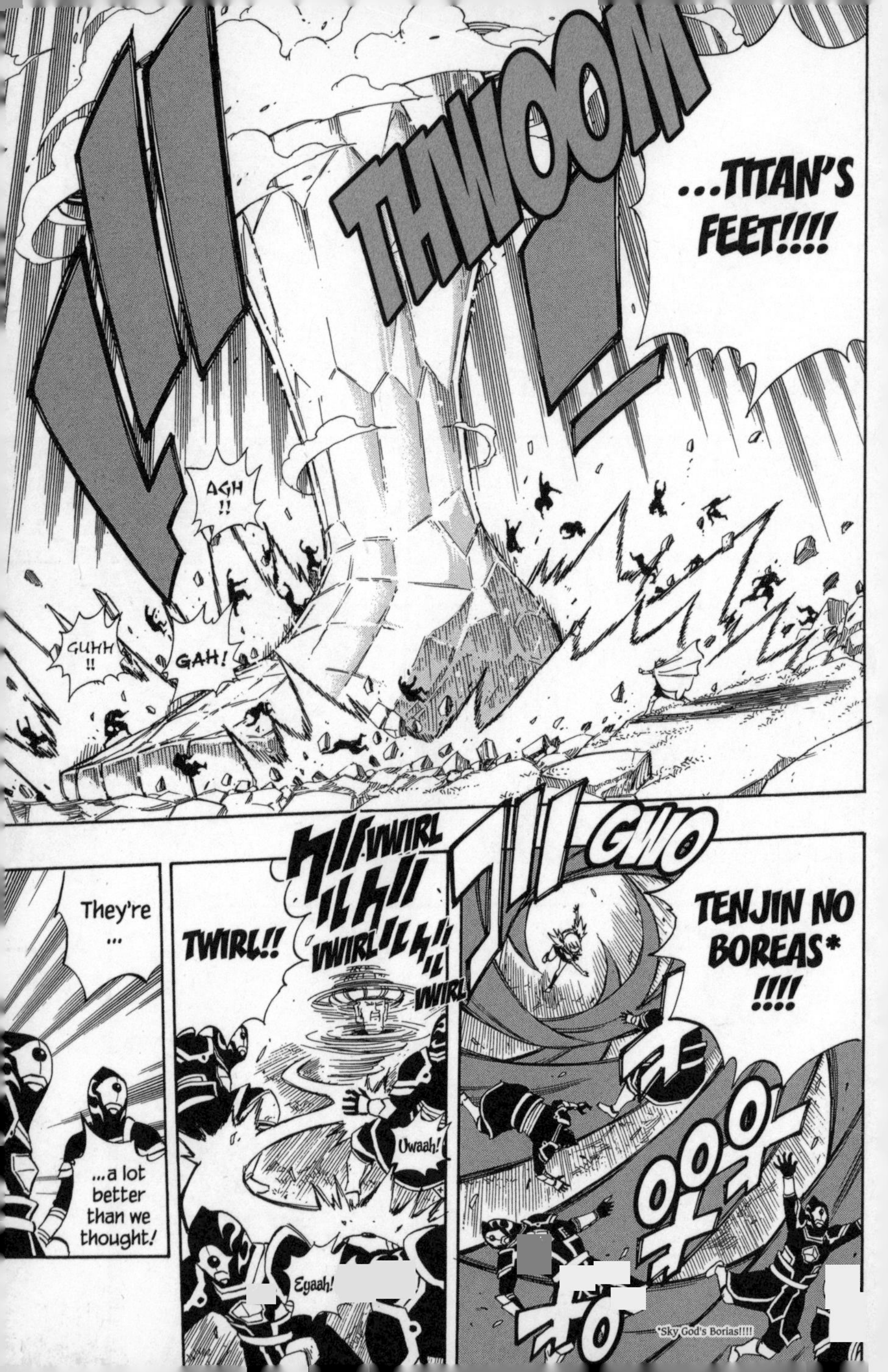
THWOOM
...TITAN'S FEET!!!!
AGH!!
GAH!
GUHH!!
GWO
TENJIN NO BOREAS* !!!!
*Sky God's Borias!!!!
VWIRL
TWIRL!!
VWIRL
VWIRL
Uwaah!
Eyaah!
They're ...
...a lot better than we thought!

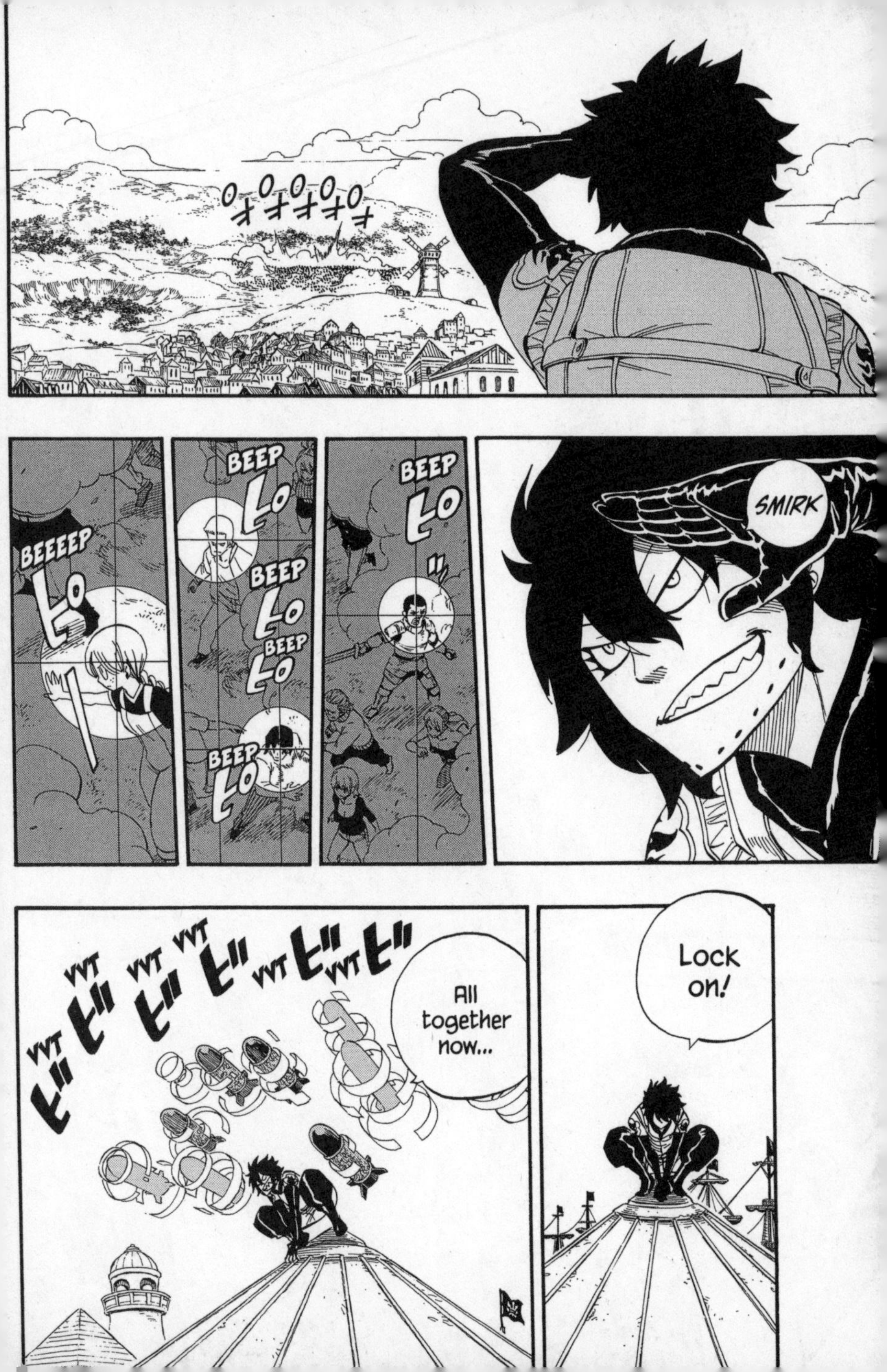

OOOOOO
SMIRK
BEEP
BEEP
BEEP
BEEP
BEEEEP
Lock on!
All together now...
VVT
VVT
VVT
VVT
VVT
VVT

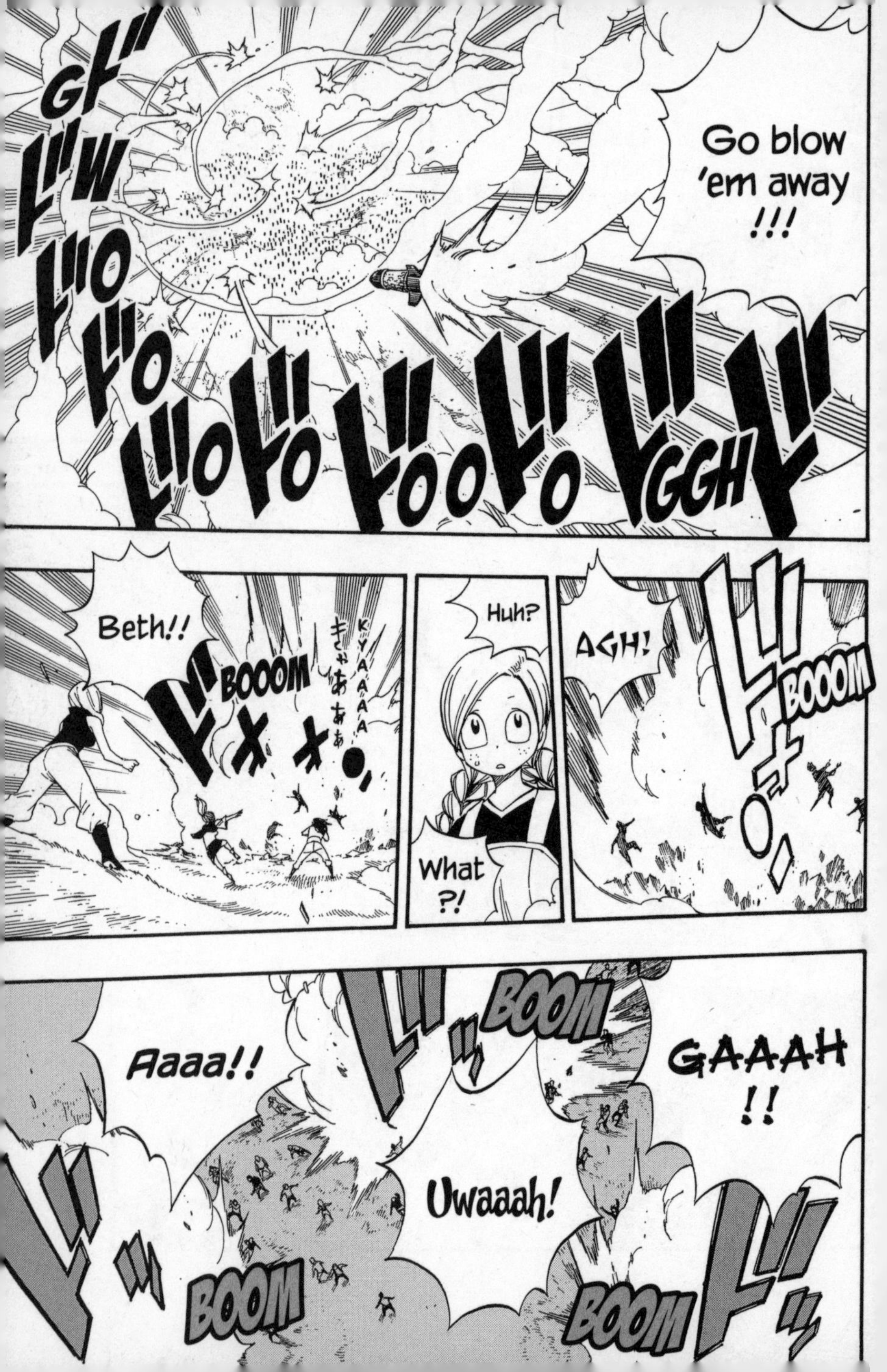
Go blow 'em away !!!
AGH!
BOOOM
Huh?
What ?!
Beth!!
BOOOM
KYAAAA
きゃあああ
GAAAH !!
BOOM
Aaaa!!
Uwaaah!
BOOM
BOOM

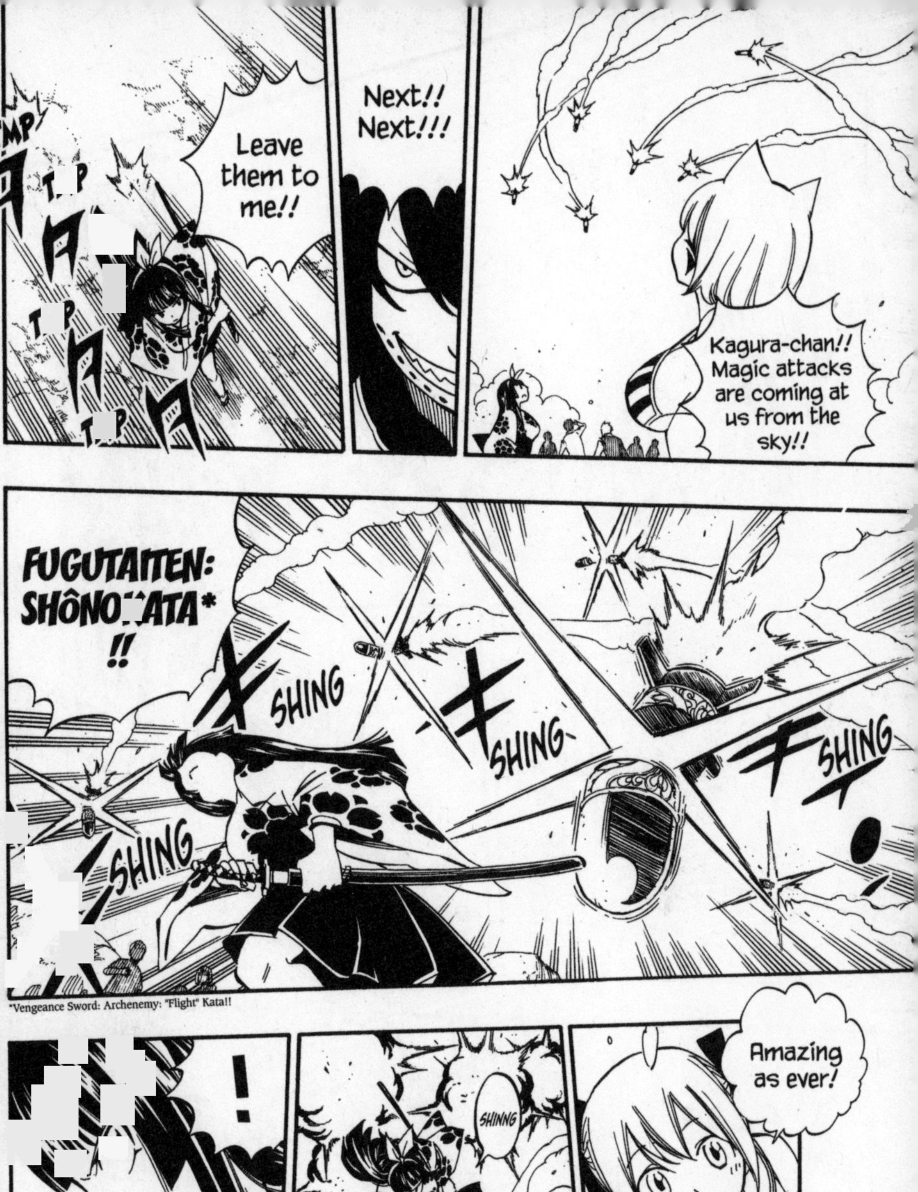
Kagura-chan!! Magic attacks are coming at us from the sky!!
Next!! Next!!!
Leave them to me!!
TMP
FUGUTAITEN:
SHING
SHING
SHING
SHING
Amazing as ever!
SHINNG
!
*Vengeance Sword: Archenemy: "Flight" Kata!!

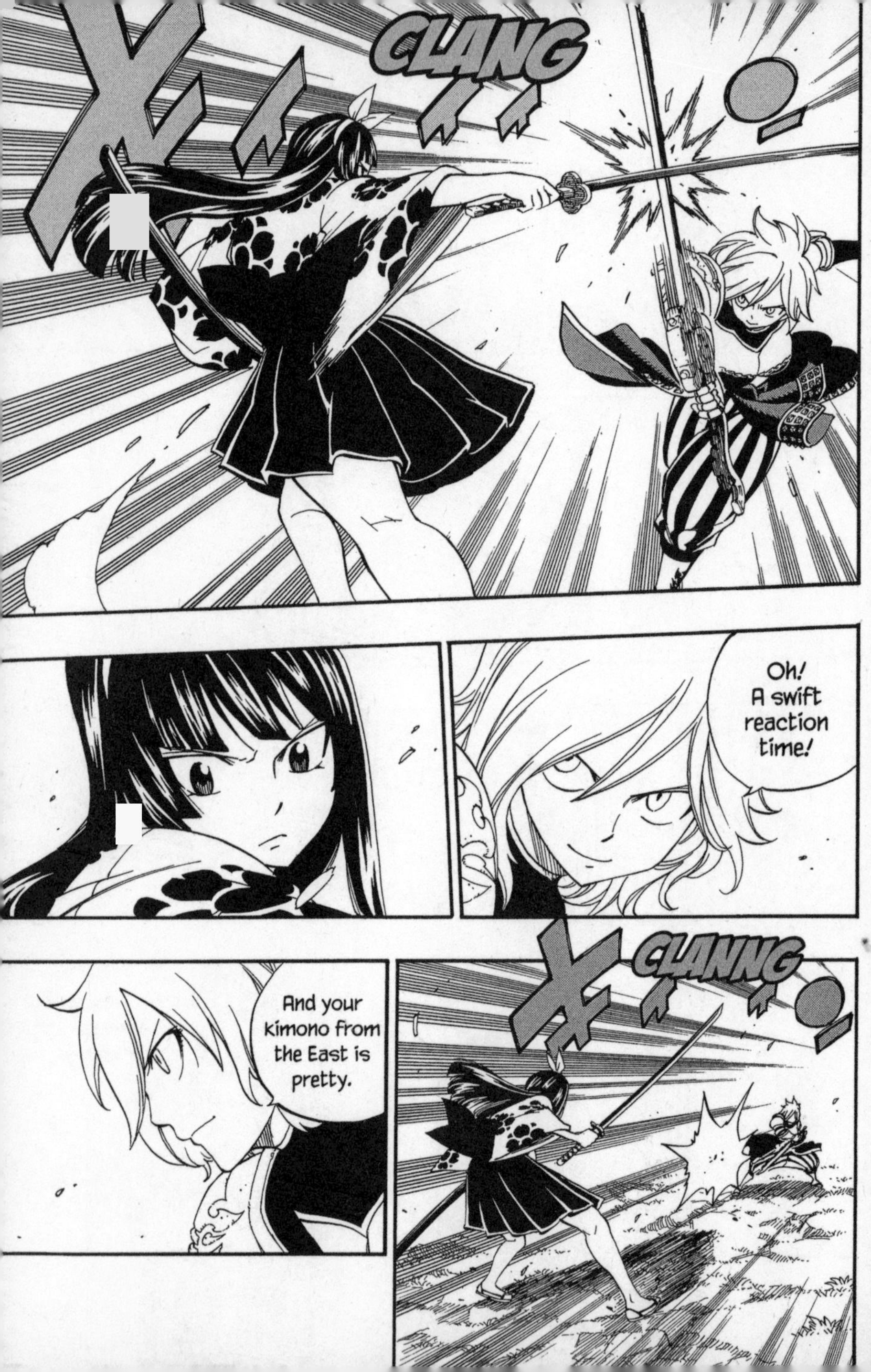
CLANG
Oh! A swift reaction time!
CLANNG
And your kimono from the East is pretty.

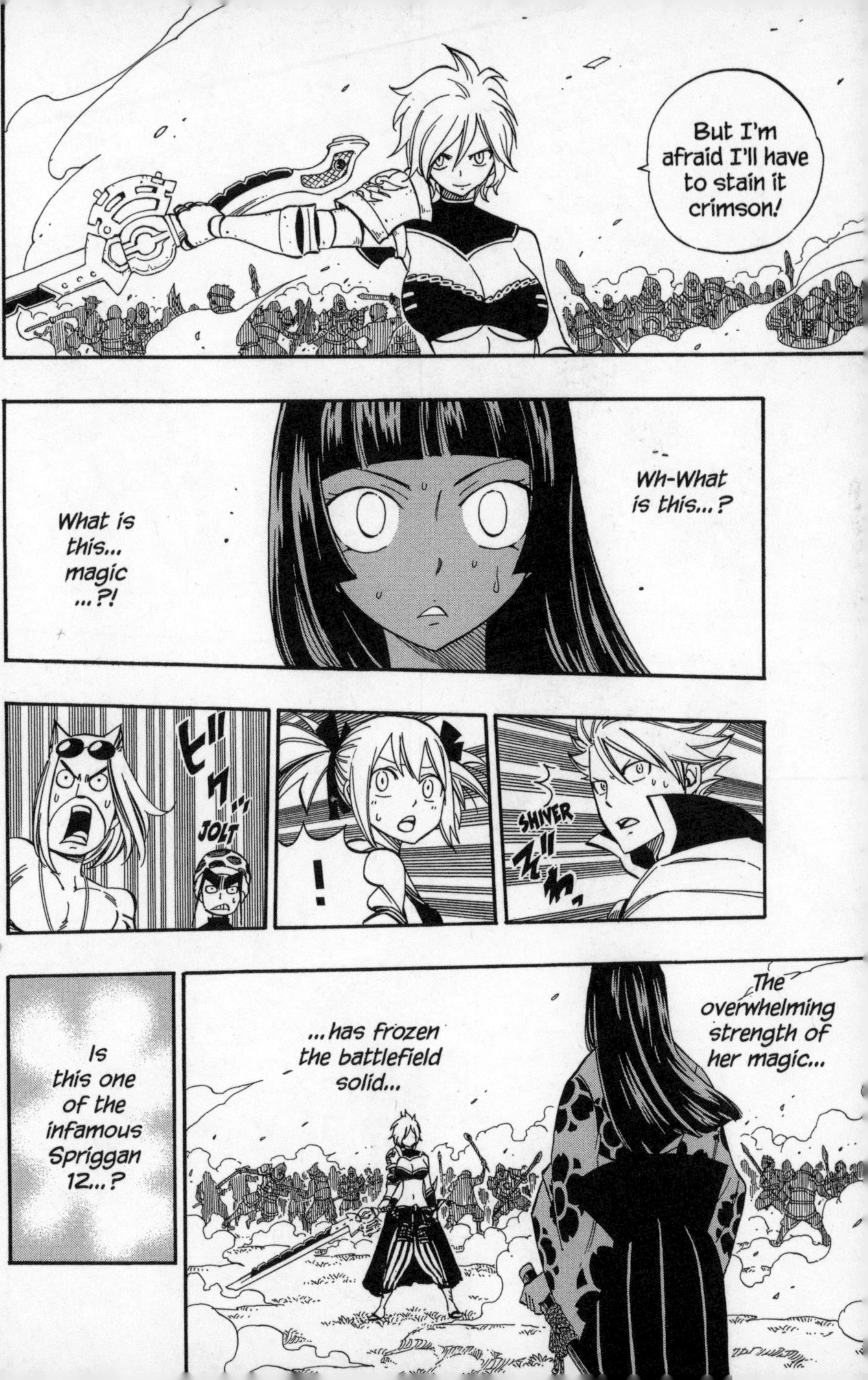
But I'm afraid I'll have to stain it crimson!
Wh-What is this...?
What is this... magic ...?!
SHIVER
!
JOLT
The overwhelming strength of her magic...
...has frozen the battlefield solid...
Is this one of the infamous Spriggan 12...?

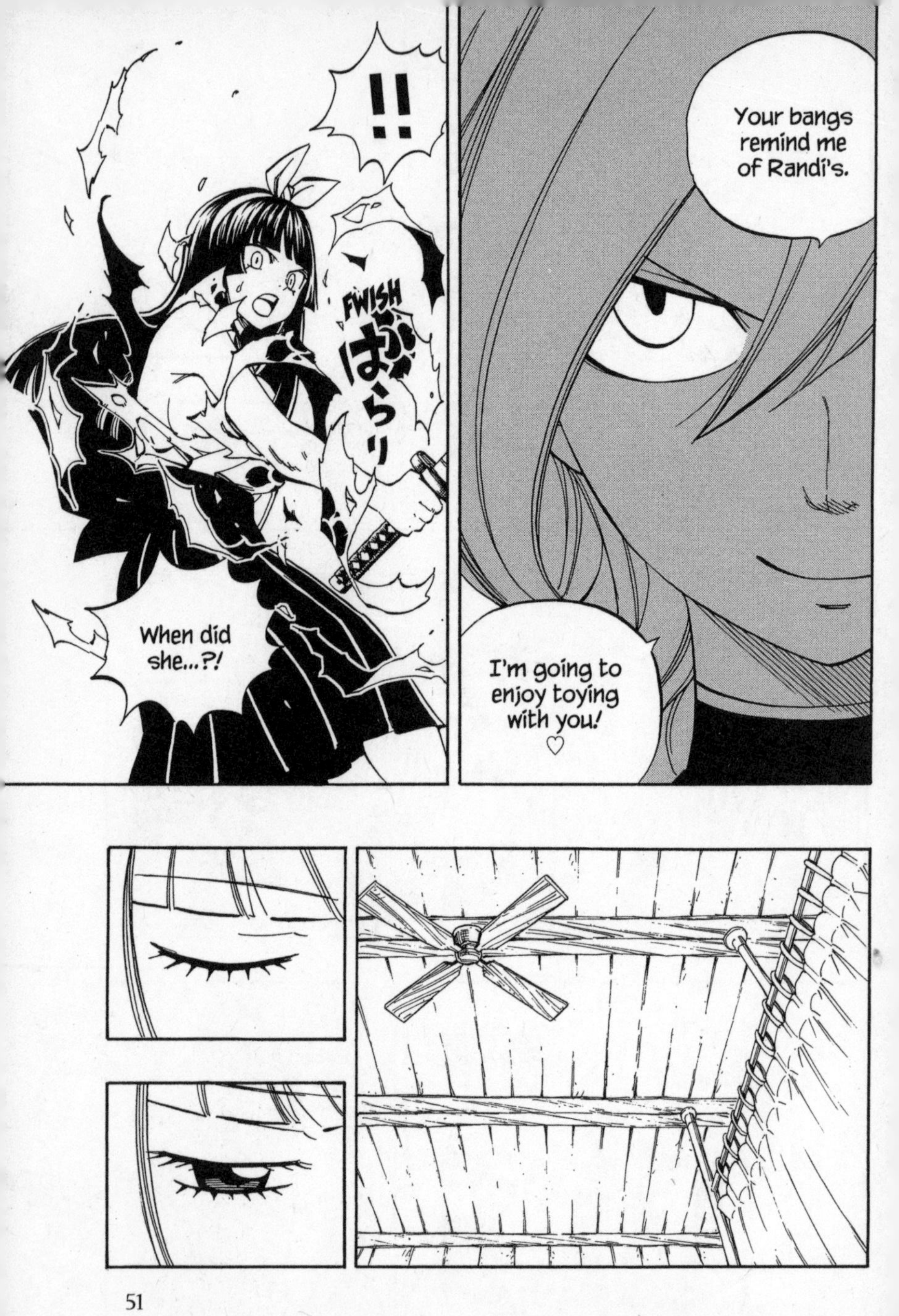
Your bangs remind me of Randi's.
I'm going to enjoy toying with you! ♡
!!
FWISH
はらり
When did she...?!

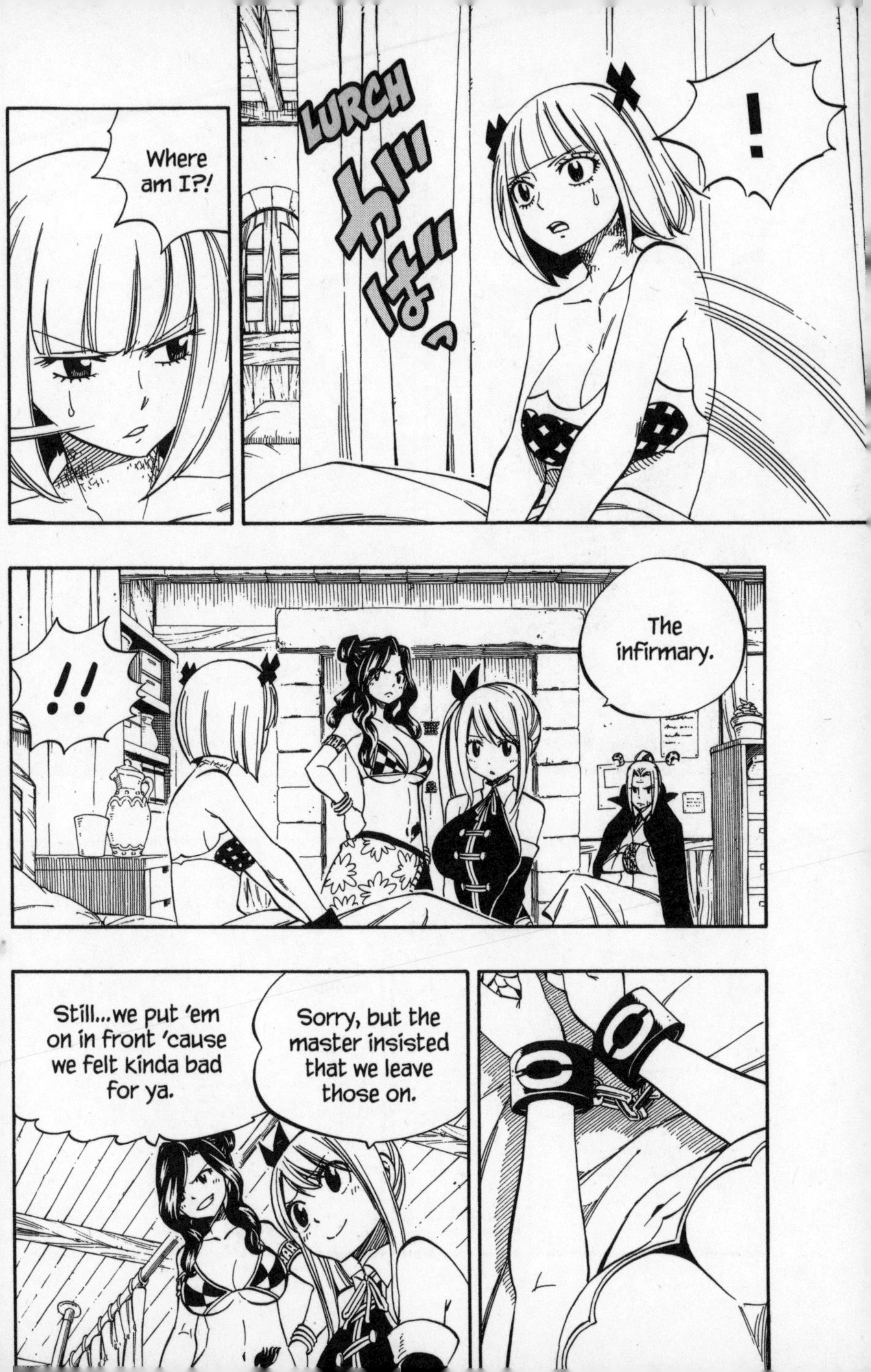

!
LURCH
Where am I?!
The infirmary.
!!
Sorry, but the master insisted that we leave those on.
Still...we put 'em on in front 'cause we felt kinda bad for ya.

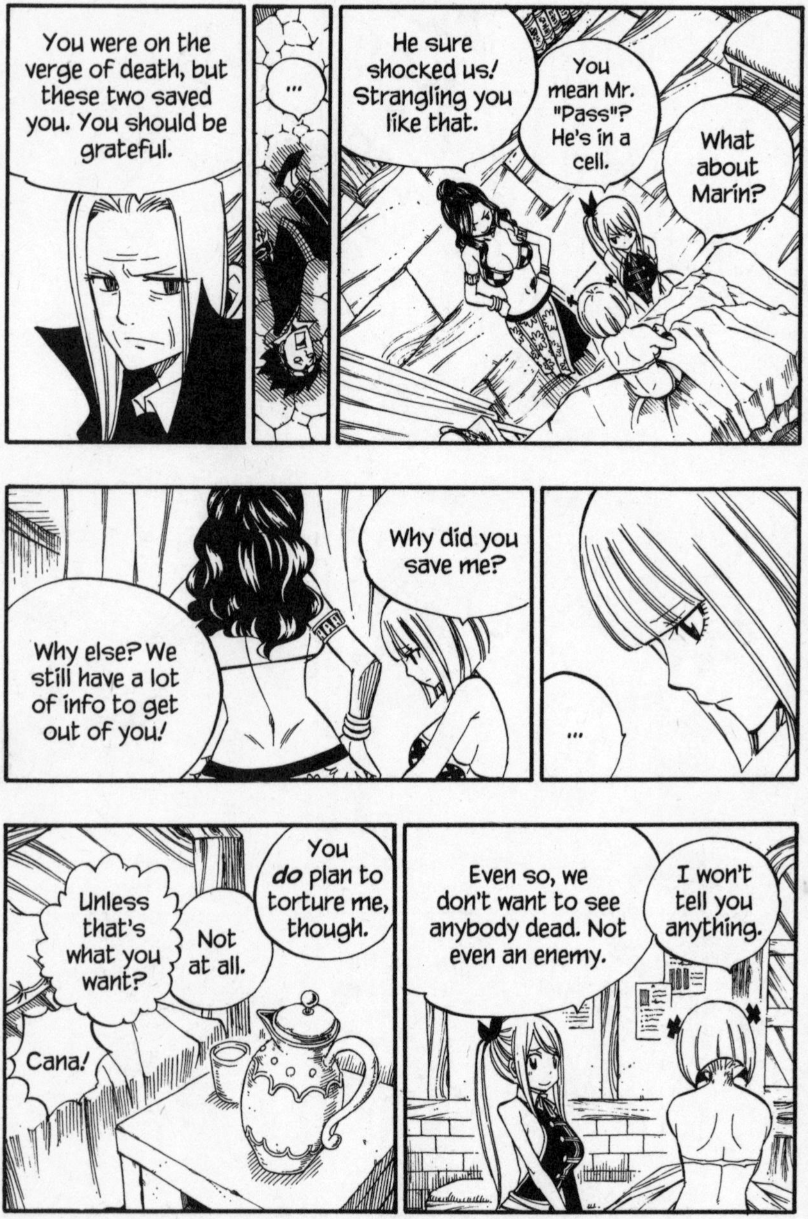
What about Marin?
You mean Mr. "Pass"? He's in a cell.
He sure shocked us! Strangling you like that.
...
You were on the verge of death, but these two saved you. You should be grateful.
...
Why did you save me?
Why else? We still have a lot of info to get out of you!
I won't tell you anything.
Even so, we don't want to see anybody dead. Not even an enemy.
You *do* plan to torture me, though.
Not at all.
Unless that's what you want?
Cana!

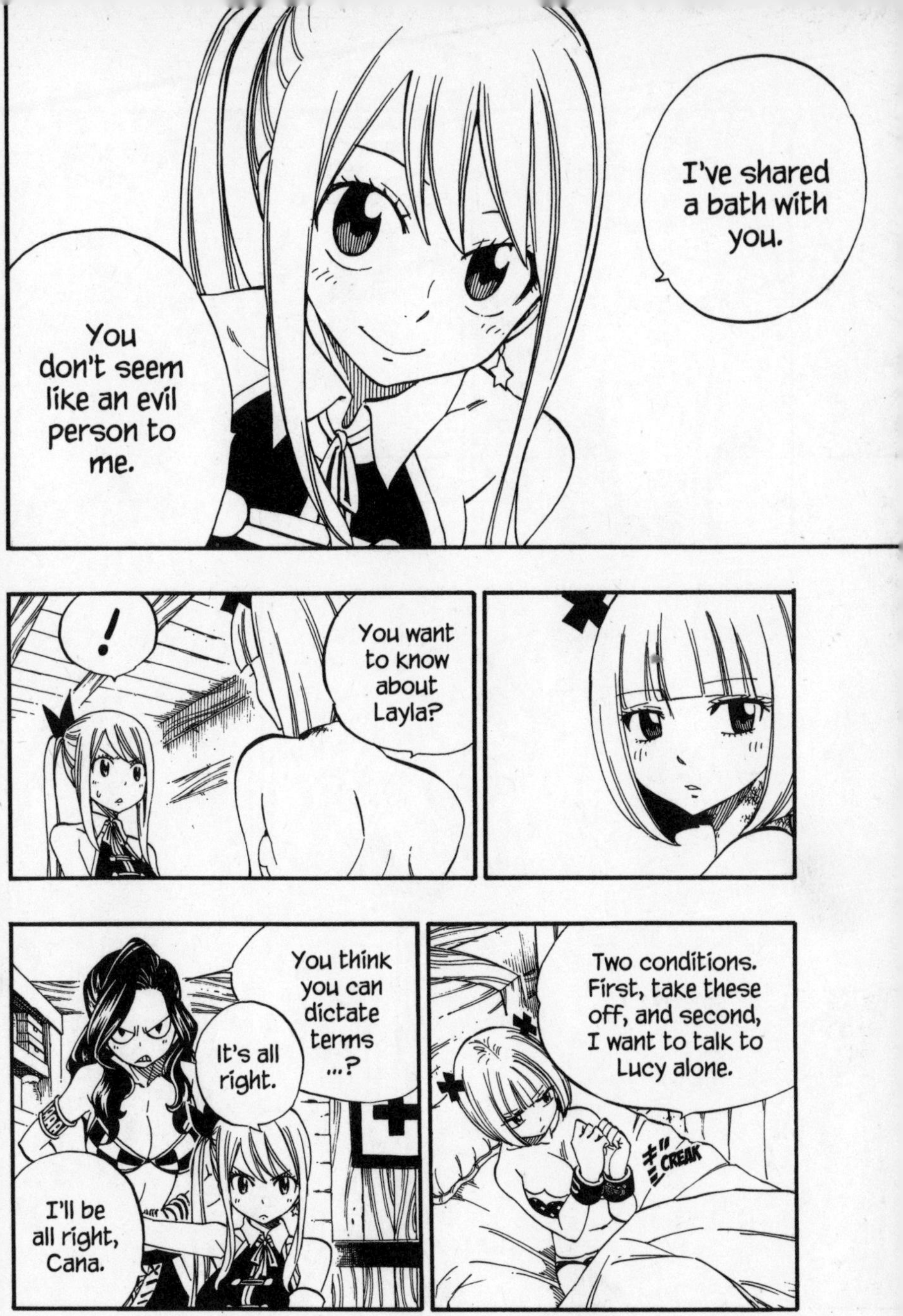
I've shared a bath with you.
You don't seem like an evil person to me.
You want to know about Layla?
!
Two conditions. First, take these off, and second, I want to talk to Lucy alone.
CREAK
You think you can dictate terms ...?
It's all right.
I'll be all right, Cana.

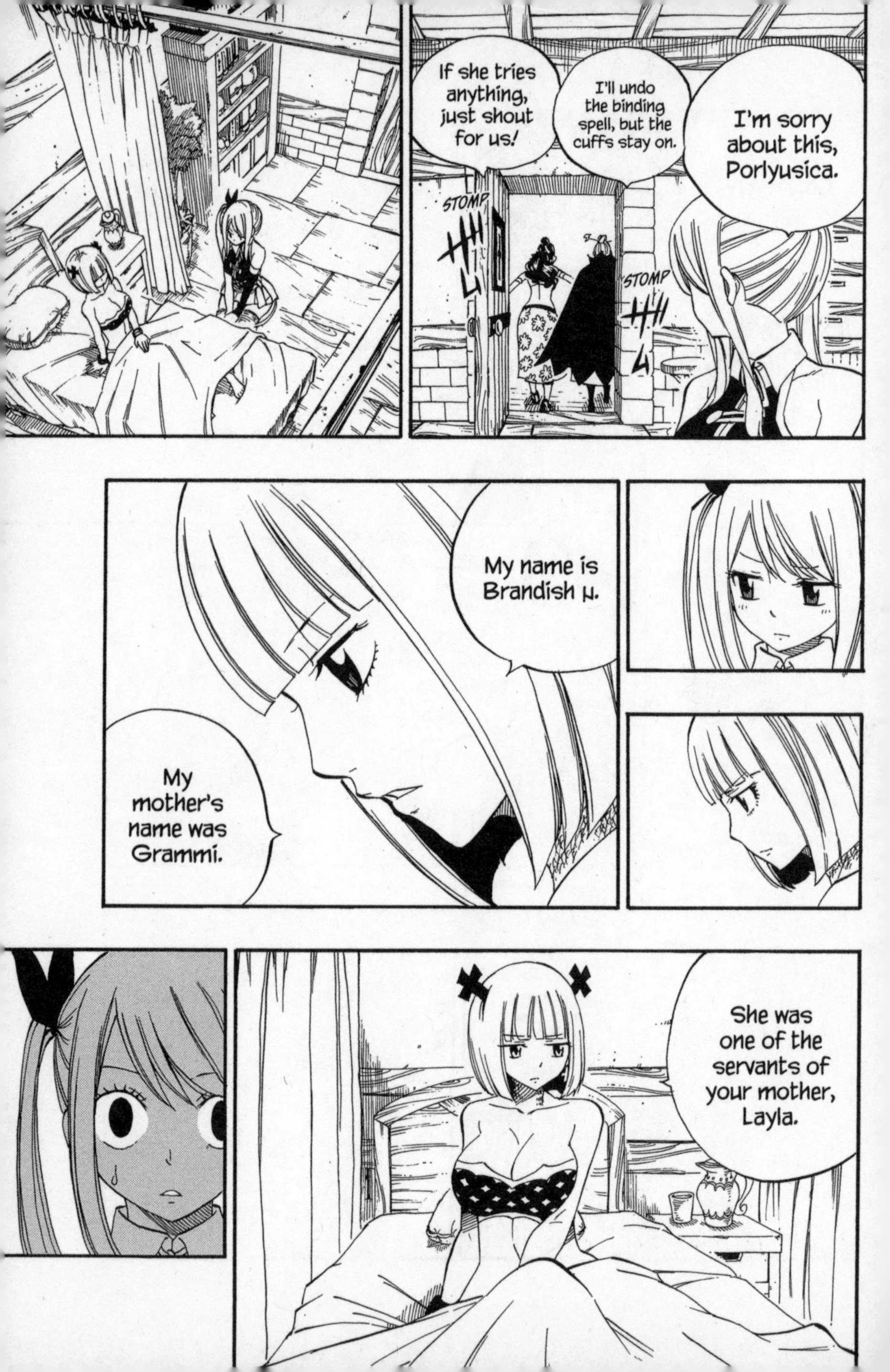
I'm sorry about this, Porlyusica.
I'll undo the binding spell, but the cuffs stay on.
If she tries anything, just shout for us!
STOMP
STOMP
My name is Brandish μ.
My mother's name was Grammi.
She was one of the servants of your mother, Layla.

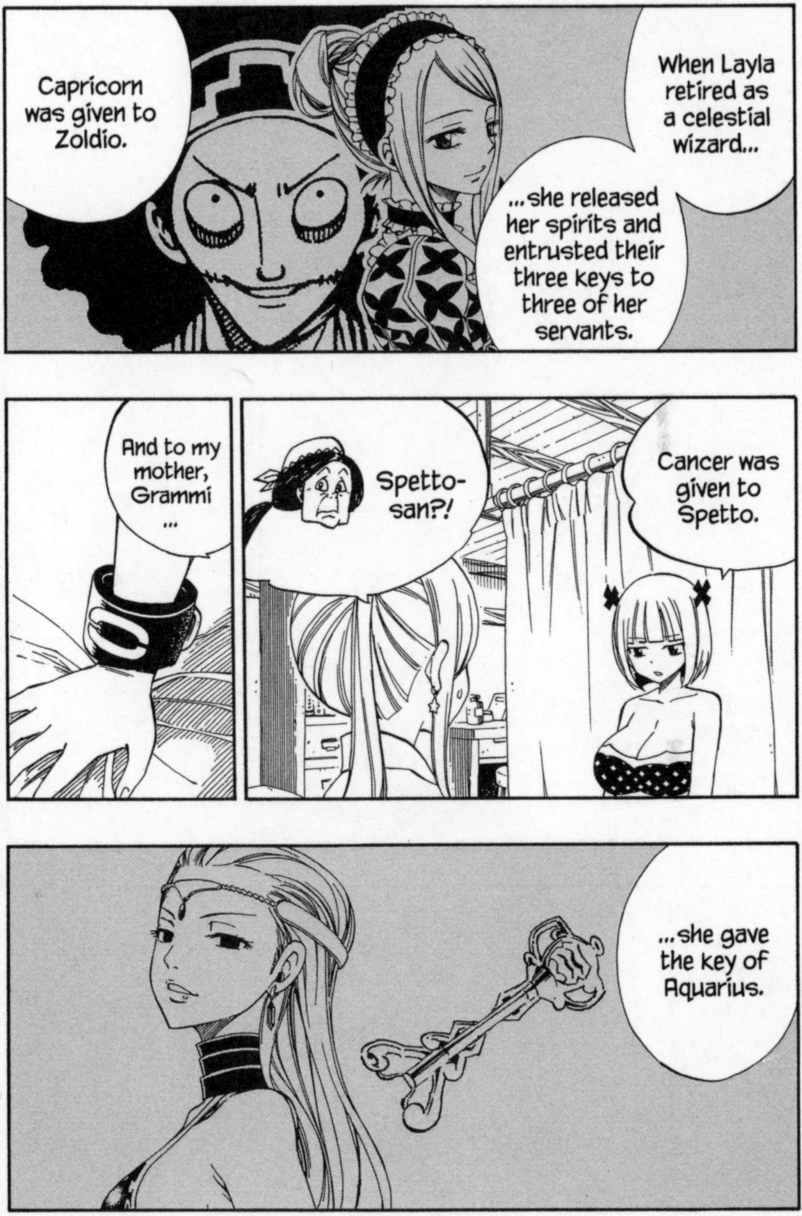
When Layla retired as a celestial wizard...
...she released her spirits and entrusted their three keys to three of her servants.
Capricorn was given to Zoldio.
Cancer was given to Spetto.
Spetto-san?!
And to my mother, Grammi ...
...she gave the key of Aquarius.

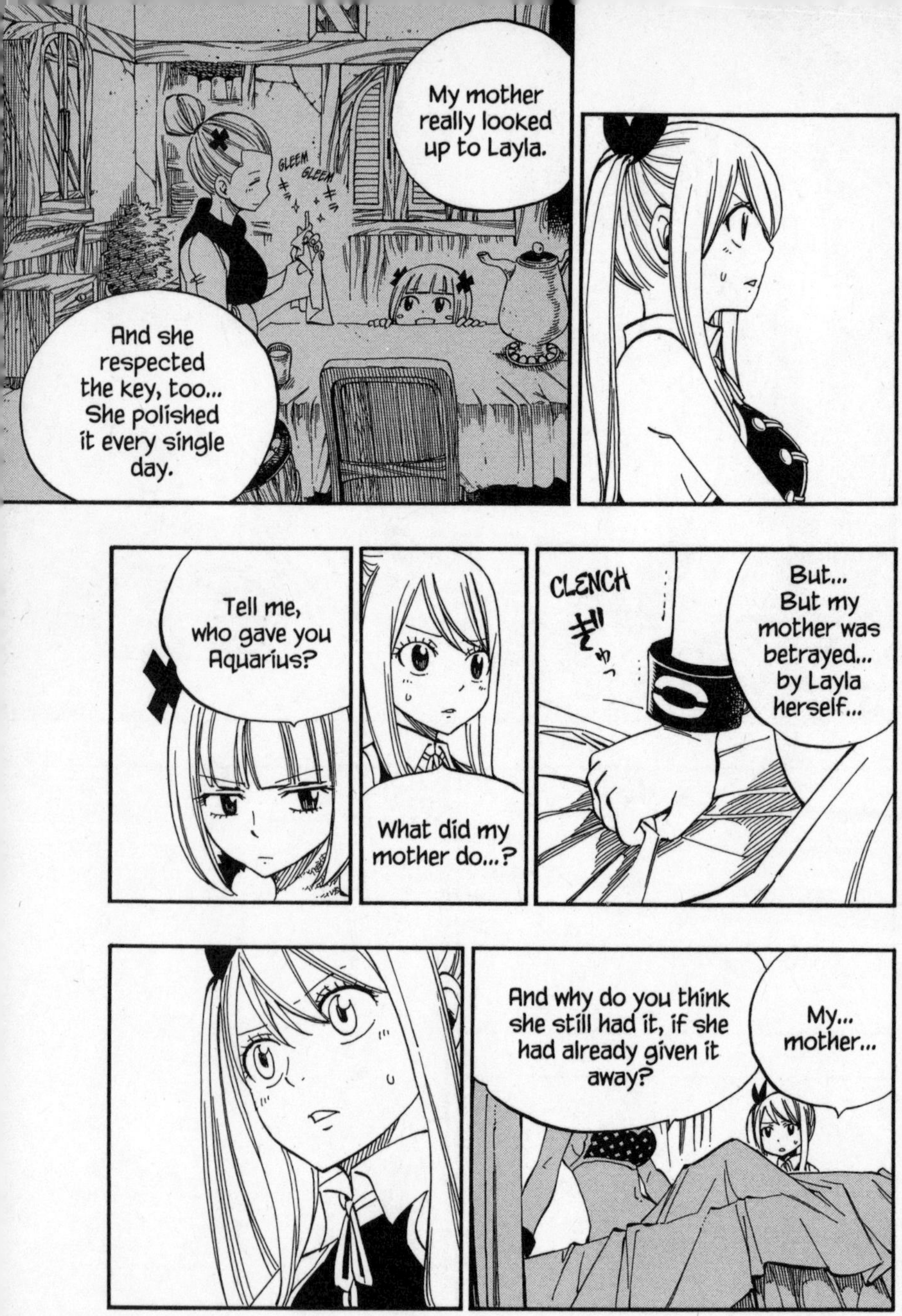
My mother really looked up to Layla.
GLEEM GLEEM
And she respected the key, too... She polished it every single day.
But... But my mother was betrayed... by Layla herself...
CLENCH
What did my mother do...?
Tell me, who gave you Aquarius?
My... mother...
And why do you think she still had it, if she had already given it away?

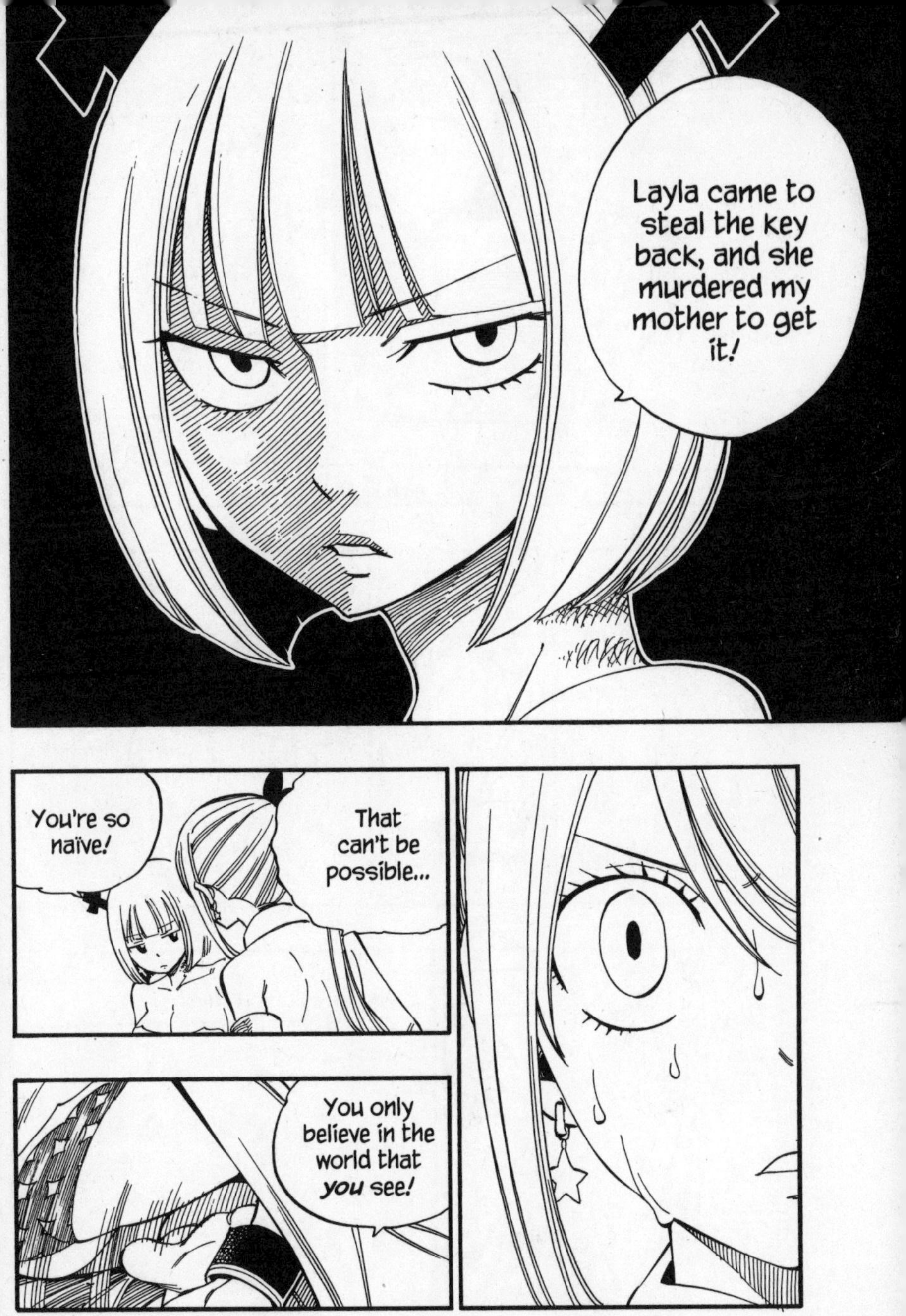
Layla came to steal the key back, and she murdered my mother to get it!
That can't be possible...
You're so naïve!
You only believe in the world that *you* see!

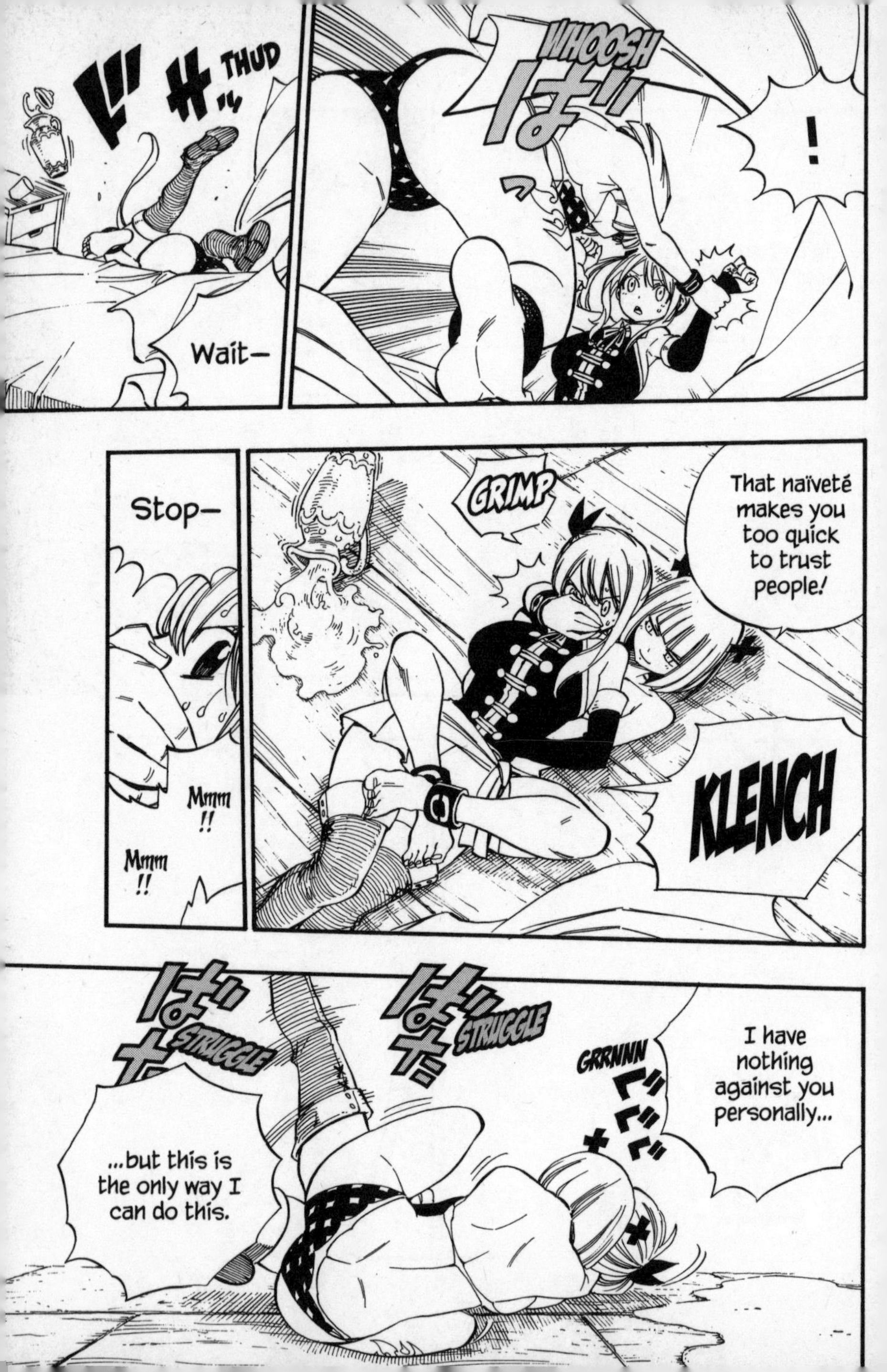
WHOOSH
!
THUD
Wait—
That naïveté makes you too quick to trust people!
GRIMP
KLENCH
Stop—
Mmm !!
Mmm !!
I have nothing against you personally...
GRRNNN
STRUGGLE
STRUGGLE
...but this is the only way I can do this.

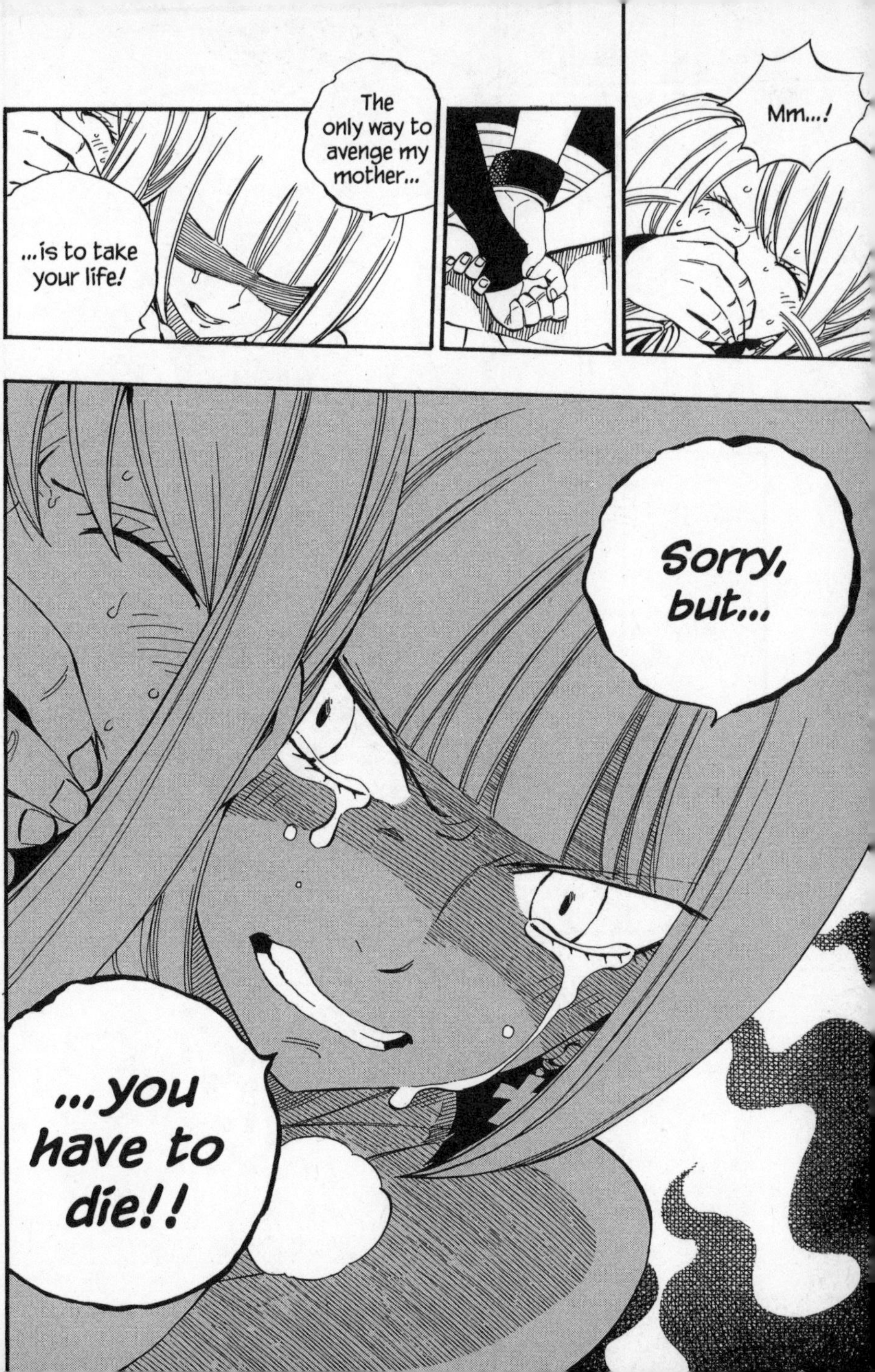
Mm...!
The only way to avenge my mother...
...is to take your life!
Sorry, but...
...you have to die!!

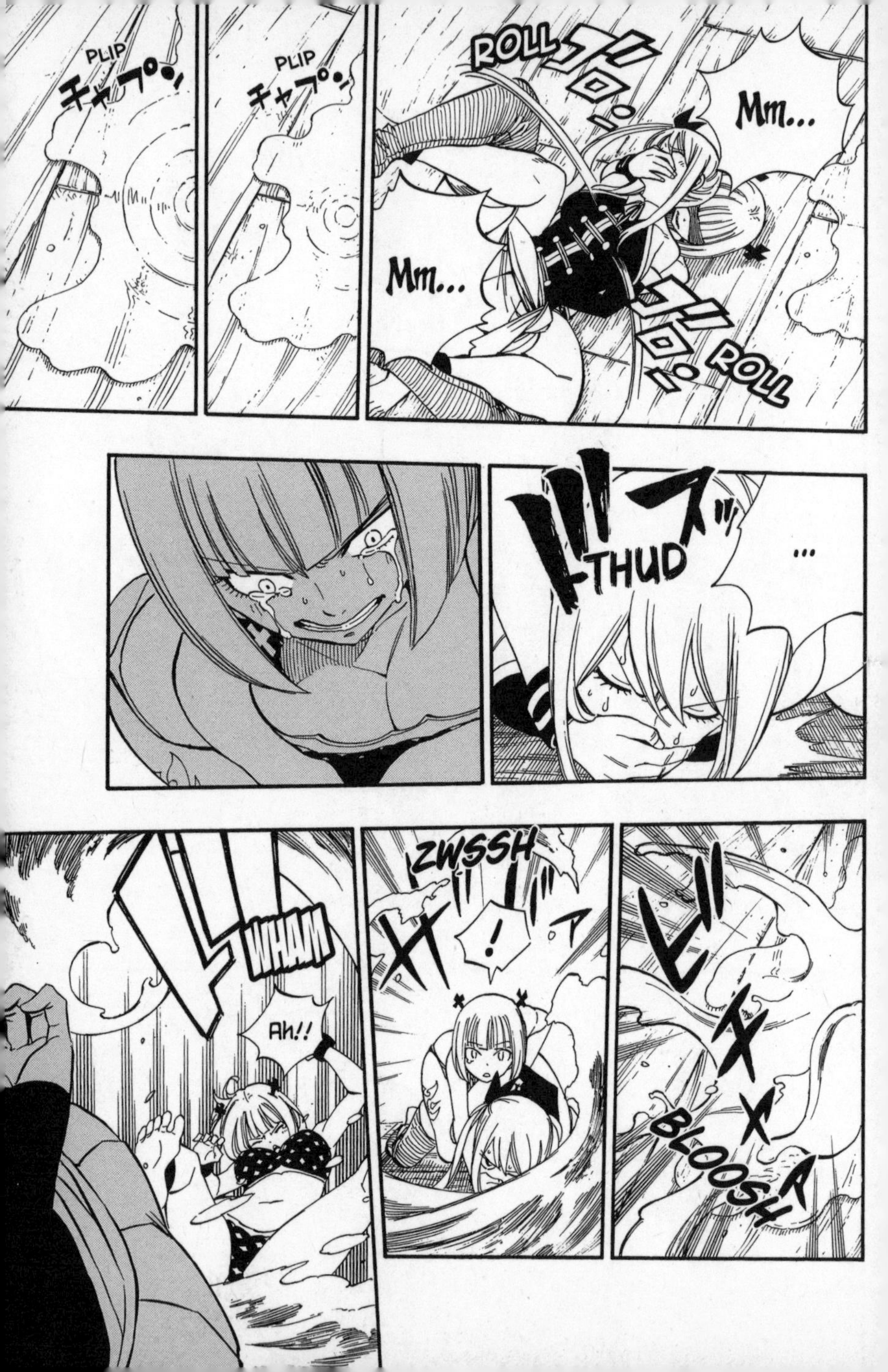
Mm...
ROLL
Mm...
ROLL
PLIP
チャプ
PLIP
チャプ
THUD
...
BLOOSH
ZWSSH
!
WHAM
Ah!!

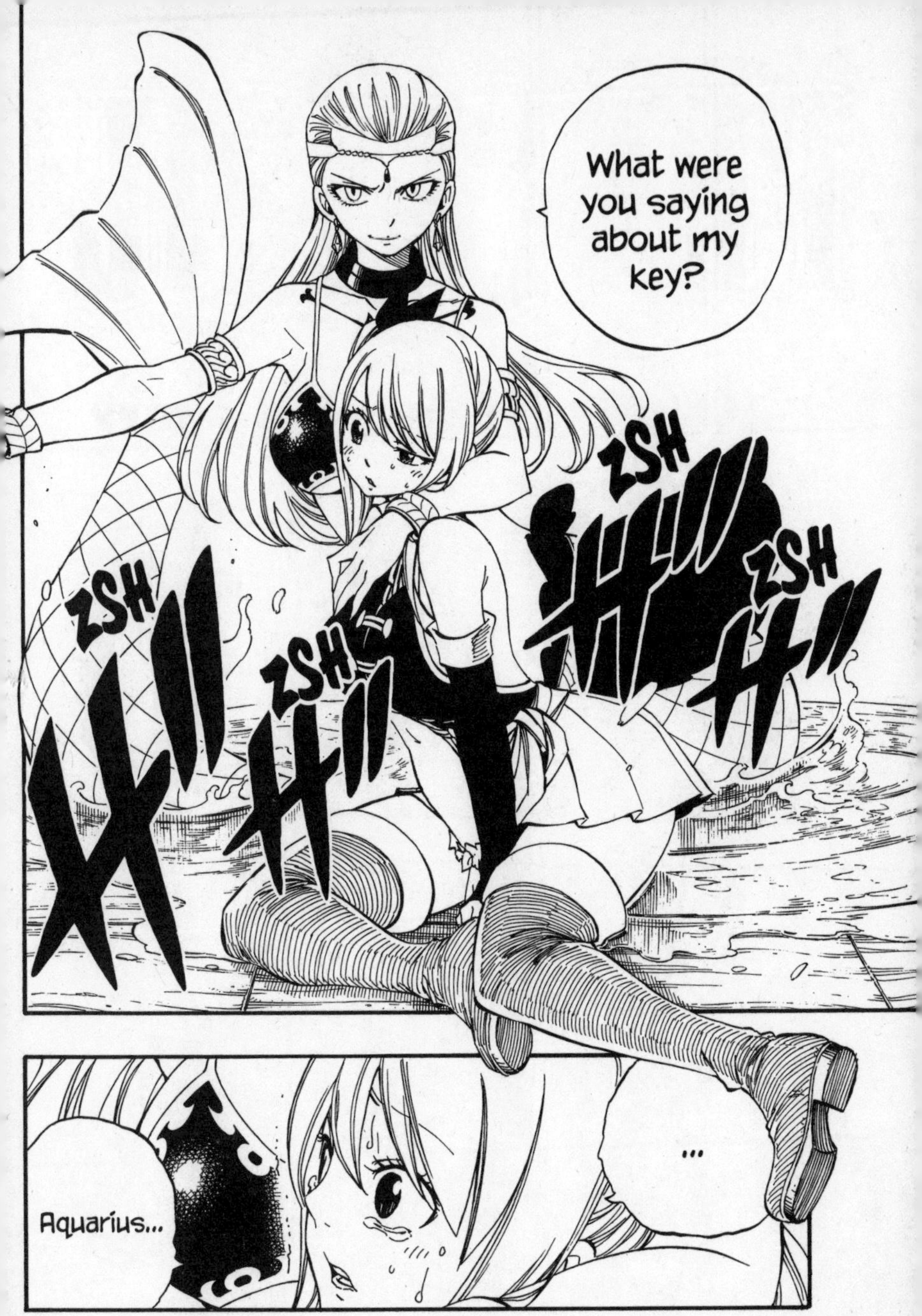
What were you saying about my key?
ZSH
ZSH
ZSH
ZSH
...
Aquarius...

FAIRY TAIL

フェアリーテイル

Chapter 468: Star Memory

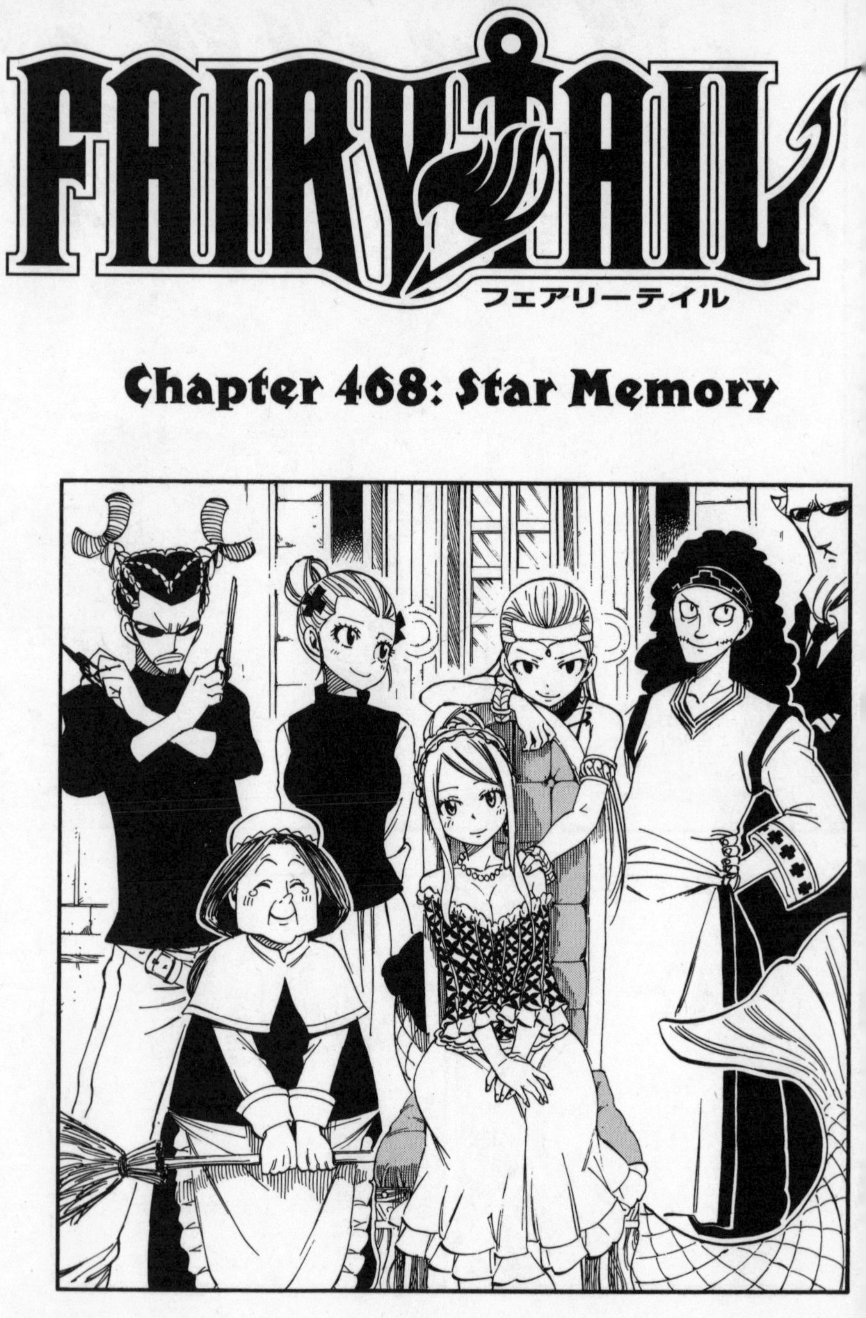

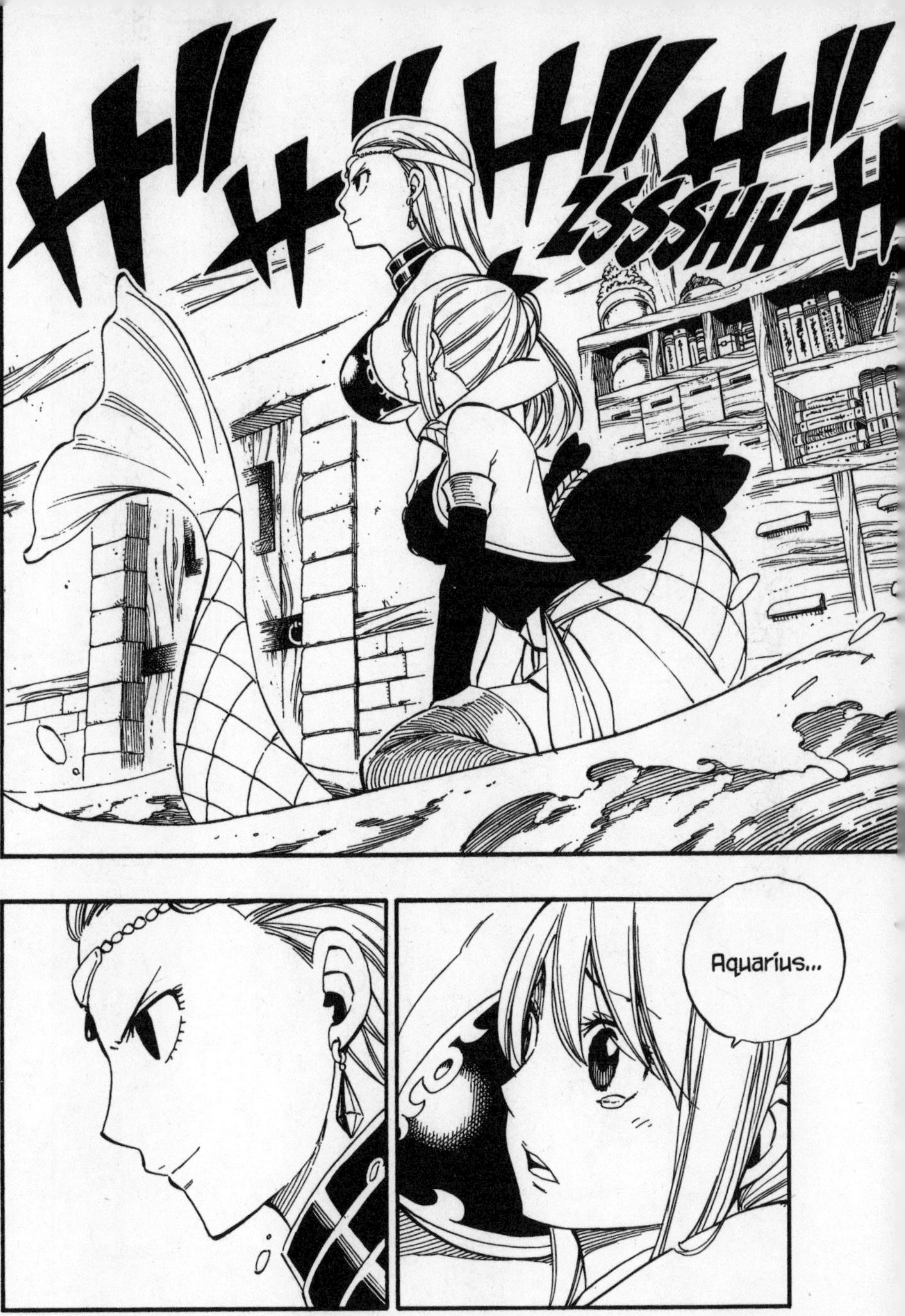
ZSSSHH
Aquarius...

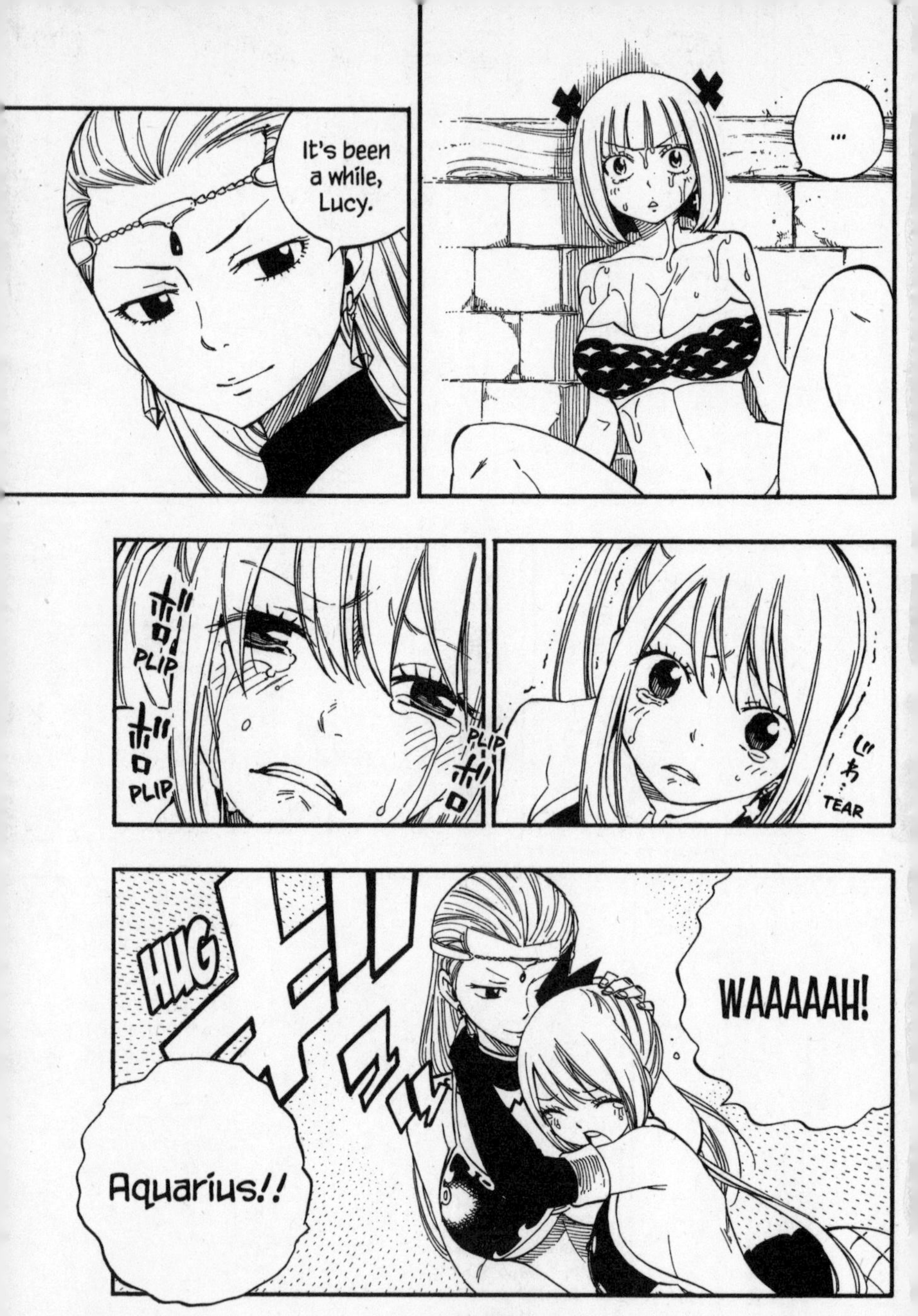
...
It's been a while, Lucy.
じわ…
TEAR
ポロ
PLIP
ポロ
PLIP
ポロ
PLIP
WAAAAH!
HUG
Aquarius!!

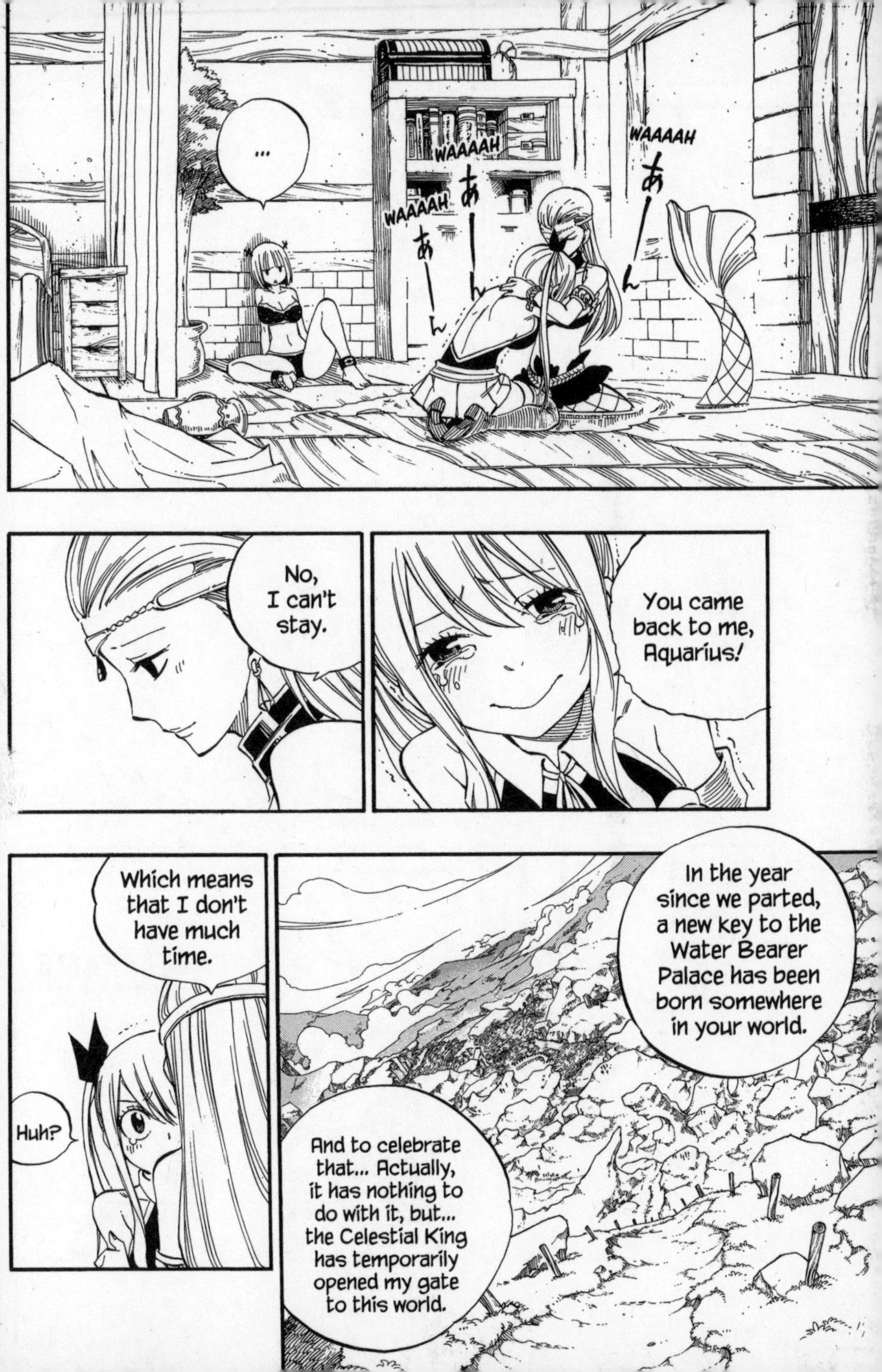
WAAAAH
あーん
WAAAAH
あーん
WAAAAH
あーん
...
You came back to me, Aquarius!
No, I can't stay.
In the year since we parted, a new key to the Water Bearer Palace has been born somewhere in your world.
And to celebrate that... Actually, it has nothing to do with it, but... the Celestial King has temporarily opened my gate to this world.
Which means that I don't have much time.
Huh?

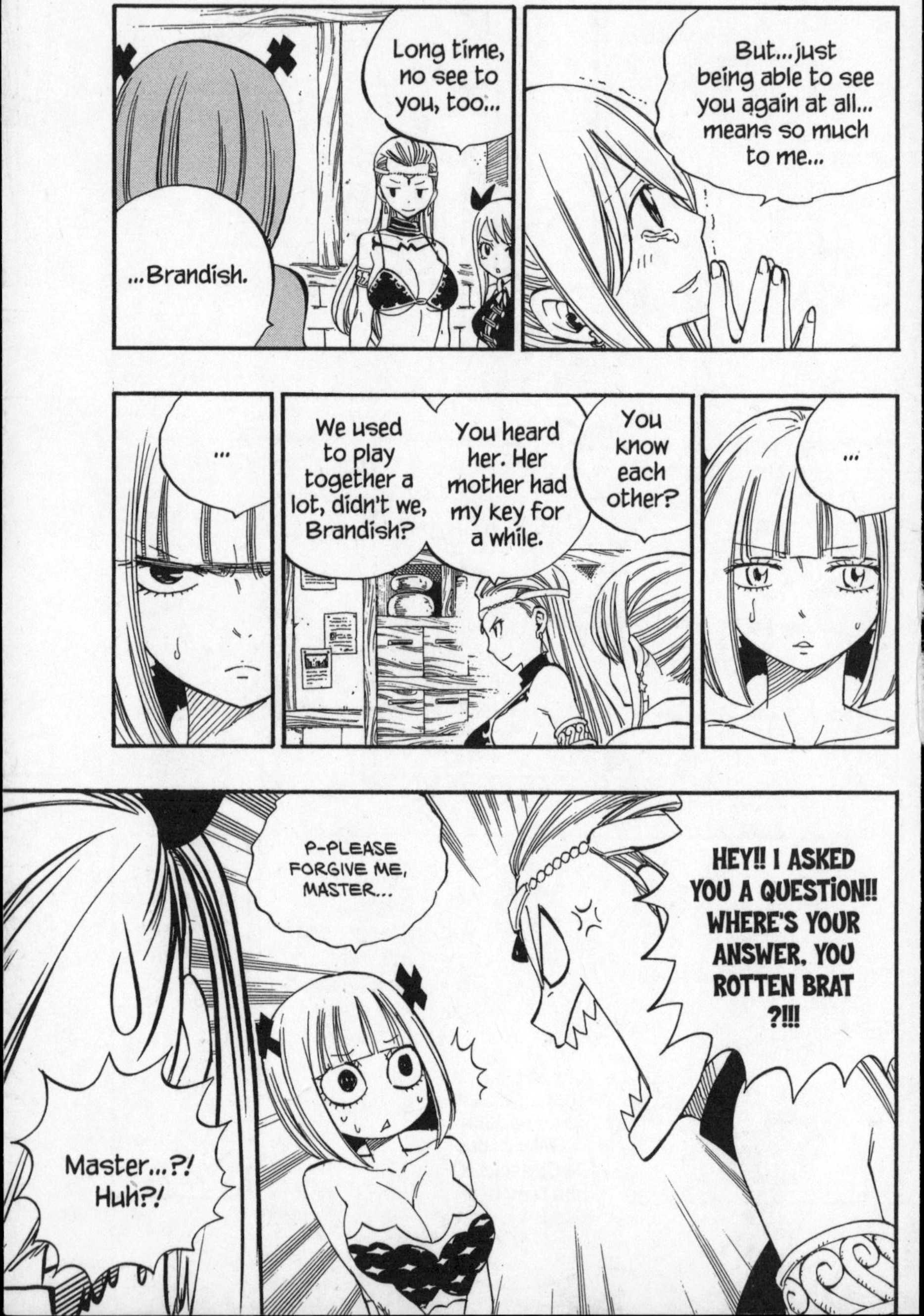
But...just being able to see you again at all... means so much to me...
Long time, no see to you, too...
...Brandish.
...
You know each other?
You heard her. Her mother had my key for a while.
We used to play together a lot, didn't we, Brandish?
...
HEY!! I ASKED YOU A QUESTION!! WHERE'S YOUR ANSWER, YOU ROTTEN BRAT ?!!!
P-PLEASE FORGIVE ME, MASTER...
Master...?! Huh?!

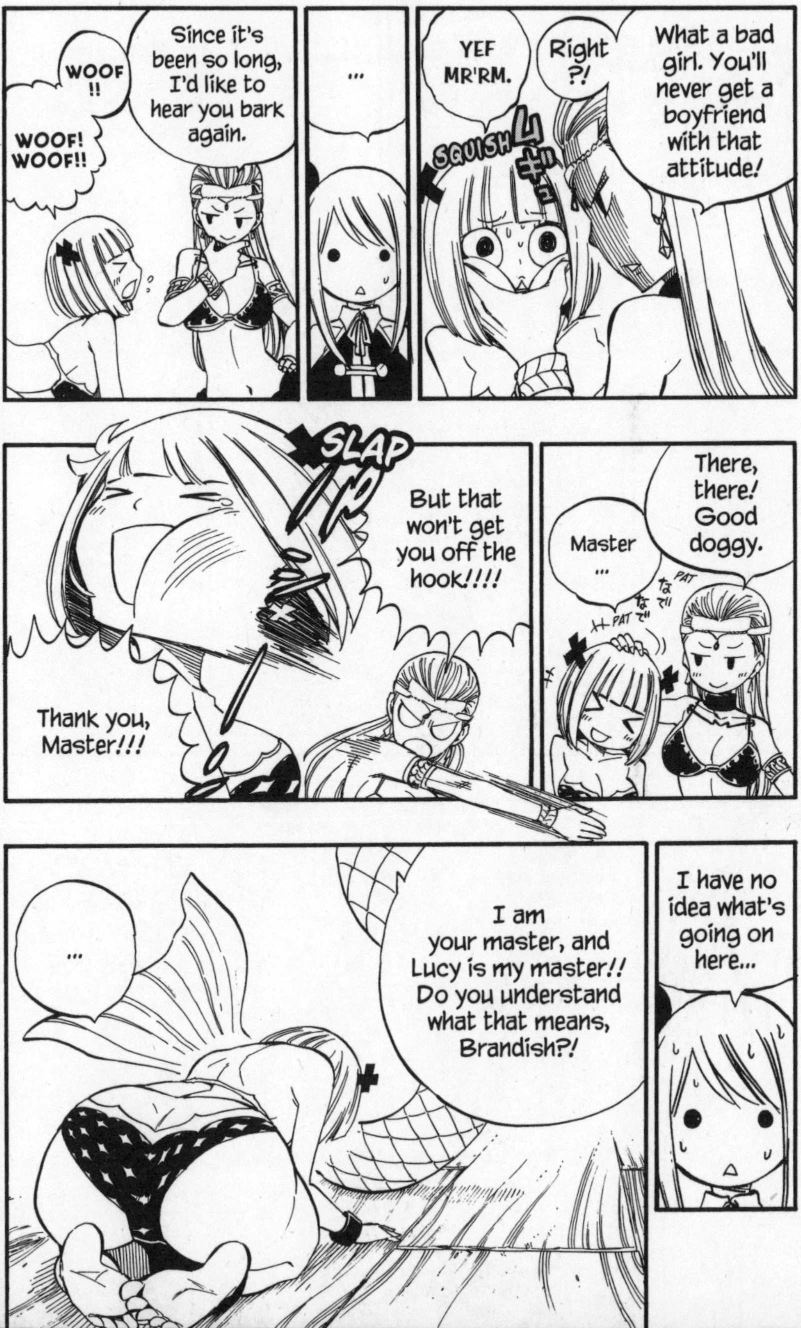
What a bad girl. You'll never get a boyfriend with that attitude!
Right?!
YEF MR'RM.
SQUISH
...
Since it's been so long, I'd like to hear you bark again.
WOOF!!
WOOF! WOOF!!
There, there! Good doggy.
PAT
PAT
Master ...
SLAP
But that won't get you off the hook!!!!
Thank you, Master!!!
I have no idea what's going on here...
I am your master, and Lucy is my master!! Do you understand what that means, Brandish?!
...

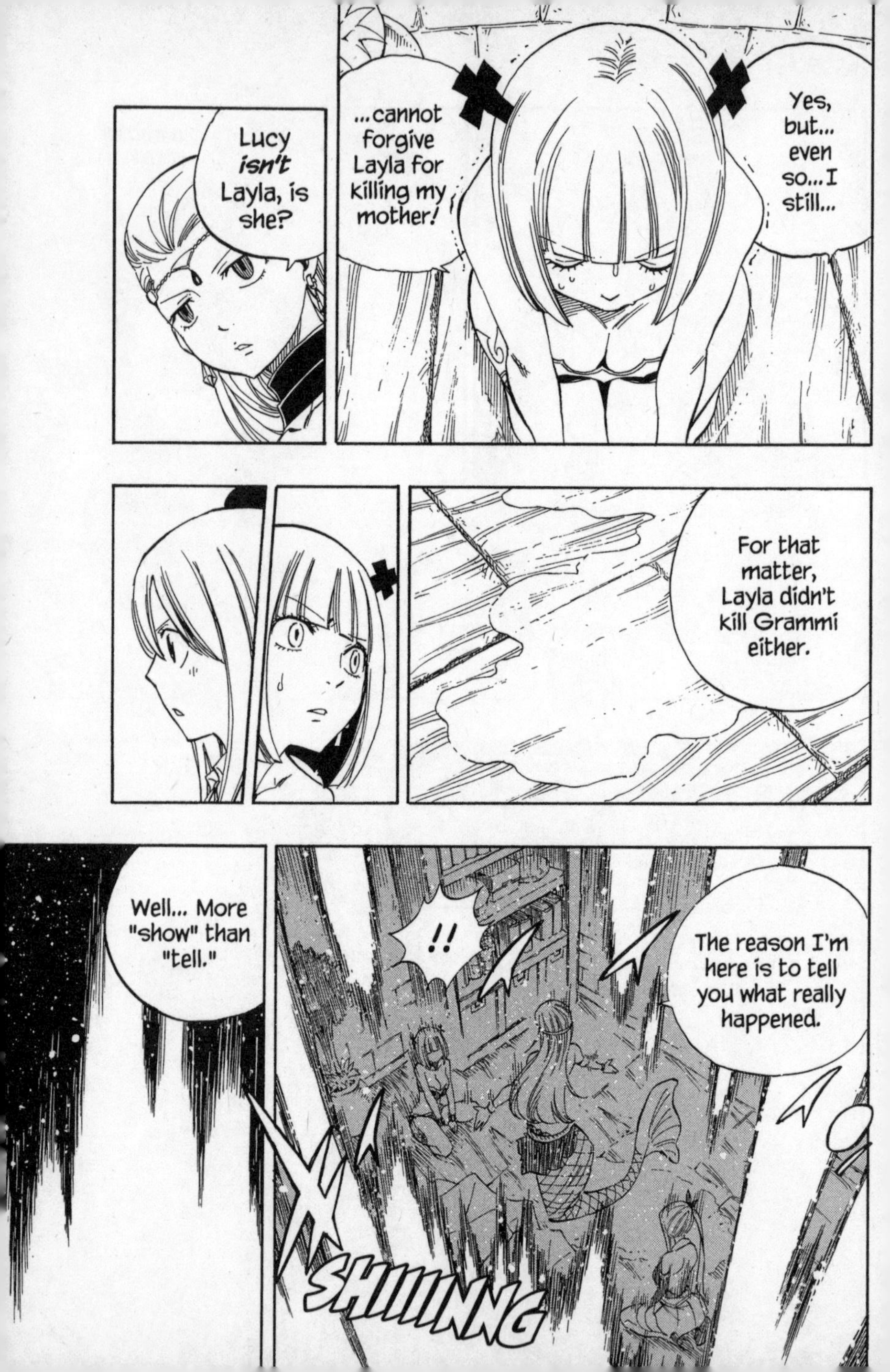
Yes, but... even so...I still...
...cannot forgive Layla for killing my mother!
Lucy *isn't* Layla, is she?
For that matter, Layla didn't kill Grammi either.
The reason I'm here is to tell you what really happened.
!!
Well... More "show" than "tell."
SHIIINNG

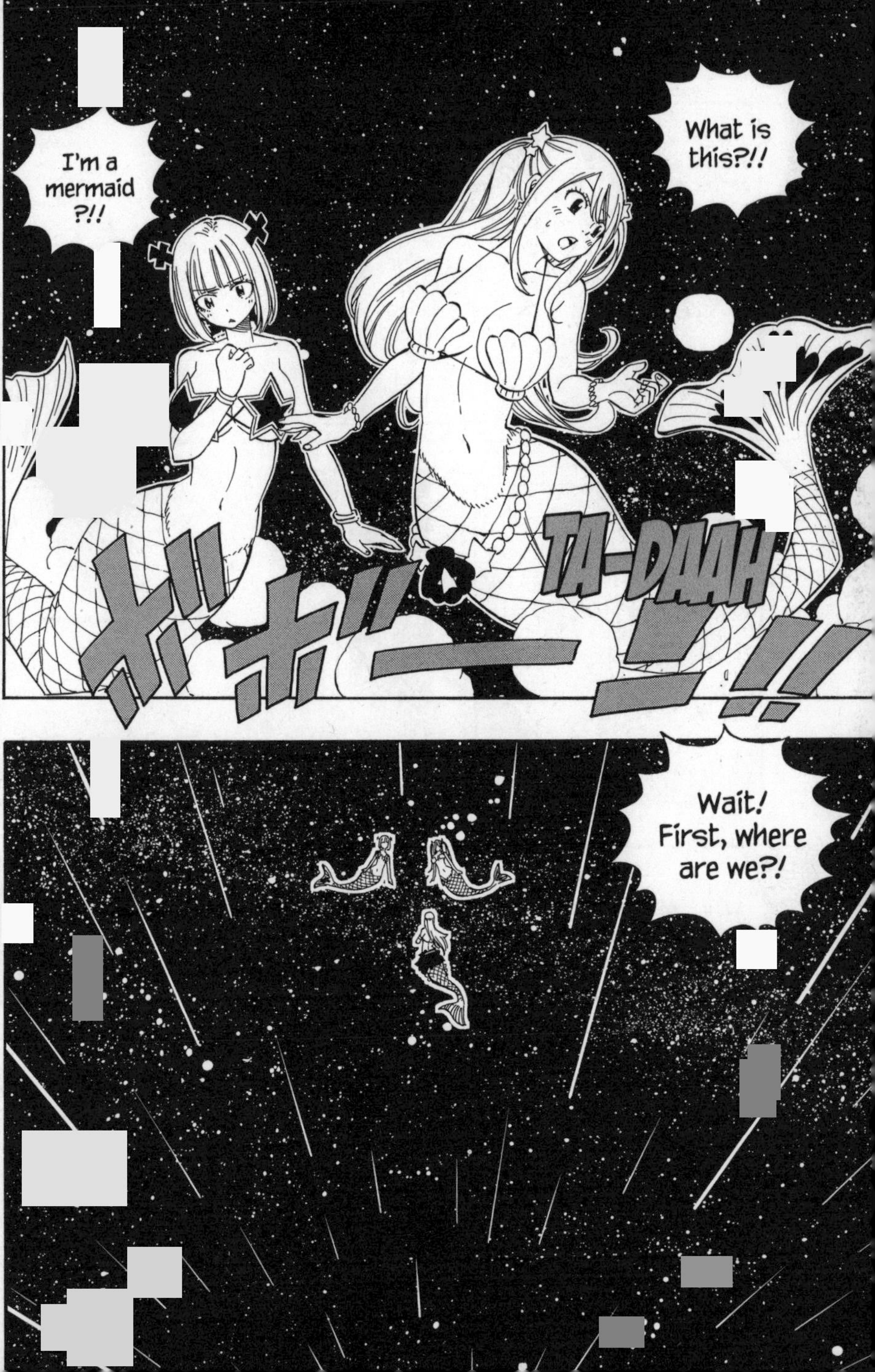
What is this?!!
I'm a mermaid ?!!
TA-DAAH
Wait! First, where are we?!

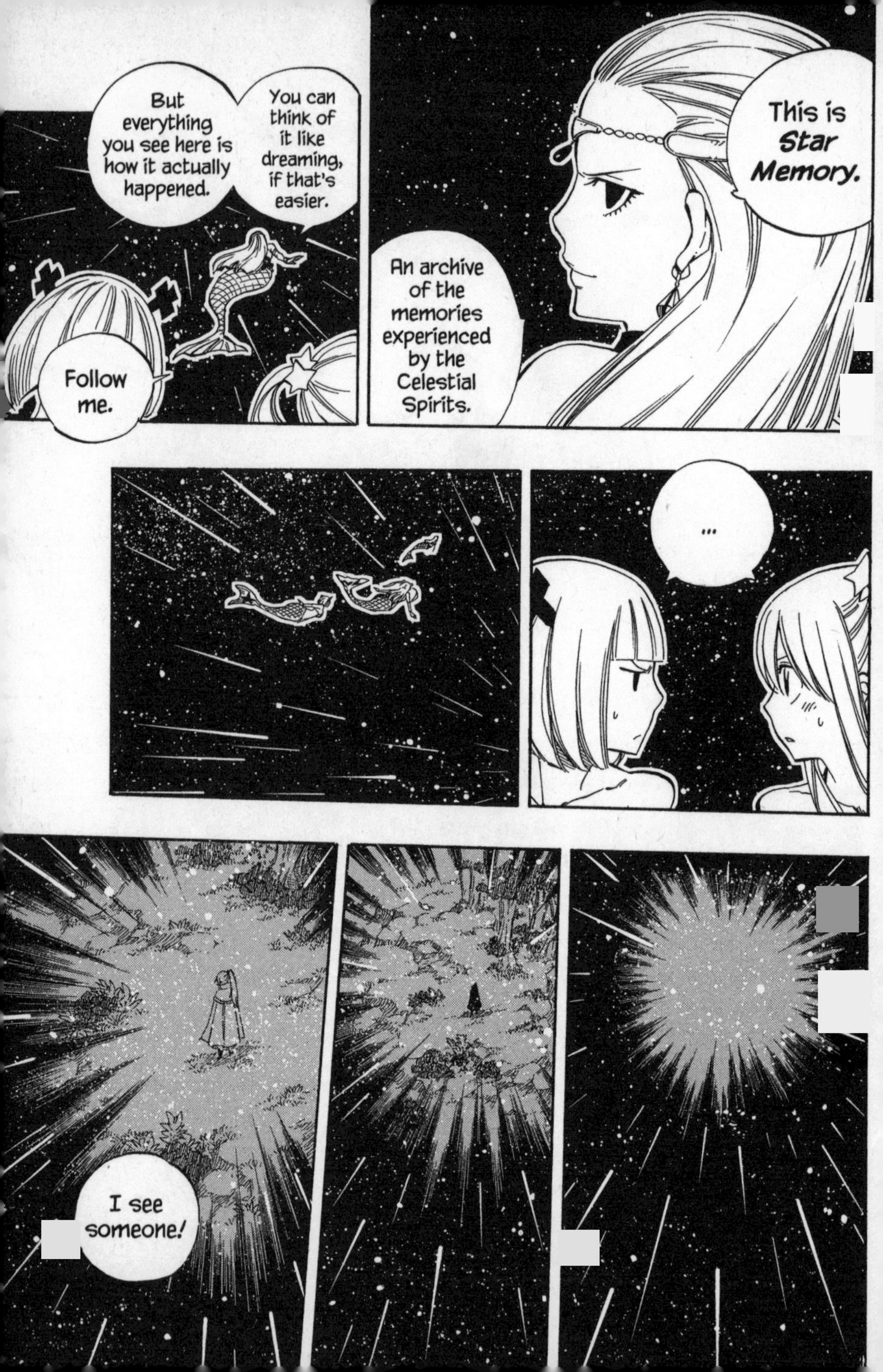
This is Star Memory.
An archive of the memories experienced by the Celestial Spirits.
You can think of it like dreaming, if that's easier.
But everything you see here is how it actually happened.
Follow me.
...
I see someone!

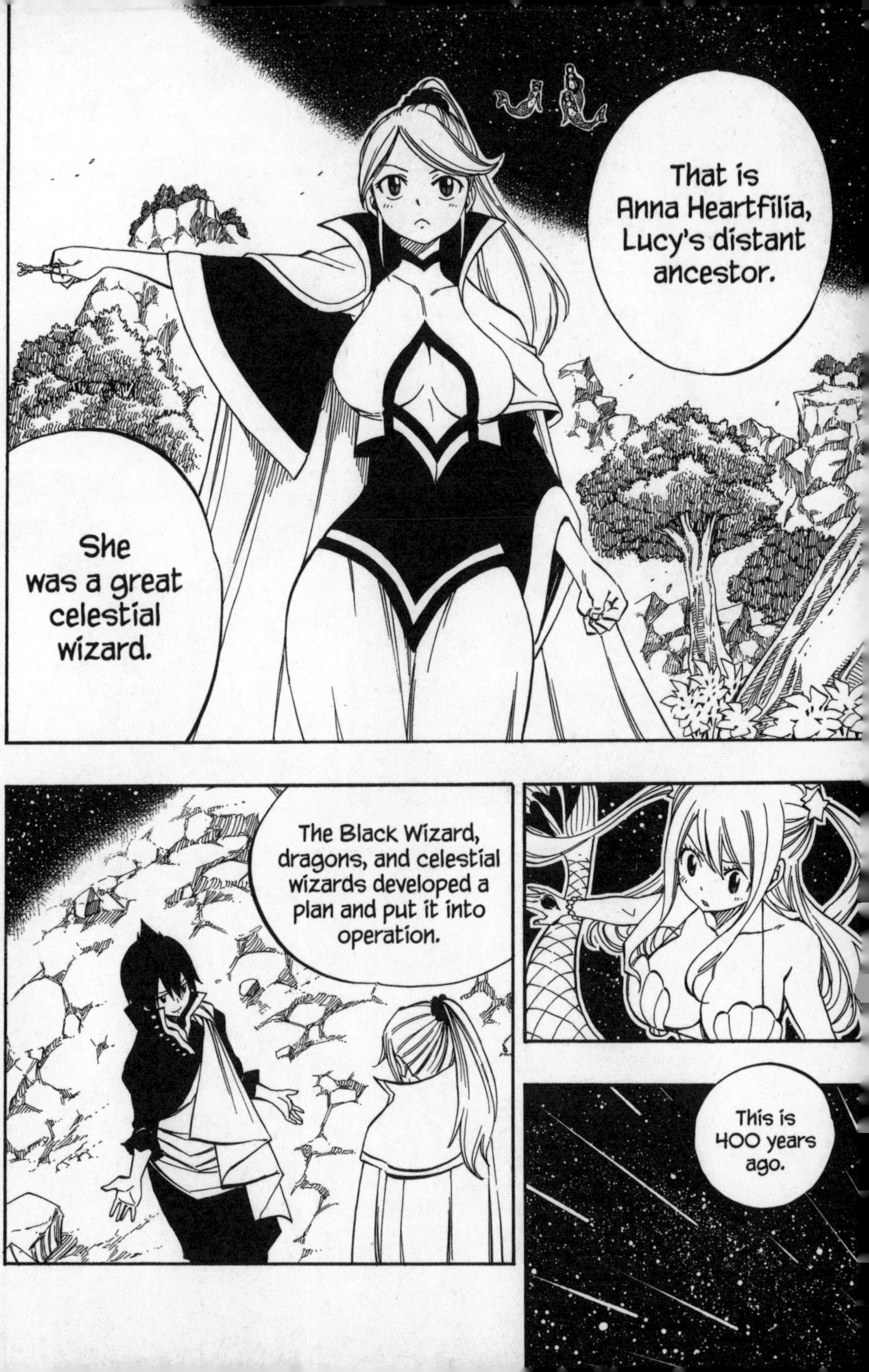
That is Anna Heartfilia, Lucy's distant ancestor.
She was a great celestial wizard.
This is 400 years ago.
The Black Wizard, dragons, and celestial wizards developed a plan and put it into operation.

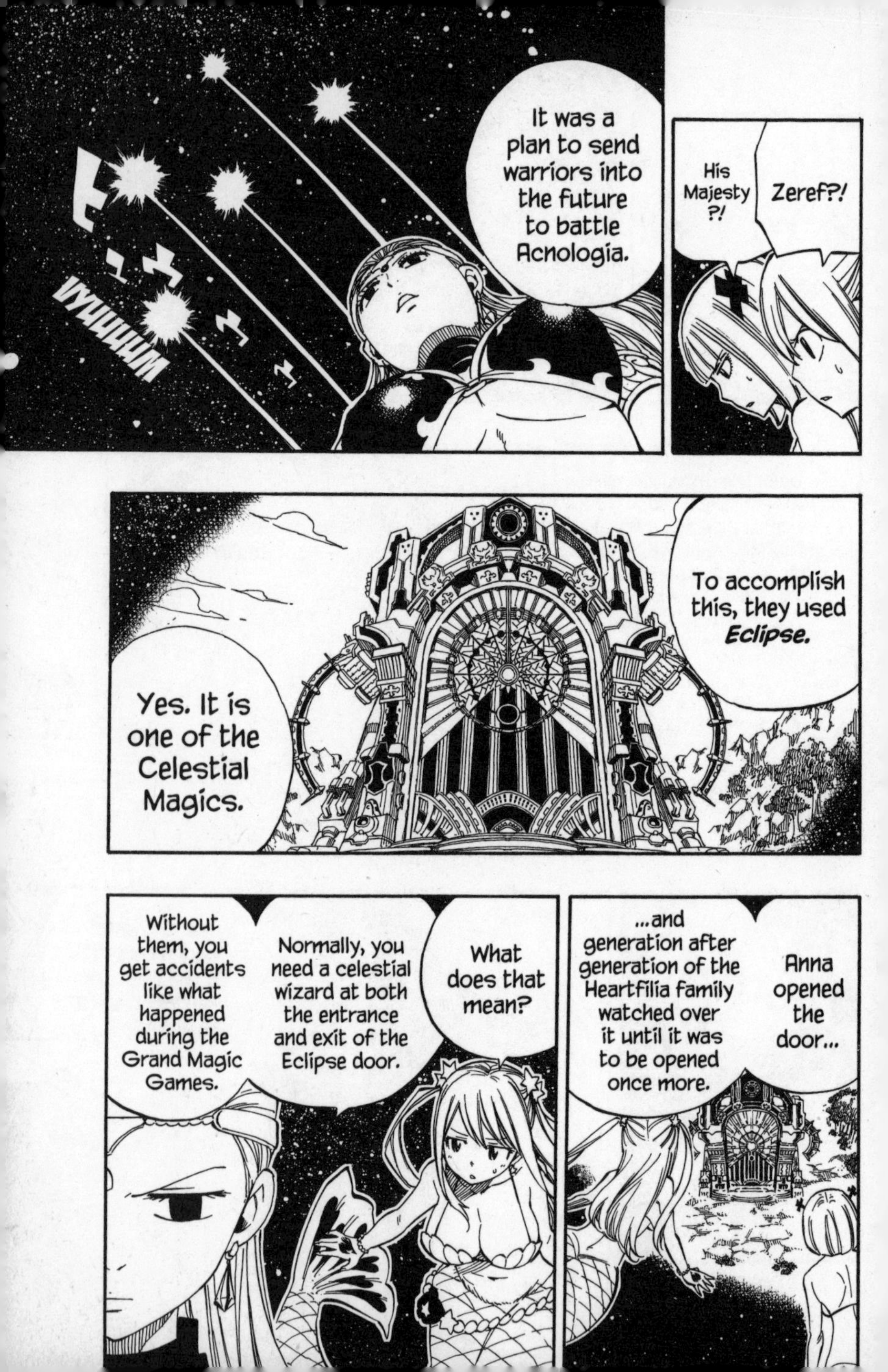
Zeref?!
His Majesty ?!
It was a plan to send warriors into the future to battle Acnologia.
To accomplish this, they used *Eclipse.*
Yes. It is one of the Celestial Magics.
Anna opened the door...
...and generation after generation of the Heartfilia family watched over it until it was to be opened once more.
What does that mean?
Normally, you need a celestial wizard at both the entrance and exit of the Eclipse door.
Without them, you get accidents like what happened during the Grand Magic Games.

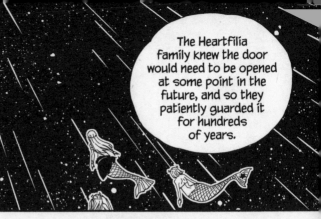

The Heartfilia family knew the door would need to be opened at some point in the future, and so they patiently guarded it for hundreds of years.
The responsibility of opening it ultimately fell upon Layla.
To open the door, you need all twelve of the Golden Keys. To assemble them, Layla called a gathering of all the celestial wizards, and attempted to retrieve the three keys she had entrusted to her servants as well.
But Grammi had crossed to the western continent, and could not be reached.
So there was one key missing. Mine.

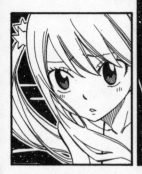

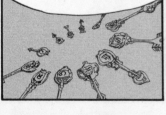

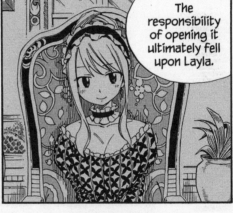

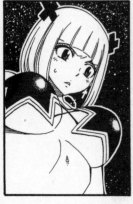

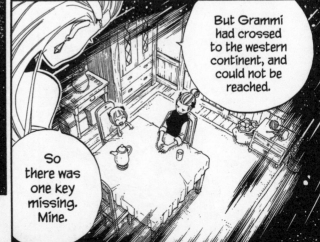

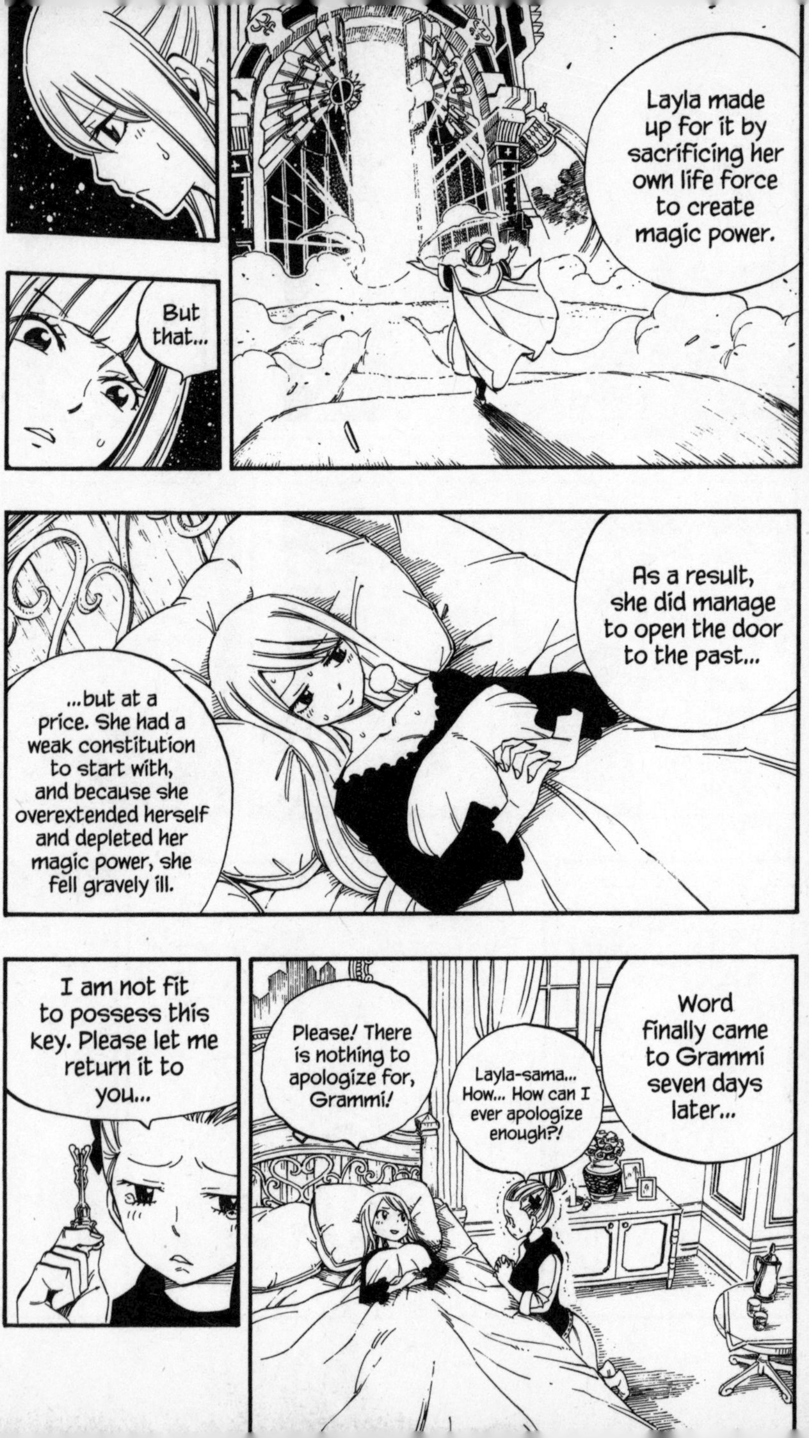
Layla made up for it by sacrificing her own life force to create magic power.
But that...
As a result, she did manage to open the door to the past...
...but at a price. She had a weak constitution to start with, and because she overextended herself and depleted her magic power, she fell gravely ill.
Word finally came to Grammi seven days later...
Layla-sama... How... How can I ever apologize enough?!
Please! There is nothing to apologize for, Grammi!
I am not fit to possess this key. Please let me return it to you...

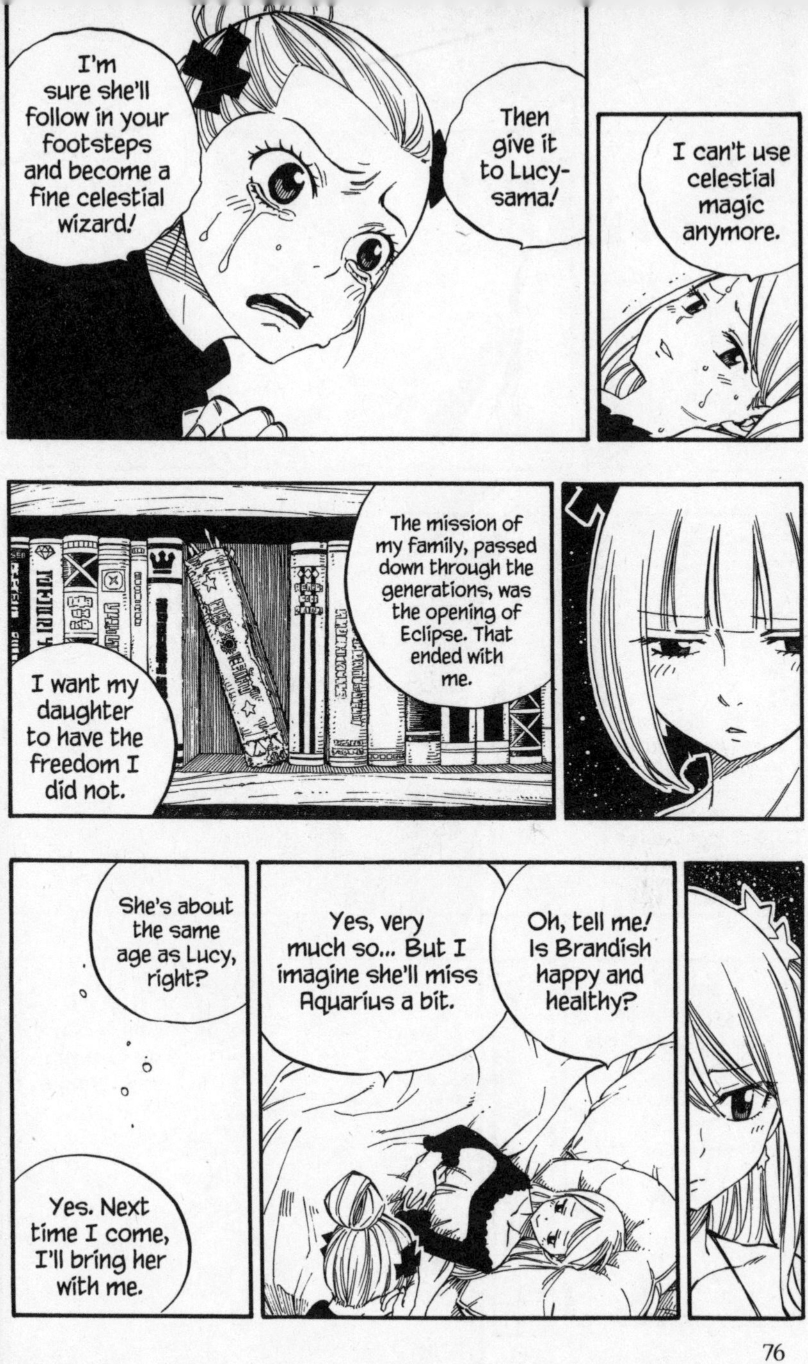
I can't use celestial magic anymore.
Then give it to Lucy-sama!
I'm sure she'll follow in your footsteps and become a fine celestial wizard!
The mission of my family, passed down through the generations, was the opening of Eclipse. That ended with me.
I want my daughter to have the freedom I did not.
Oh, tell me! Is Brandish happy and healthy?
Yes, very much so... But I imagine she'll miss Aquarius a bit.
She's about the same age as Lucy, right?
Yes. Next time I come, I'll bring her with me.

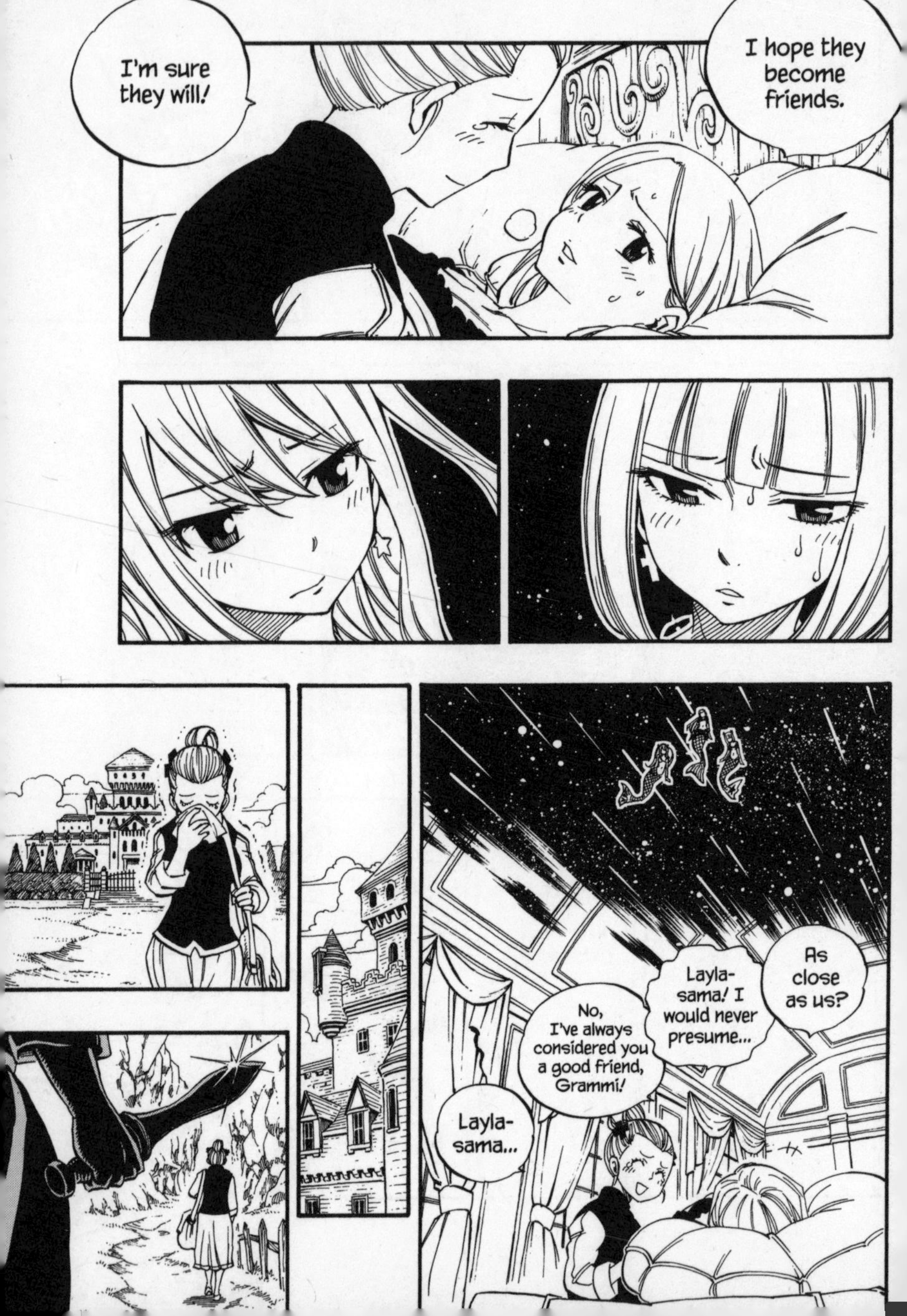
I hope they become friends.
I'm sure they will!
As close as us?
Layla-sama! I would never presume...
No, I've always considered you a good friend, Grammi!
Layla-sama...

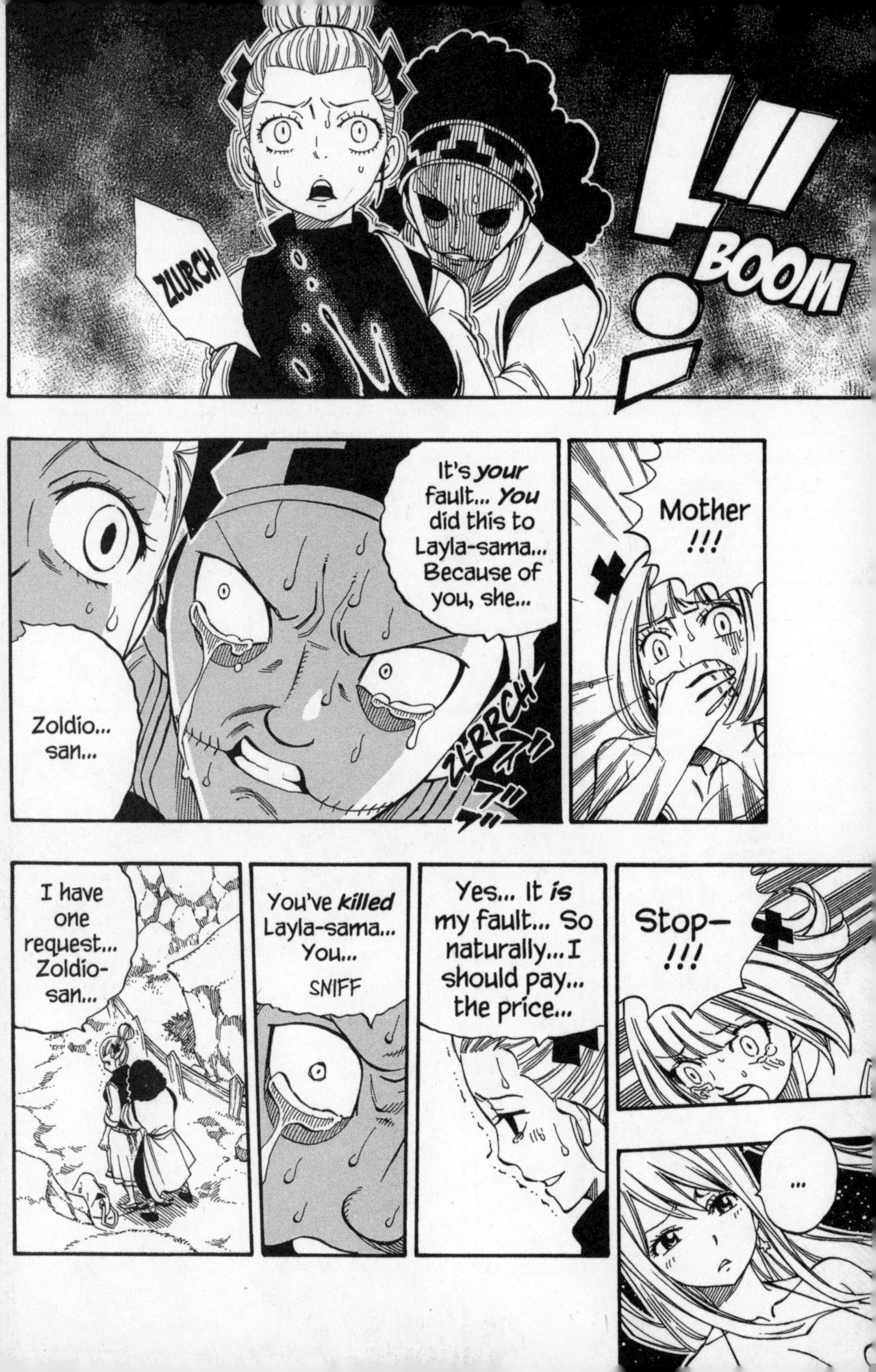
!!
BOOM
ZLURCH
Mother !!!
It's *your* fault... *You* did this to Layla-sama... Because of you, she...
ZLRRCH
Zoldio... san...
Stop— !!!
...
Yes... It *is* my fault... So naturally... I should pay... the price...
You've *killed* Layla-sama... You...
SNIFF
I have one request... Zoldio-san...

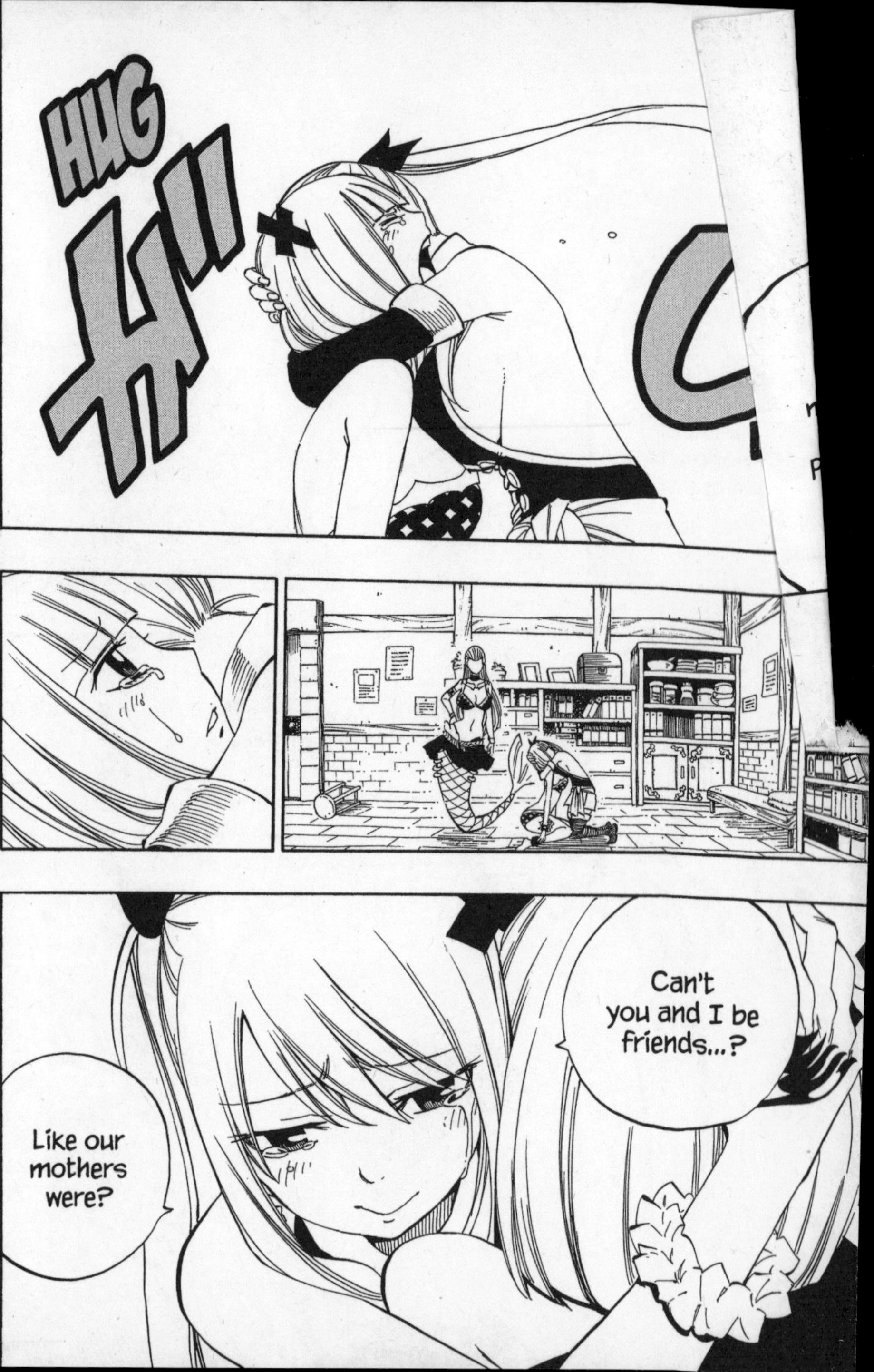
HUG
Can't you and I be friends...?
Like our mothers were?

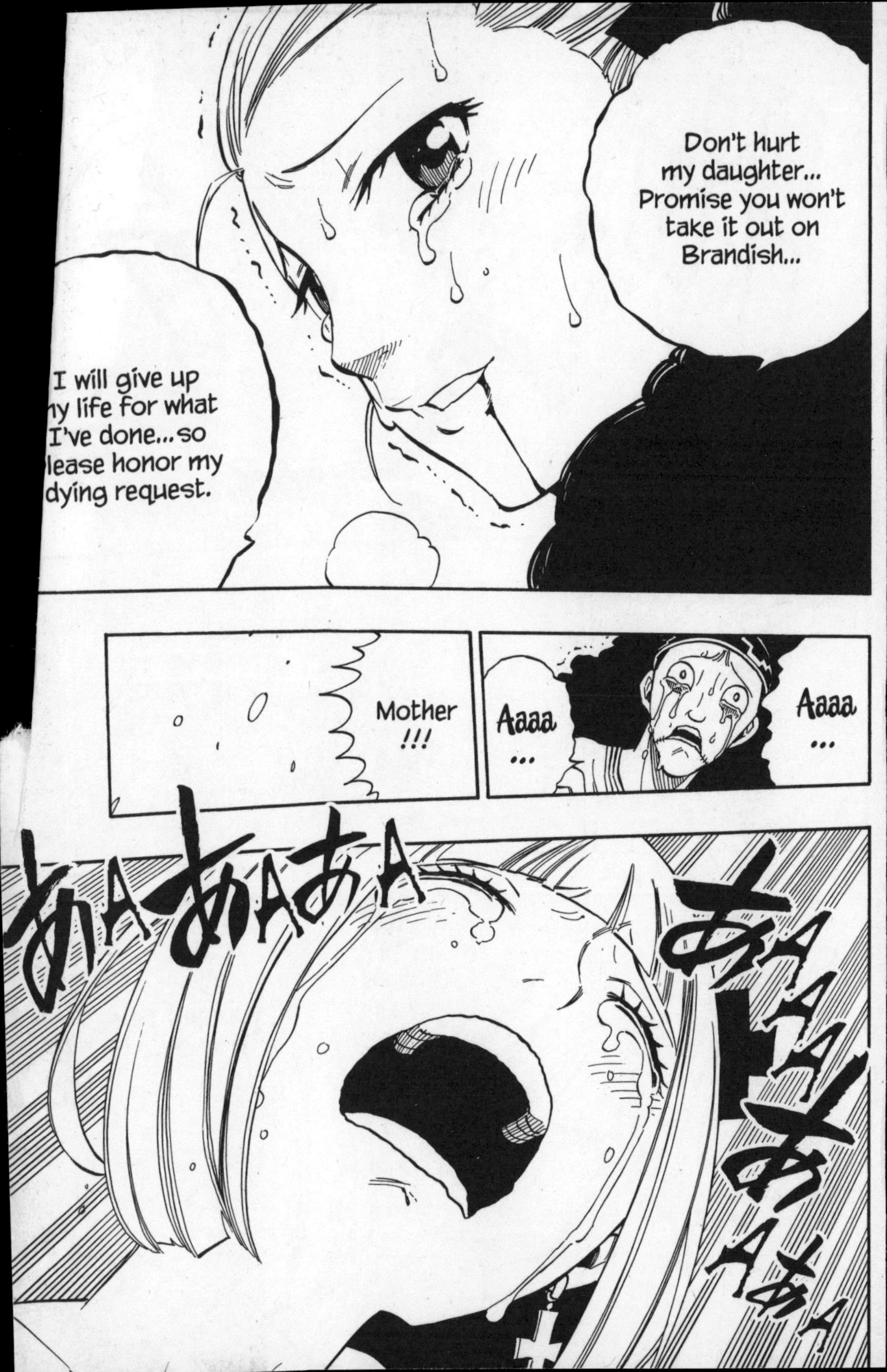
Don't hurt my daughter... Promise you won't take it out on Brandish...
I will give up ny life for what I've done...so lease honor my dying request.
Aaaa ...
Aaaa ...
Mother !!!
あAあAあA

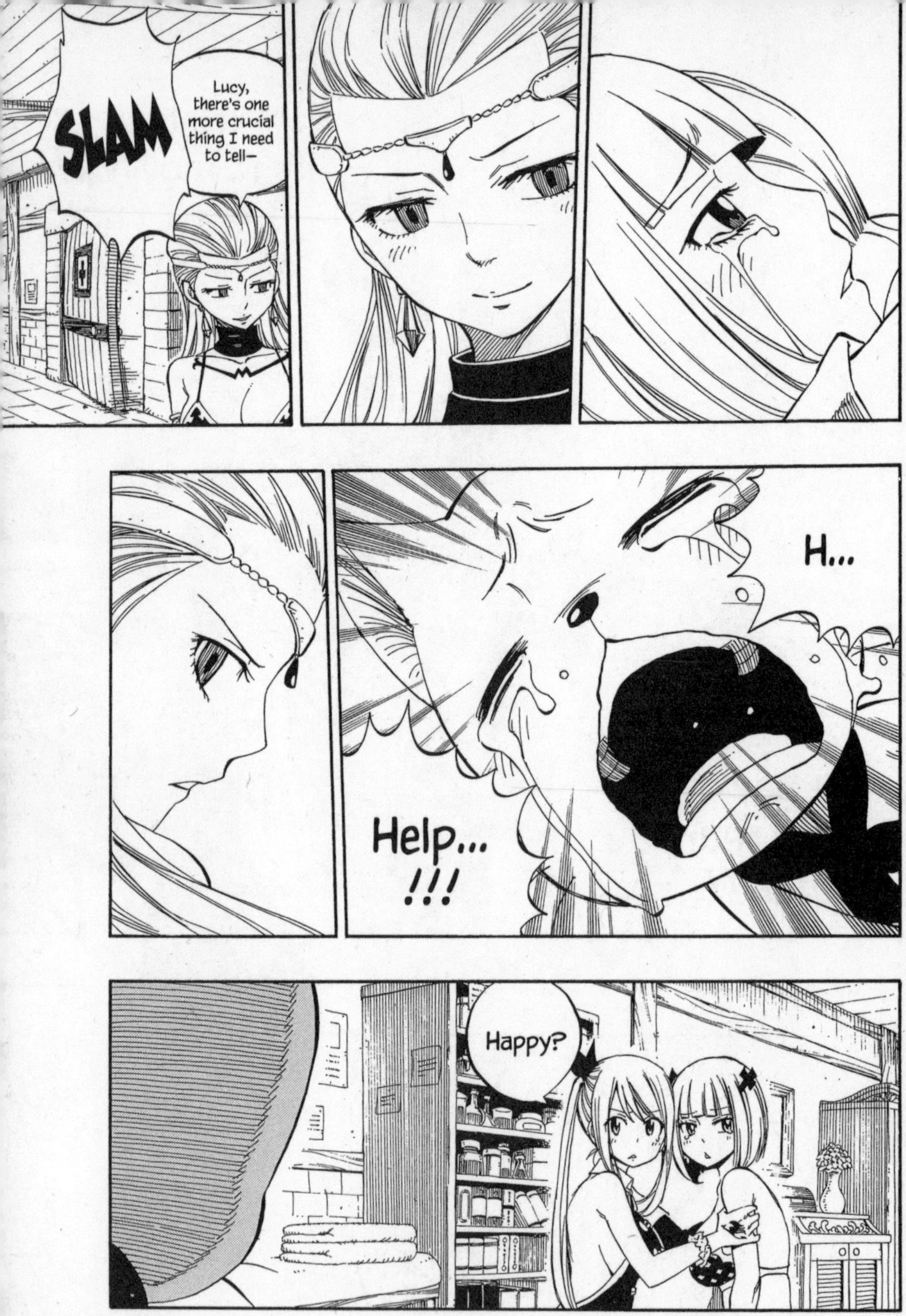
Lucy, there's one more crucial thing I need to tell—
SLAM
H...
Help... !!!
Happy?

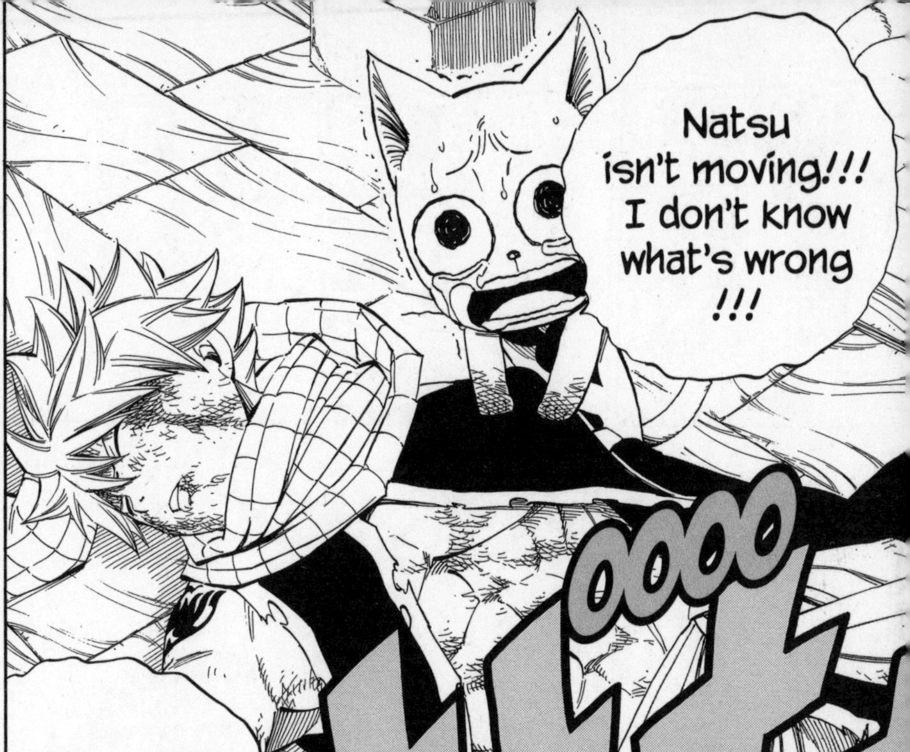
Natsu isn't moving!!! I don't know what's wrong !!!
OOOO
He needs help real bad!!!

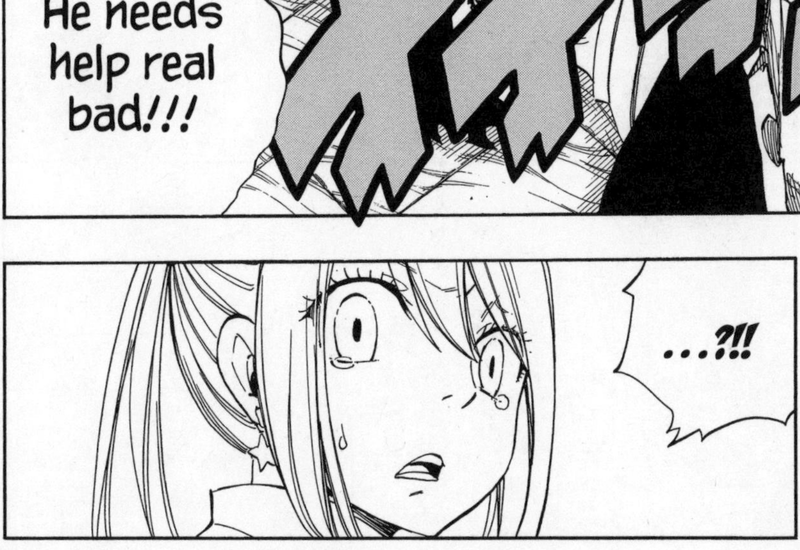
...?!!

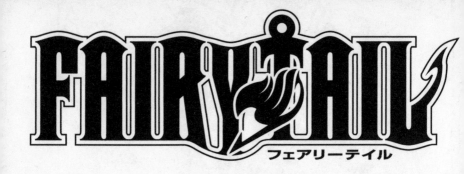

Chapter 469: What I Want to Do

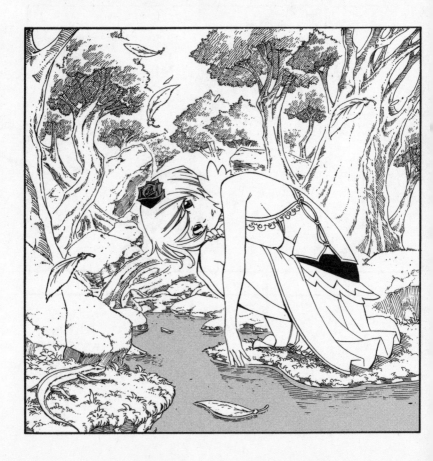

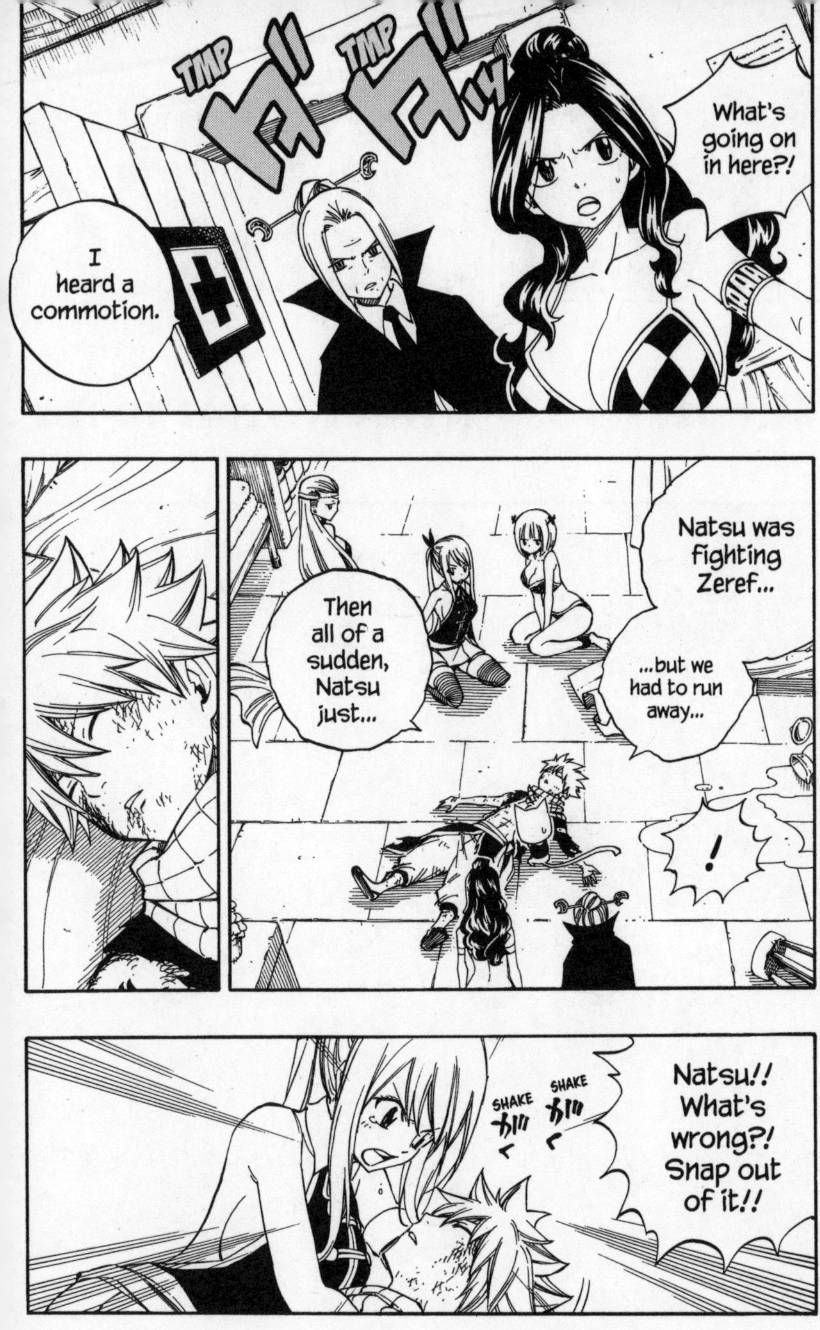
What's going on in here?!
TMP
TMP
I heard a commotion.
Natsu was fighting Zeref...
...but we had to run away...
Then all of a sudden, Natsu just...
!
Natsu!! What's wrong?! Snap out of it!!
SHAKE
SHAKE

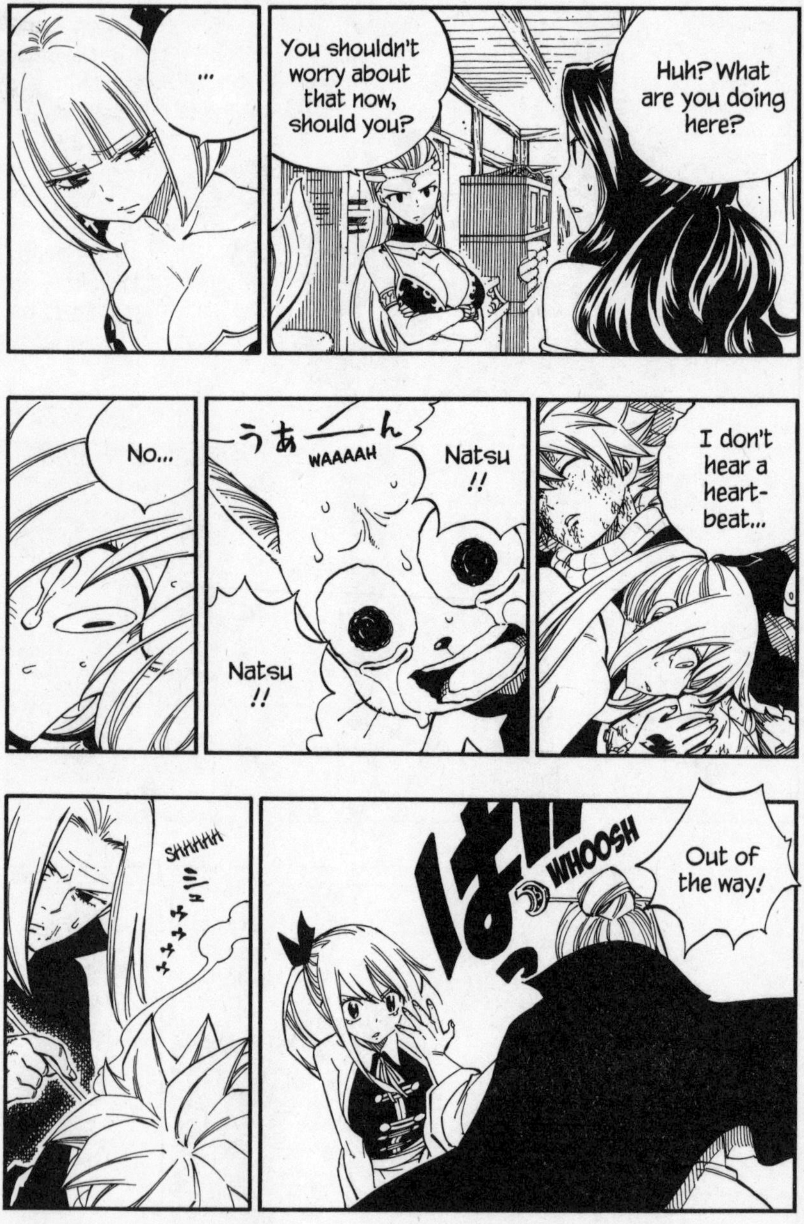
Huh? What are you doing here?
You shouldn't worry about that now, should you?
...
I don't hear a heart-beat...
うあーーん
WAAAAH
Natsu!!
Natsu!!
No...
Out of the way!
ばっ
WHOOSH
SHHHHH
シュウウウウ

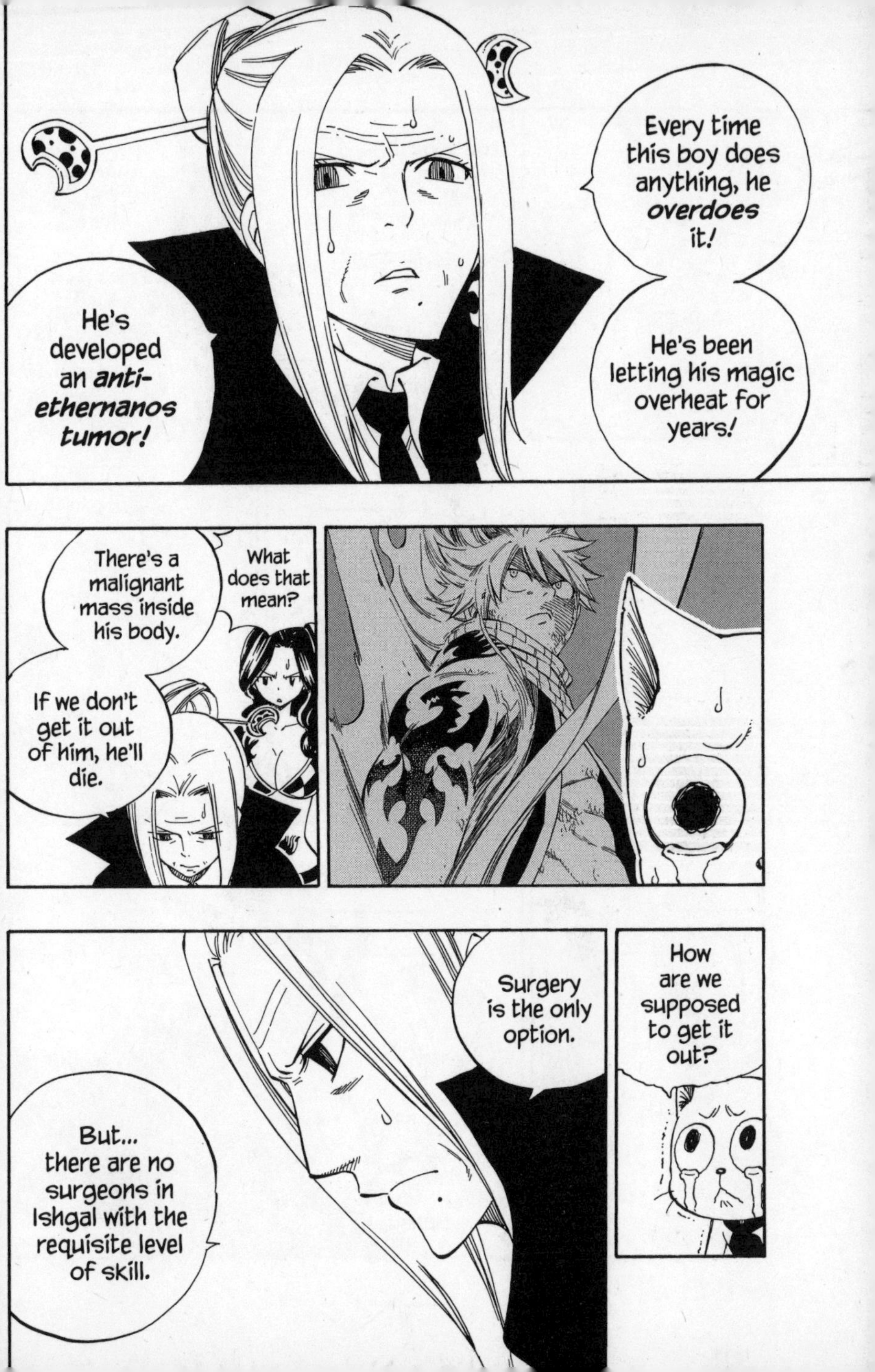
Every time this boy does anything, he overdoes it!
He's been letting his magic overheat for years!
He's developed an anti-ethernanos tumor!
What does that mean?
There's a malignant mass inside his body.
If we don't get it out of him, he'll die.
How are we supposed to get it out?
Surgery is the only option.
But... there are no surgeons in Ishgal with the requisite level of skill.

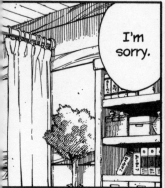

I'm sorry.

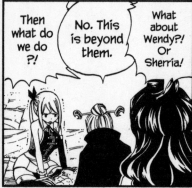

Then what do we do?!

No. This is beyond them.

What about Wendy?! Or Sherria!

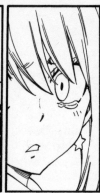

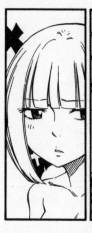

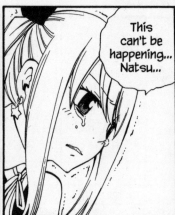

This can't be happening... Natsu...

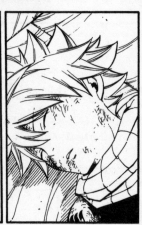

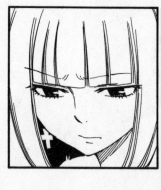

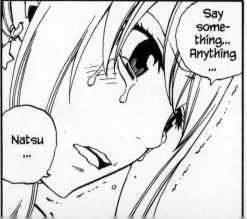

Say something... Anything...

Natsu...

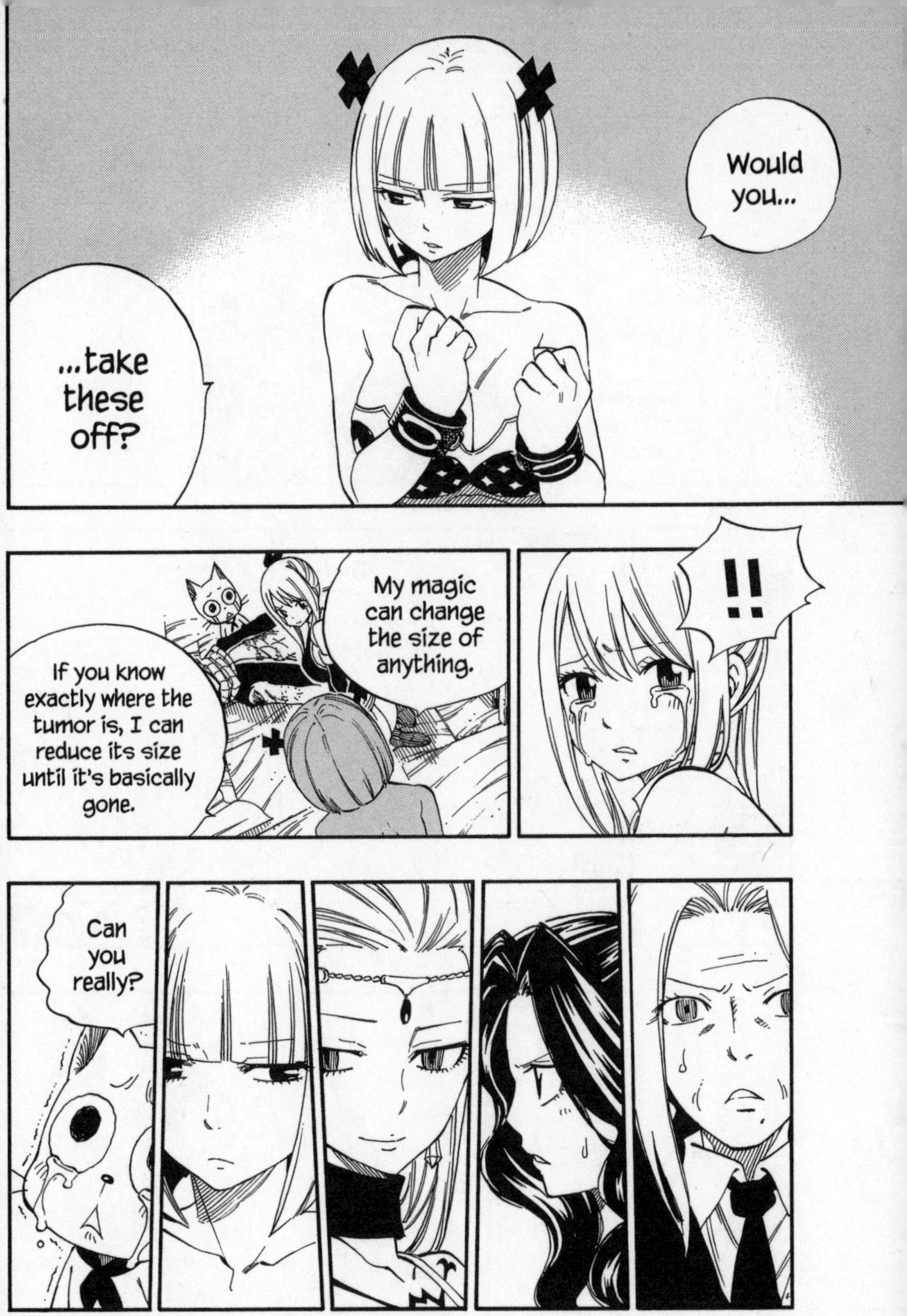
Would you...
...take these off?
!!
My magic can change the size of anything.
If you know exactly where the tumor is, I can reduce its size until it's basically gone.
Can you really?

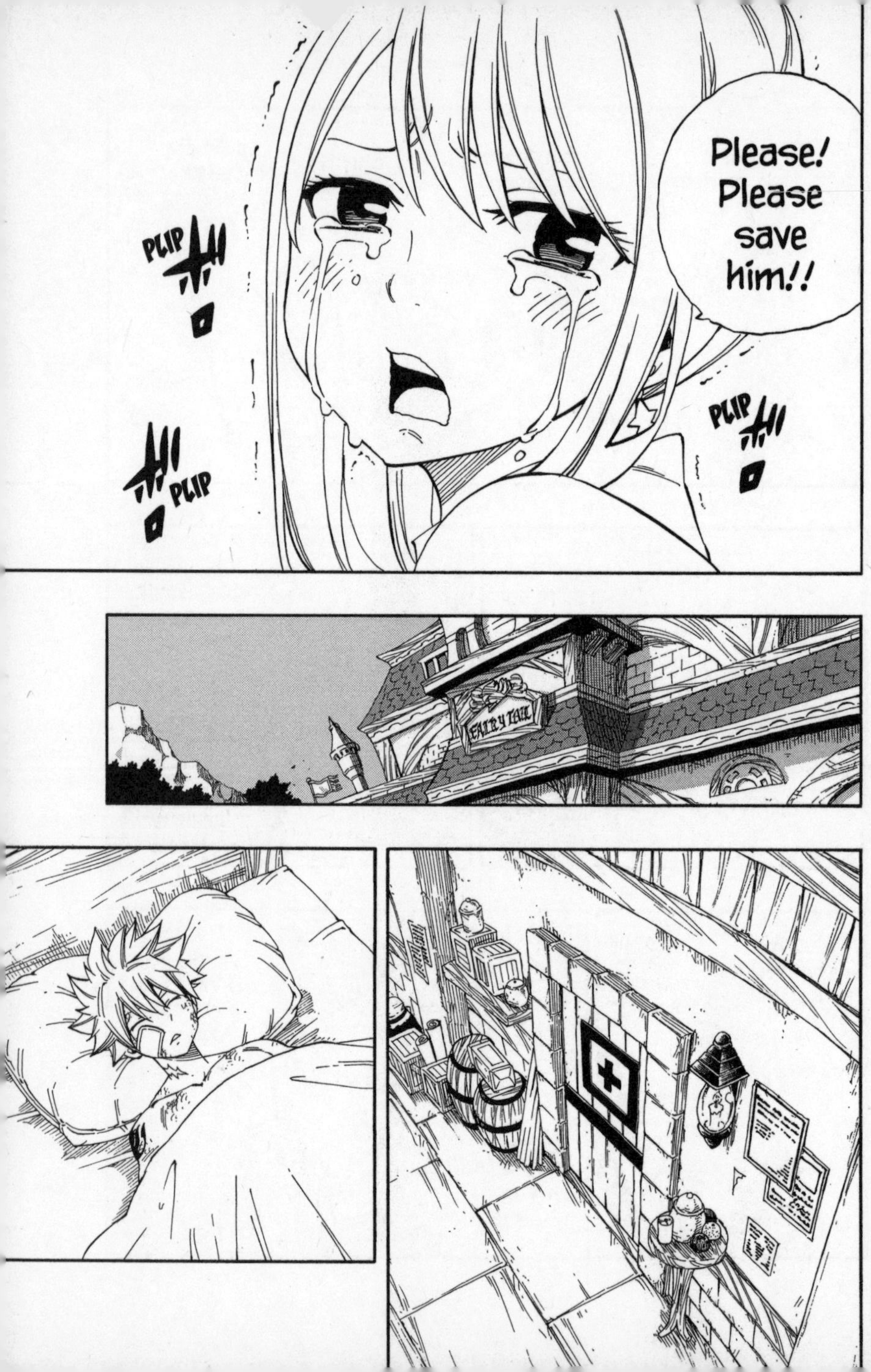
Please! Please save him!!
PLIP
PLIP
PLIP
FAIRY TAIL

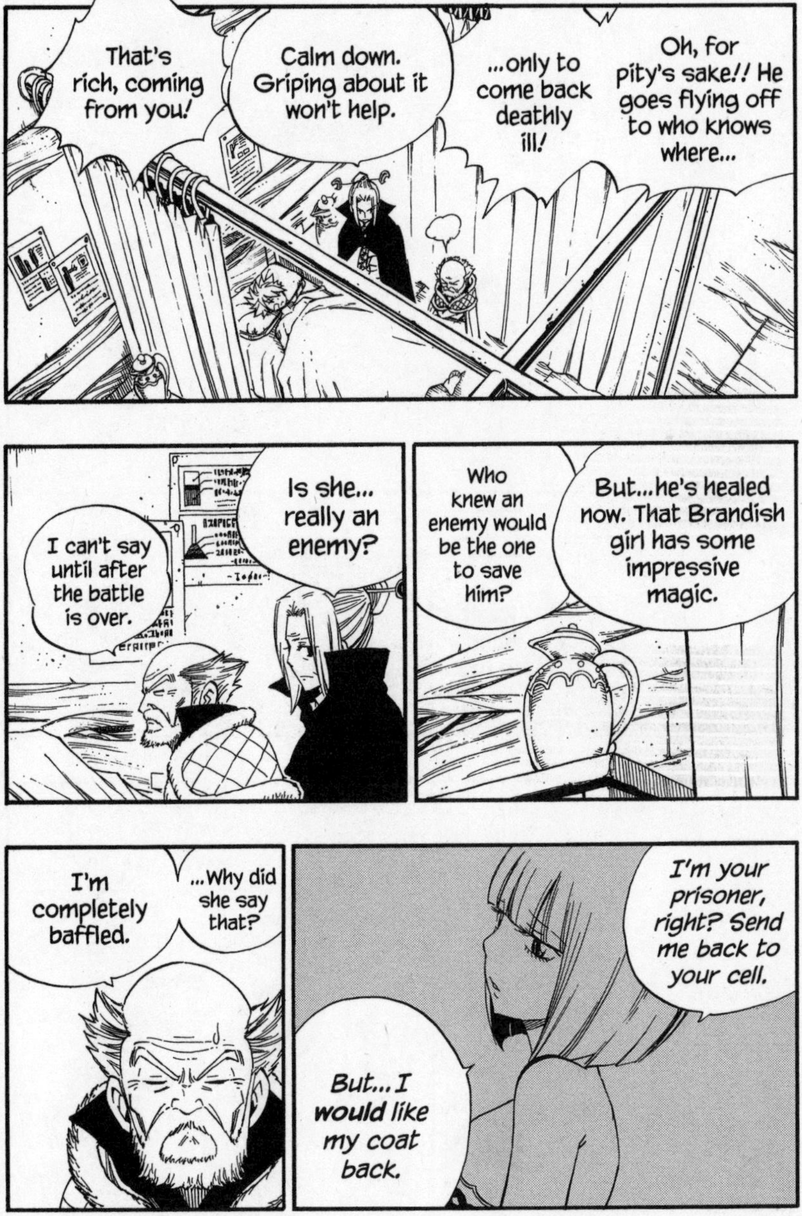
Oh, for pity's sake!! He goes flying off to who knows where...
...only to come back deathly ill!
Calm down. Griping about it won't help.
That's rich, coming from you!
But...he's healed now. That Brandish girl has some impressive magic.
Who knew an enemy would be the one to save him?
Is she... really an enemy?
I can't say until after the battle is over.
I'm your prisoner, right? Send me back to your cell.
But...I *would* like my coat back.
...Why did she say that?
I'm completely baffled.

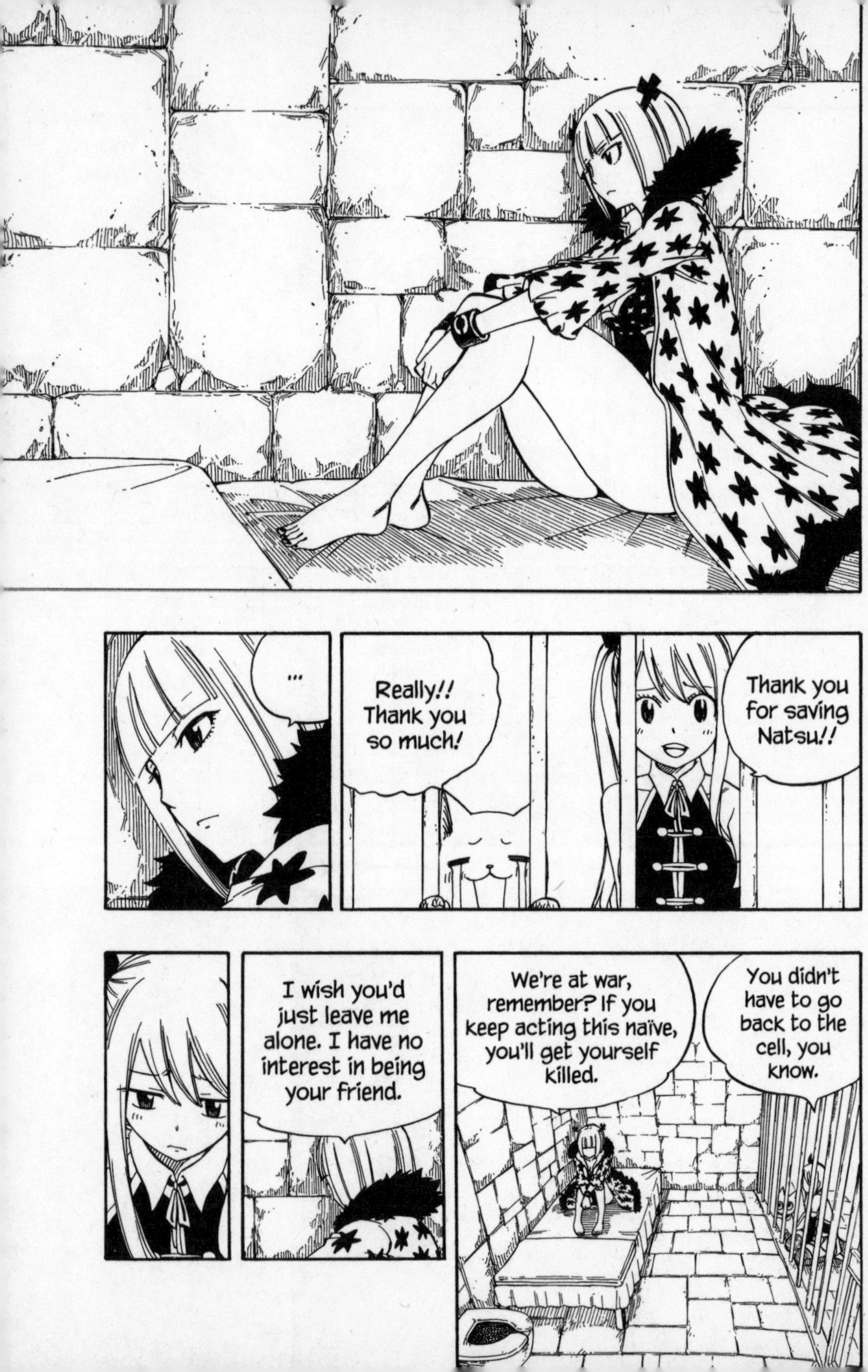
Thank you for saving Natsu!!
Really!! Thank you so much!
...
You didn't have to go back to the cell, you know.
We're at war, remember? If you keep acting this naïve, you'll get yourself killed.
I wish you'd just leave me alone. I have no interest in being your friend.

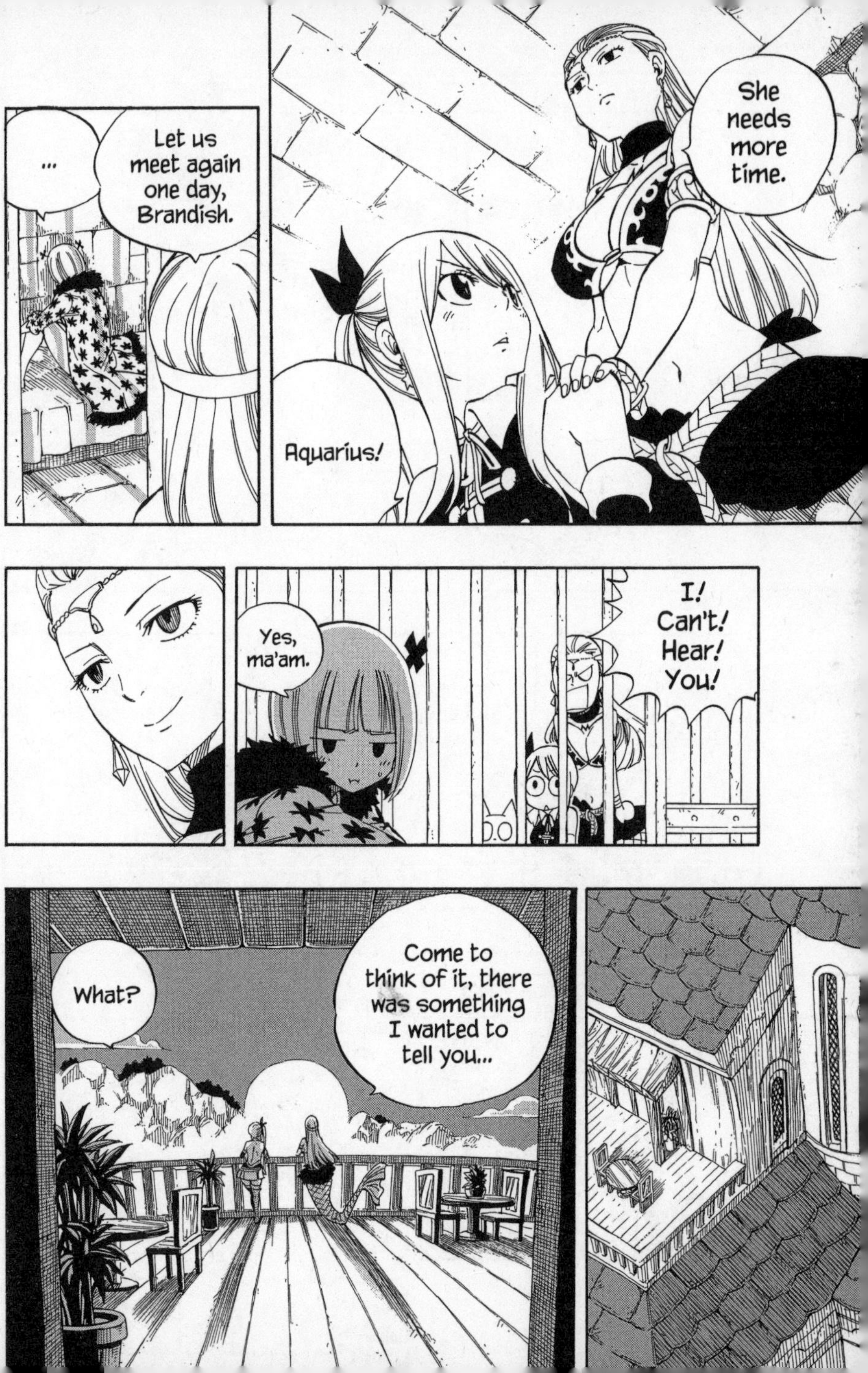
She needs more time.
Aquarius!
Let us meet again one day, Brandish.
...
I! Can't! Hear! You!
Yes, ma'am.
Come to think of it, there was something I wanted to tell you...
What?

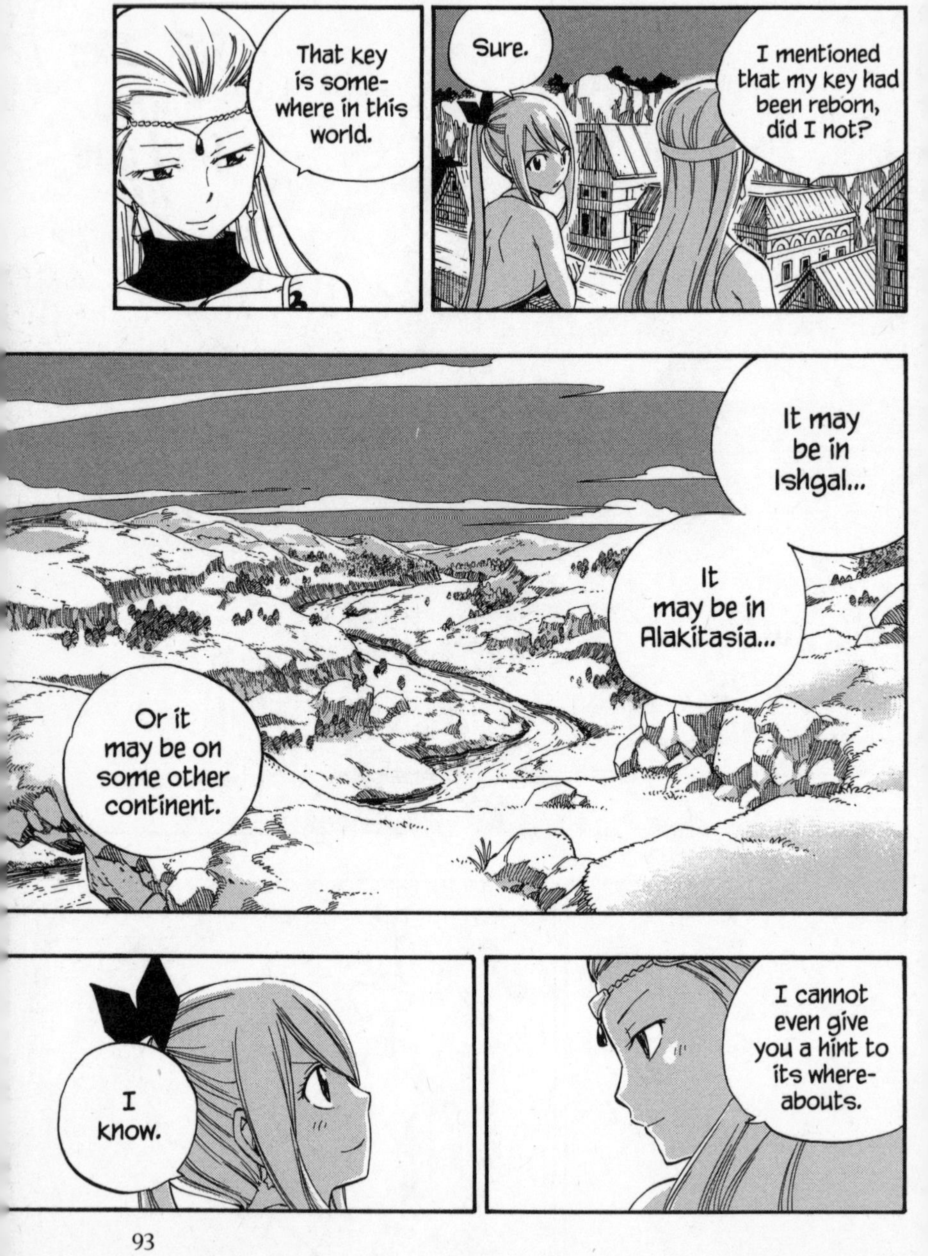

I mentioned that my key had been reborn, did I not?
Sure.
That key is somewhere in this world.
It may be in Ishgal...
It may be in Alakitasia...
Or it may be on some other continent.
I cannot even give you a hint to its whereabouts.
I know.

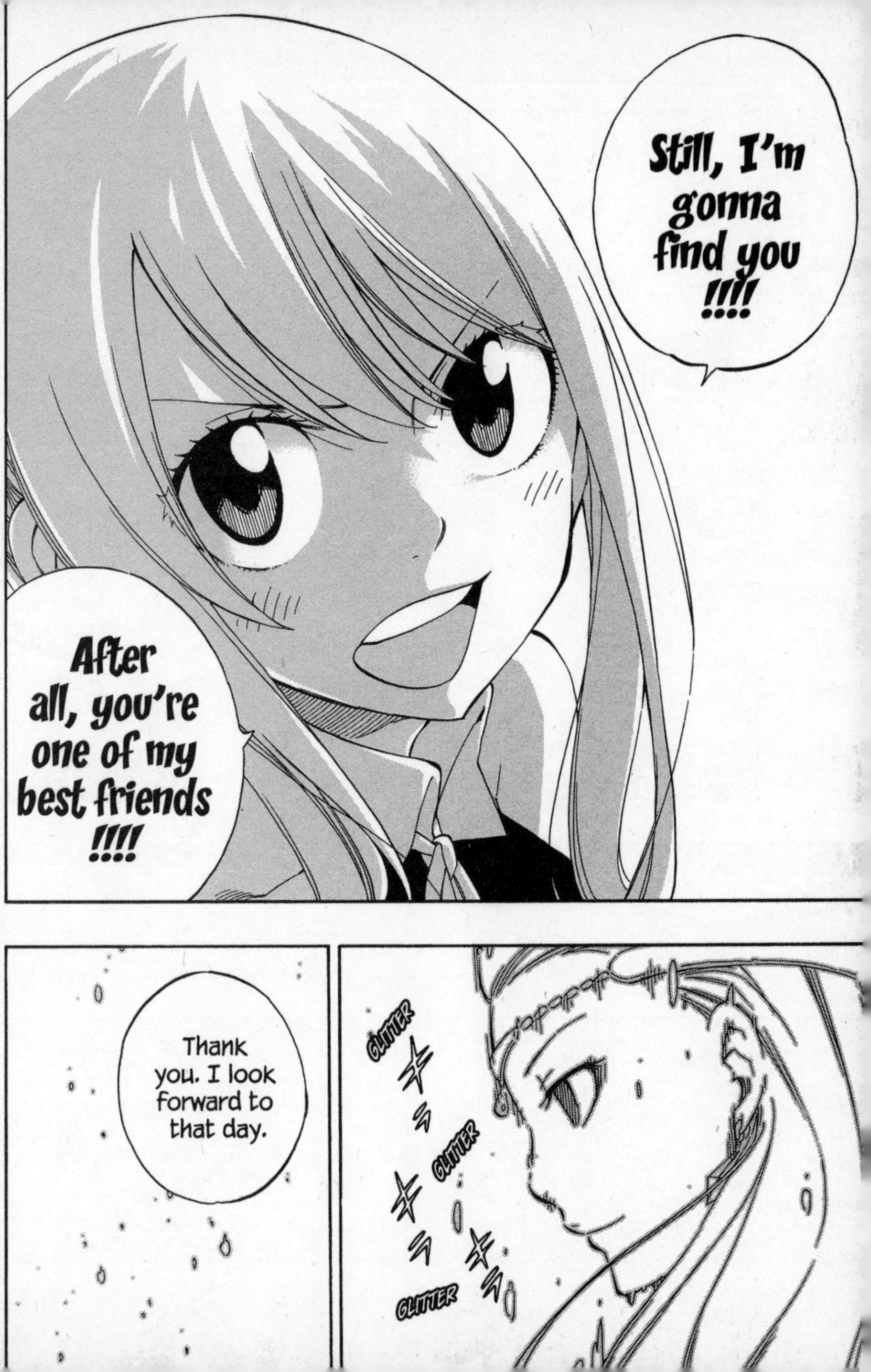
Still, I'm gonna find you !!!!
After all, you're one of my best friends !!!!
GLITTER
GLITTER
GLITTER
Thank you. I look forward to that day.

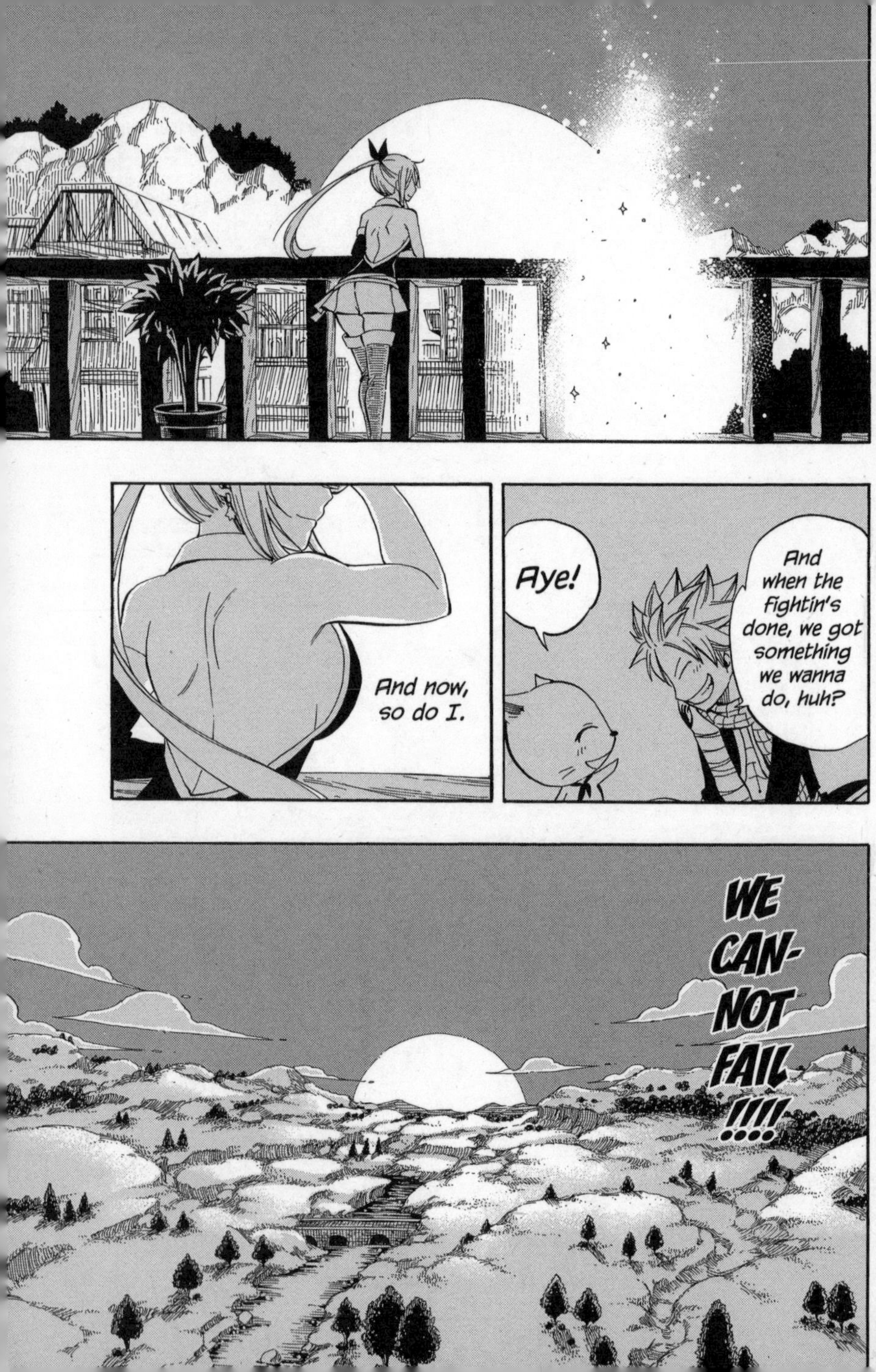
And when the fightin's done, we got something we wanna do, huh?
Aye!
And now, so do I.
WE CAN-NOT FAIL!!!!

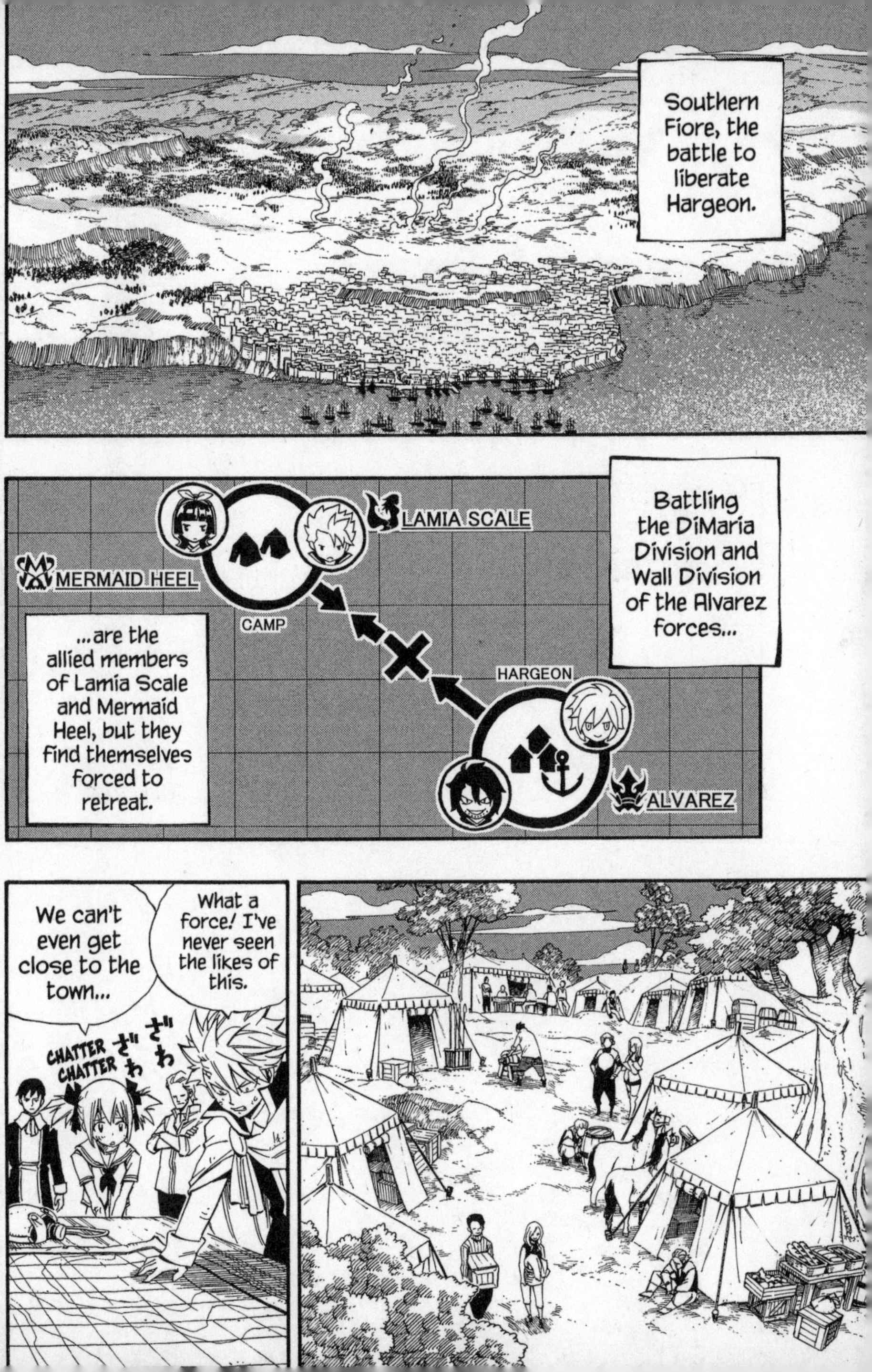
Southern Fiore, the battle to liberate Hargeon.
Battling the DiMaria Division and Wall Division of the Alvarez forces...
LAMIA SCALE
MERMAID HEEL
CAMP
HARGEON
ALVAREZ
...are the allied members of Lamia Scale and Mermaid Heel, but they find themselves forced to retreat.
What a force! I've never seen the likes of this.
We can't even get close to the town...
ざわ ざわ
CHATTER CHATTER

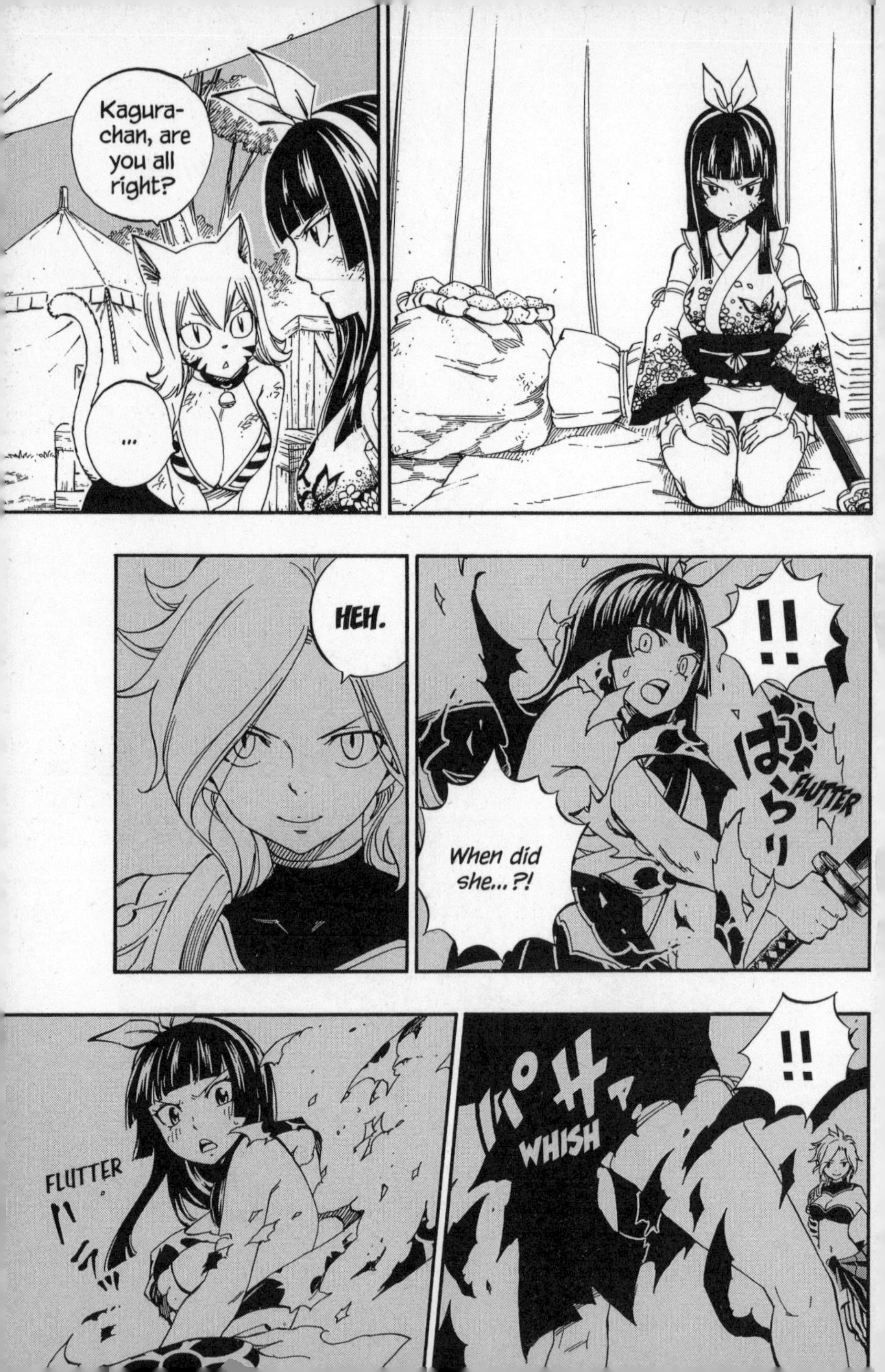
Kagura-chan, are you all right?
...
!!
ぱらり
FLUTTER
When did she...?!
HEH.
!!
パサ
WHISH
FLUTTER

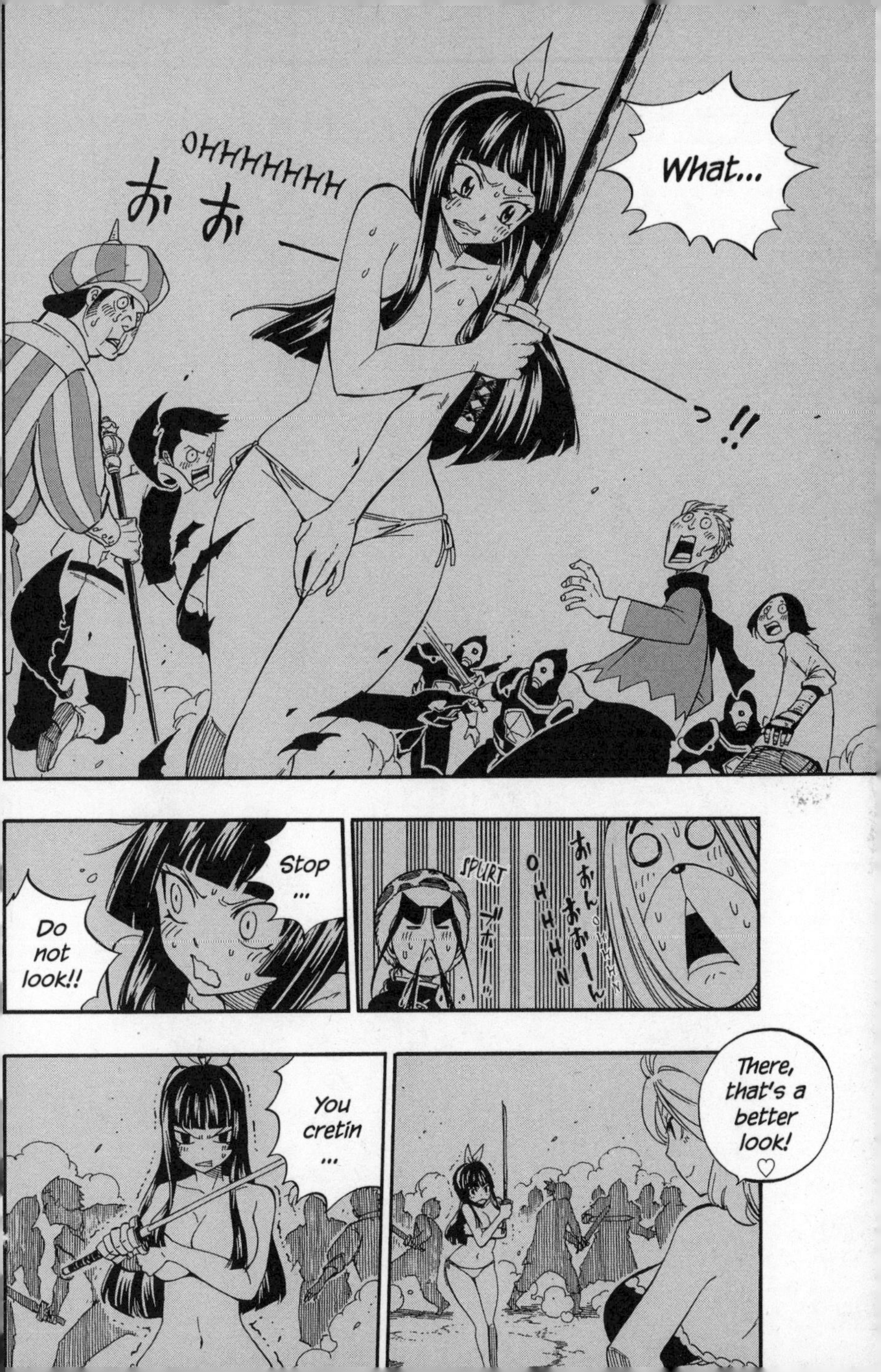
What...
OHHHHHHHH
おお
っ!!
おおん。
おお〜ん
OHHHN
OHHHN
SPURT
ブボーッ
Stop ...
Do not look!!
There, that's a better look! ♡
You cretin ...

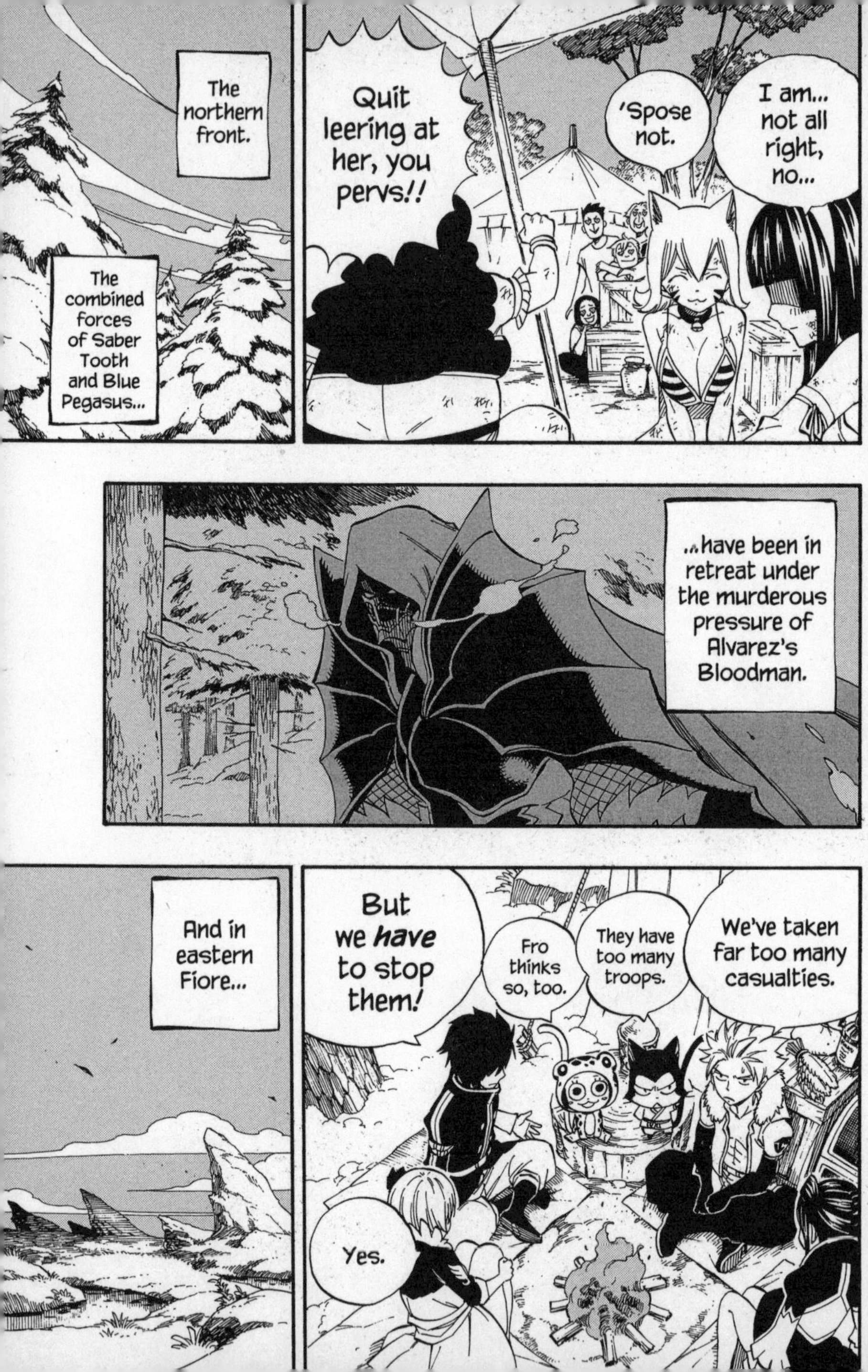
I am... not all right, no...
'Spose not.
Quit leering at her, you pervs!!
The northern front.
The combined forces of Saber Tooth and Blue Pegasus...
...have been in retreat under the murderous pressure of Alvarez's Bloodman.
We've taken far too many casualties.
They have too many troops.
Fro thinks so, too.
But we *have* to stop them!
Yes.
And in eastern Fiore...

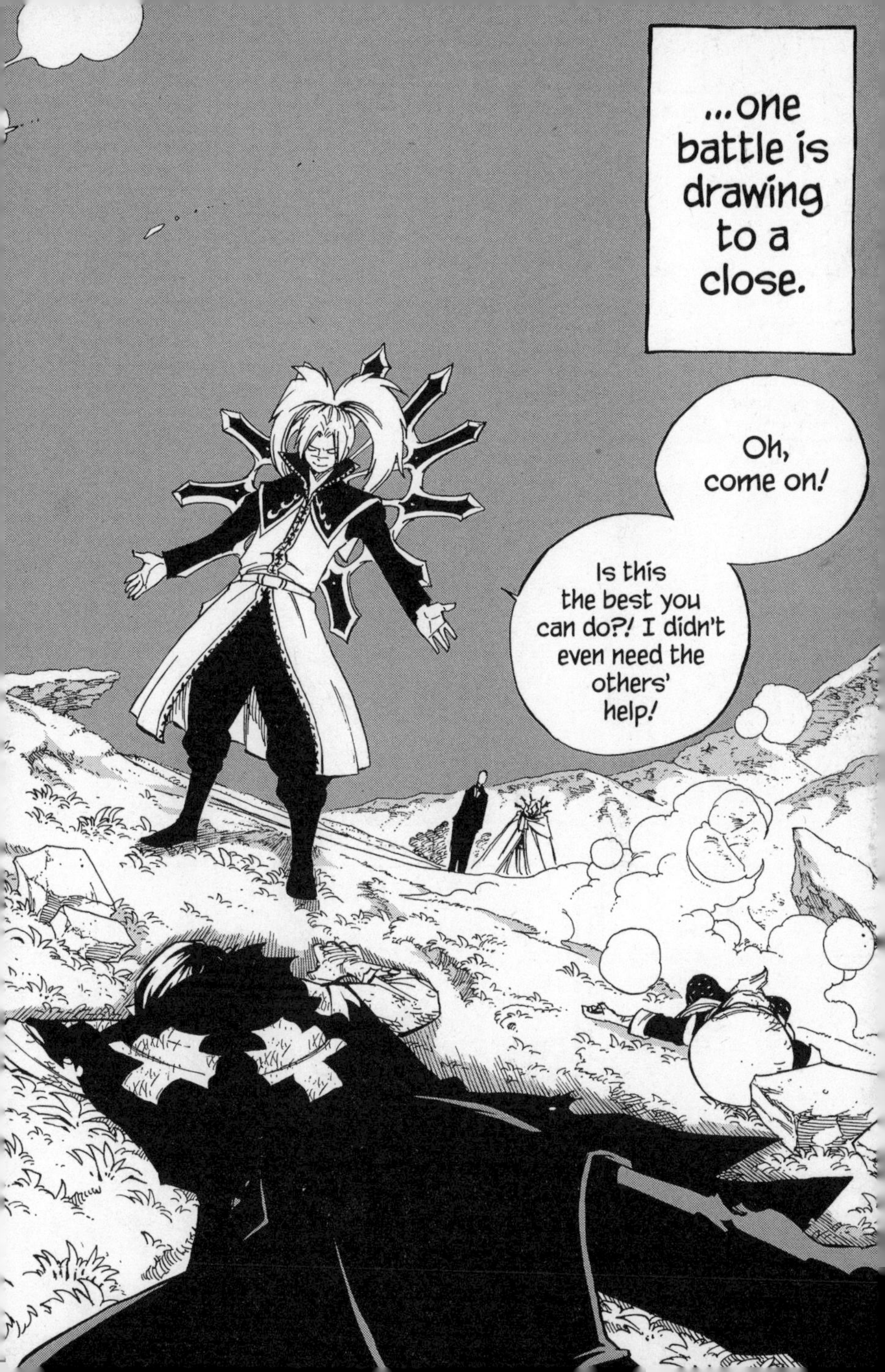
...one battle is drawing to a close.
Oh, come on!
Is this the best you can do?! I didn't even need the others' help!

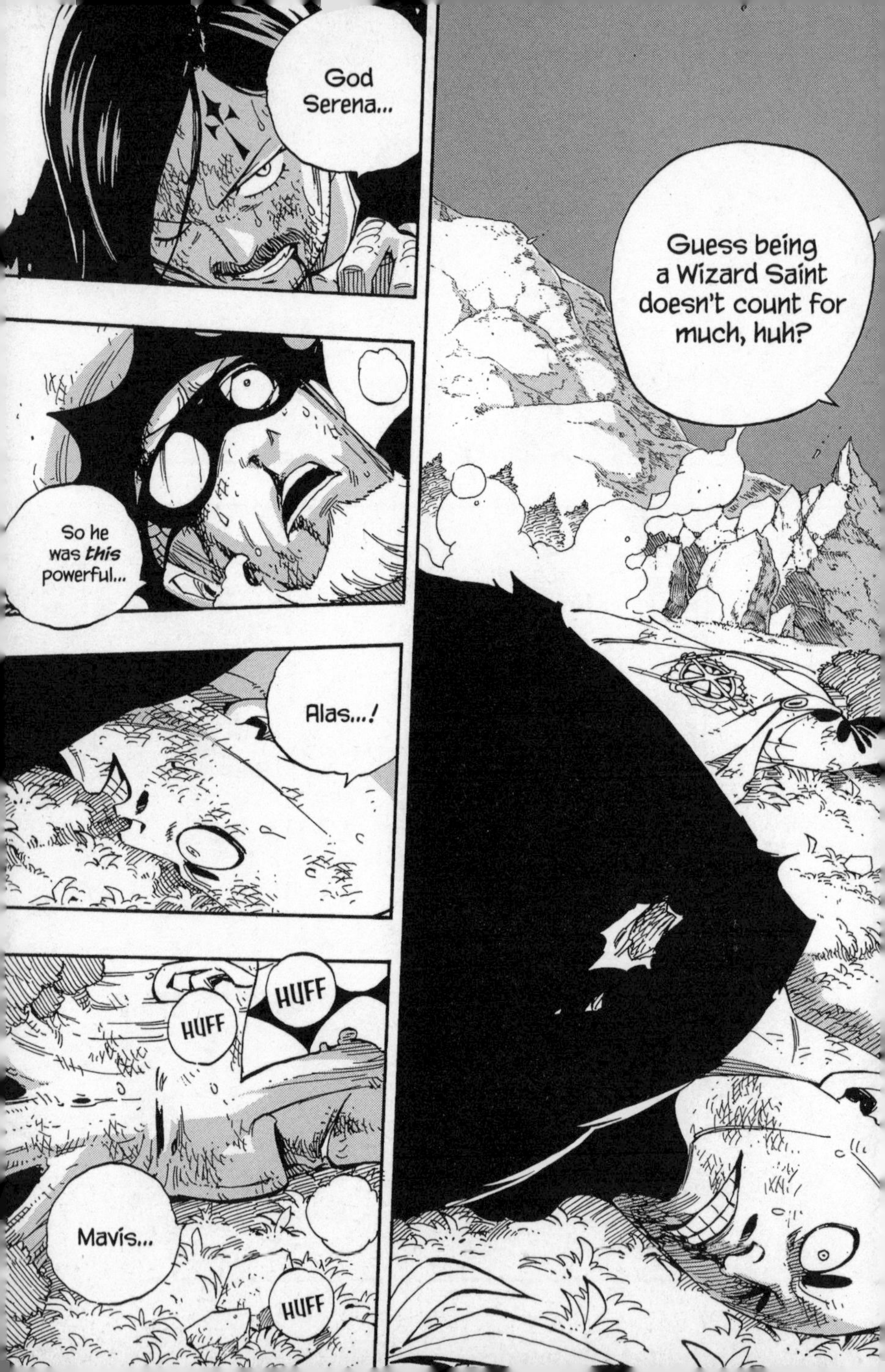
Guess being a Wizard Saint doesn't count for much, huh?
God Serena...
So he was *this* powerful...
Alas...!
HUFF
HUFF
Mavis...
HUFF

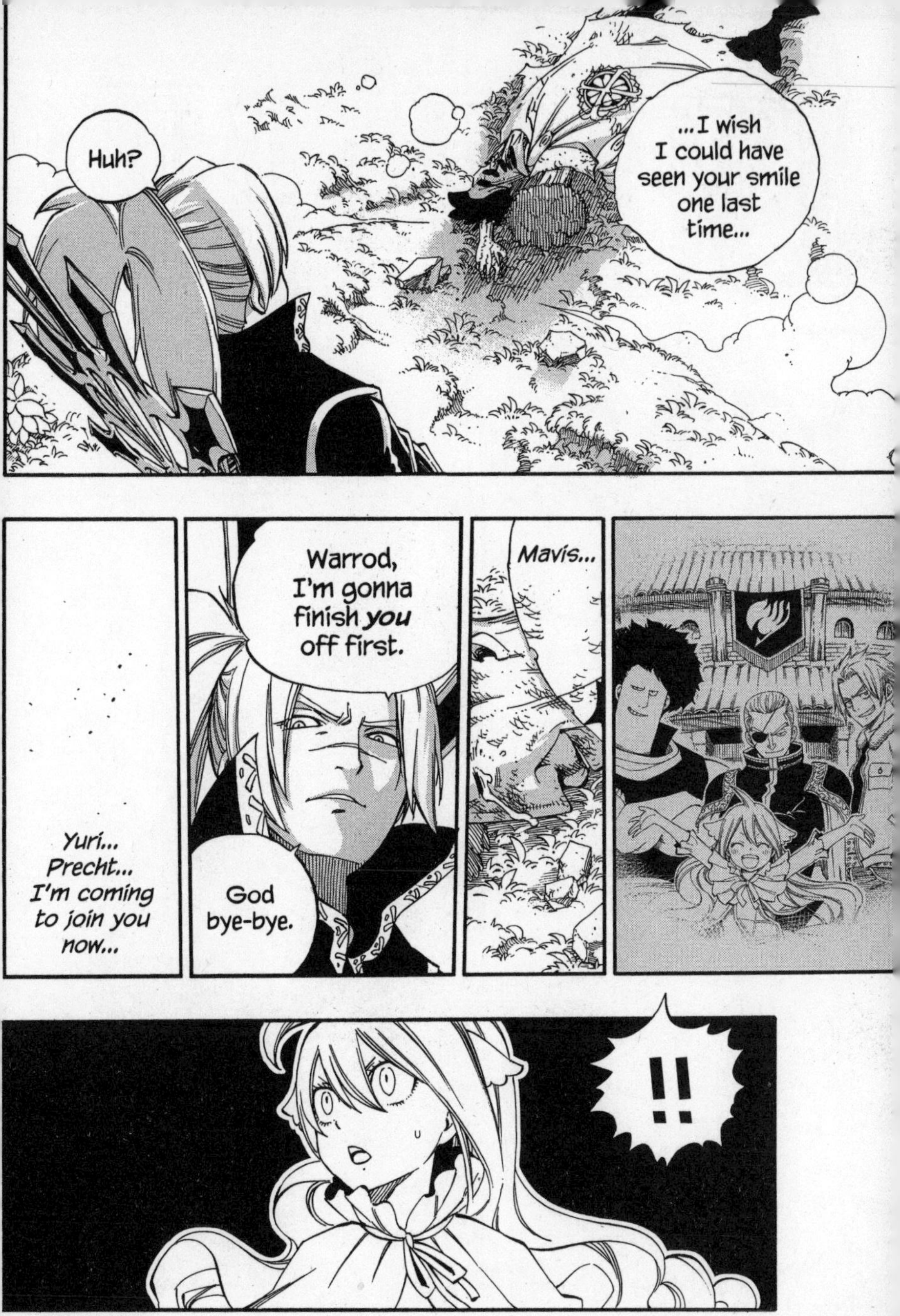
...I wish I could have seen your smile one last time...
Huh?
Mavis...
Warrod, I'm gonna finish *you* off first.
God bye-bye.
Yuri... Precht... I'm coming to join you now...
!!

FAIRY TAIL

フェアリーテイル

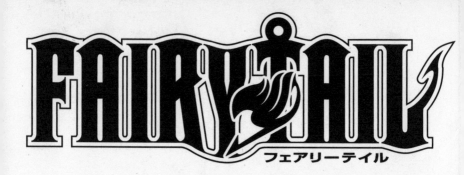

Chapter 470: Hybrid Theory

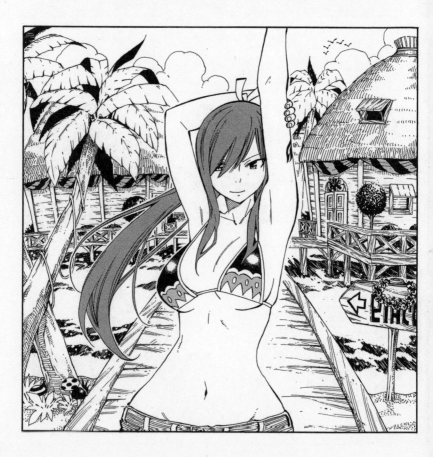

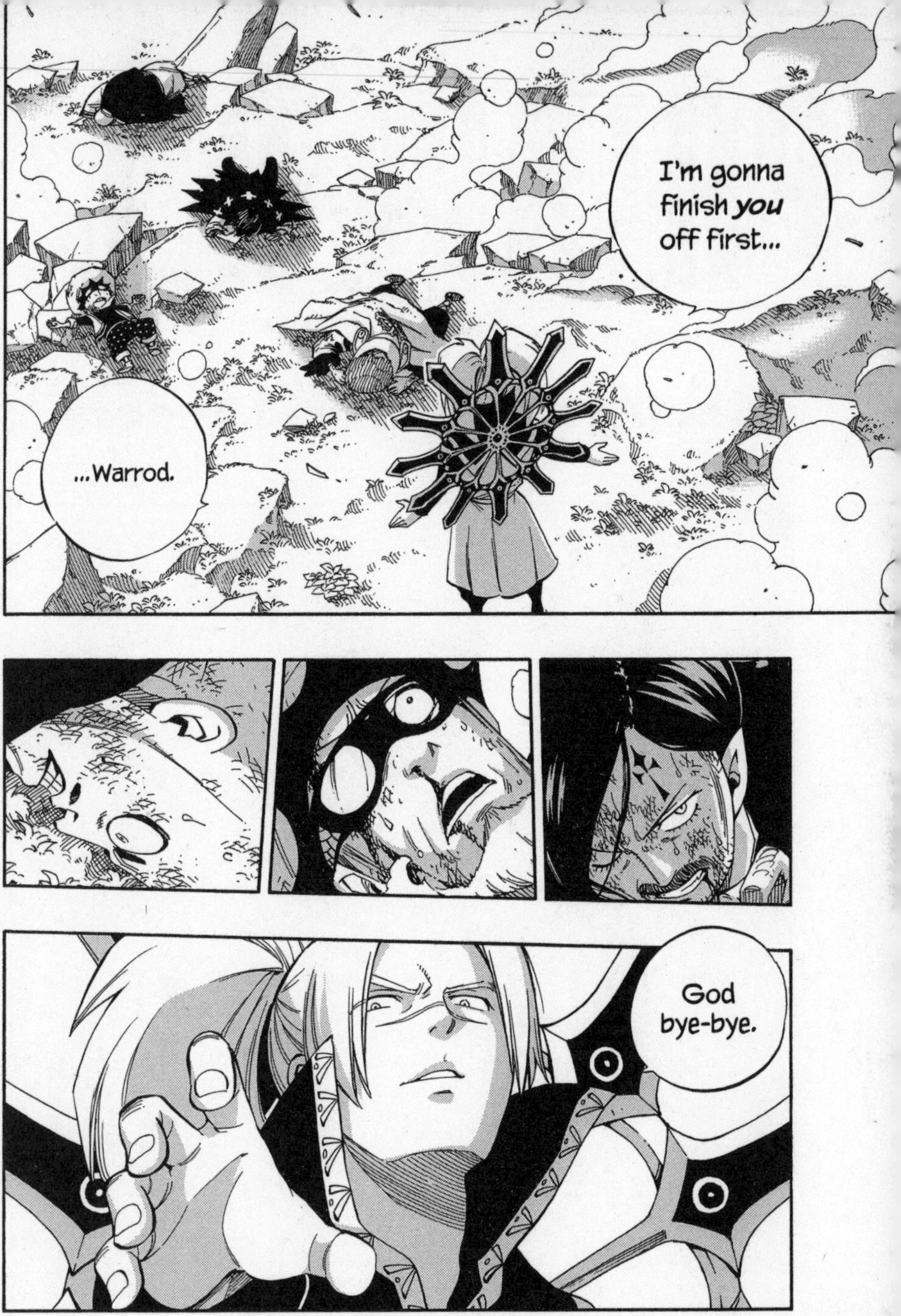
I'm gonna finish *you* off first...
...Warrod.
God bye-bye.

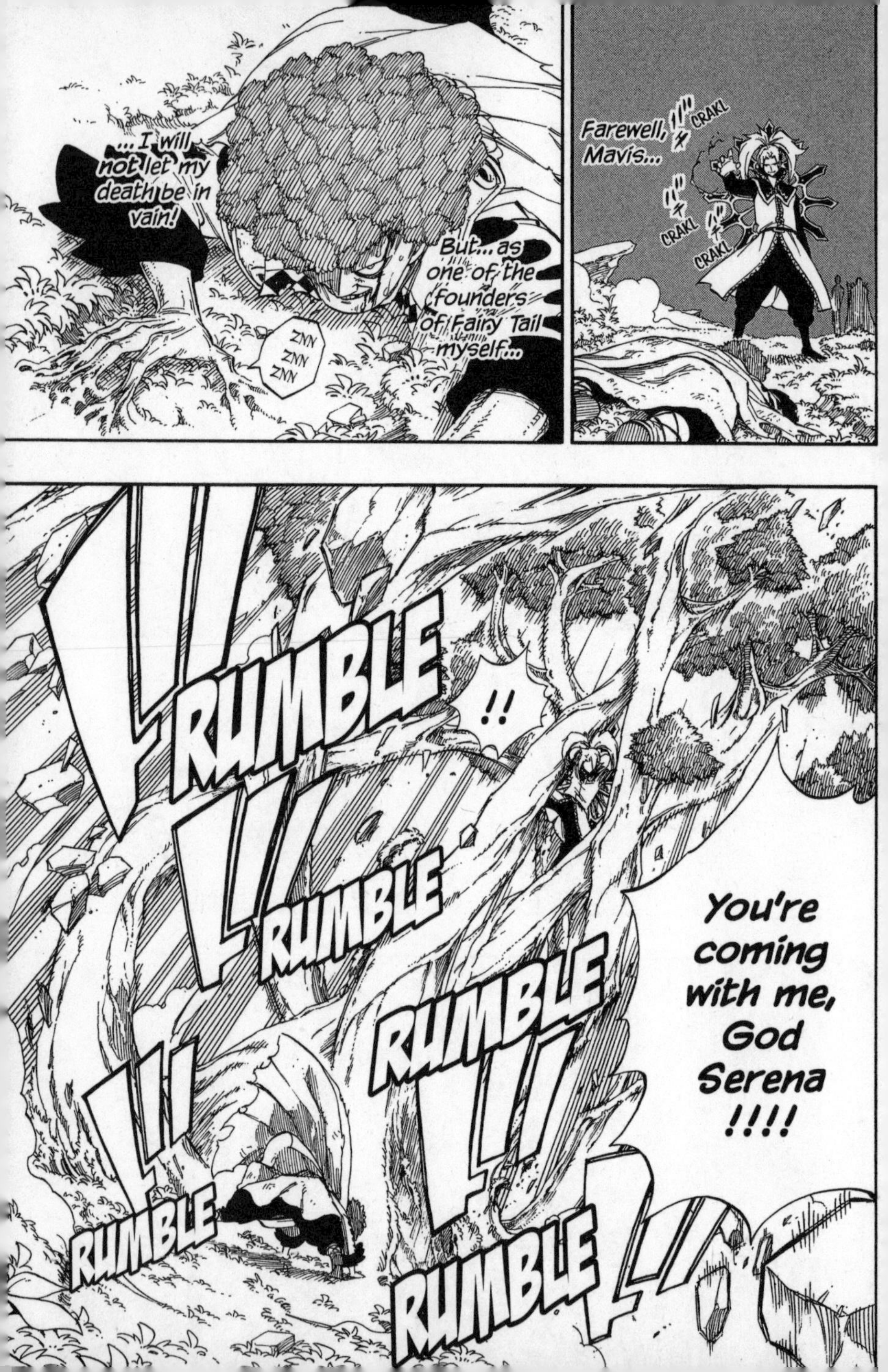
Farewell, Mavis...
CRAKL
CRAKL
CRAKL
But... as one of the founders of Fairy Tail myself...
...I will not let my death be in vain!
ZNN ZNN ZNN
You're coming with me, God Serena !!!!
!!
RUMBLE
RUMBLE
RUMBLE
RUMBLE
RUMBLE

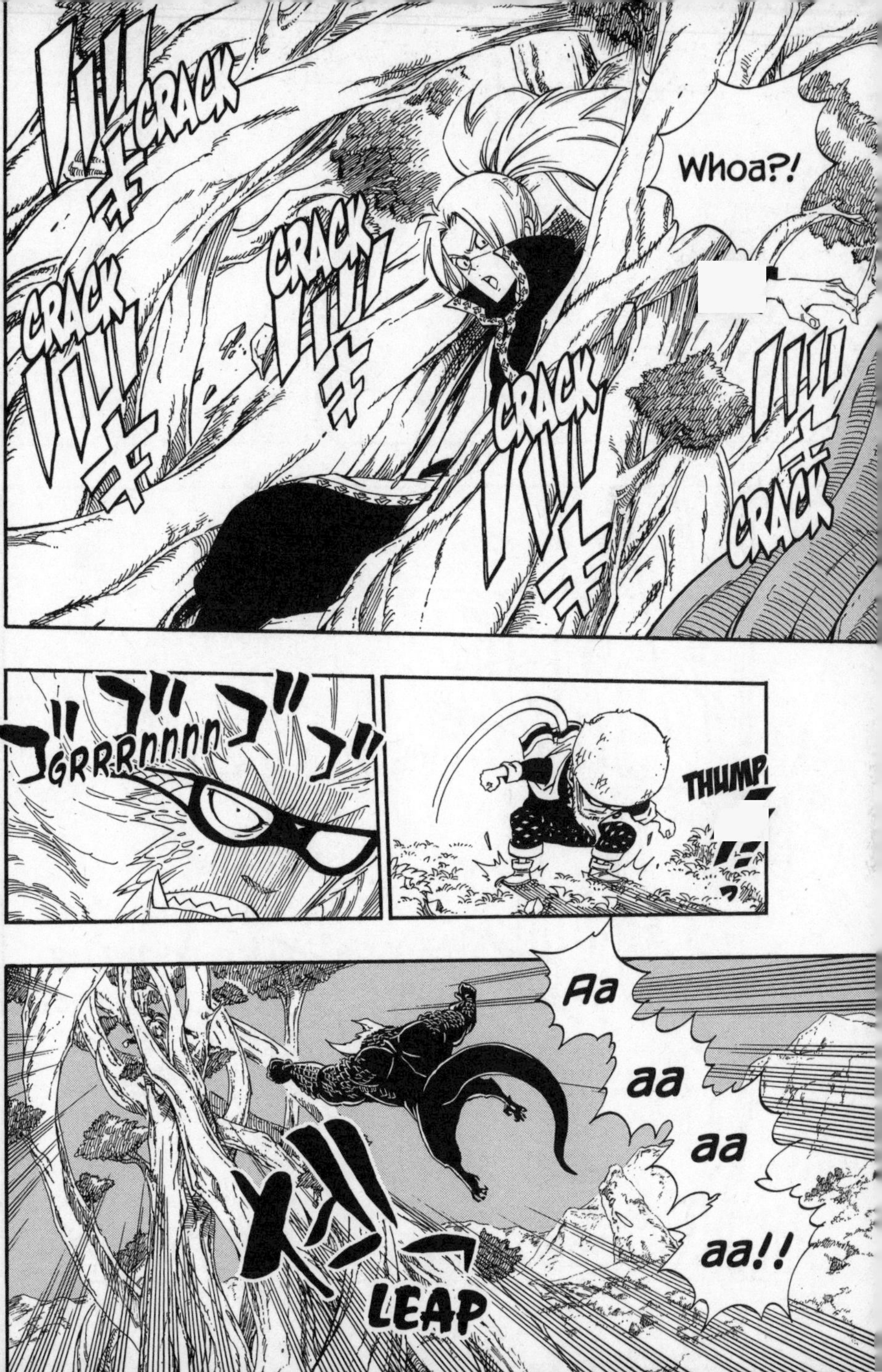
Whoa?!
CRACK
CRACK
CRACK
CRACK
CRACK
THUMP
GRRRnnnn
Aa
aa
aa
aa!!
LEAP

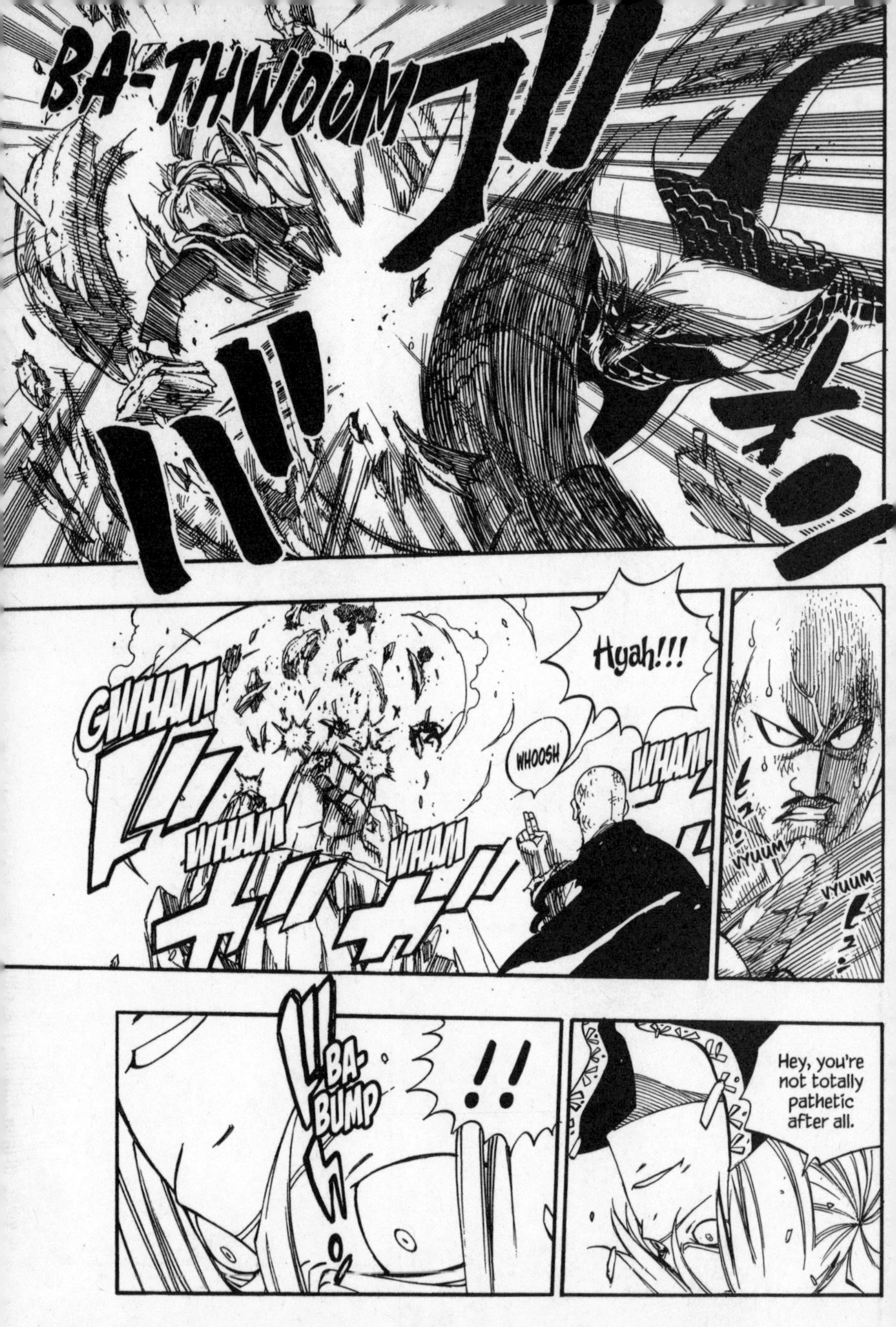
BA-THWOOM
VYUUM
VYUUM
Hyah!!!
WHAM
WHOOSH
WHAM
WHAM
GWHAM
Hey, you're not totally pathetic after all.
!!
BA-BUMP

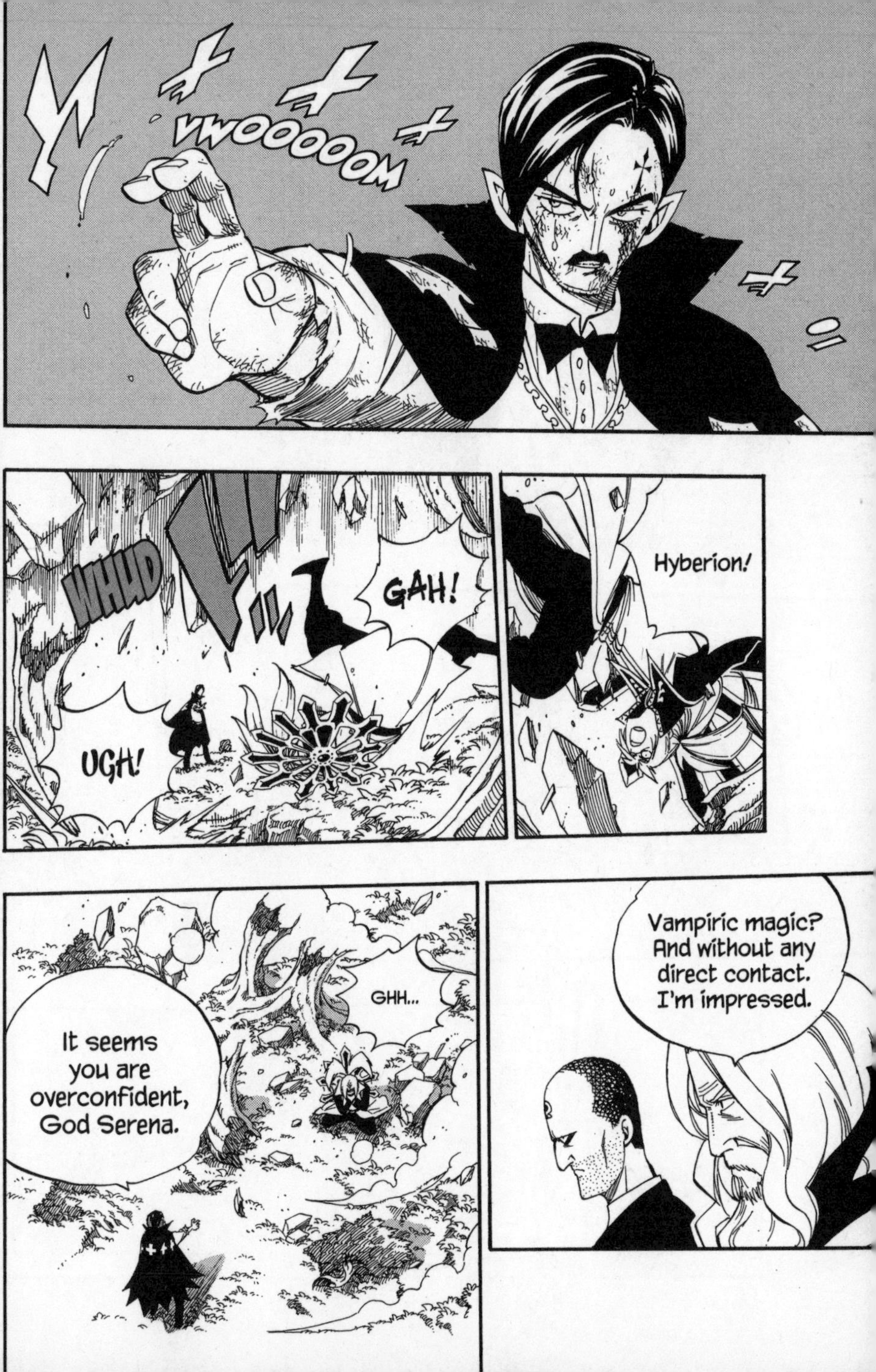
VWOOOOOM
Hyberion!
GAH!
WHUD
UGH!
Vampiric magic? And without any direct contact. I'm impressed.
GHH...
It seems you are overconfident, God Serena.

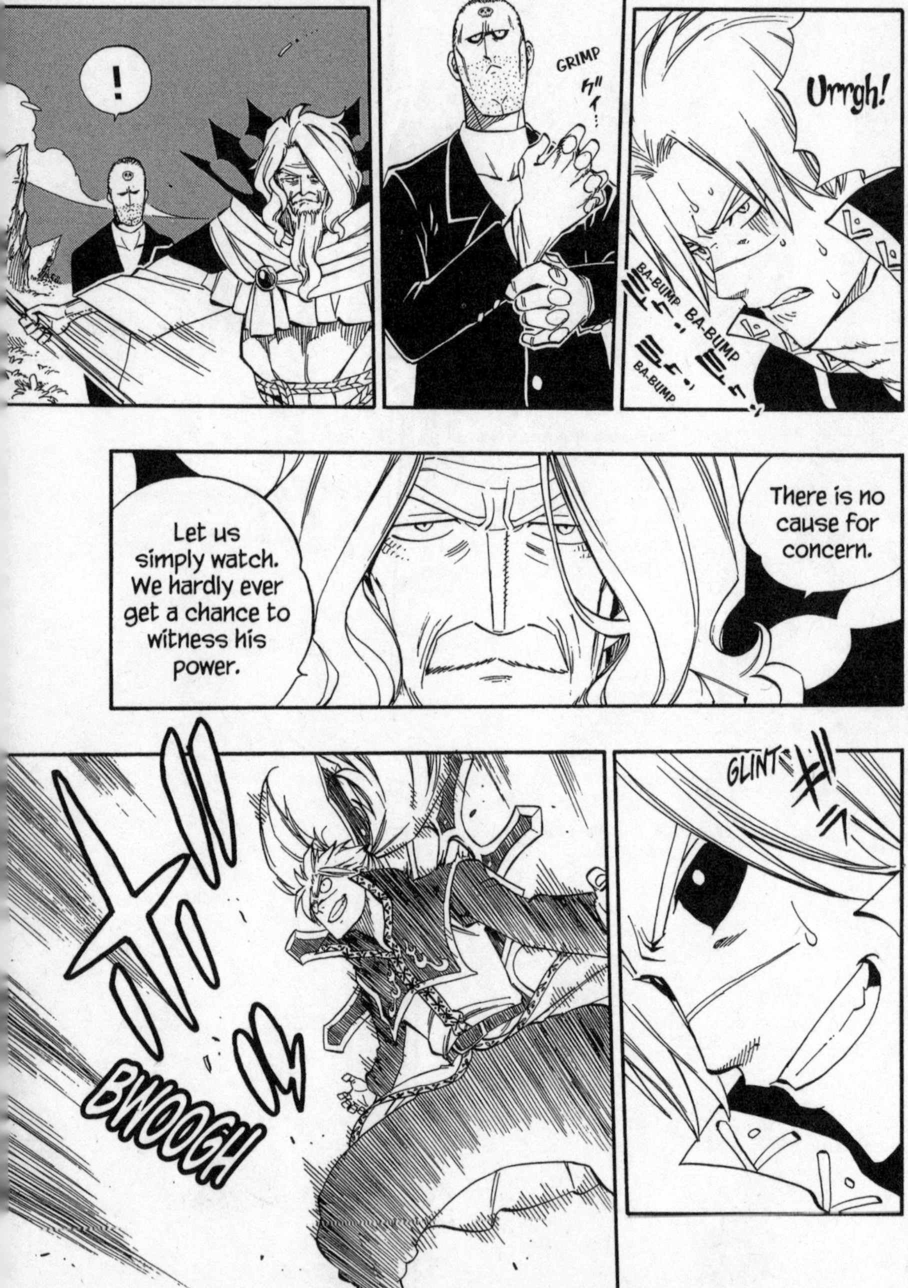
Urrgh!
BA-BUMP
BA-BUMP
BA-BUMP
GRIMP
!
There is no cause for concern.
Let us simply watch. We hardly ever get a chance to witness his power.
GLINT
BWOOGH

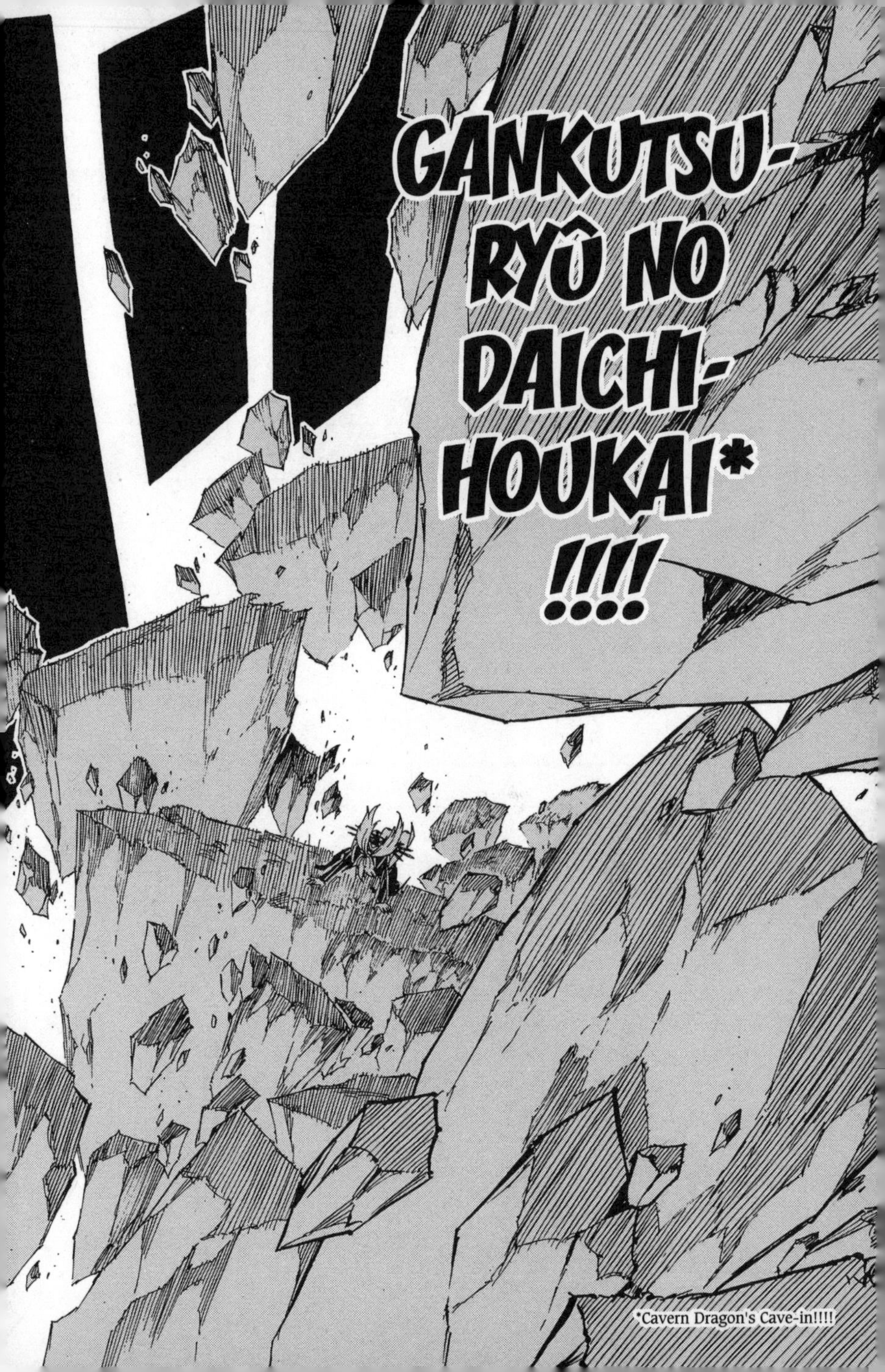
GANKUTSU-RYÛ NO DAICHI-HOUKAI* !!!!
*Cavern Dragon's Cave-in!!!!

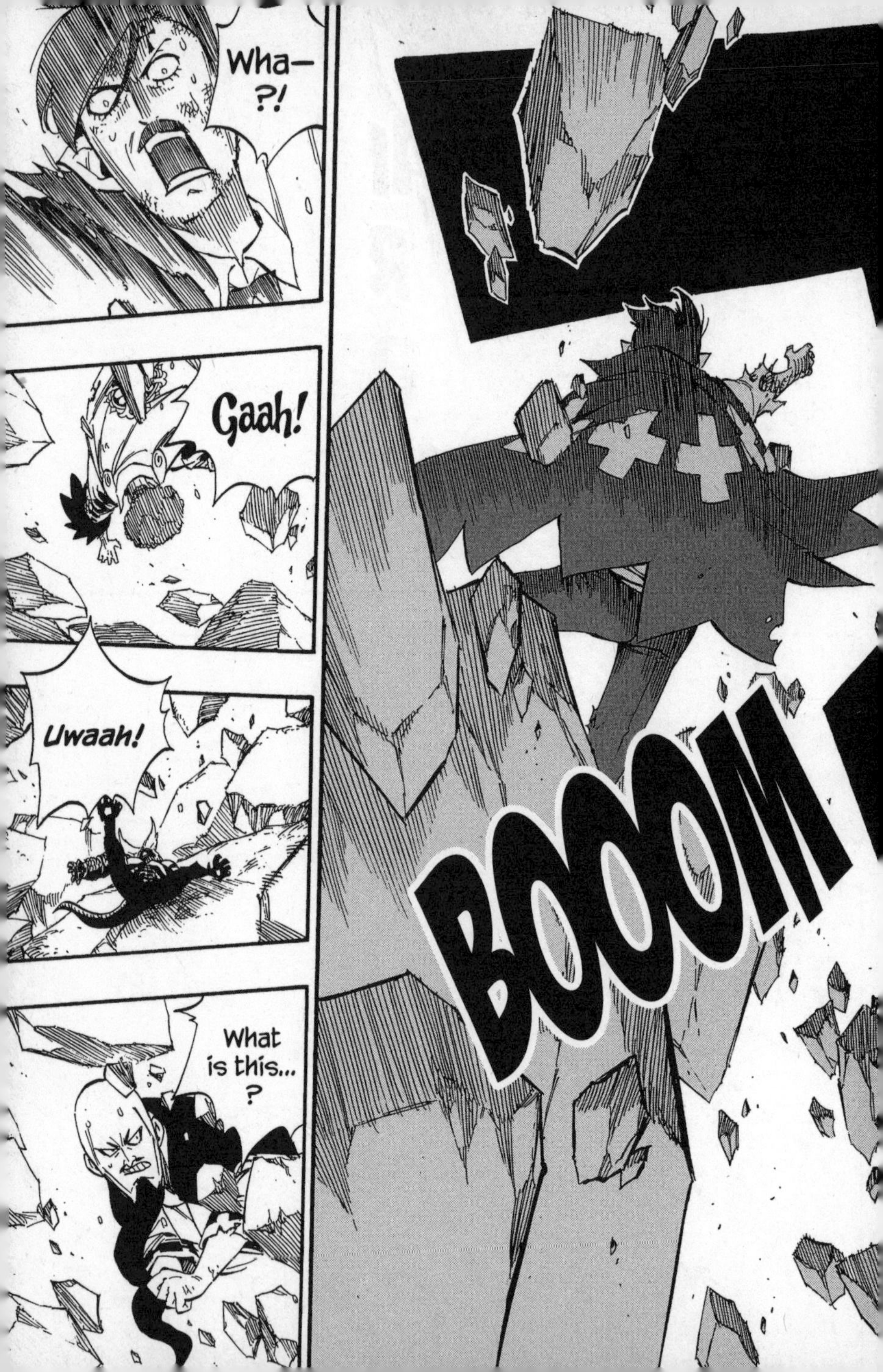
BOOOM
Wha—?!
Gaah!
Uwaah!
What is this...?

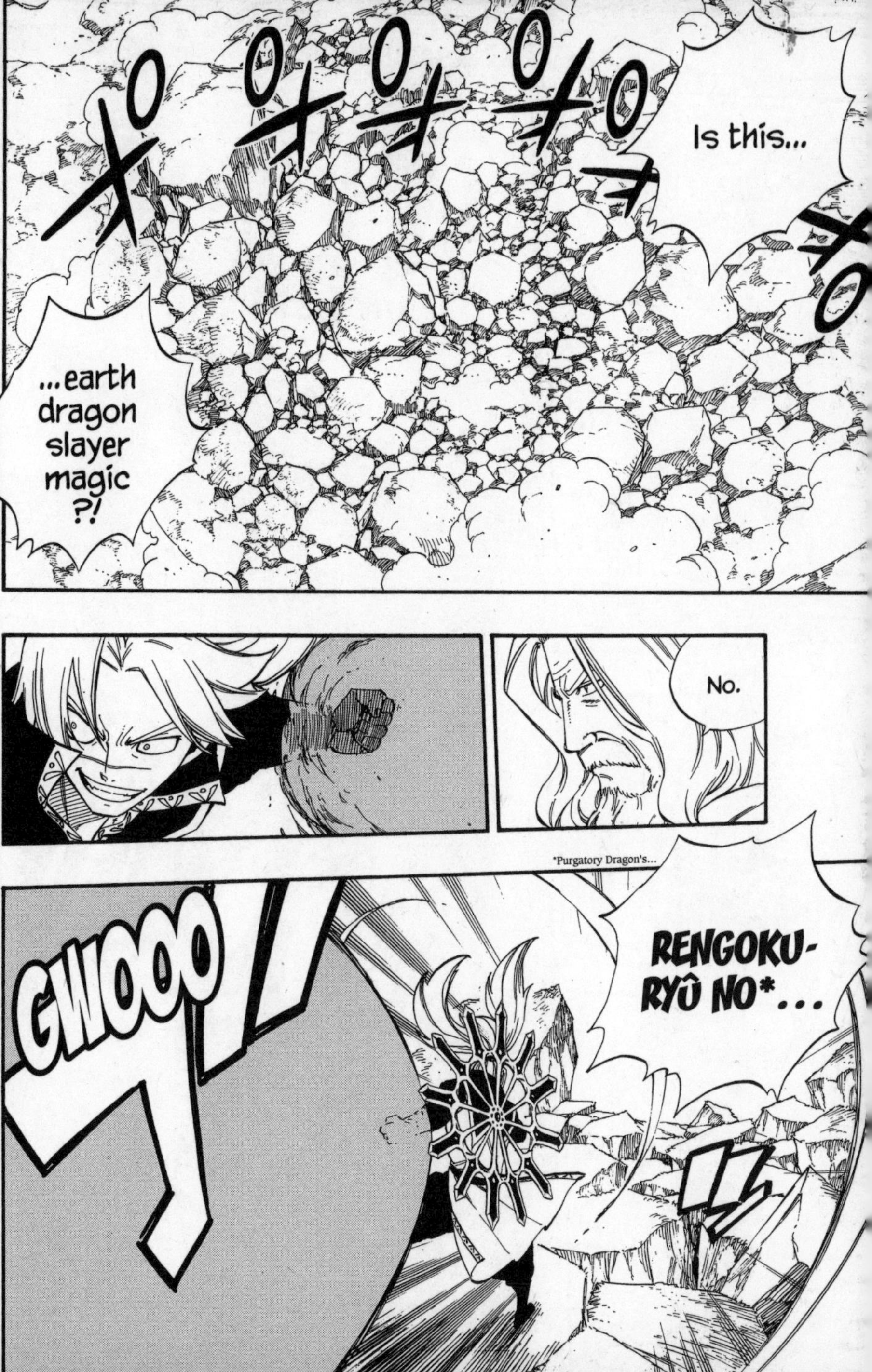
Is this...
...earth dragon slayer magic?!
No.
RENGOKU-RYÛ NO*...
GWOOO
*Purgatory Dragon's...

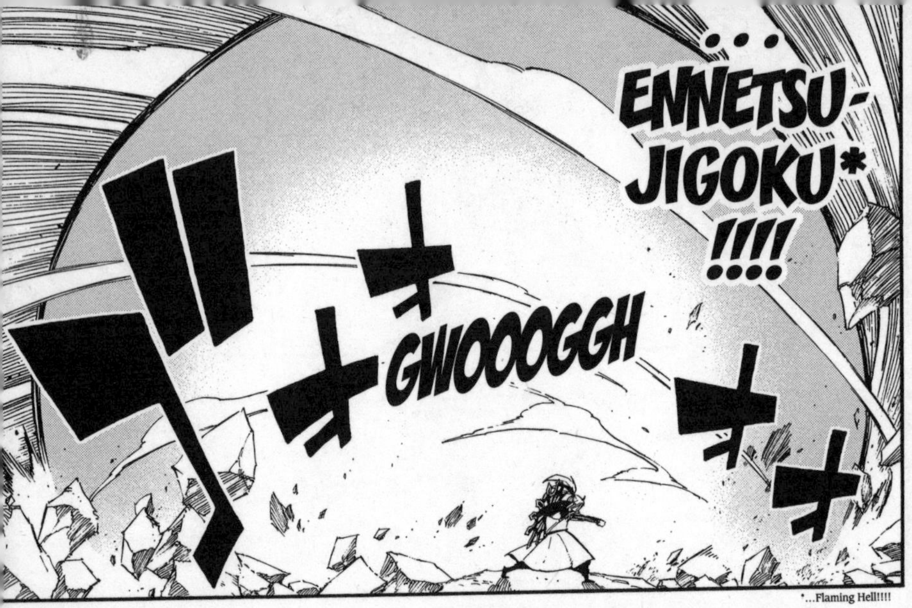
...ENNETSU-JIGOKU* !!!!
GWOOOGGH

*...Flaming Hell!!!!

**Sea King Dragon's Encircling Deluge!!!!

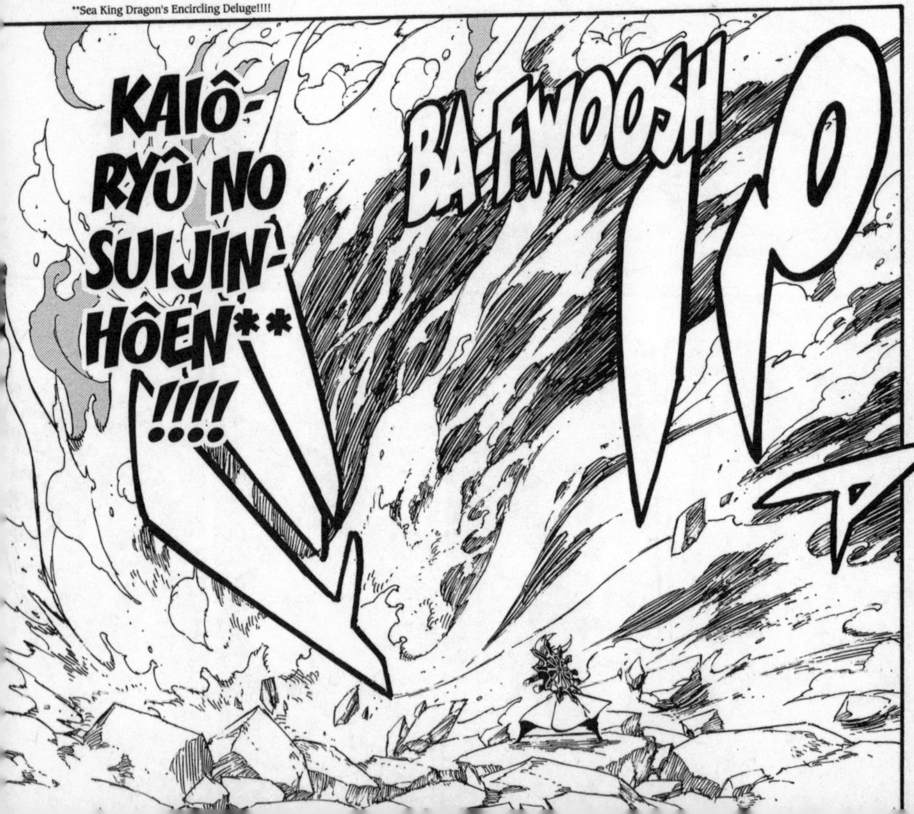
KAIÔ-RYÛ NO SUIJIN-HÔEN** !!!!
BA-FWOOSH

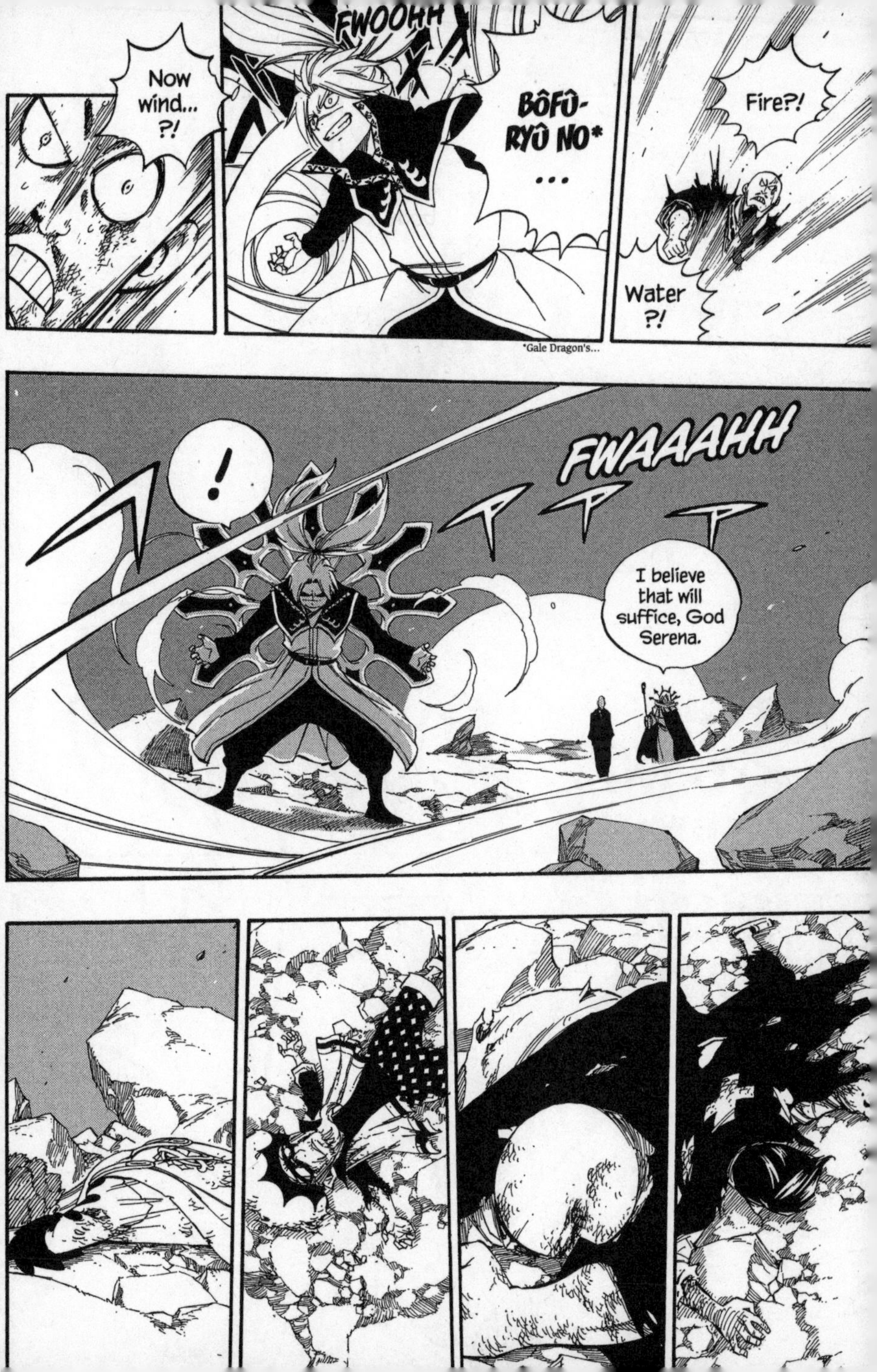
Fire?!
Water ?!
FWOOHH
BÔFÛ-RYÛ NO* ...
Now wind... ?!
FWAAAHH
!
I believe that will suffice, God Serena.
*Gale Dragon's...

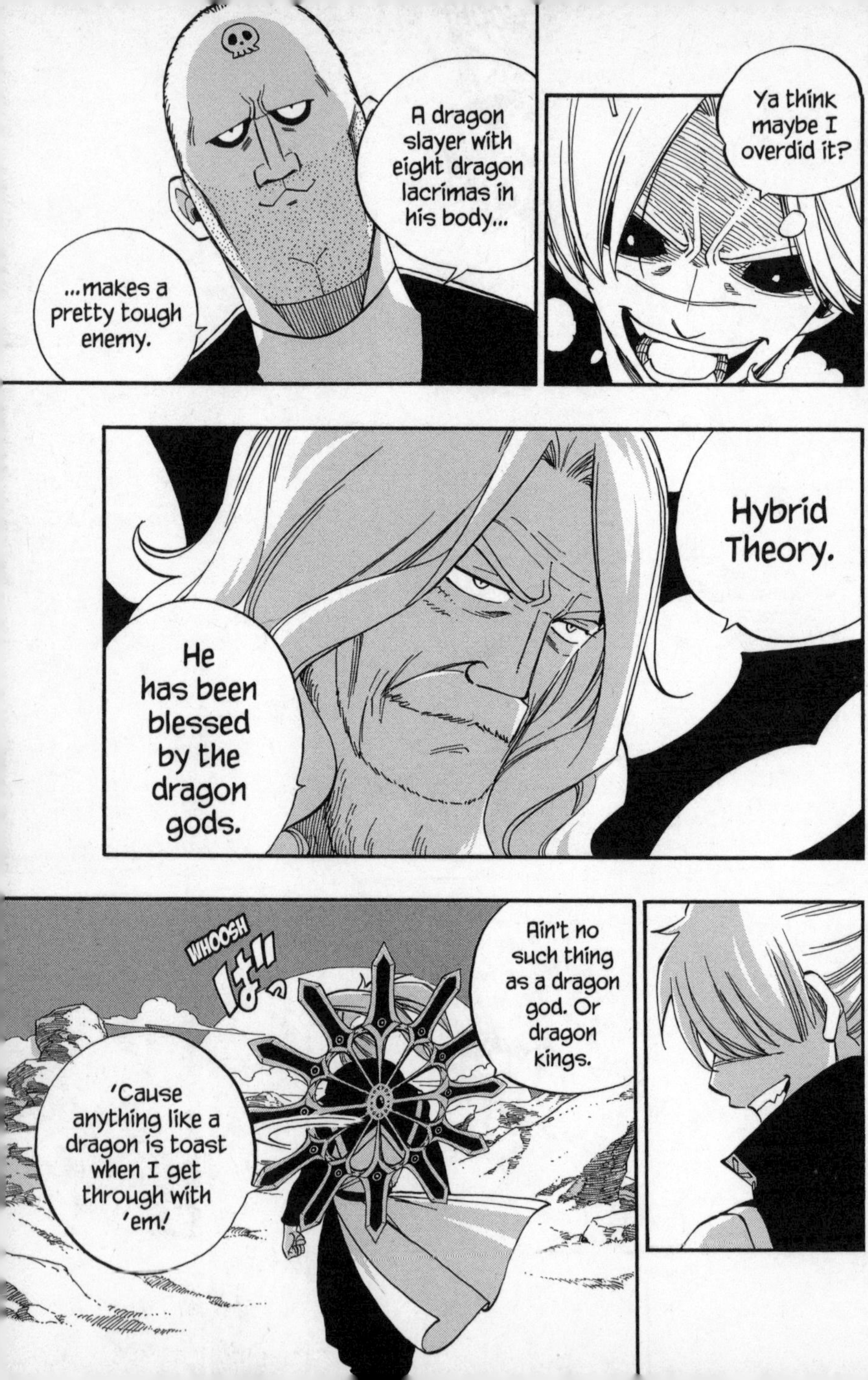
Ya think maybe I overdid it?
A dragon slayer with eight dragon lacrimas in his body...
...makes a pretty tough enemy.
Hybrid Theory.
He has been blessed by the dragon gods.
Ain't no such thing as a dragon god. Or dragon kings.
WHOOSH
'Cause anything like a dragon is toast when I get through with 'em!

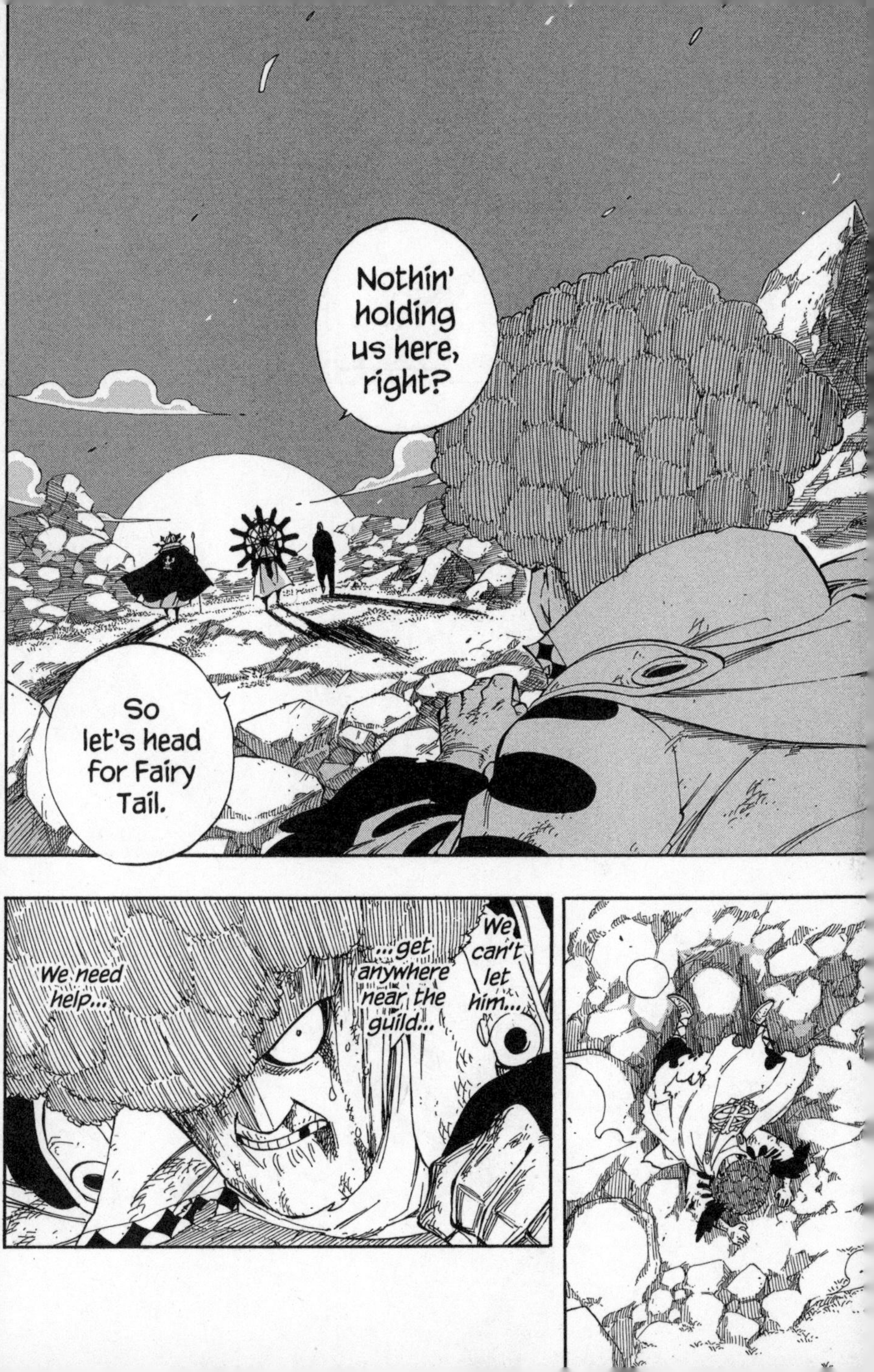
Nothin' holding us here, right?
So let's head for Fairy Tail.
We can't let him...
...get anywhere near the guild...
We need help...

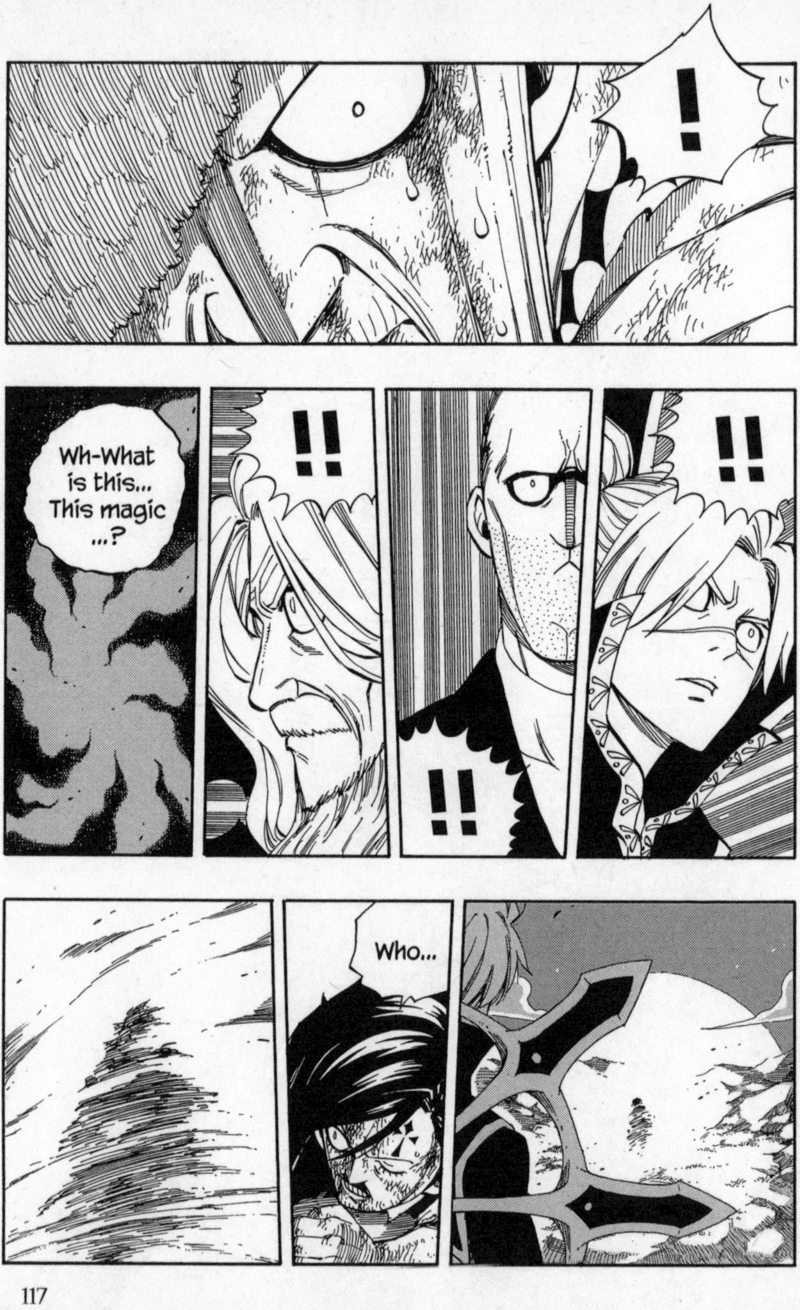
!
!!
!!
!!
Wh-What is this... This magic ...?
Who...

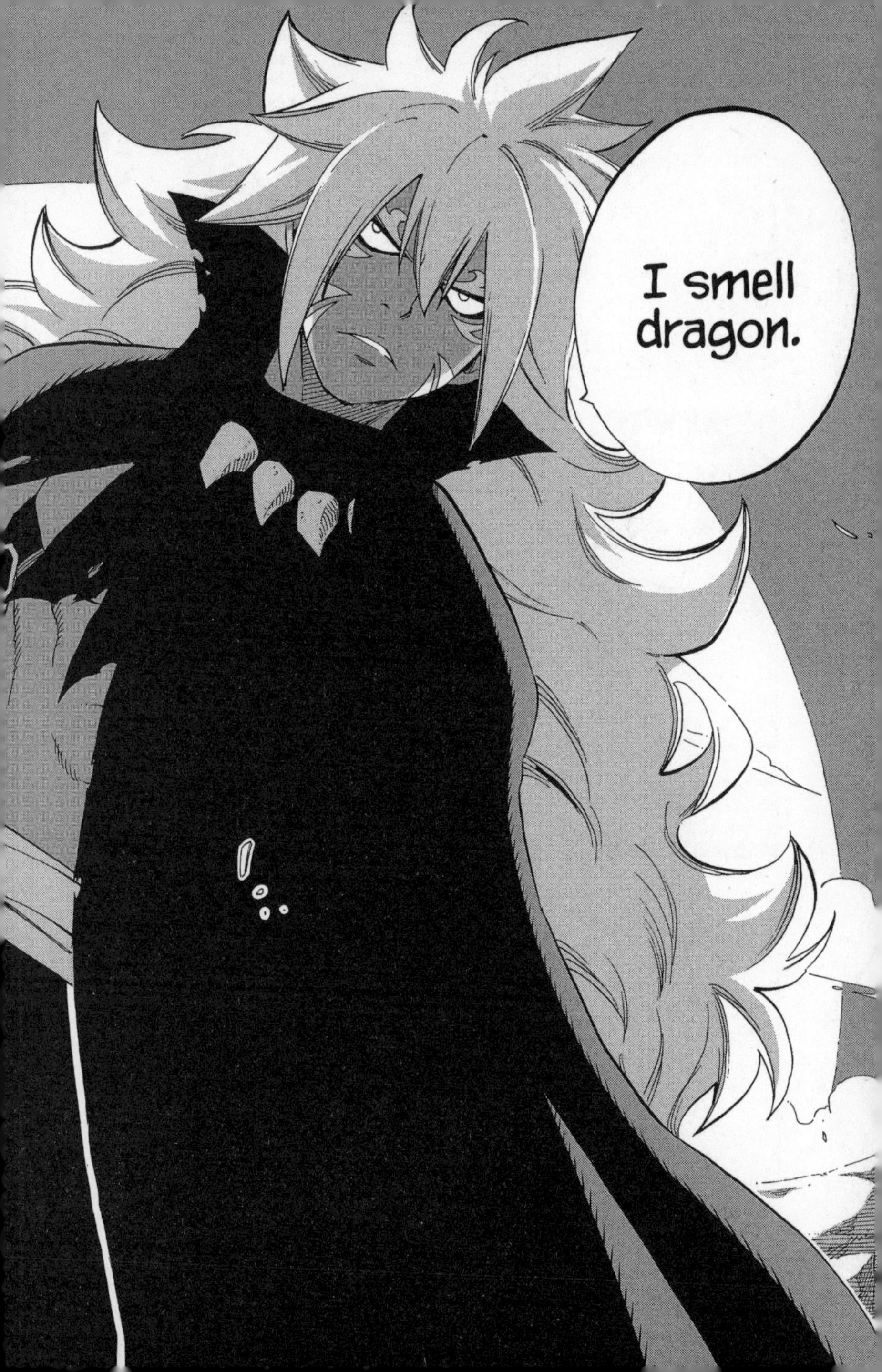
I smell dragon.

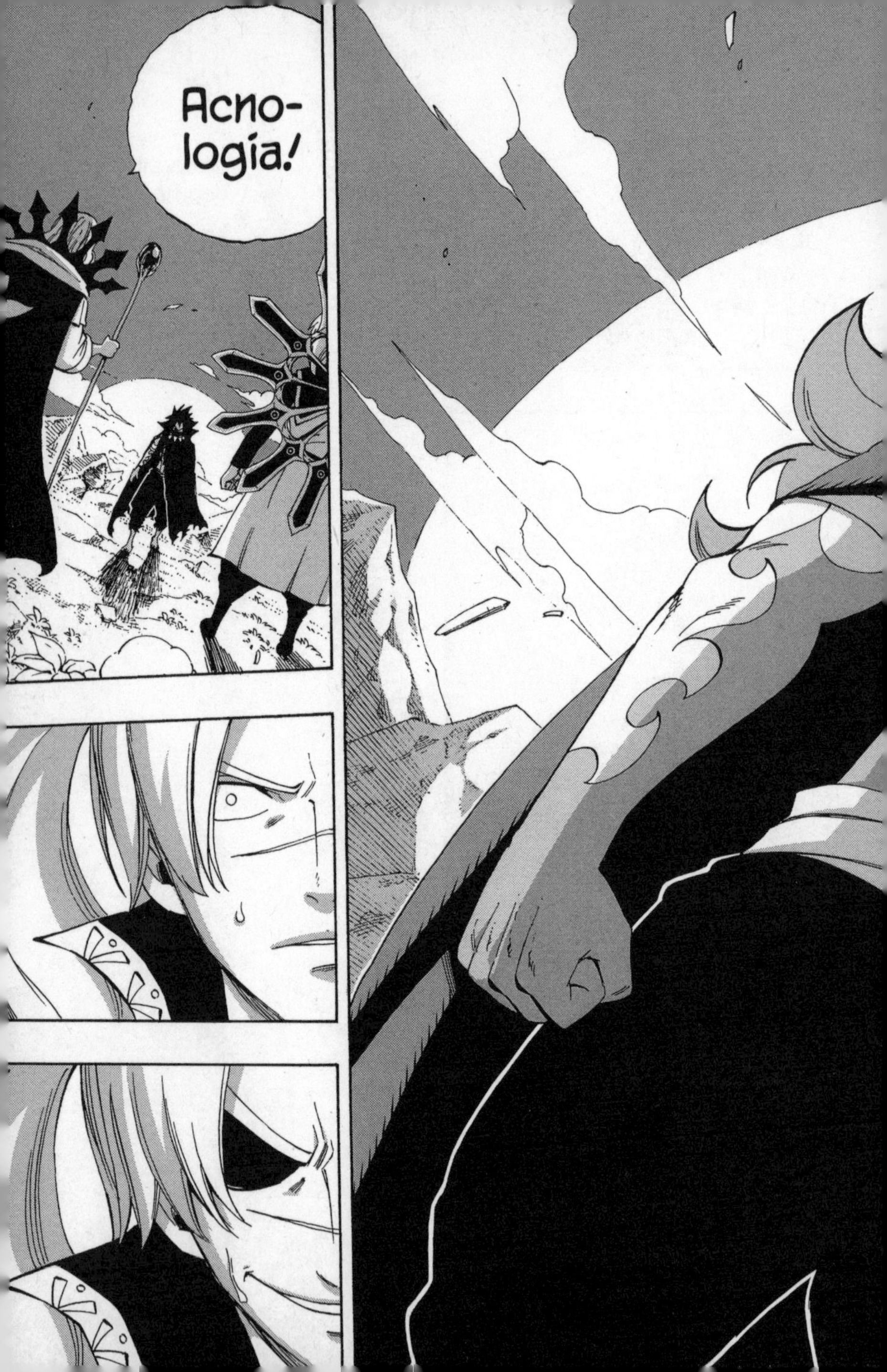
Acno-
logia!

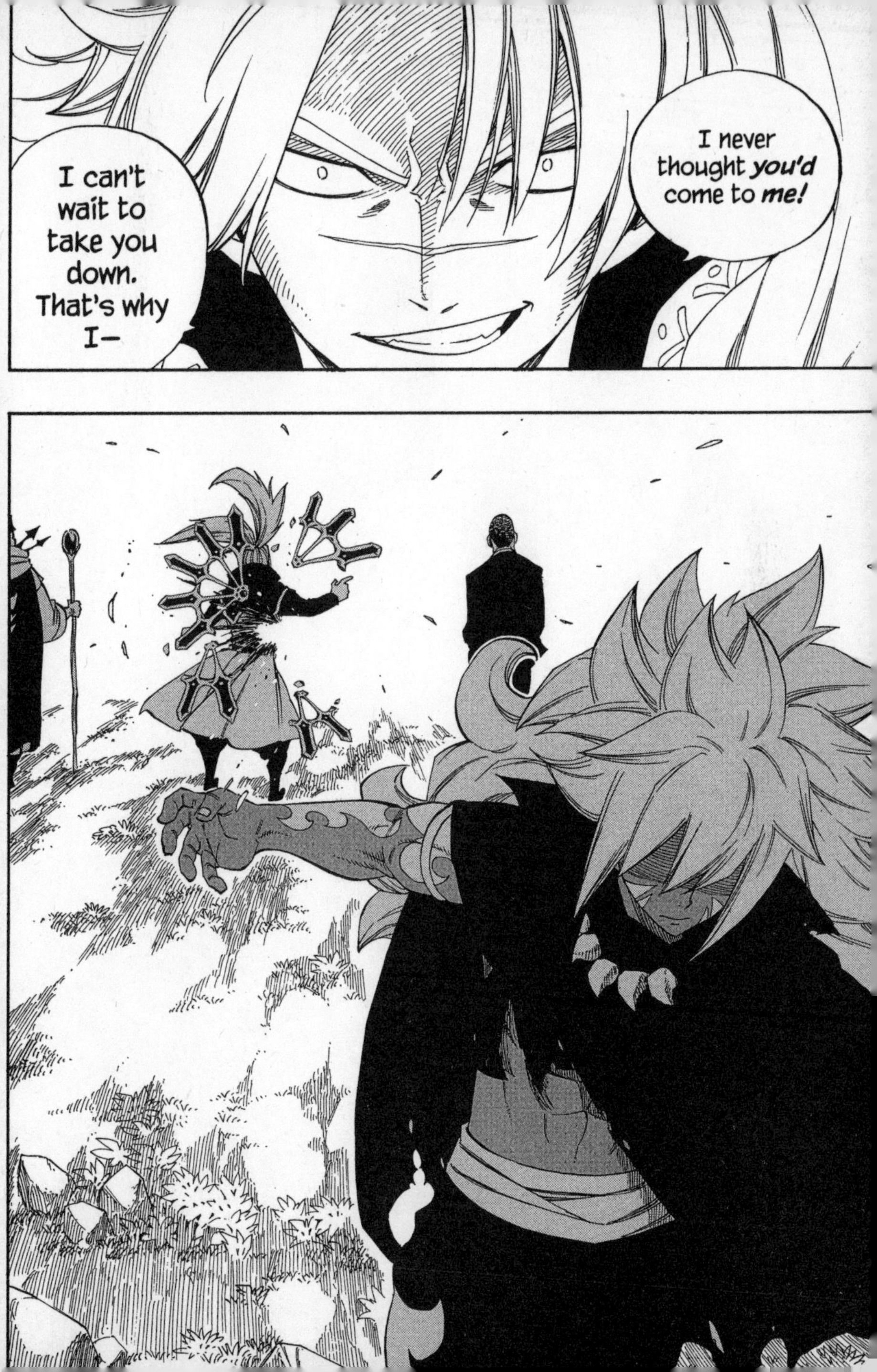
I never thought *you'd* come to *me!*
I can't wait to take you down. That's why I—

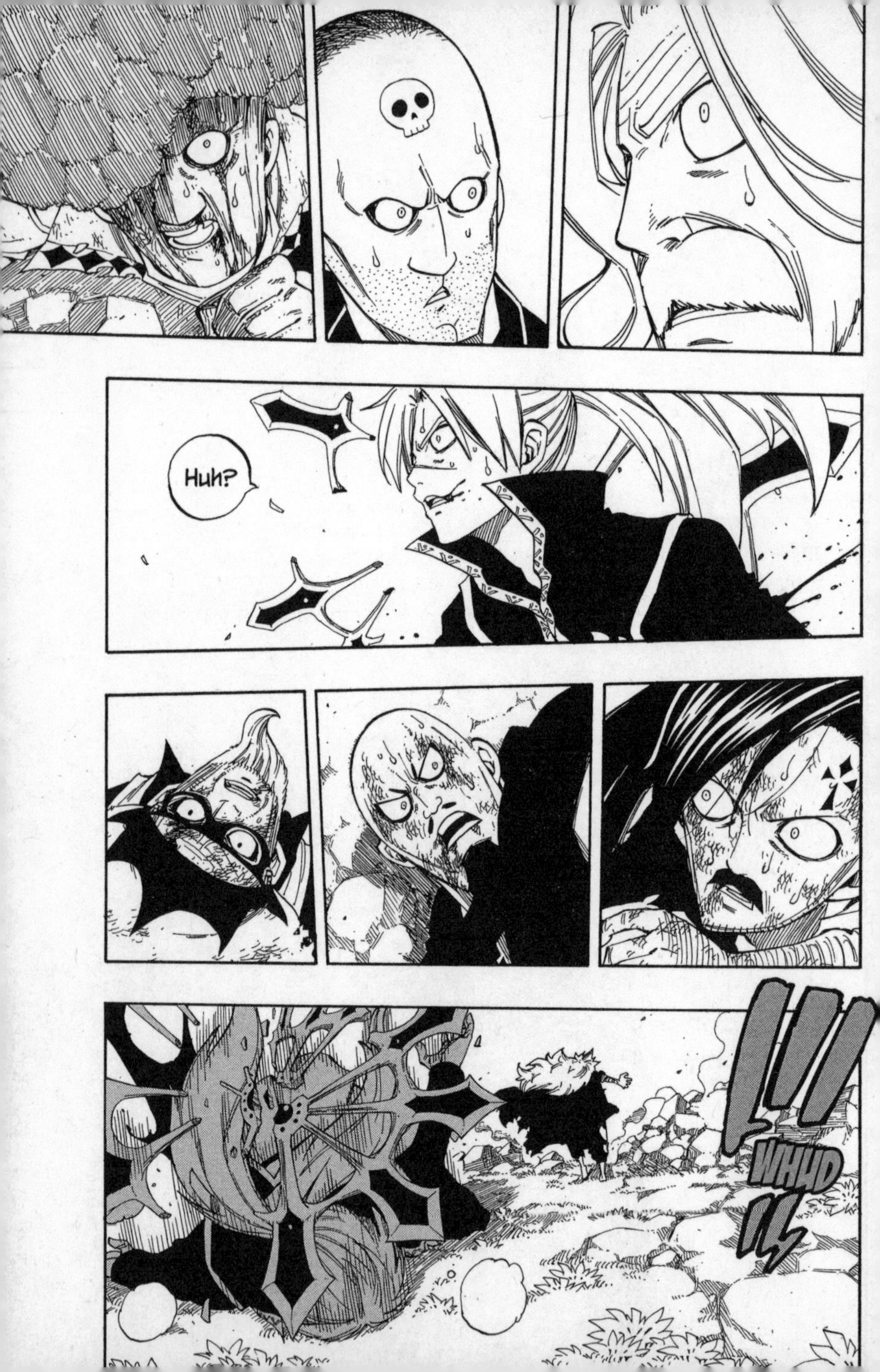
Huh?
WHUD

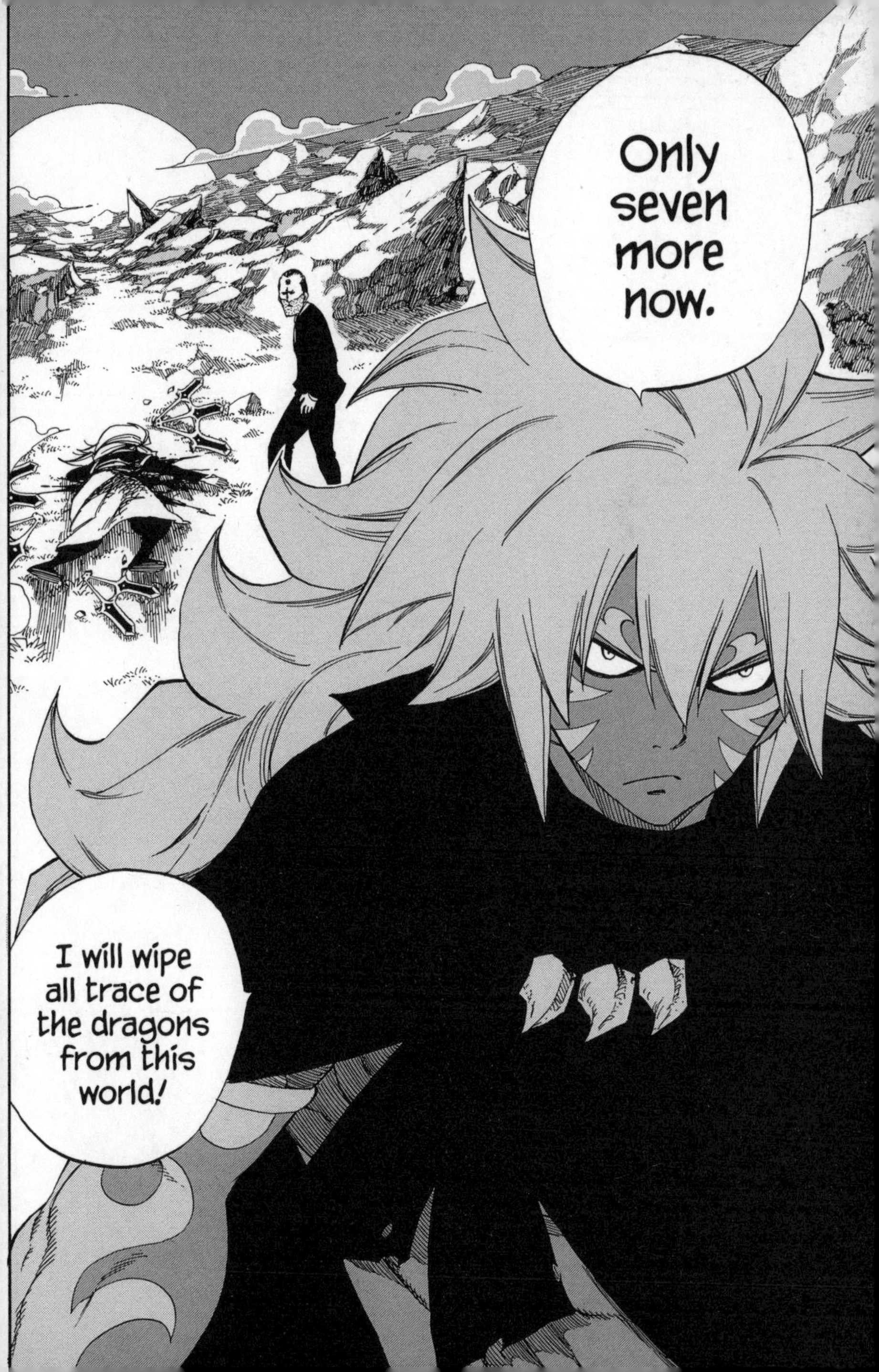
Only seven more now.
I will wipe all trace of the dragons from this world!

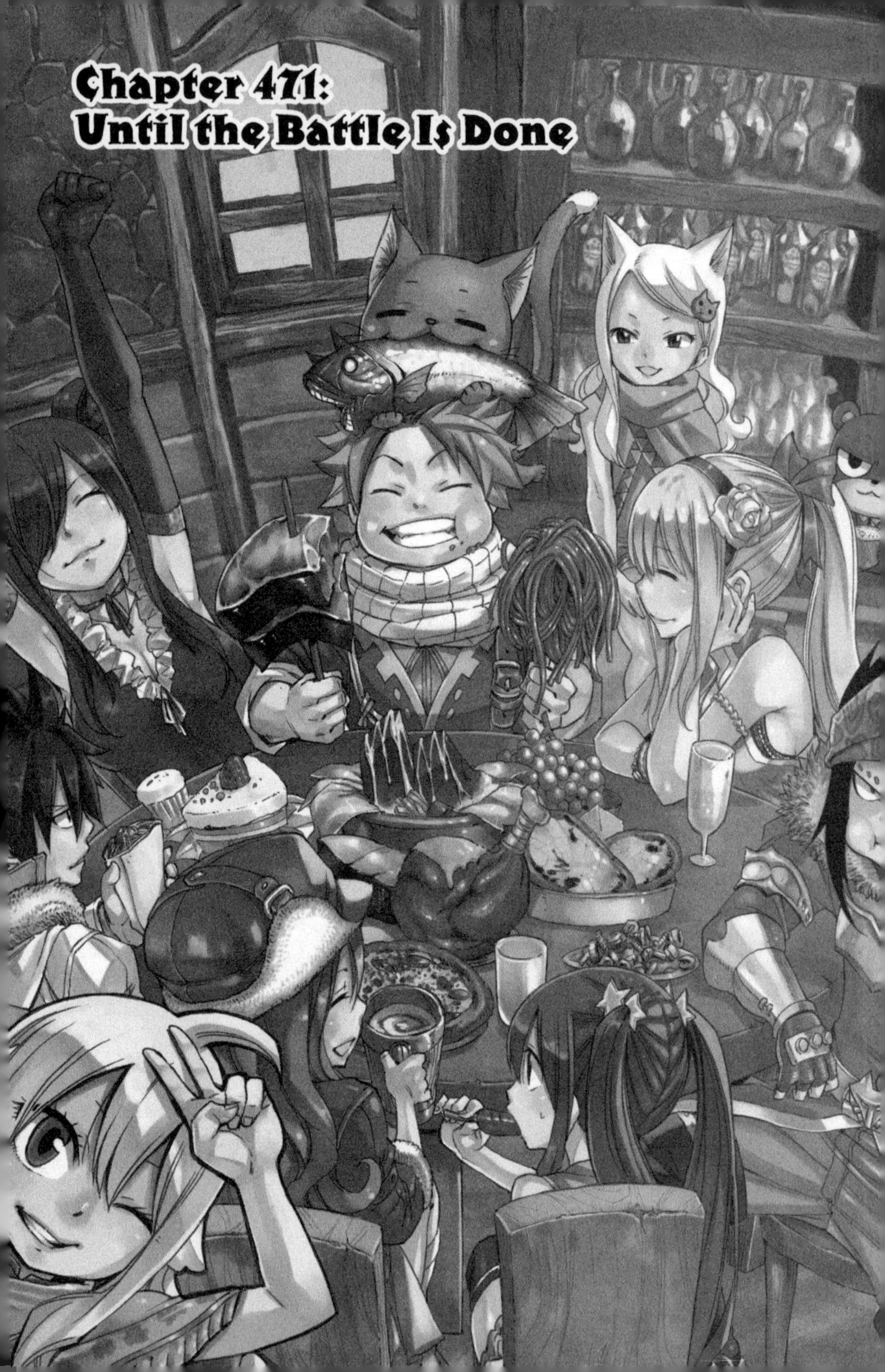
Chapter 471:
Until the Battle Is Done

FAIRY TAIL
フェアリーテイル

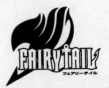

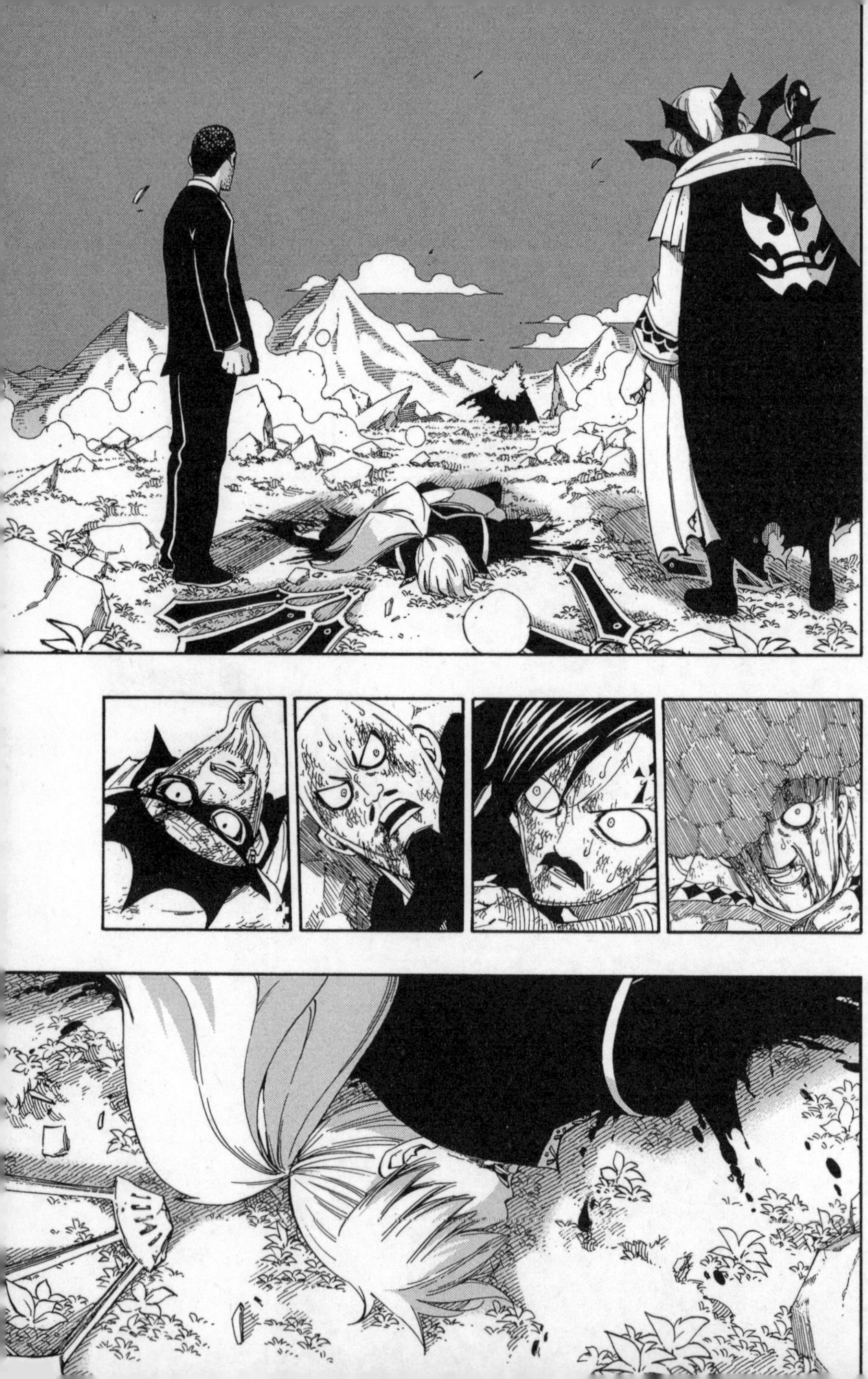

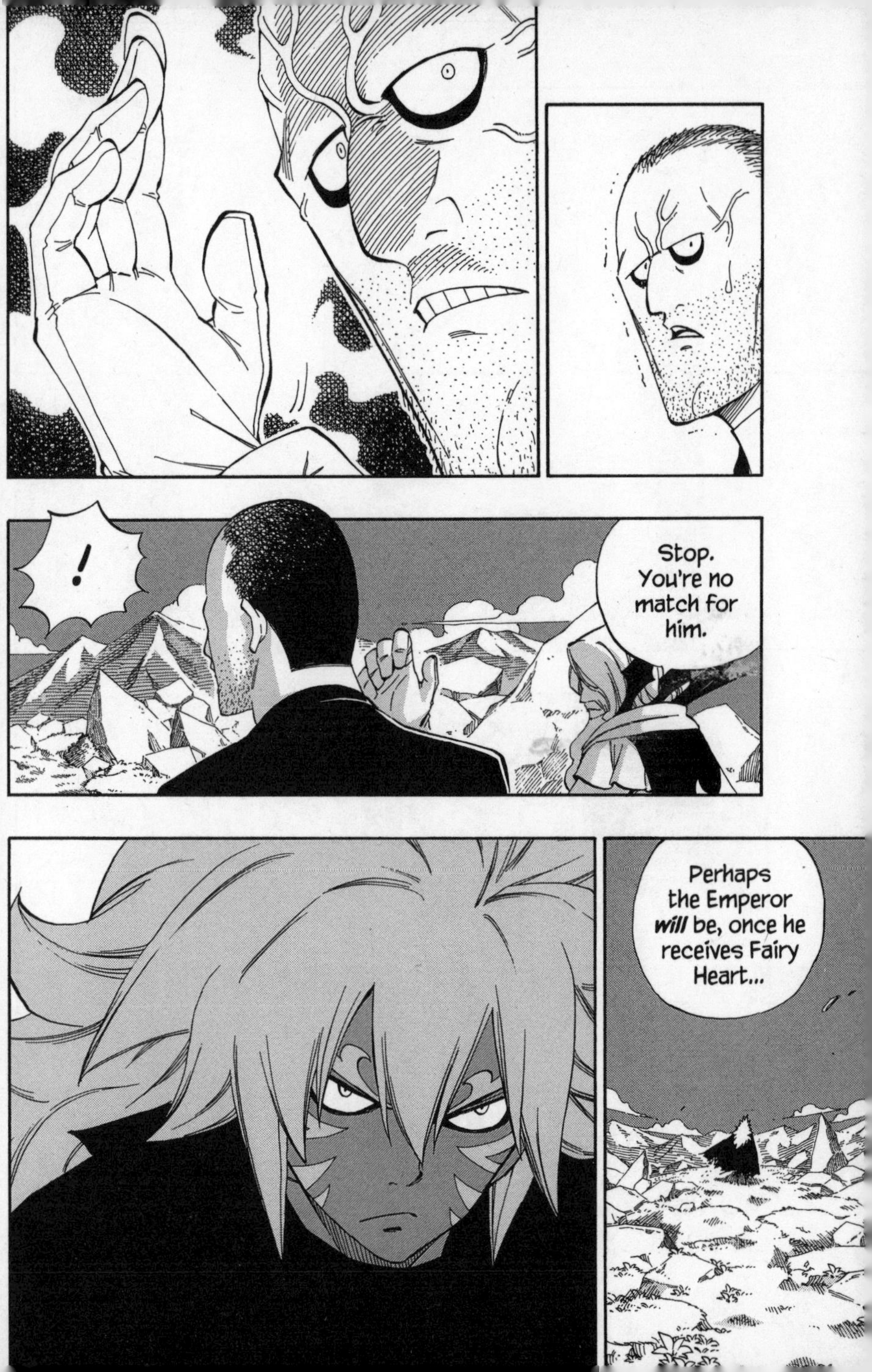
Stop. You're no match for him.
!
Perhaps the Emperor *will* be, once he receives Fairy Heart...

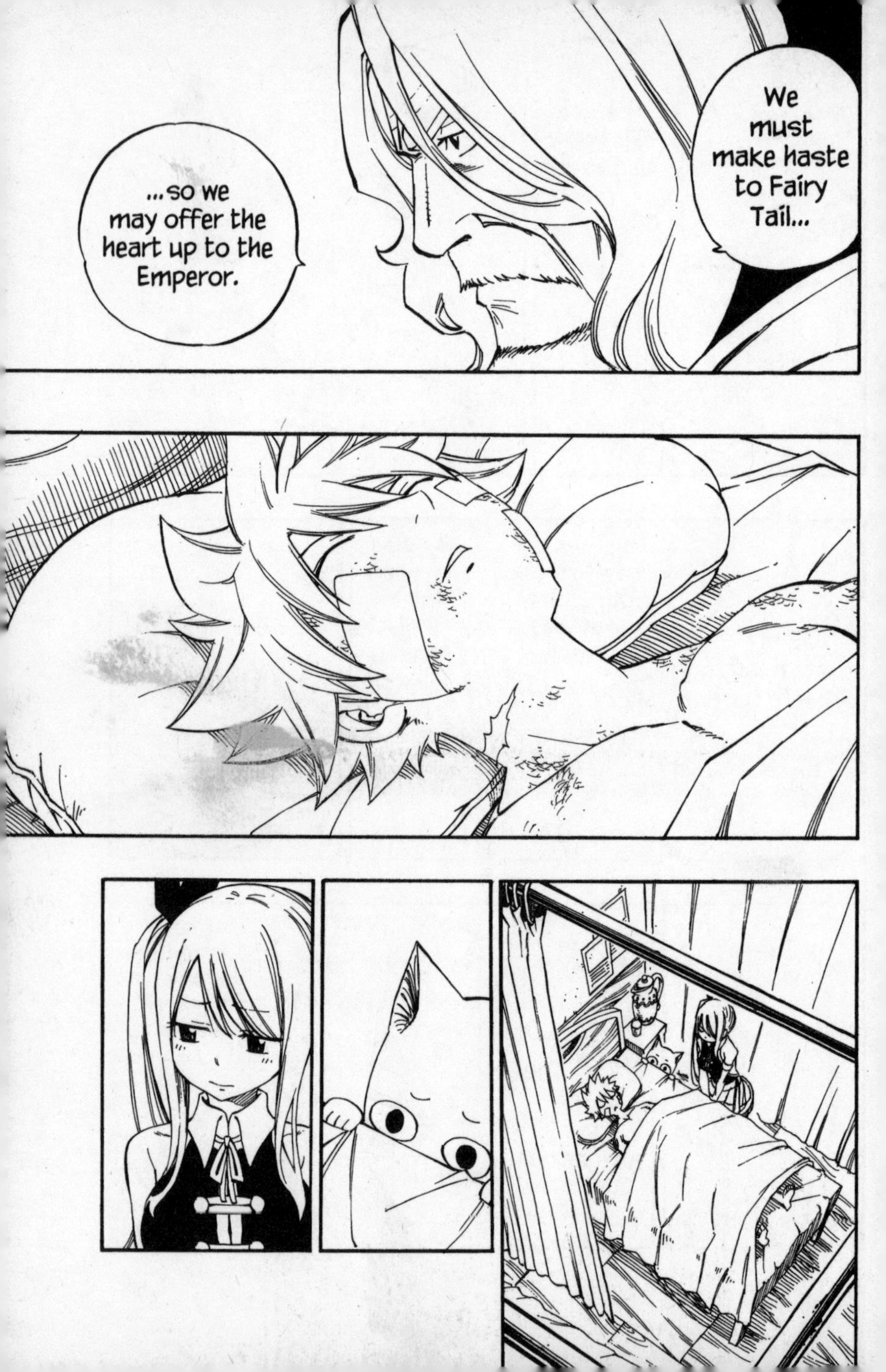
We must make haste to Fairy Tail...
...so we may offer the heart up to the Emperor.

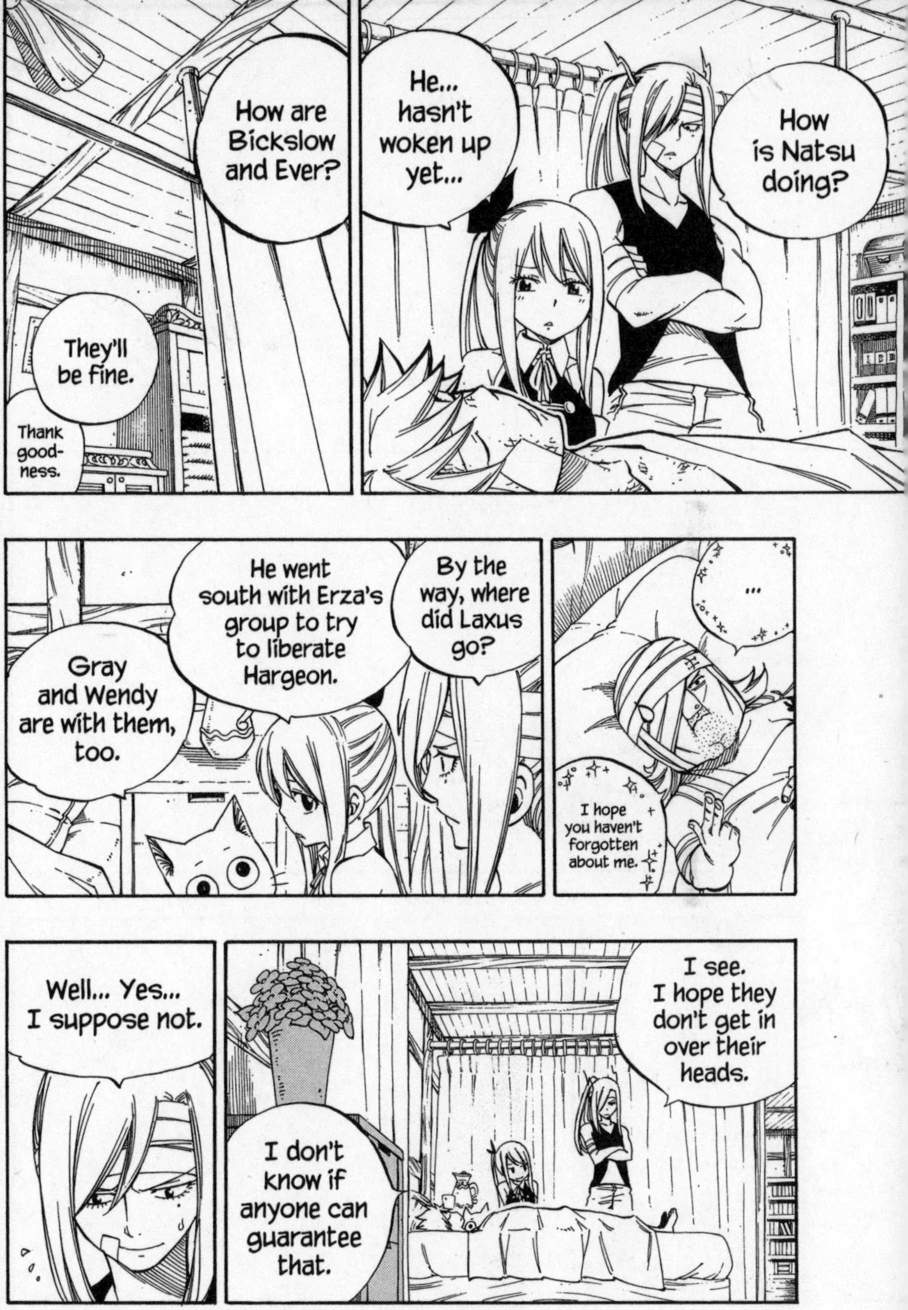
How is Natsu doing?
He... hasn't woken up yet...
How are Bickslow and Ever?
They'll be fine.
Thank goodness.
...
I hope you haven't forgotten about me.
By the way, where did Laxus go?
He went south with Erza's group to try to liberate Hargeon.
Gray and Wendy are with them, too.
I see. I hope they don't get in over their heads.
I don't know if anyone can guarantee that.
Well... Yes... I suppose not.

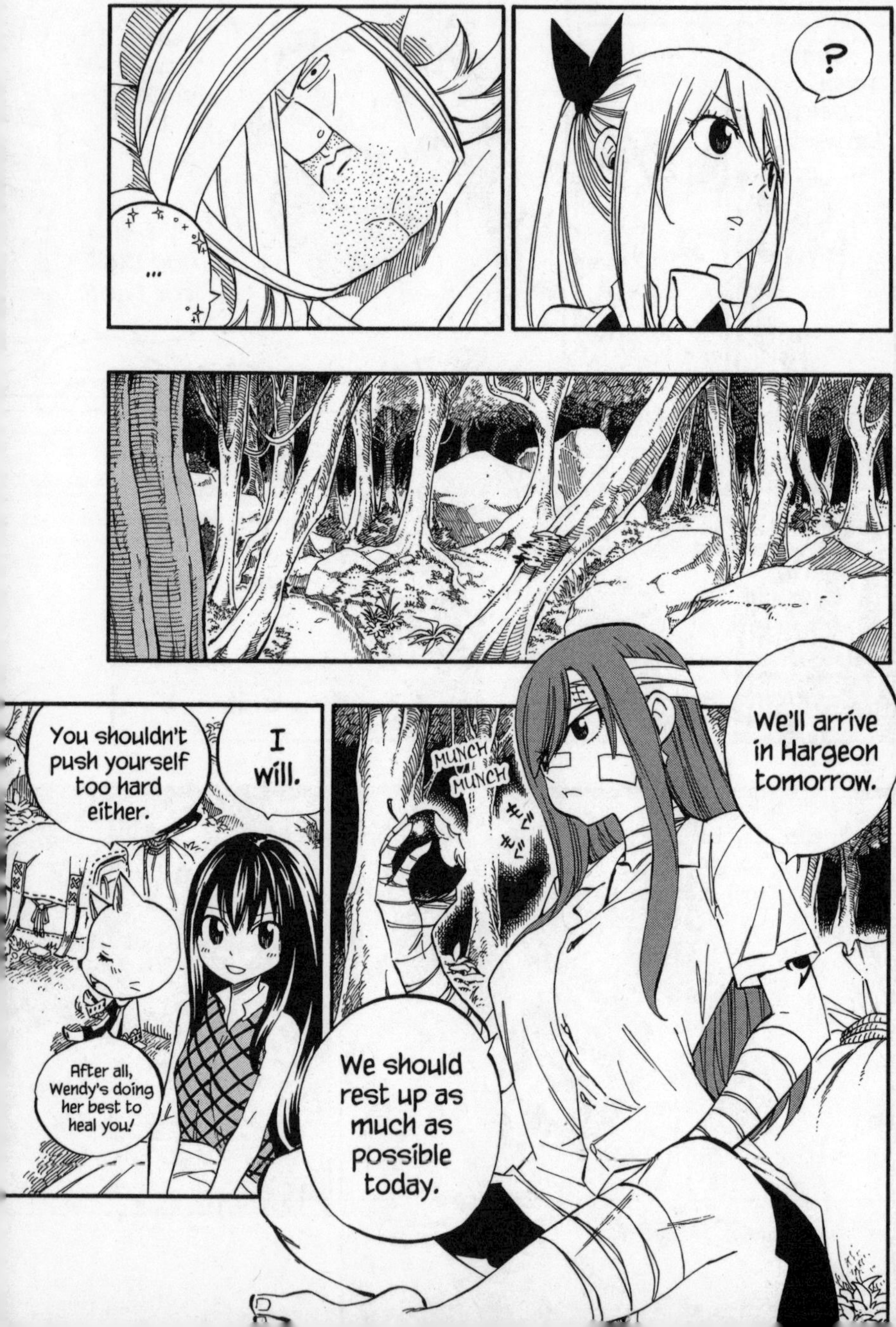
?
...
We'll arrive in Hargeon tomorrow.
MUNCH MUNCH
もぐもぐ
We should rest up as much as possible today.
I will.
You shouldn't push yourself too hard either.
After all, Wendy's doing her best to heal you!

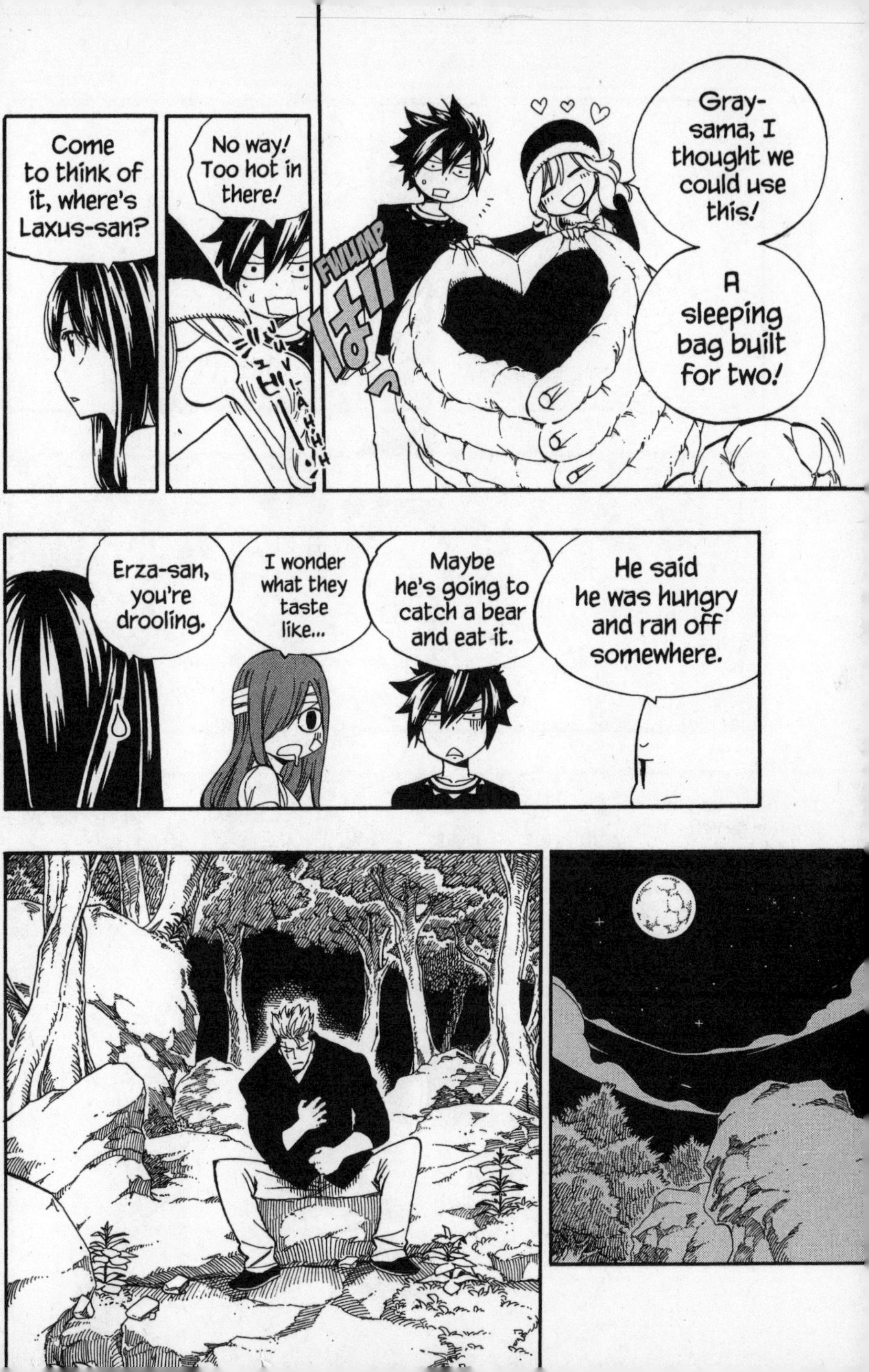

Gray-sama, I thought we could use this!
A sleeping bag built for two!
FWUMP
No way! Too hot in there!
JUVI-AHHH!
Come to think of it, where's Laxus-san?
He said he was hungry and ran off somewhere.
Maybe he's going to catch a bear and eat it.
I wonder what they taste like...
Erza-san, you're drooling.

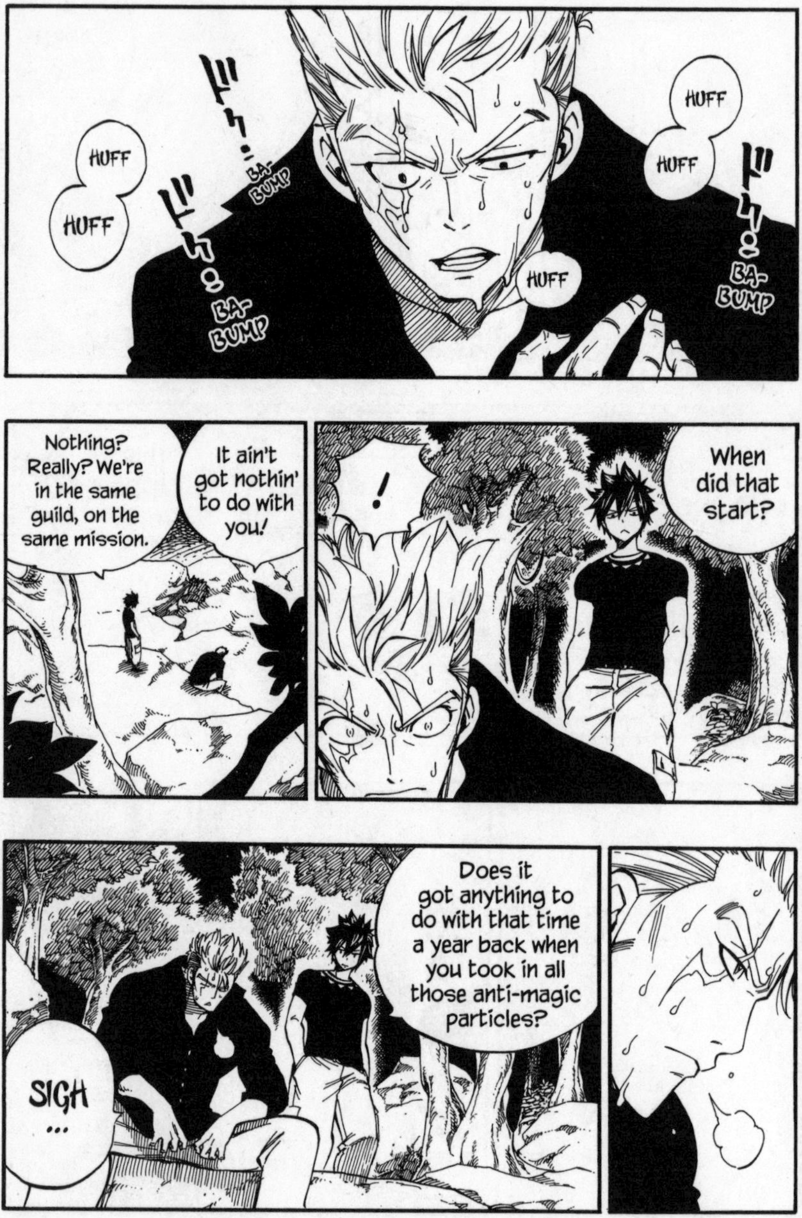
HUFF
HUFF
BA-BUMP
HUFF
BA-BUMP
HUFF
HUFF
BA-BUMP
When did that start?
!
It ain't got nothin' to do with you!
Nothing? Really? We're in the same guild, on the same mission.
Does it got anything to do with that time a year back when you took in all those anti-magic particles?
SIGH...

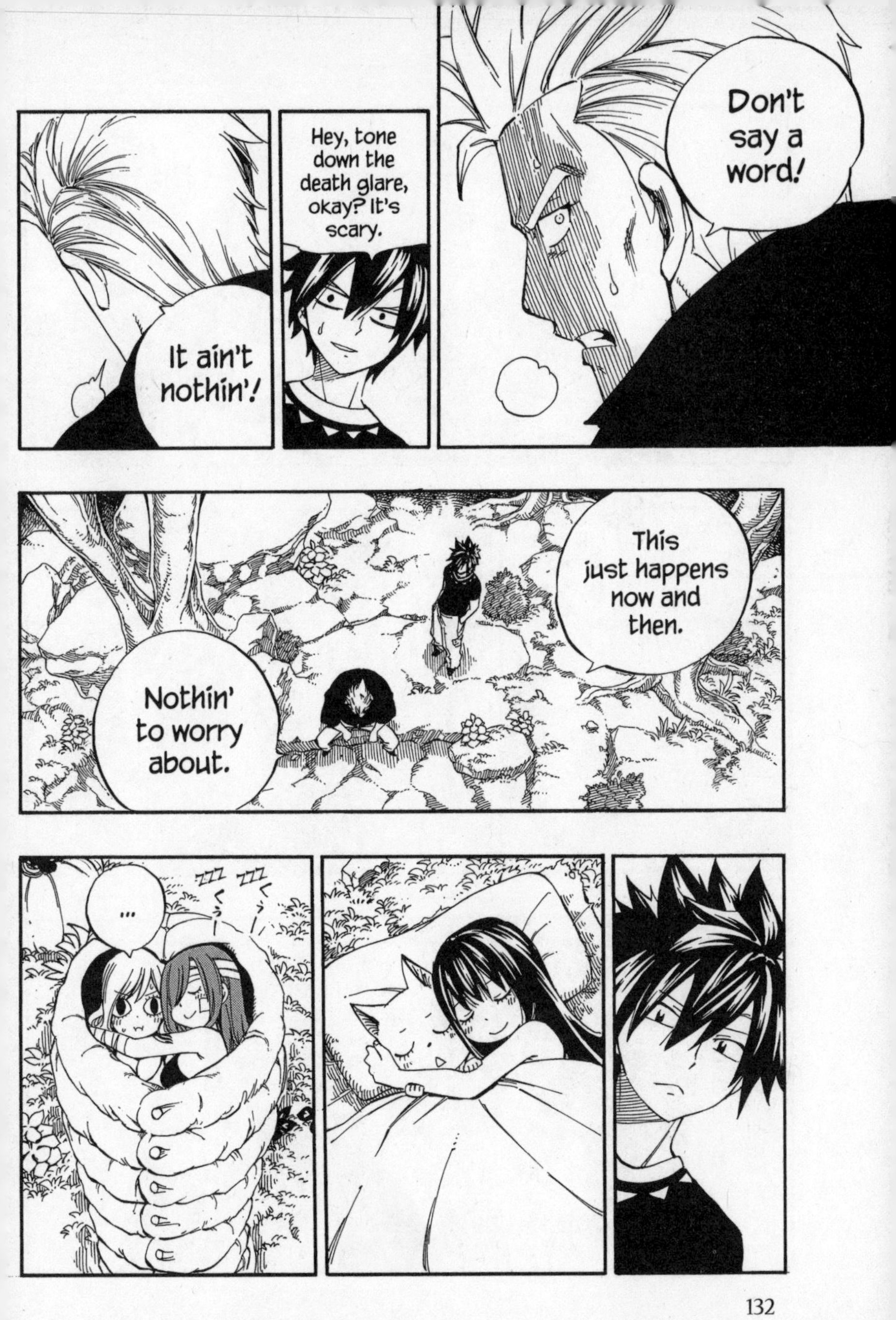

Don't say a word!
Hey, tone down the death glare, okay? It's scary.
It ain't nothin'!
This just happens now and then.
Nothin' to worry about.
ZZZ ZZZ
...

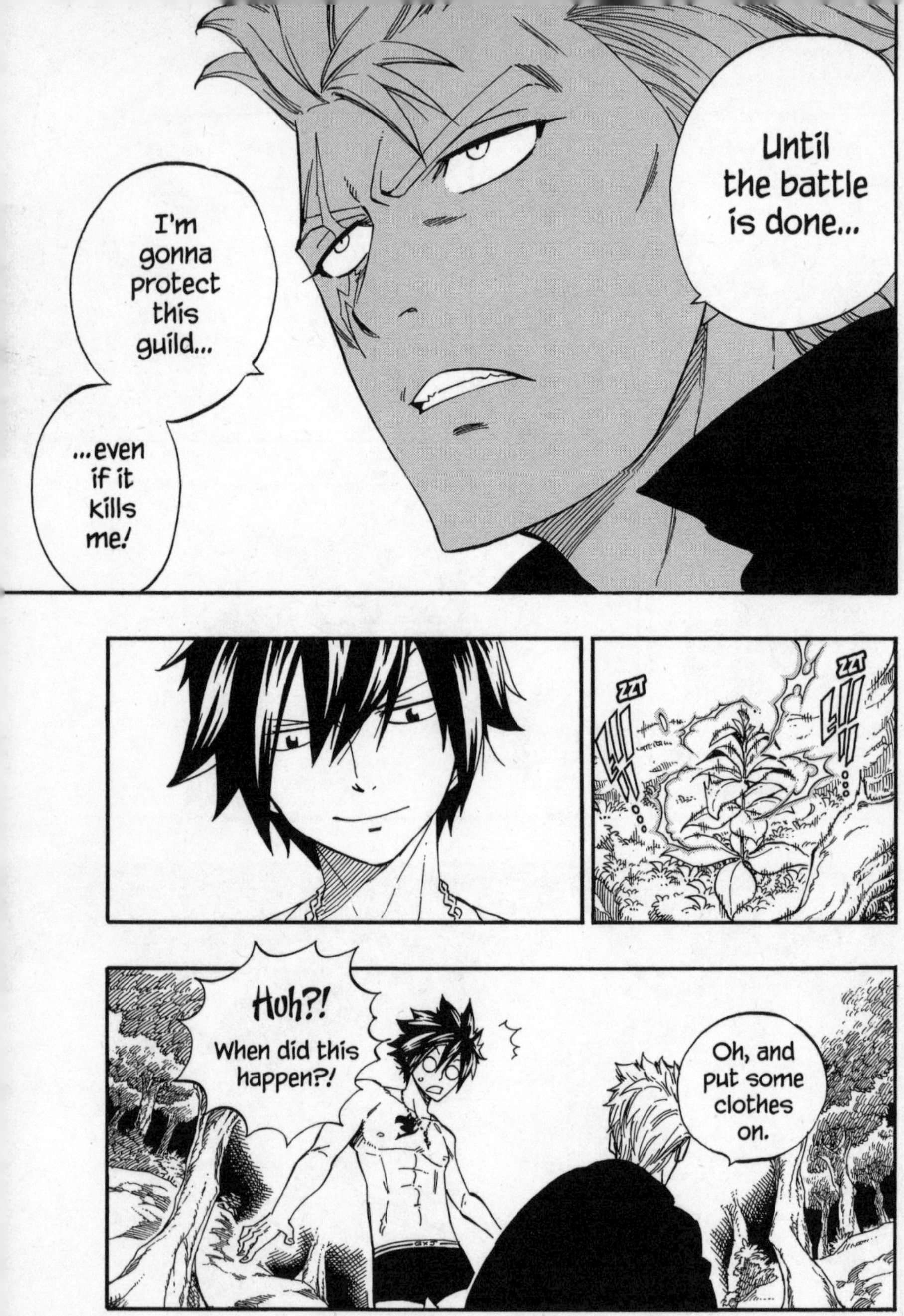
Until the battle is done...
I'm gonna protect this guild...
...even if it kills me!
ZZT
ZZT
Oh, and put some clothes on.
Huh?! When did this happen?!

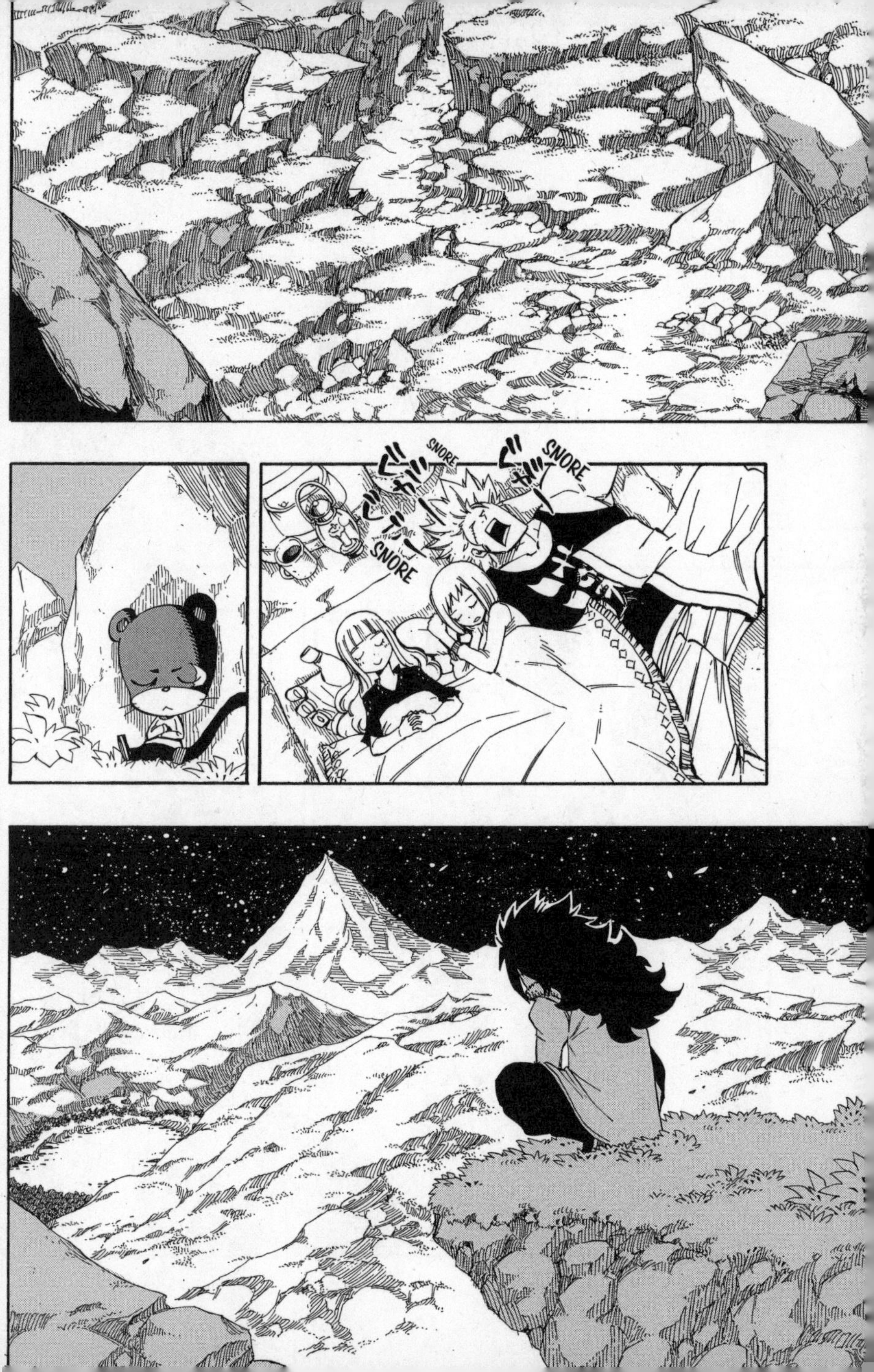
SNORE
SNORE
SNORE

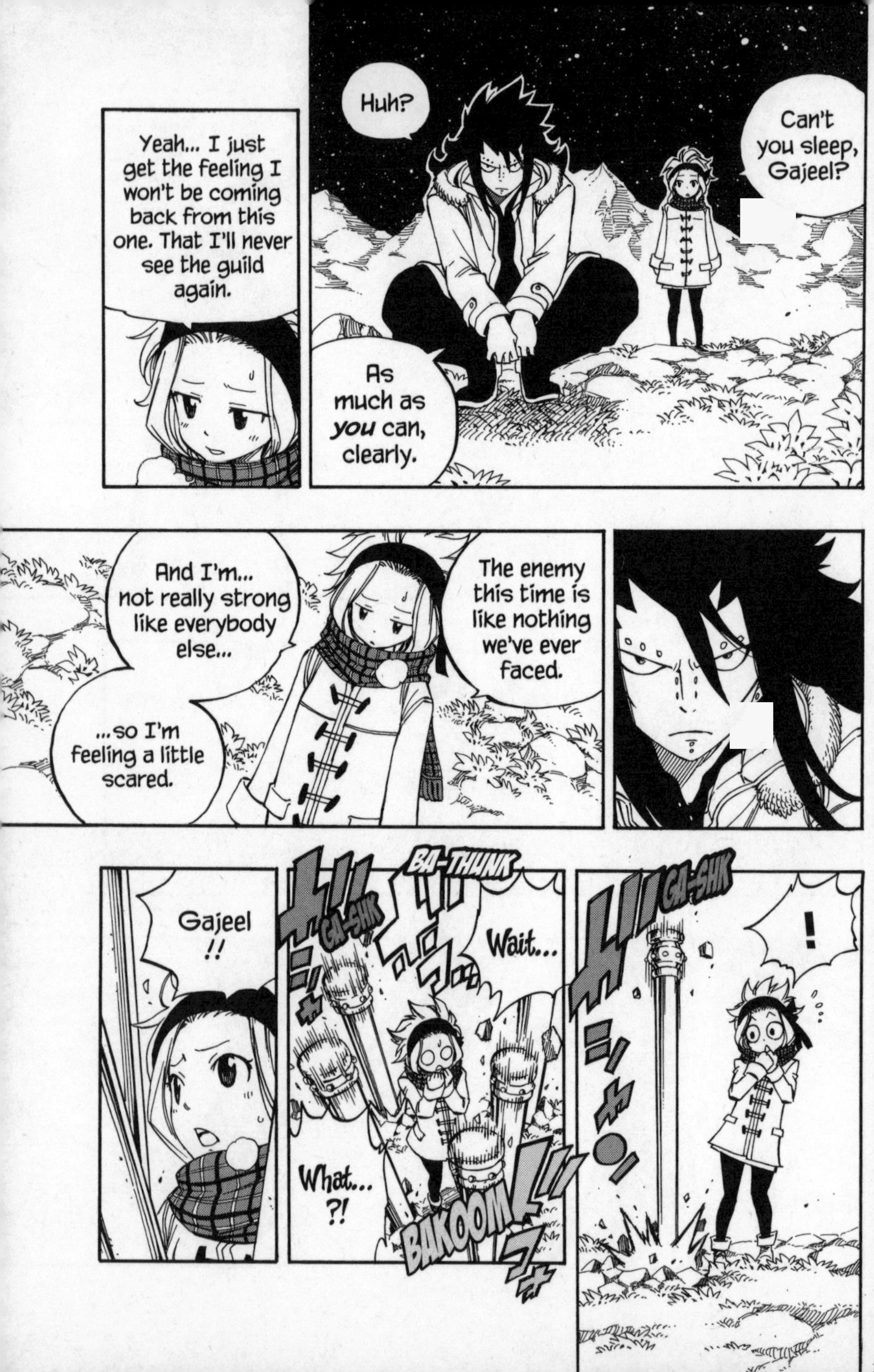
Can't you sleep, Gajeel?
Huh?
As much as *you* can, clearly.
Yeah... I just get the feeling I won't be coming back from this one. That I'll never see the guild again.
The enemy this time is like nothing we've ever faced.
And I'm... not really strong like everybody else...
...so I'm feeling a little scared.
!
GA-SHK
BA-THUNK
Wait...
GA-SHK
What... ?!
BAKOOM
Gajeel !!

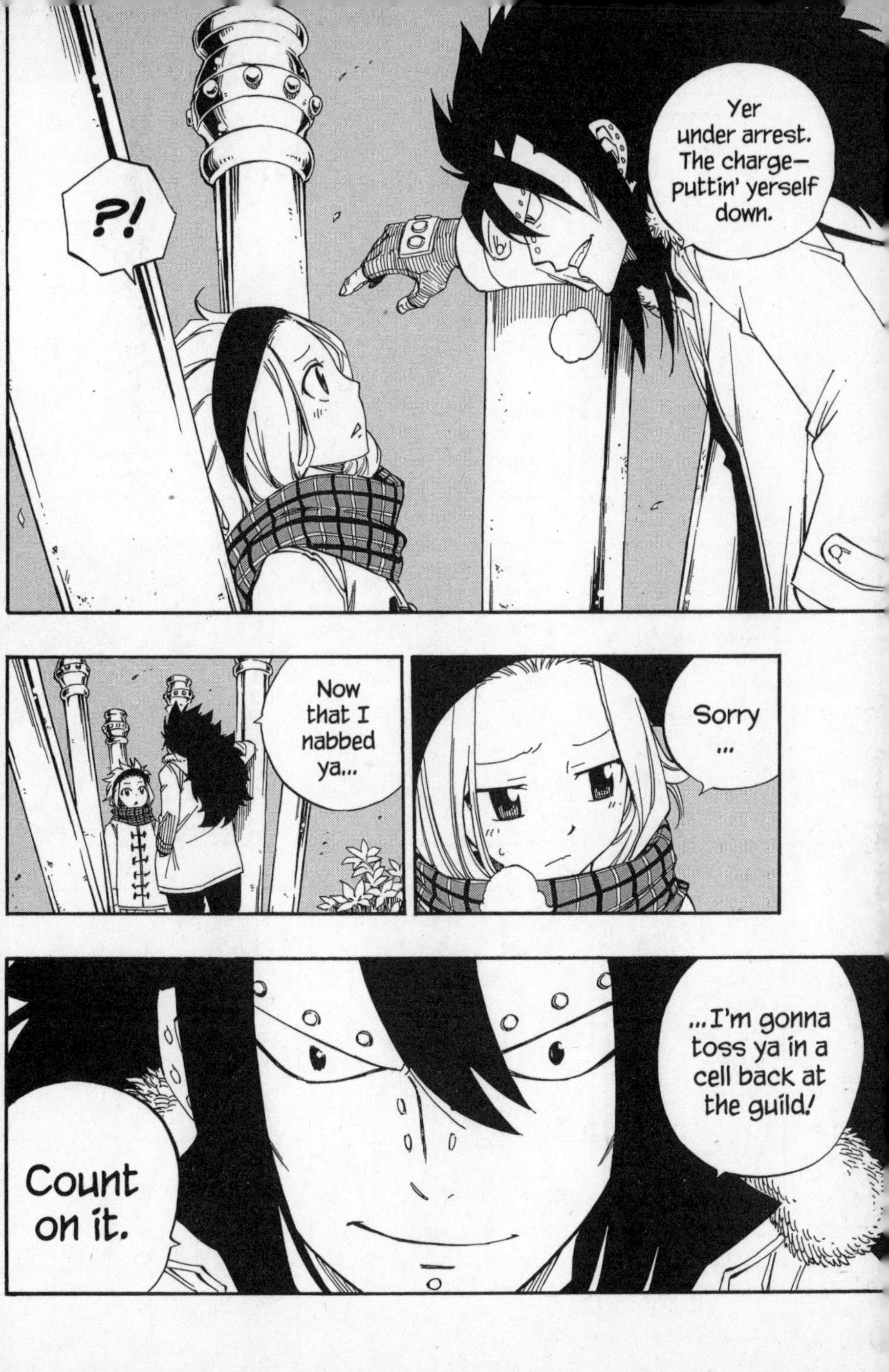
Yer under arrest. The charge— puttin' yerself down.
?!
Sorry ...
Now that I nabbed ya...
...I'm gonna toss ya in a cell back at the guild!
Count on it.

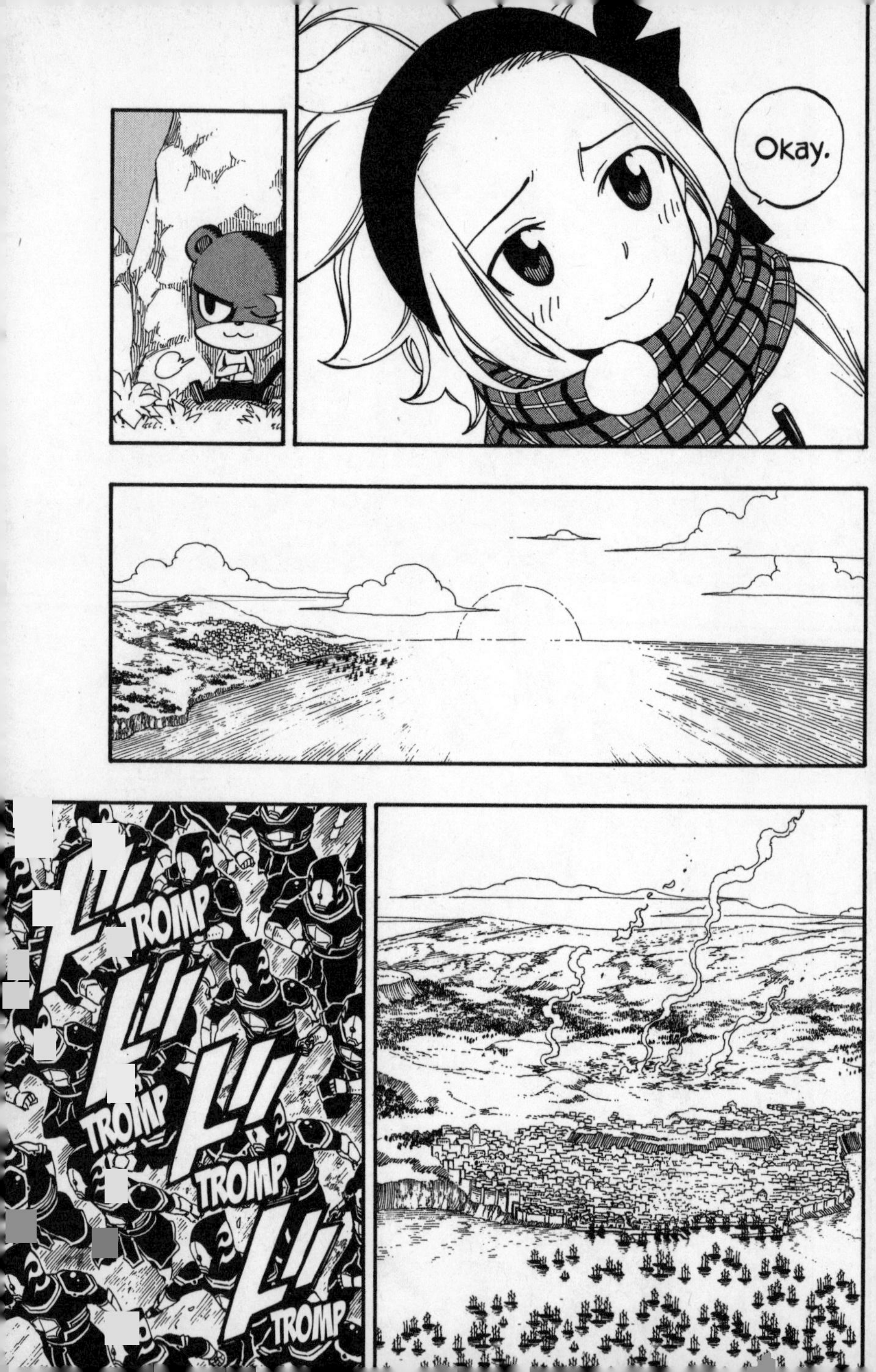
Okay.
TROMP
TROMP
TROMP
TROMP

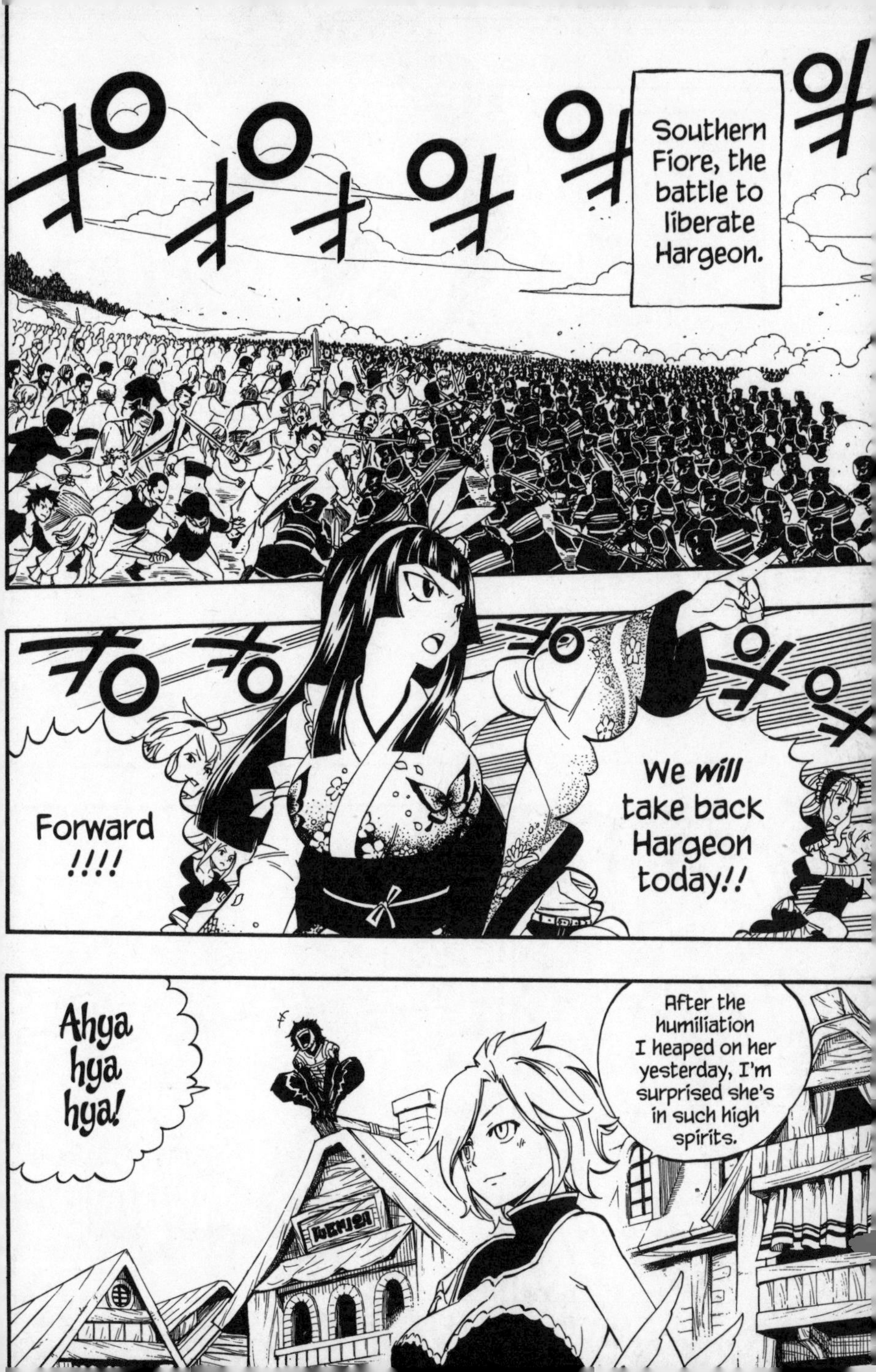

Southern Fiore, the battle to liberate Hargeon.
We *will* take back Hargeon today!!
Forward !!!!
After the humiliation I heaped on her yesterday, I'm surprised she's in such high spirits.
Ahya hya hya!

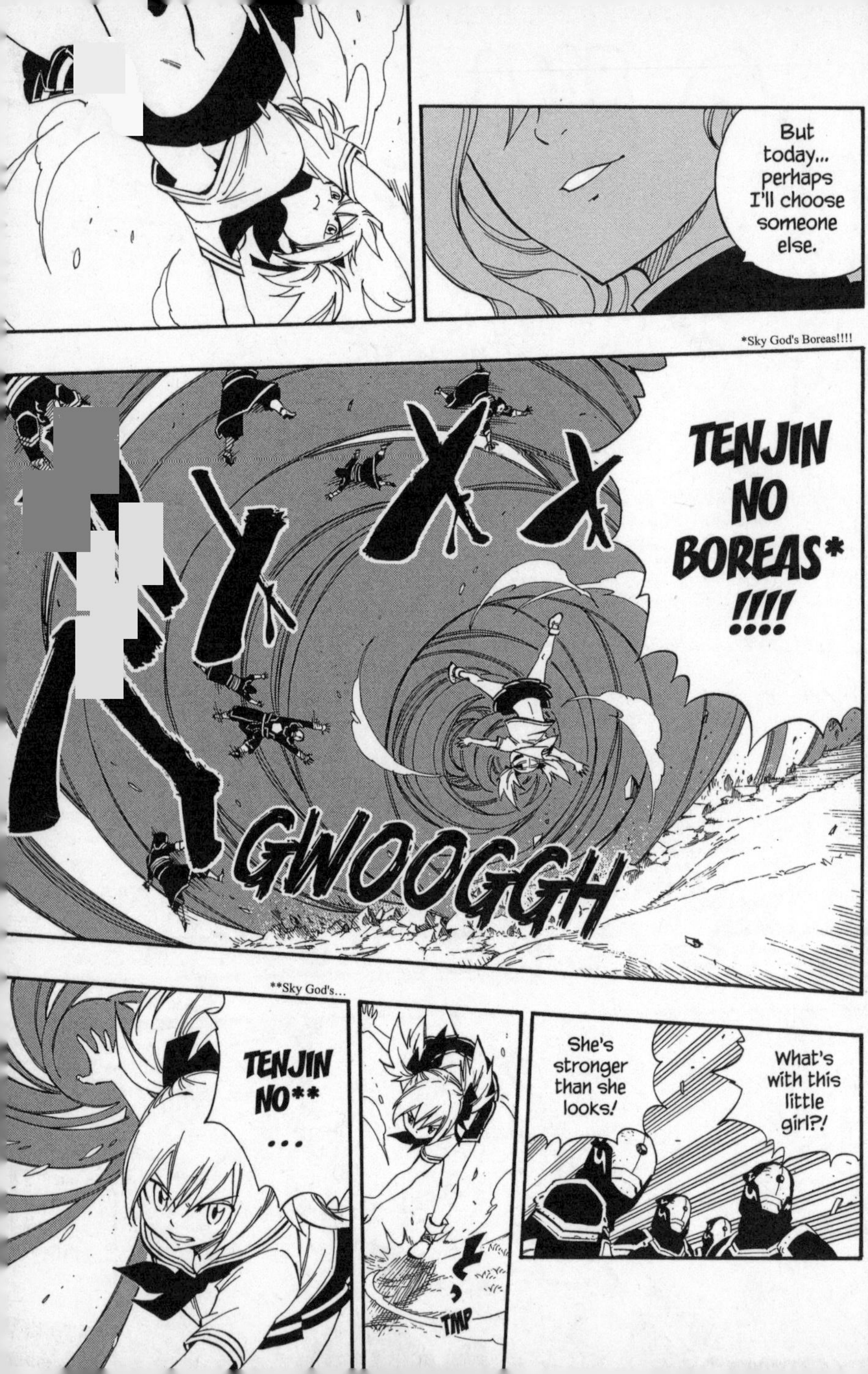
But today... perhaps I'll choose someone else.
*Sky God's Boreas!!!!
TENJIN NO BOREAS* !!!!
GWOOGGH
**Sky God's...
What's with this little girl?!
She's stronger than she looks!
TIMP
TENJIN NO** ...

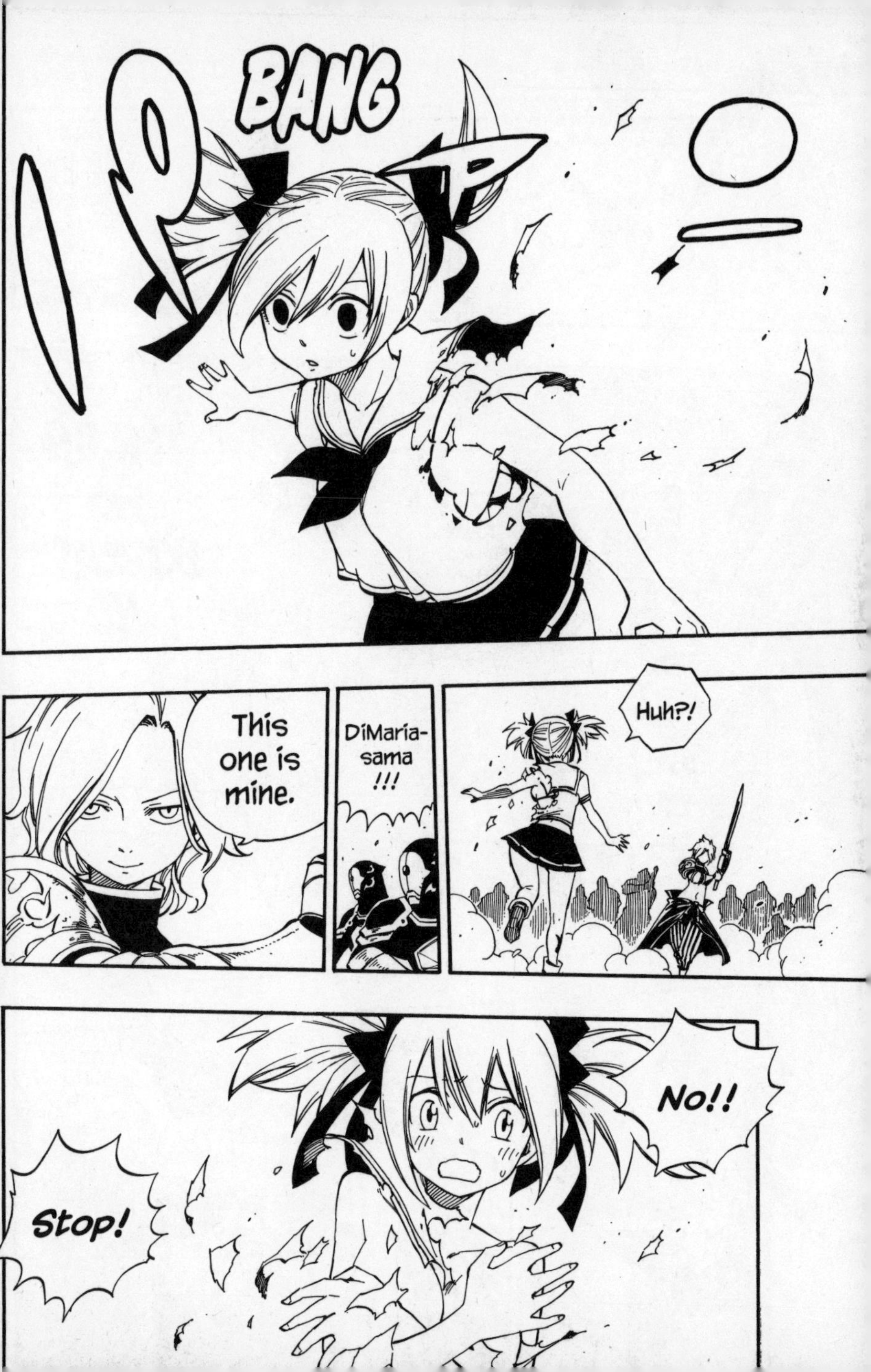
BANG
Huh?!
DiMaria-sama !!!
This one is mine.
No!!
Stop!

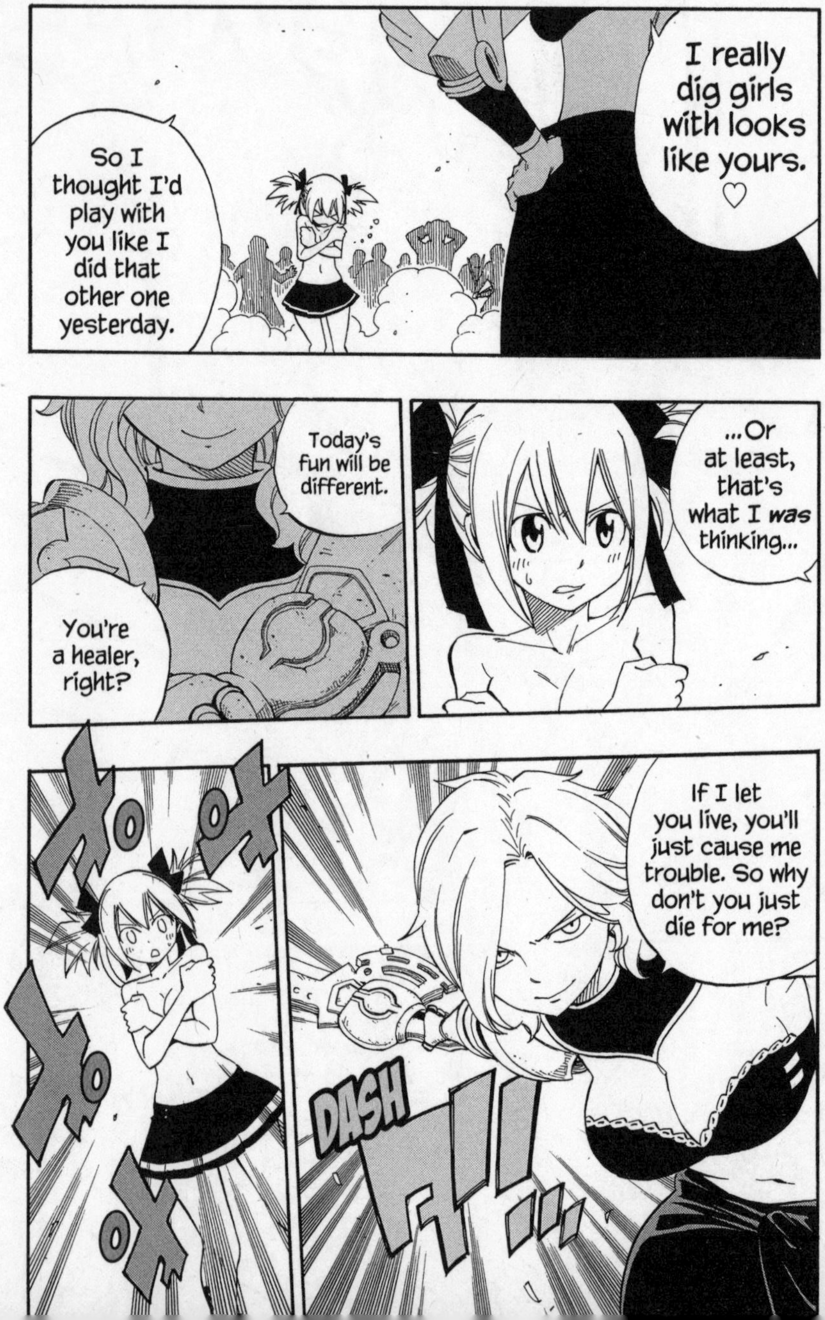
I really dig girls with looks like yours. ♡
So I thought I'd play with you like I did that other one yesterday.
...Or at least, that's what I *was* thinking...
Today's fun will be different.
You're a healer, right?
If I let you live, you'll just cause me trouble. So why don't you just die for me?
DASH

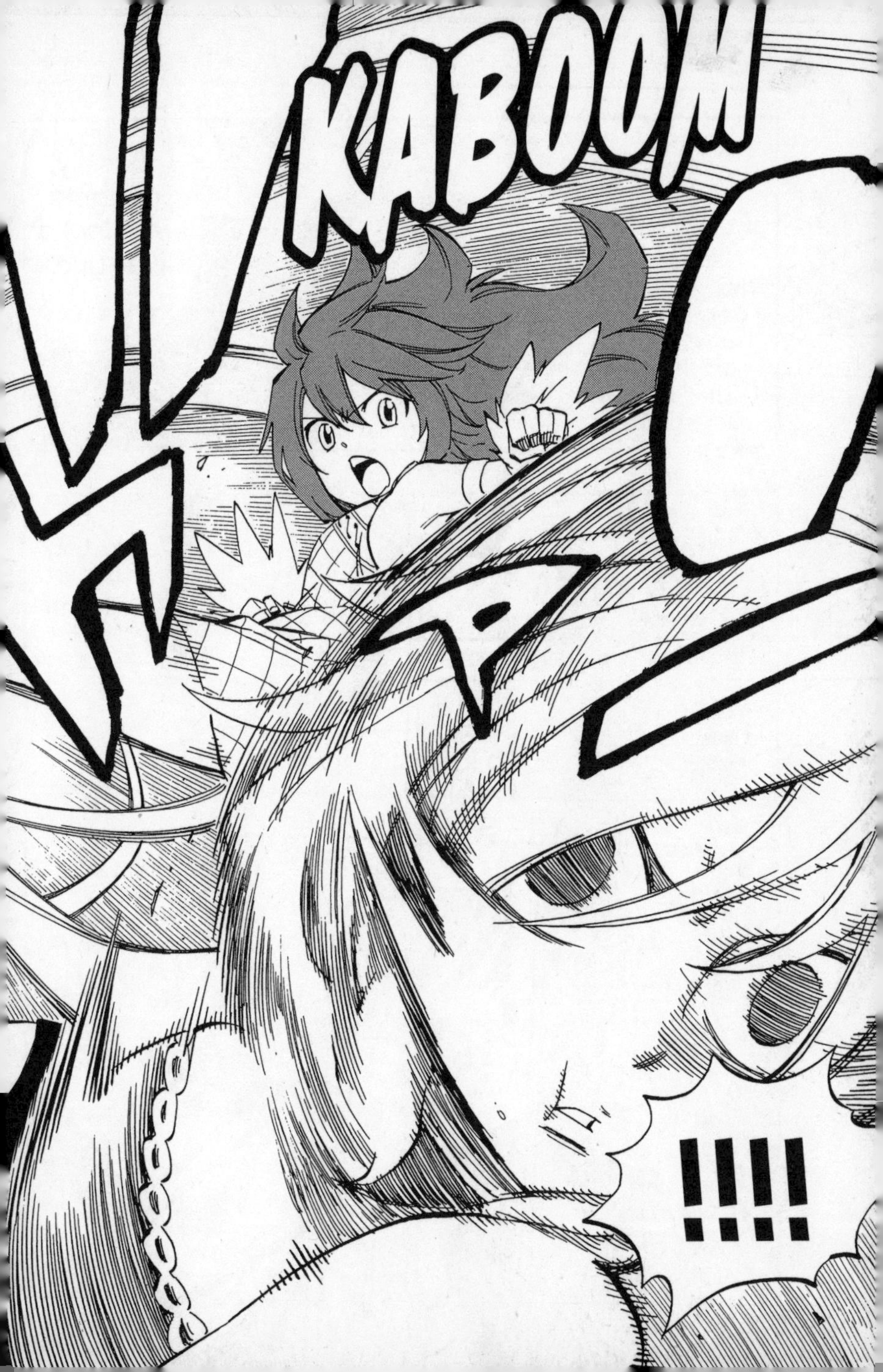
KABOOM
!!!!

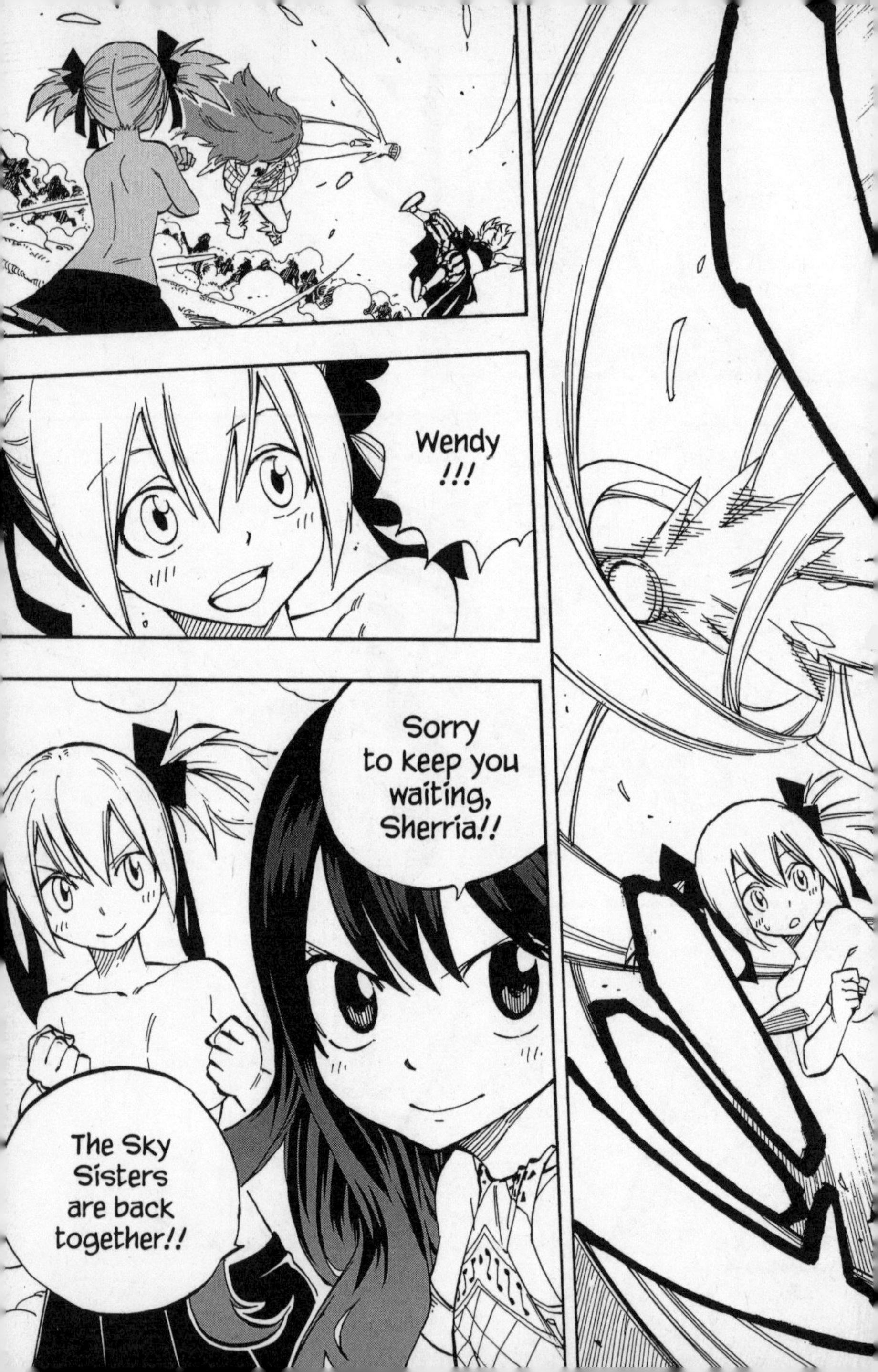
Wendy !!!
Sorry to keep you waiting, Sherria!!
The Sky Sisters are back together!!

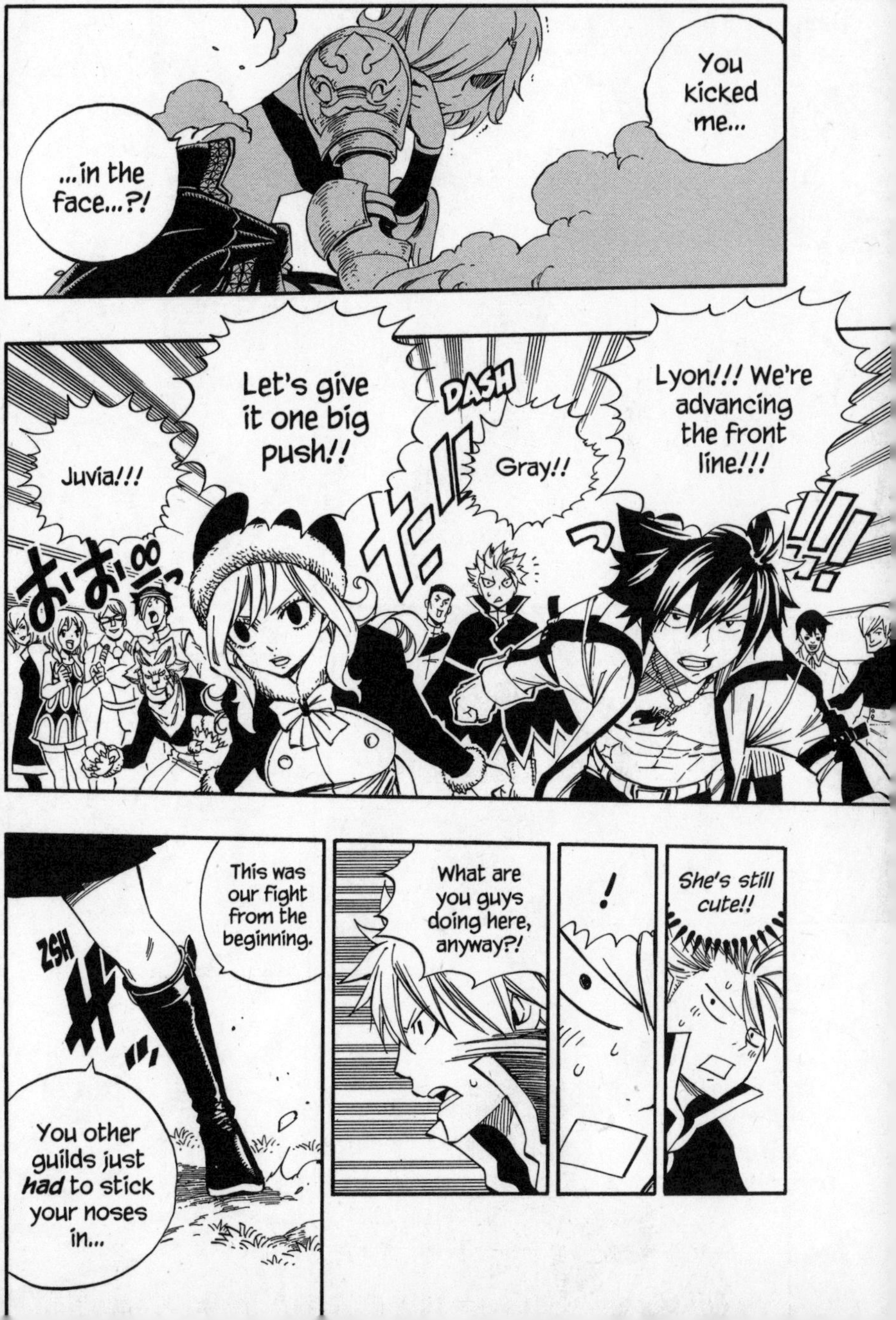
You kicked me...
...in the face...?!
Lyon!!! We're advancing the front line!!!
Gray!!
DASH
Let's give it one big push!!
Juvia!!!
She's still cute!!
!
What are you guys doing here, anyway?!
This was our fight from the beginning.
ZSH
You other guilds just *had* to stick your noses in...

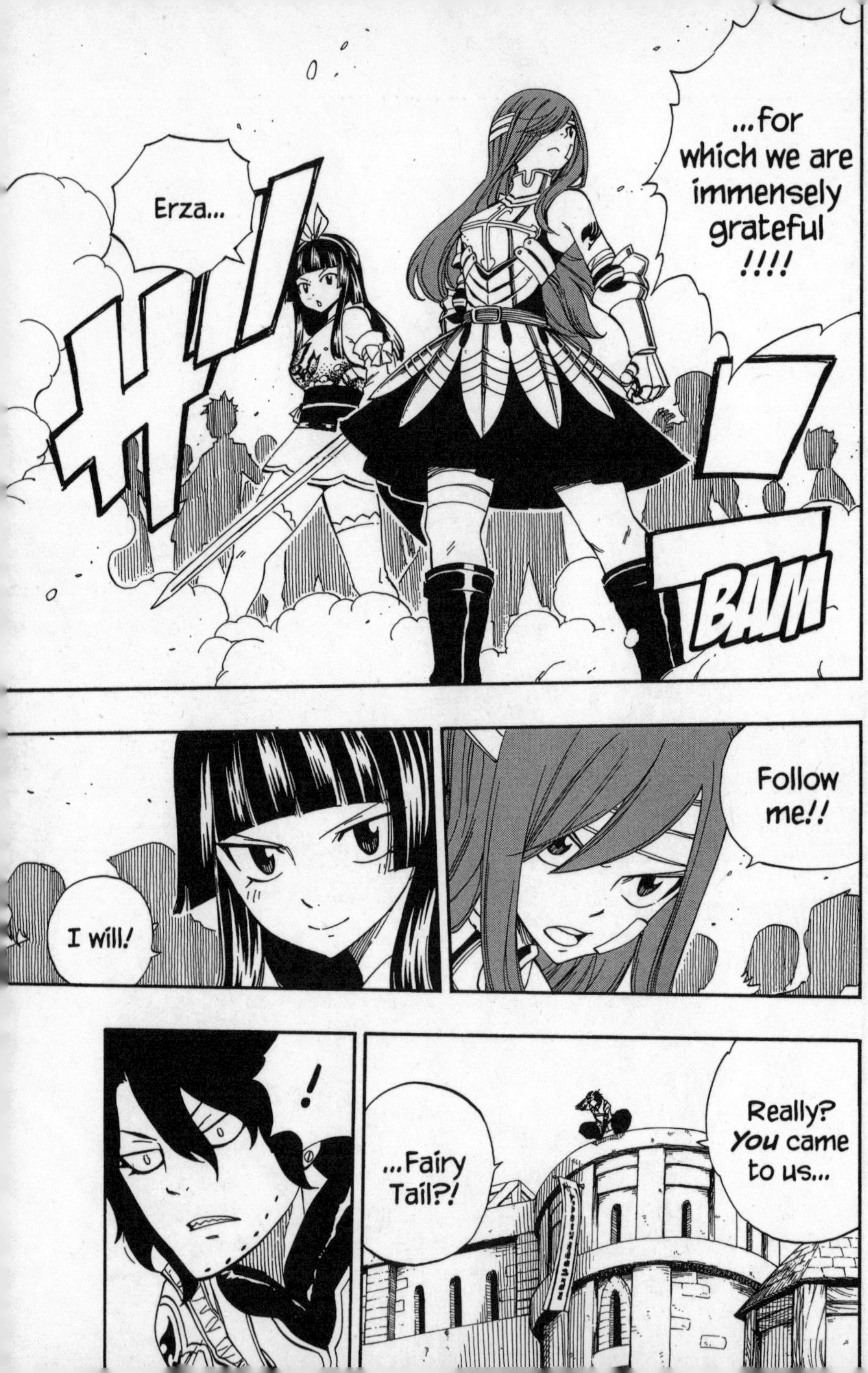
...for which we are immensely grateful!!!!
Erza...
BAM
Follow me!!
I will!
Really? *You* came to us...
...Fairy Tail?!
!

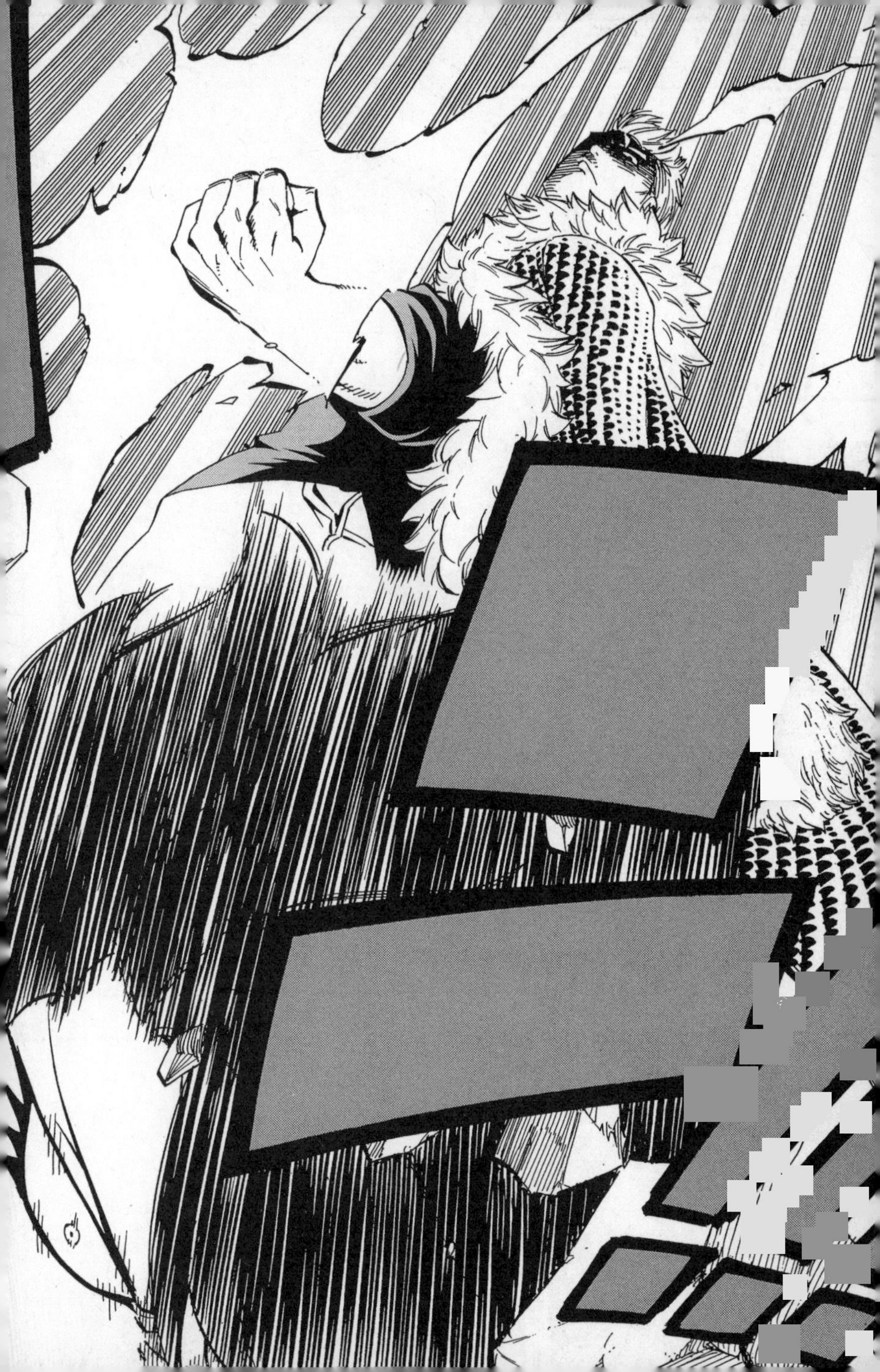

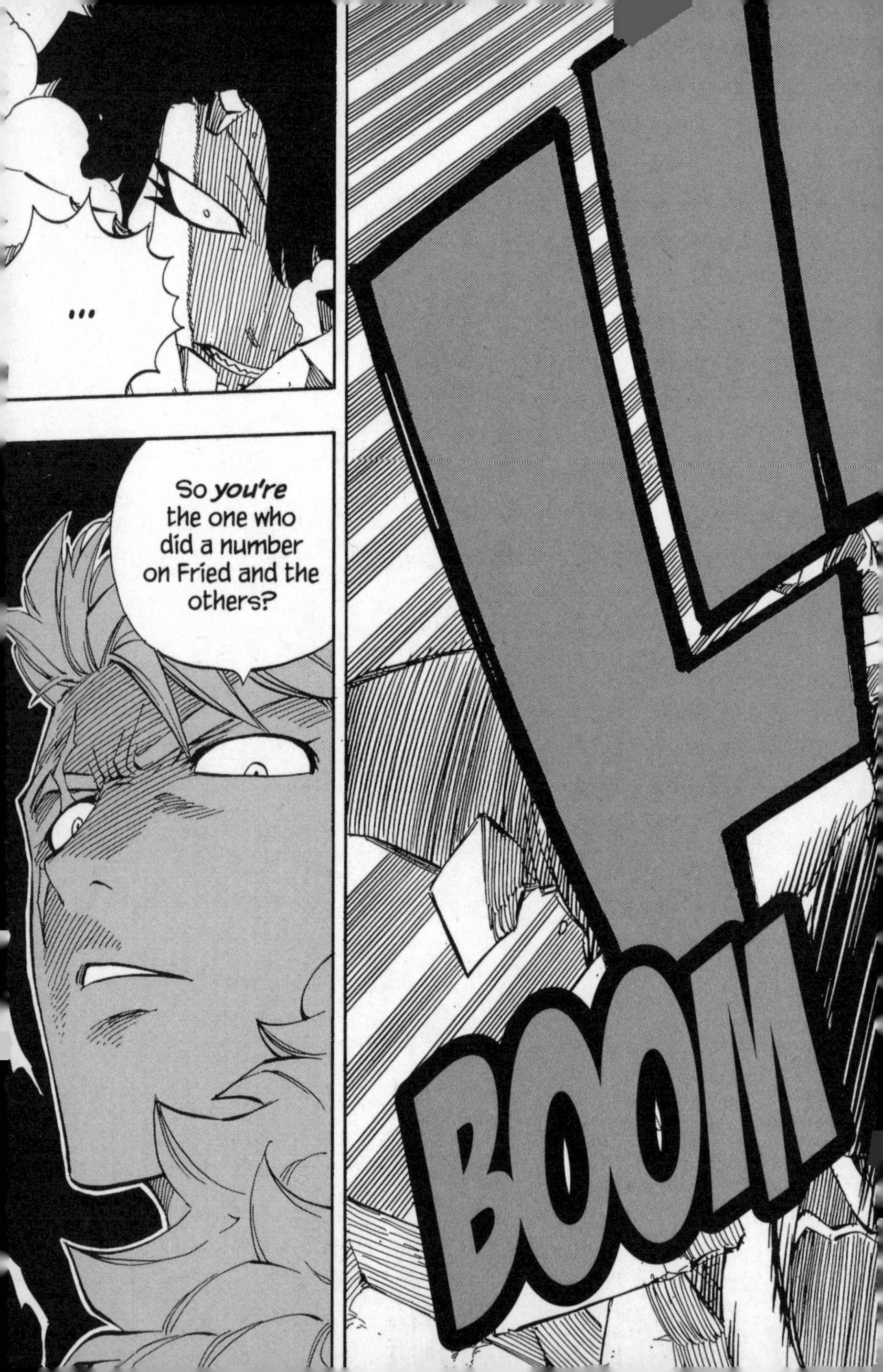
BOOM
...
So *you're* the one who did a number on Fried and the others?

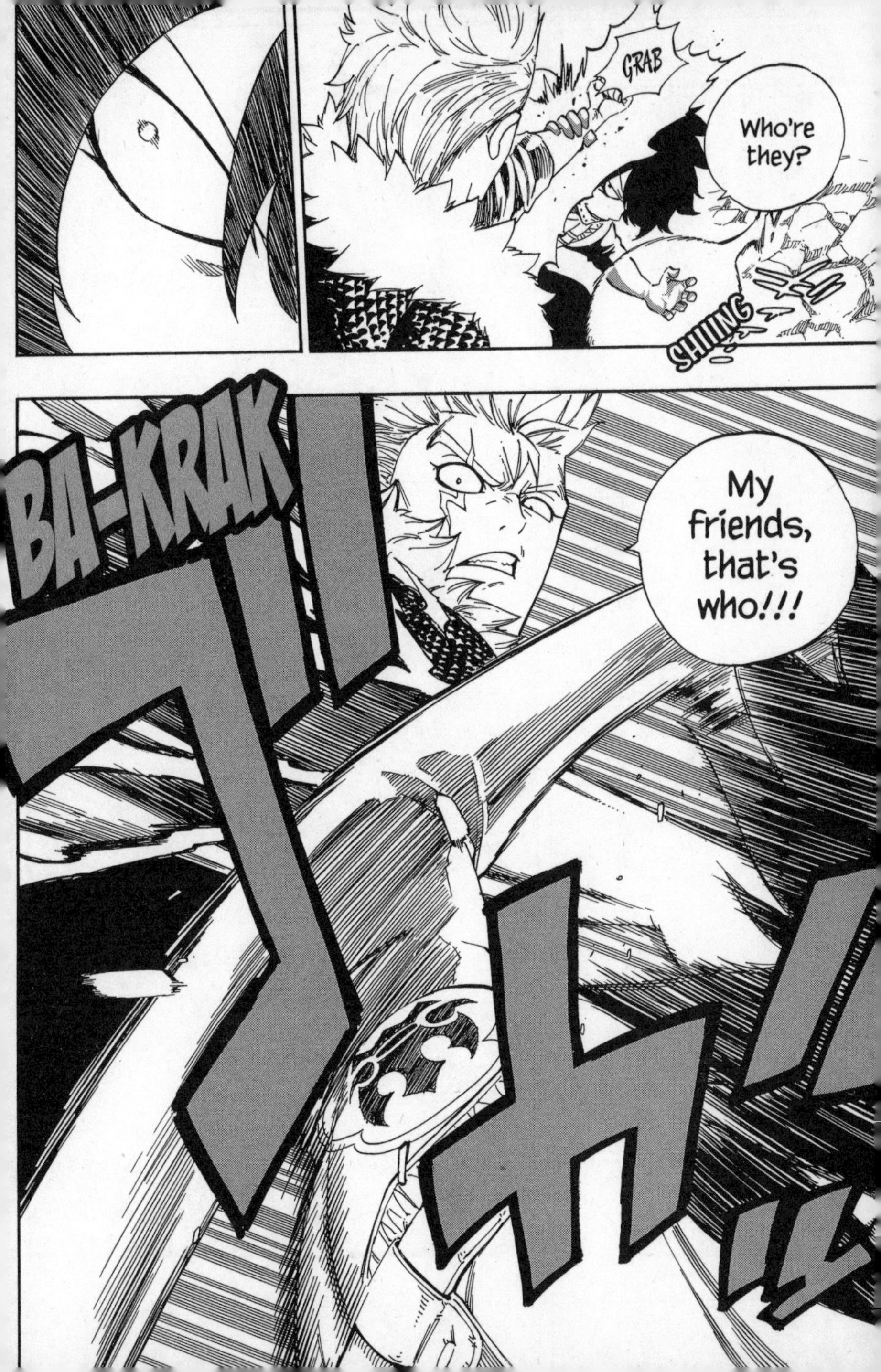
GRAB
Who're they?
SHIIING
My friends, that's who!!!
BA-KRAK

FAIRY TAIL

フェアリーテイル

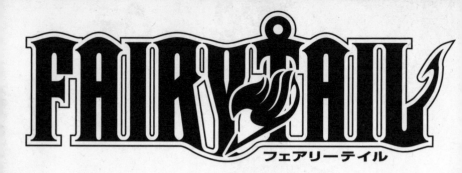

Chapter 472: Laxus vs. Wall

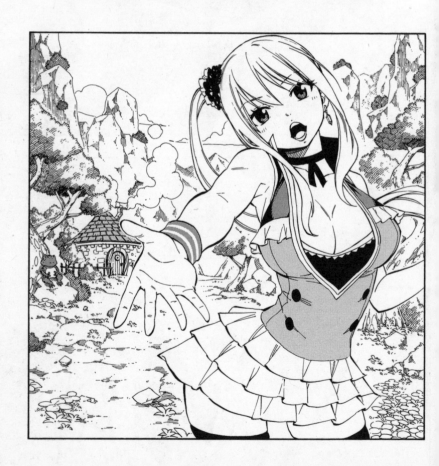

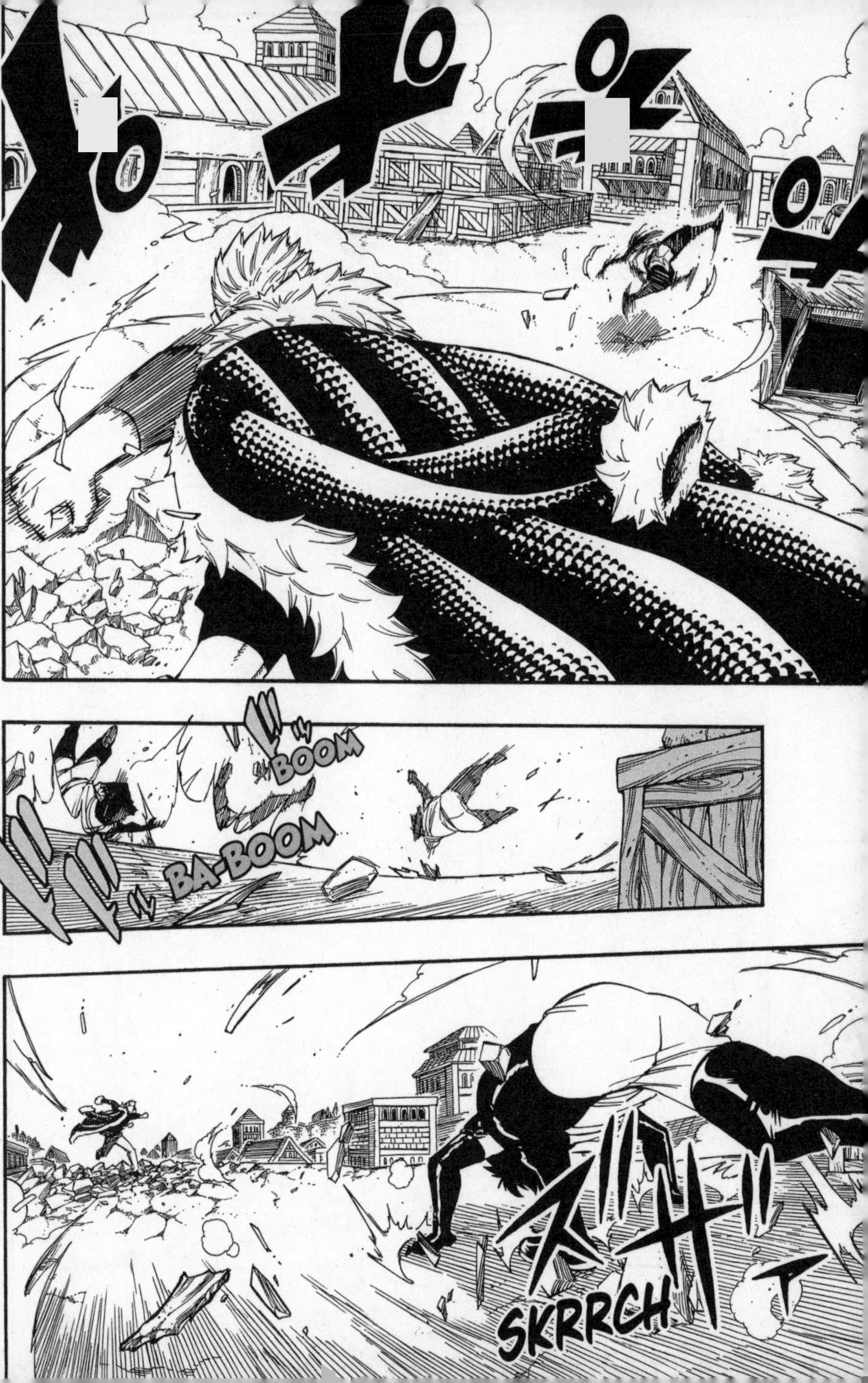
BOOM
BA-BOOM
SKRRCH

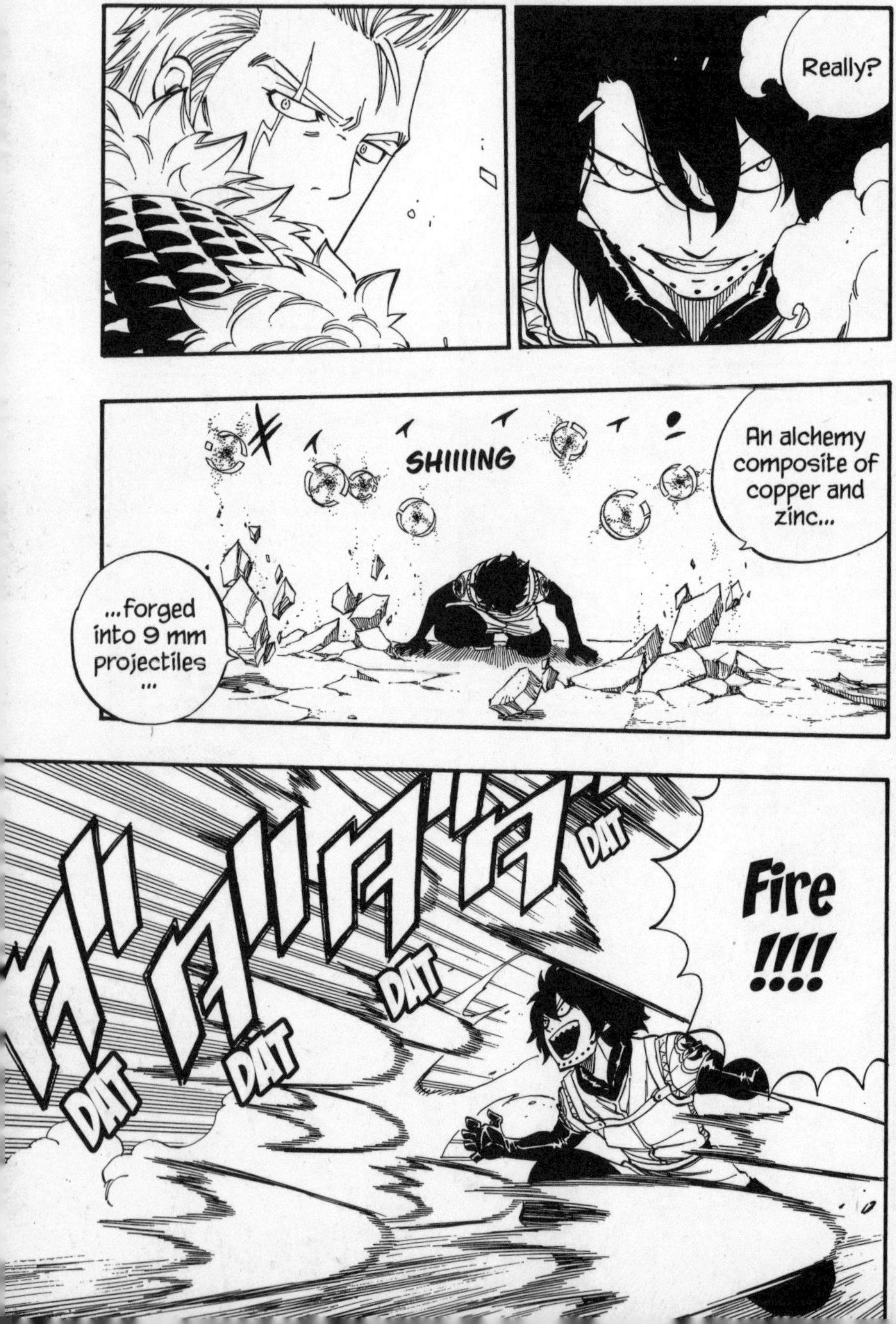
Really?
An alchemy composite of copper and zinc...
SHIIIING
...forged into 9 mm projectiles ...
Fire !!!!
DAT
DAT
DAT
DAT

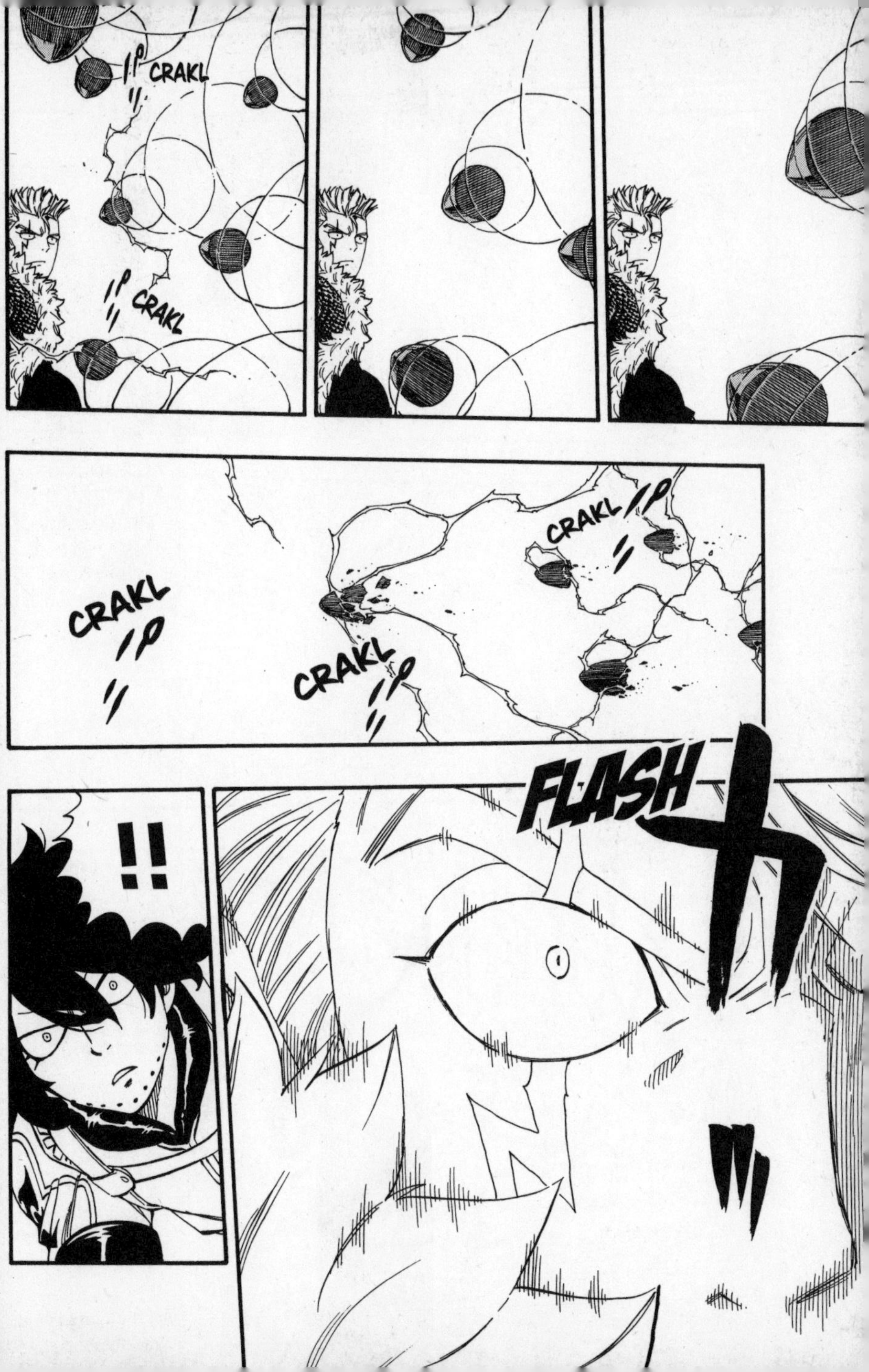
CRAKL
CRAKL
CRAKL
CRAKL
CRAKL
FLASH
!!

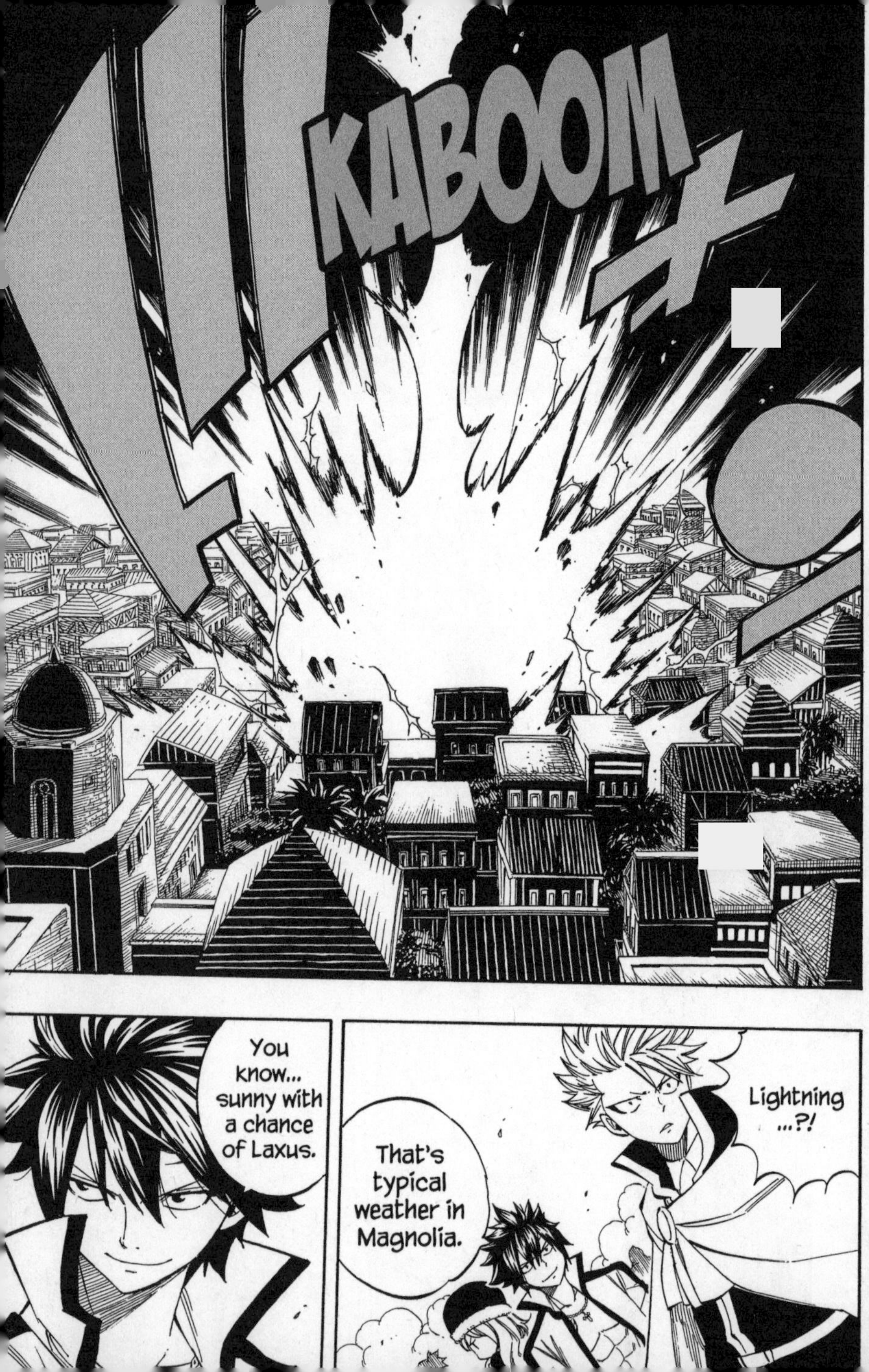
KABOOM
Lightning ...?!
That's typical weather in Magnolia.
You know... sunny with a chance of Laxus.

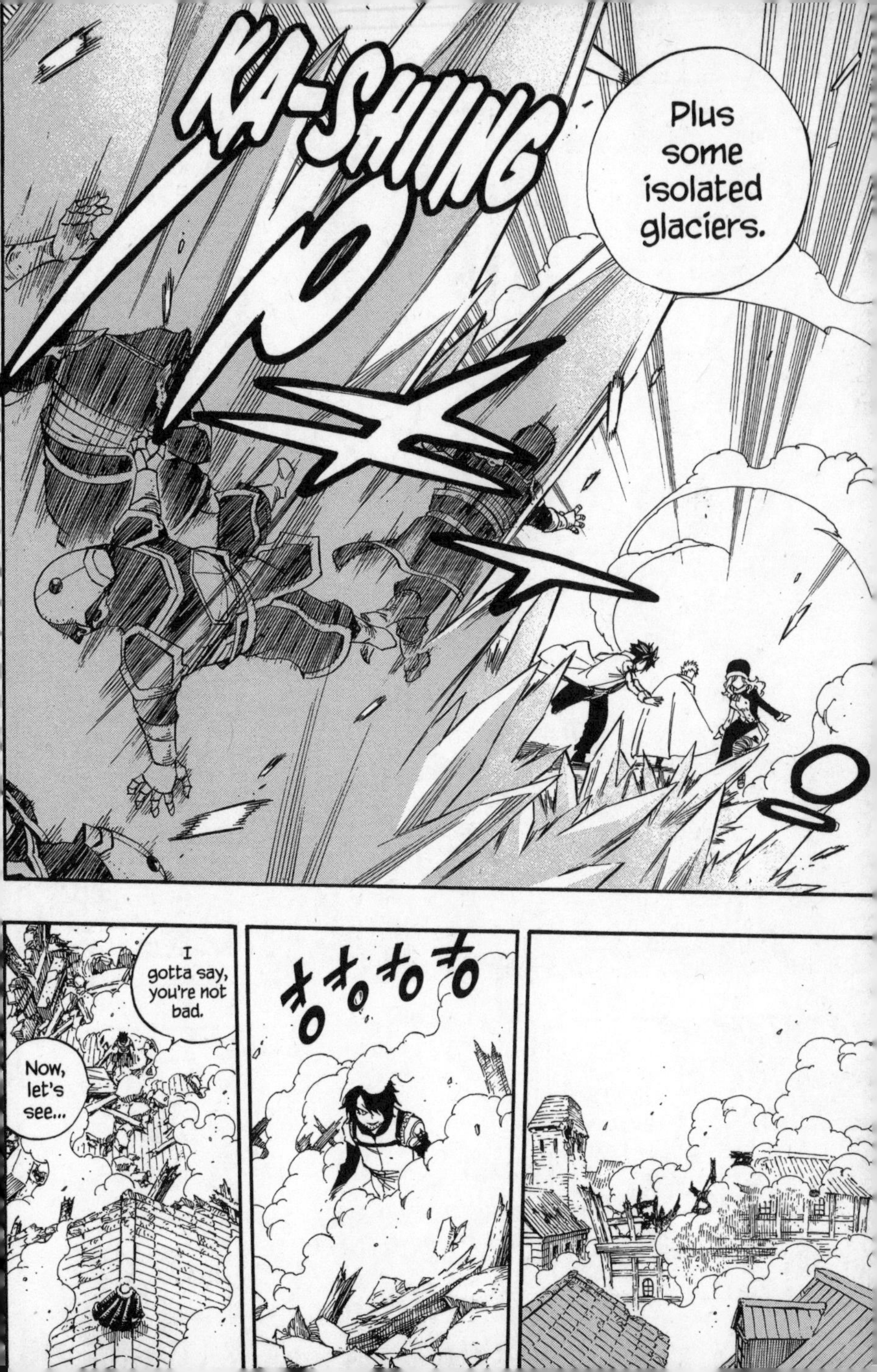
KA-SHIING
Plus some isolated glaciers.
I gotta say, you're not bad.
Now, let's see...

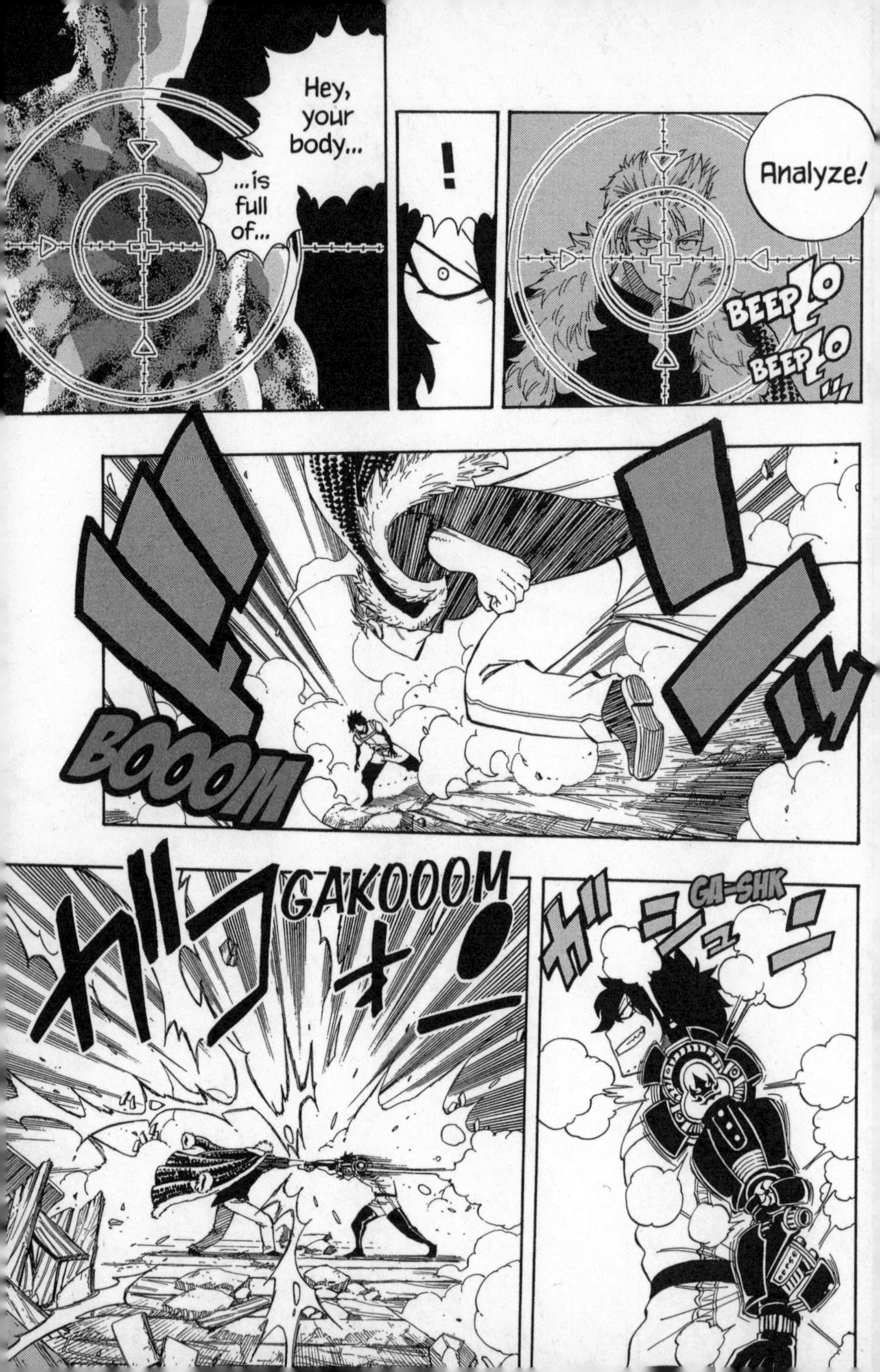
Analyze!
BEEP BEEP
BEEP BEEP
!
Hey, your body...
...is full of...
BOOOM
GA-SHK
GAKOOOM

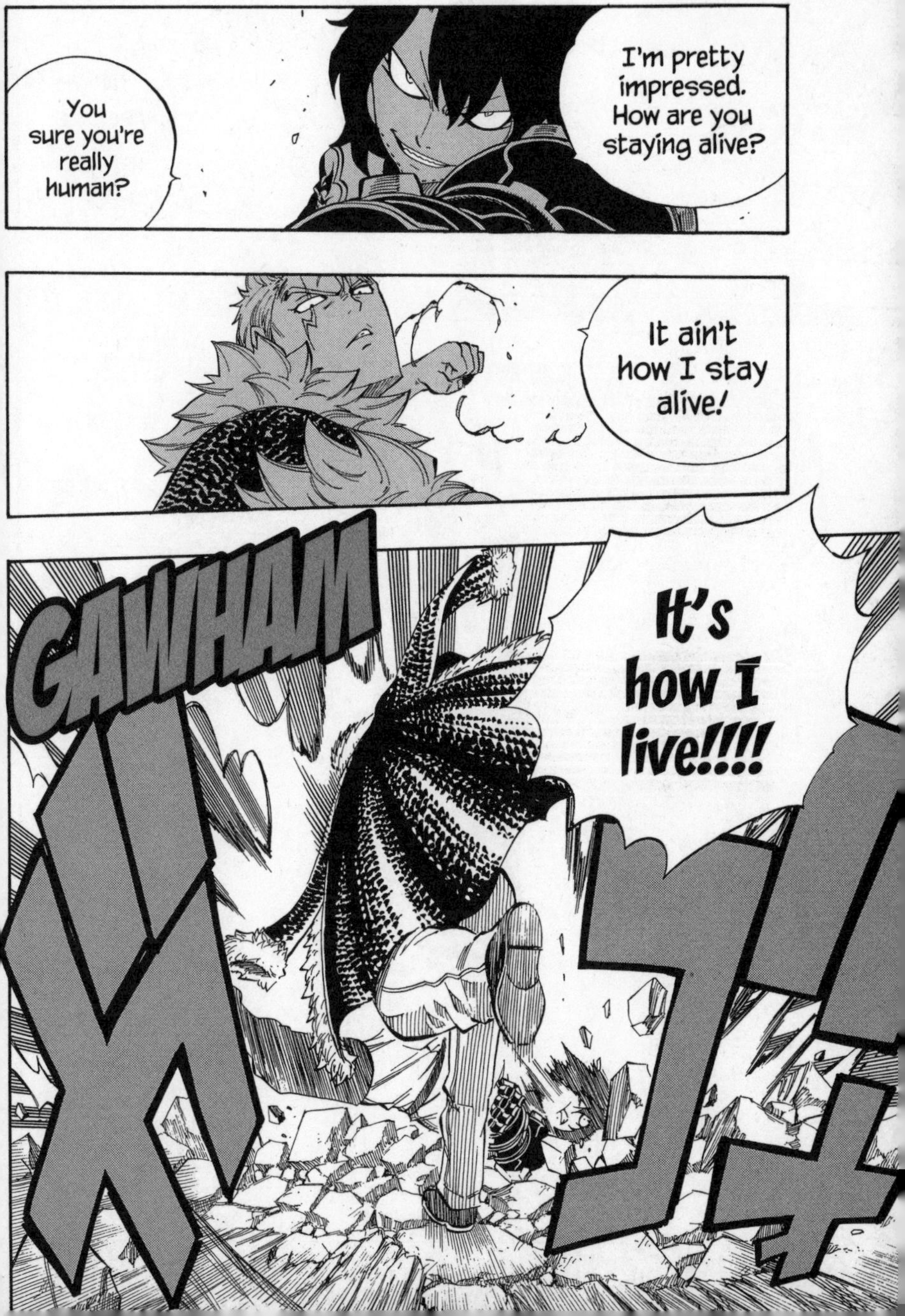
I'm pretty impressed. How are you staying alive?
You sure you're really human?
It ain't how I stay alive!
It's how I live!!!!
GAWHAM

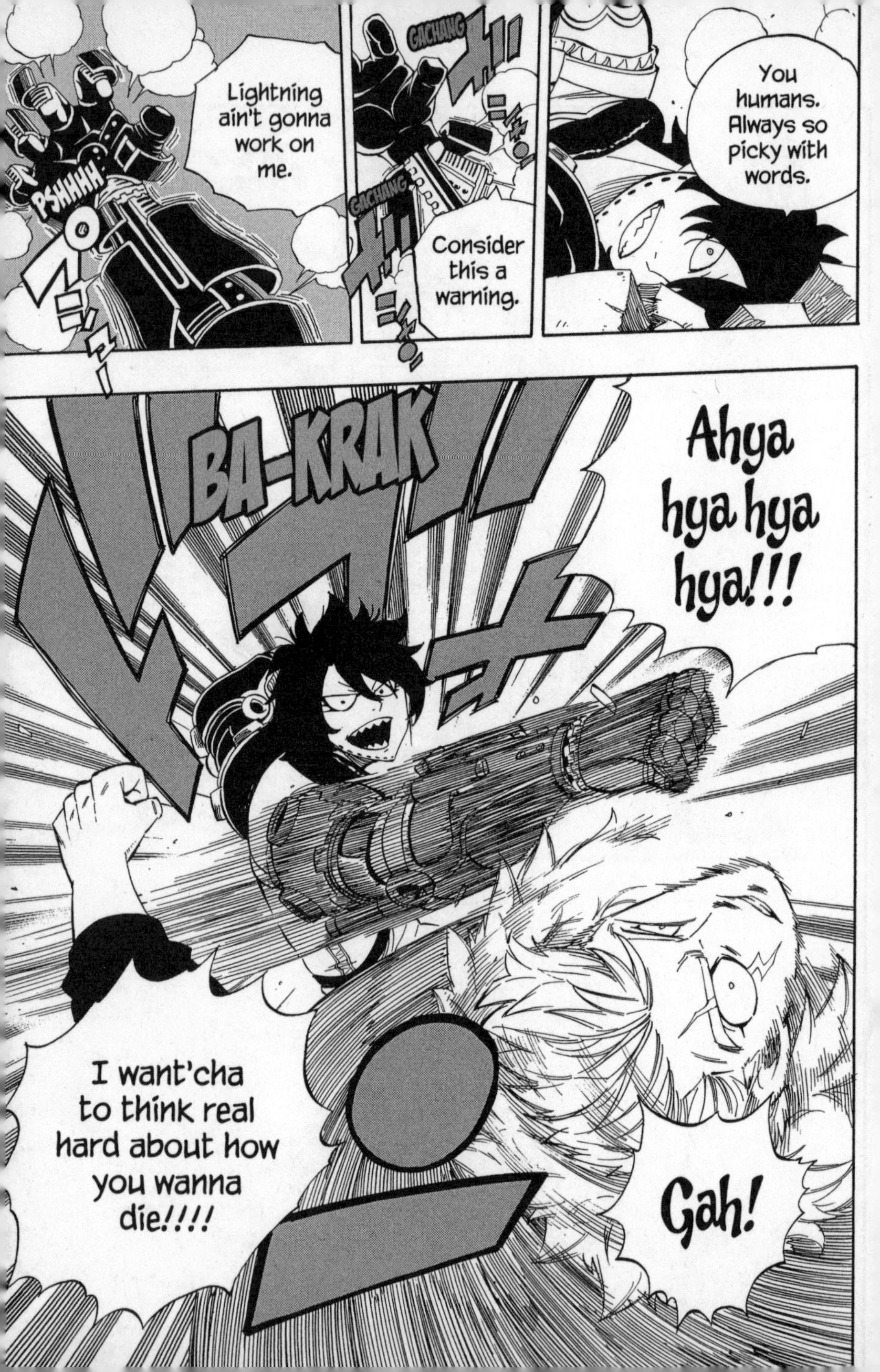
You humans. Always so picky with words.
GACHANG
GACHANG
Consider this a warning.
Lightning ain't gonna work on me.
PSHHHH
Ahya hya hya hya!!!
BA-KRAK
Gah!
I want'cha to think real hard about how you wanna die!!!!

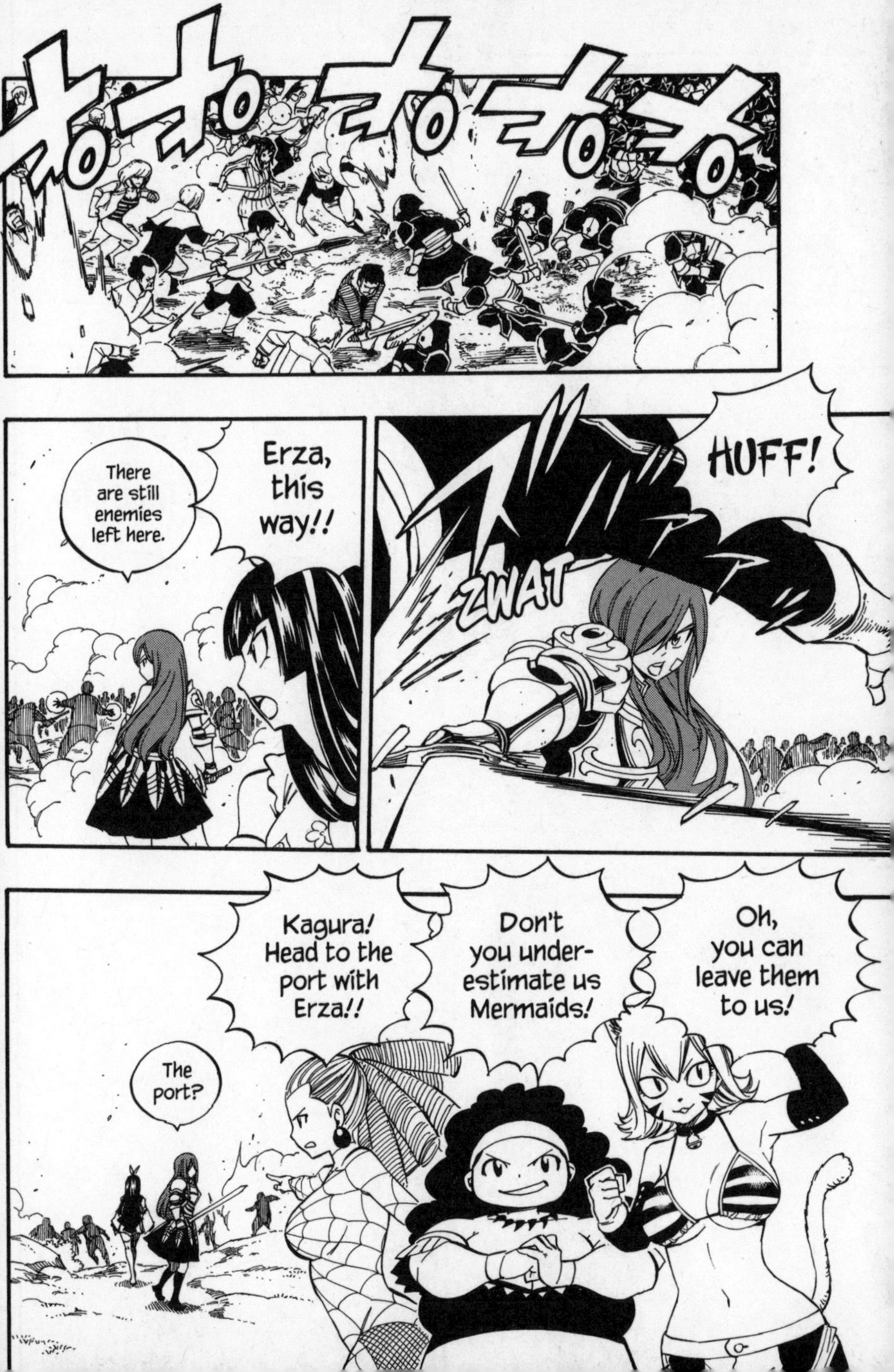
HUFF!
ZWAT
Erza, this way!!
There are still enemies left here.
Oh, you can leave them to us!
Don't you under-estimate us Mermaids!
Kagura! Head to the port with Erza!!
The port?

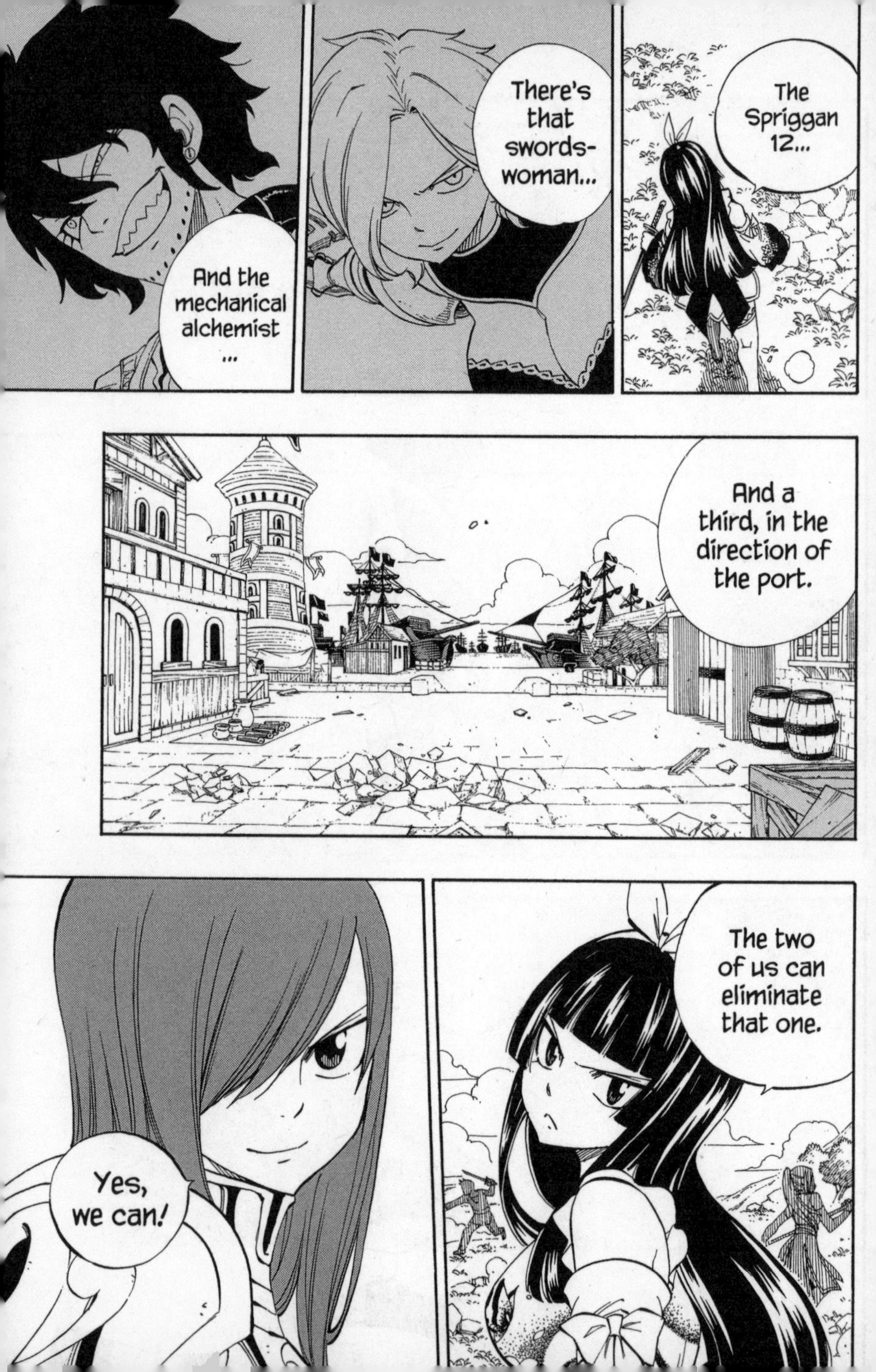

The Spriggan 12...
There's that swords-woman...
And the mechanical alchemist ...
And a third, in the direction of the port.
The two of us can eliminate that one.
Yes, we can!

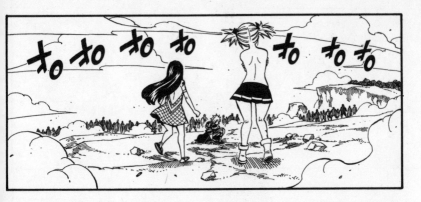

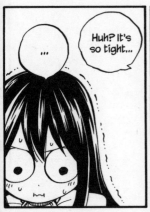

You can't go walking around looking like that!
Here, take this. It's Wendy's, but...
Thanks, Carla.
Huh? It's so tight...
...
Hey, little girls...
Do you know where you are?

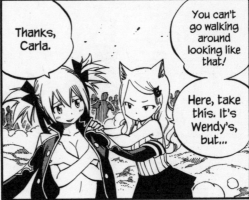

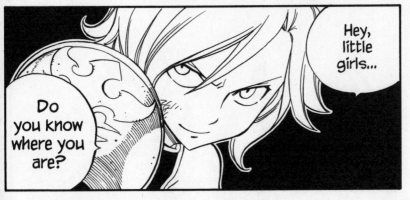

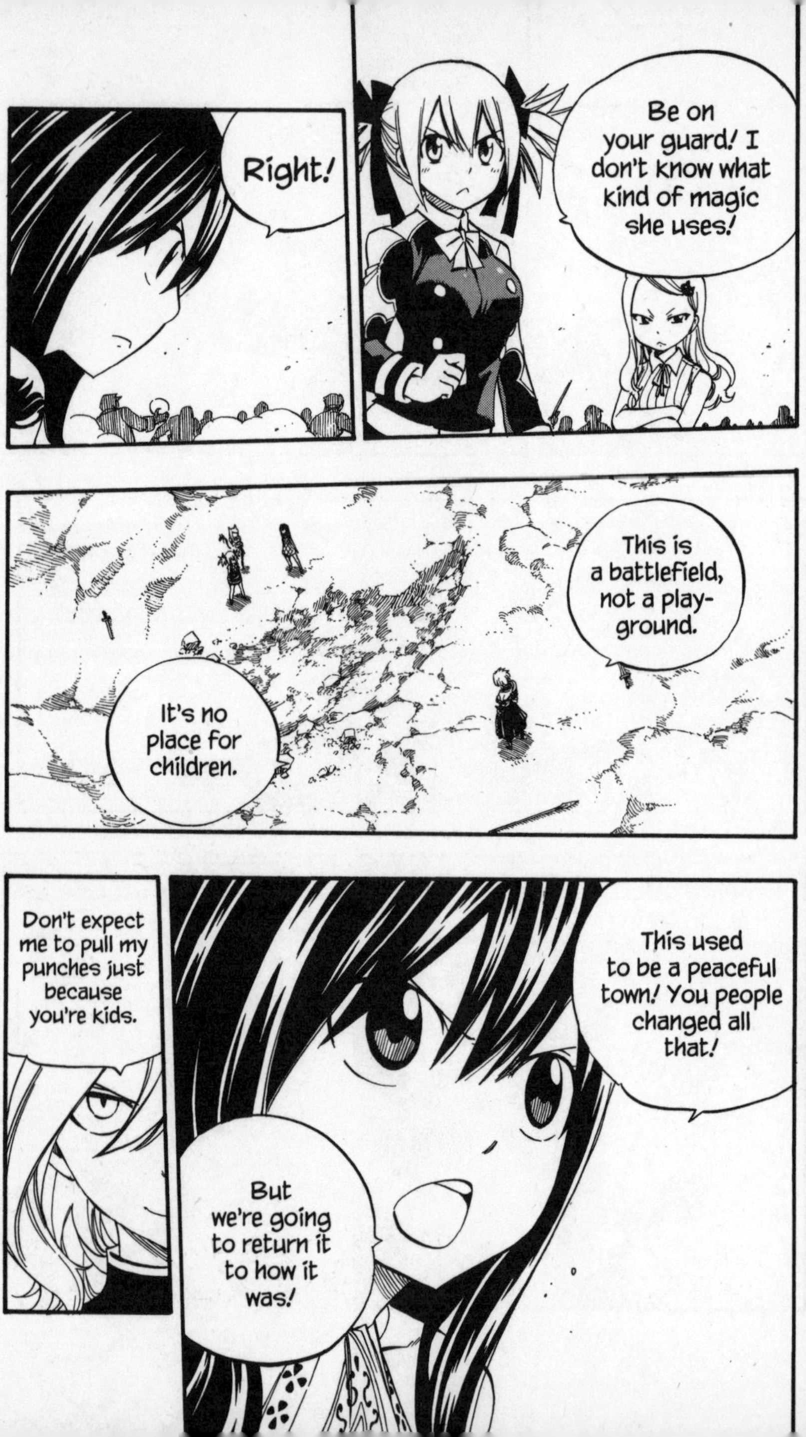
Be on your guard! I don't know what kind of magic she uses!
Right!
This is a battlefield, not a play-ground.
It's no place for children.
This used to be a peaceful town! You people changed all that!
But we're going to return it to how it was!
Don't expect me to pull my punches just because you're kids.

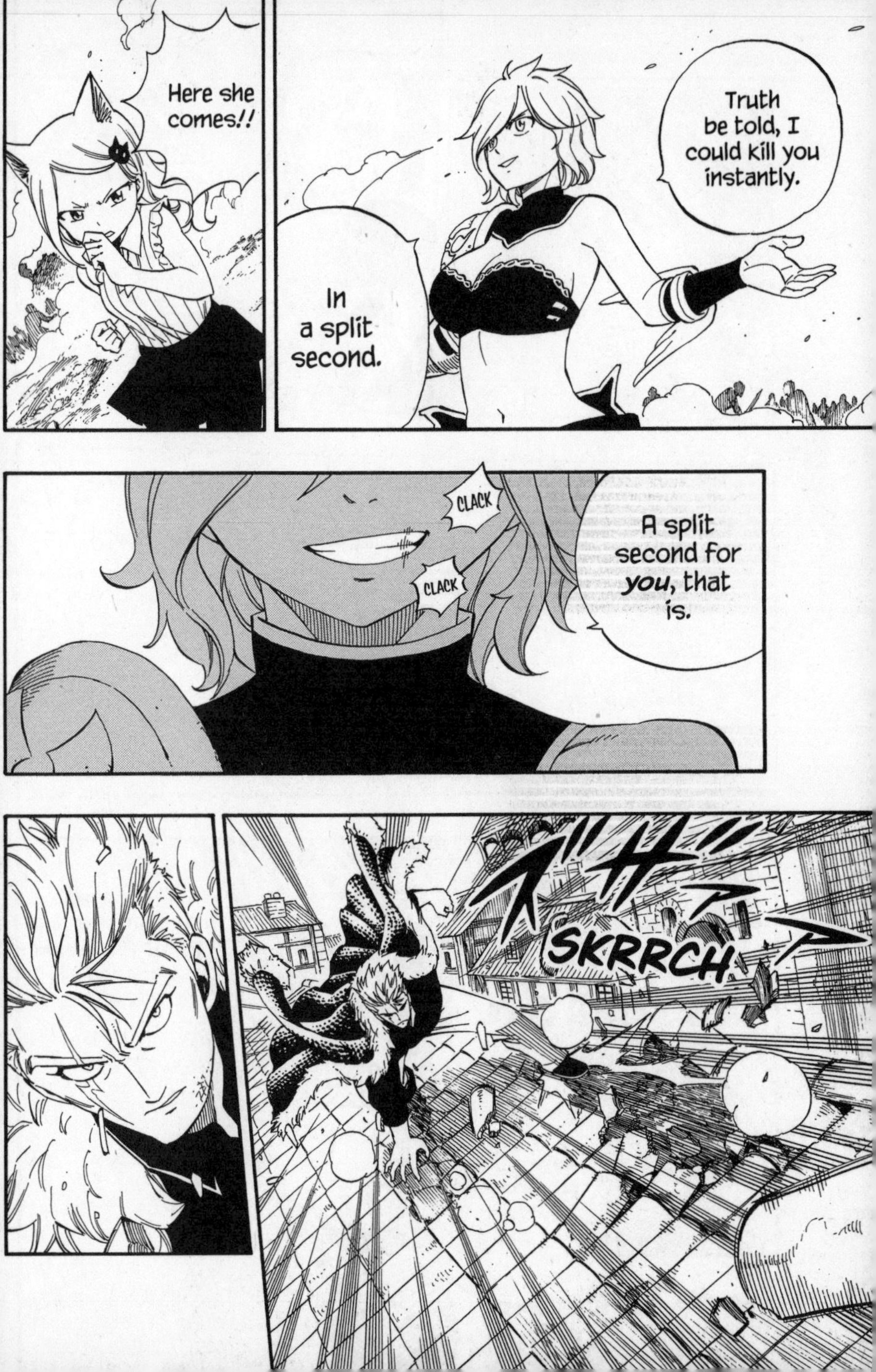
Truth be told, I could kill you instantly.
In a split second.
Here she comes!!
A split second for *you*, that is.
CLACK
CLACK
SKRRCH

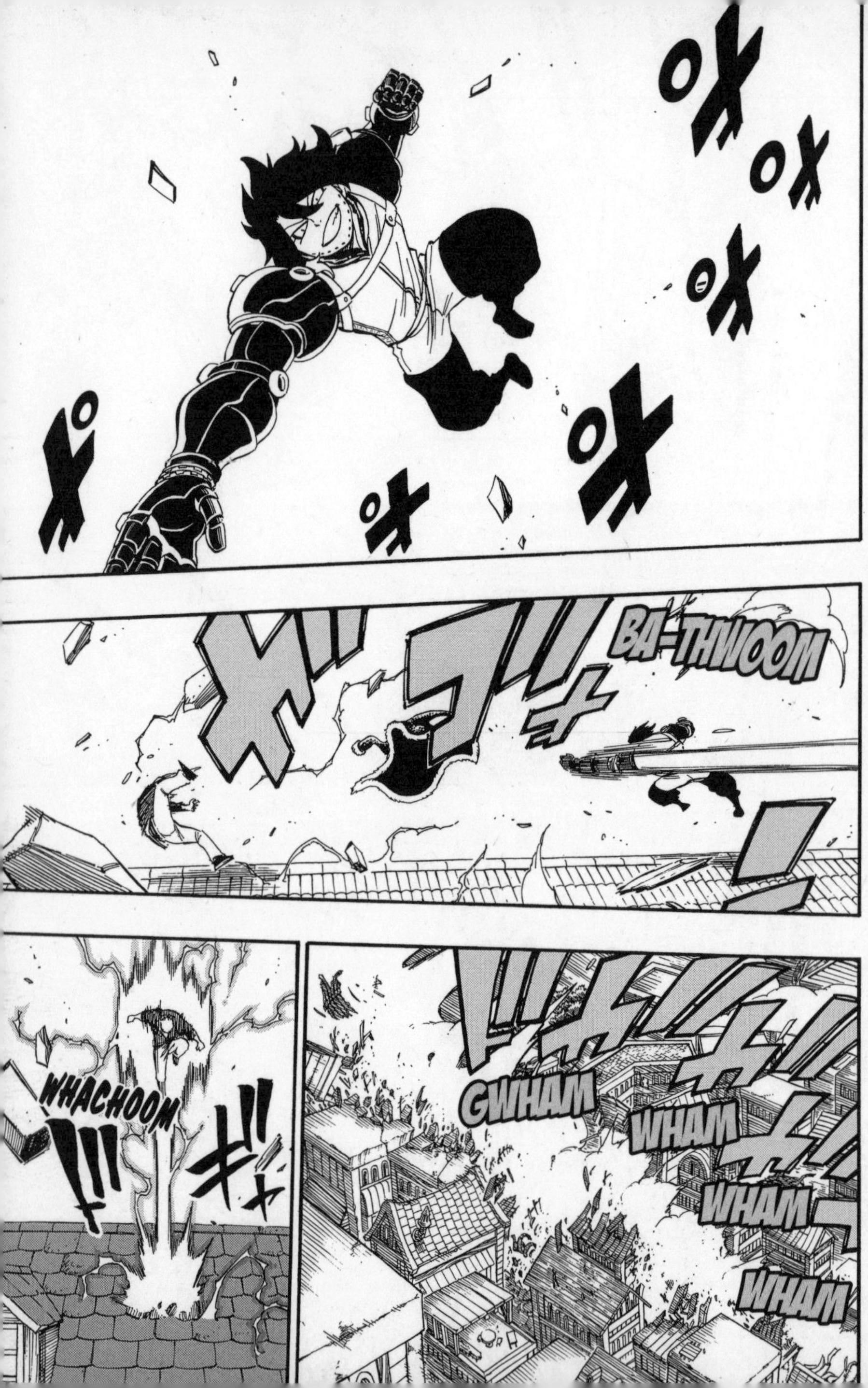
BA-THWOOM
GWHAM
WHAM
WHAM
WHAM
WHACHOOM

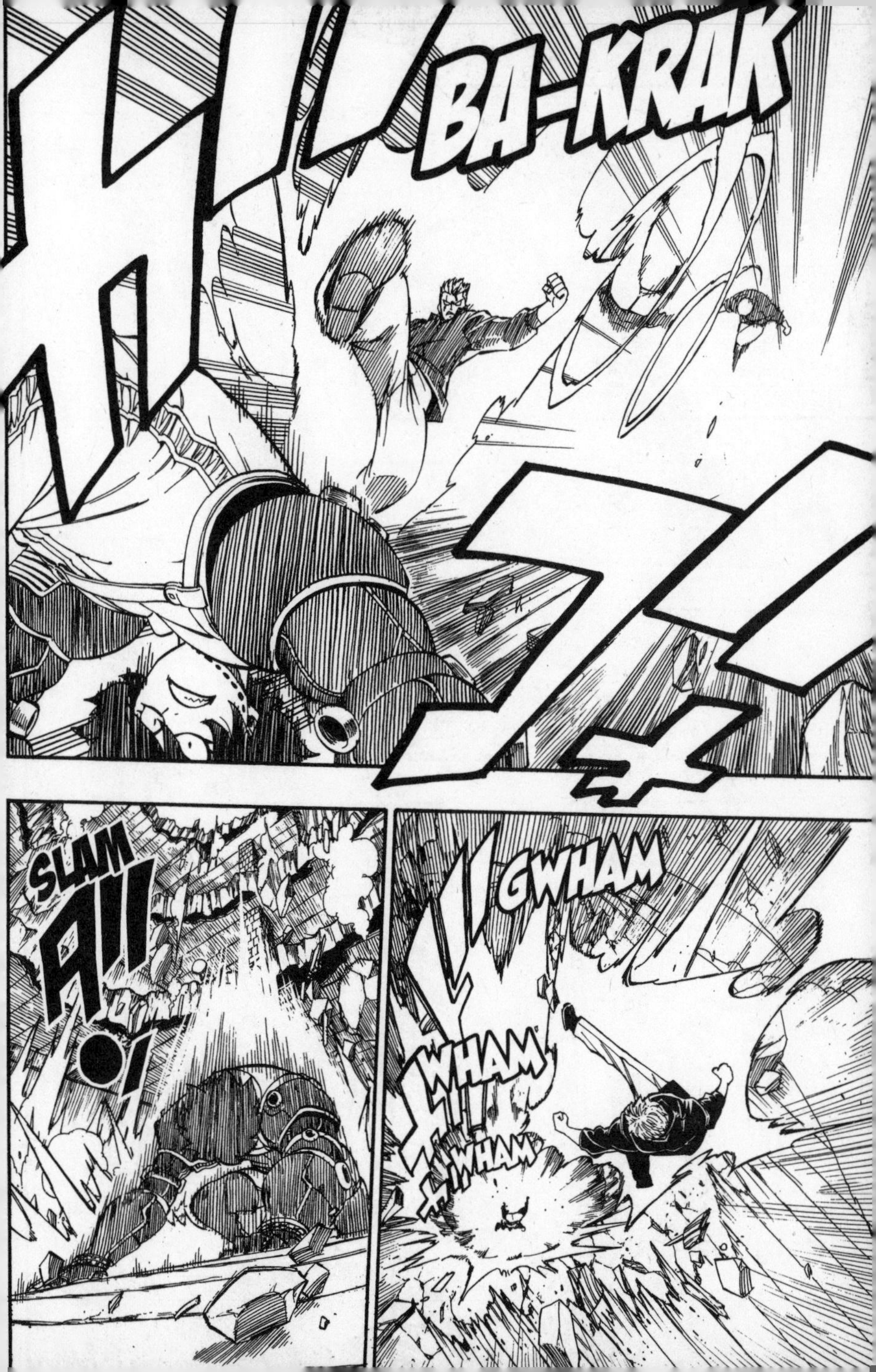
BA-KRAK
GWHAM
WHAM
WHAM
SLAM

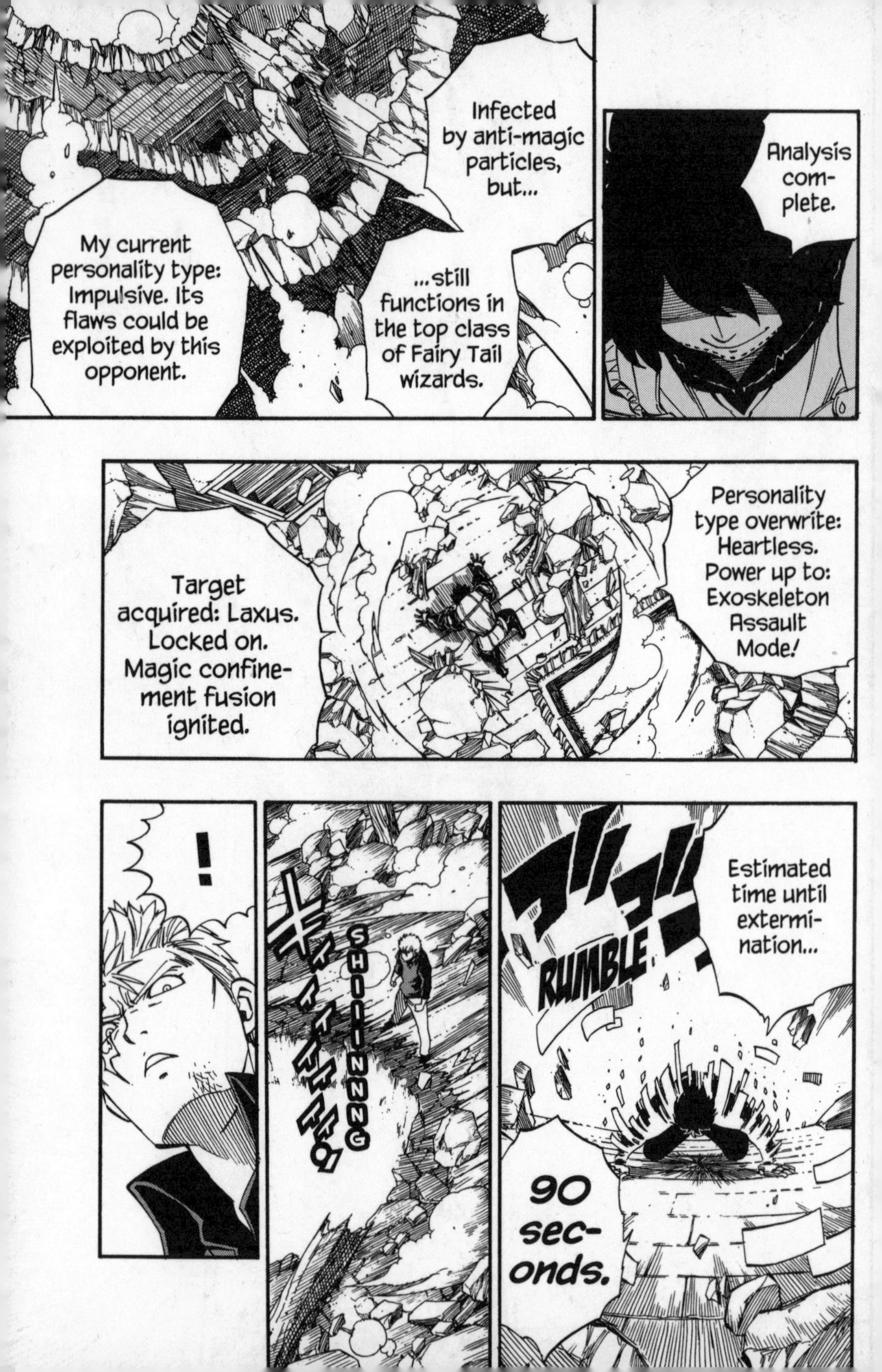

Analysis complete.
Infected by anti-magic particles, but...
...still functions in the top class of Fairy Tail wizards.
My current personality type: Impulsive. Its flaws could be exploited by this opponent.
Personality type overwrite: Heartless. Power up to: Exoskeleton Assault Mode!
Target acquired: Laxus. Locked on. Magic confinement fusion ignited.
Estimated time until extermination...
RUMBLE
90 seconds.
SHIIIINNNG
!

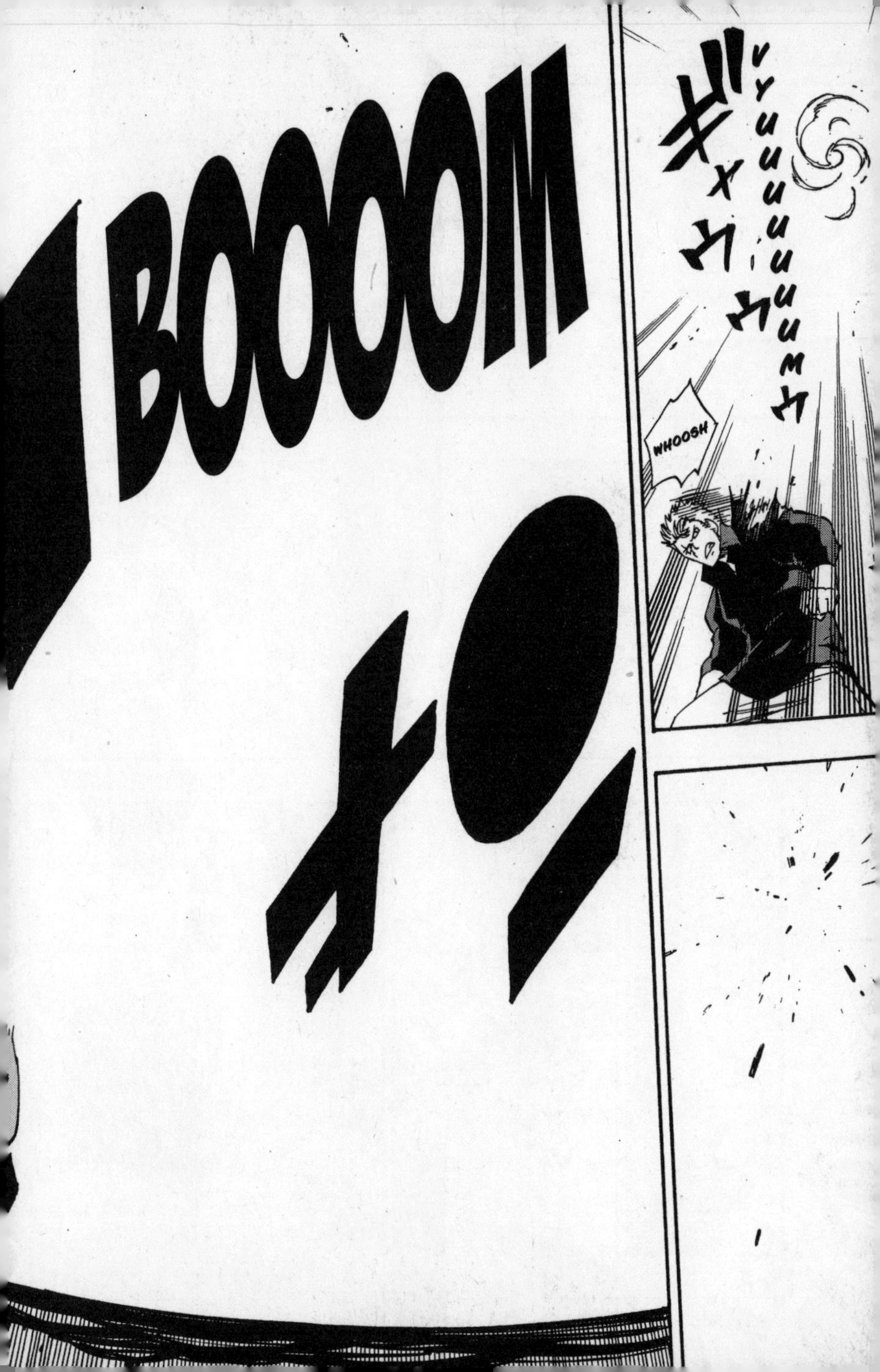

VRUUUUUUUUUUUMM
WHOOSH
BOOOOM

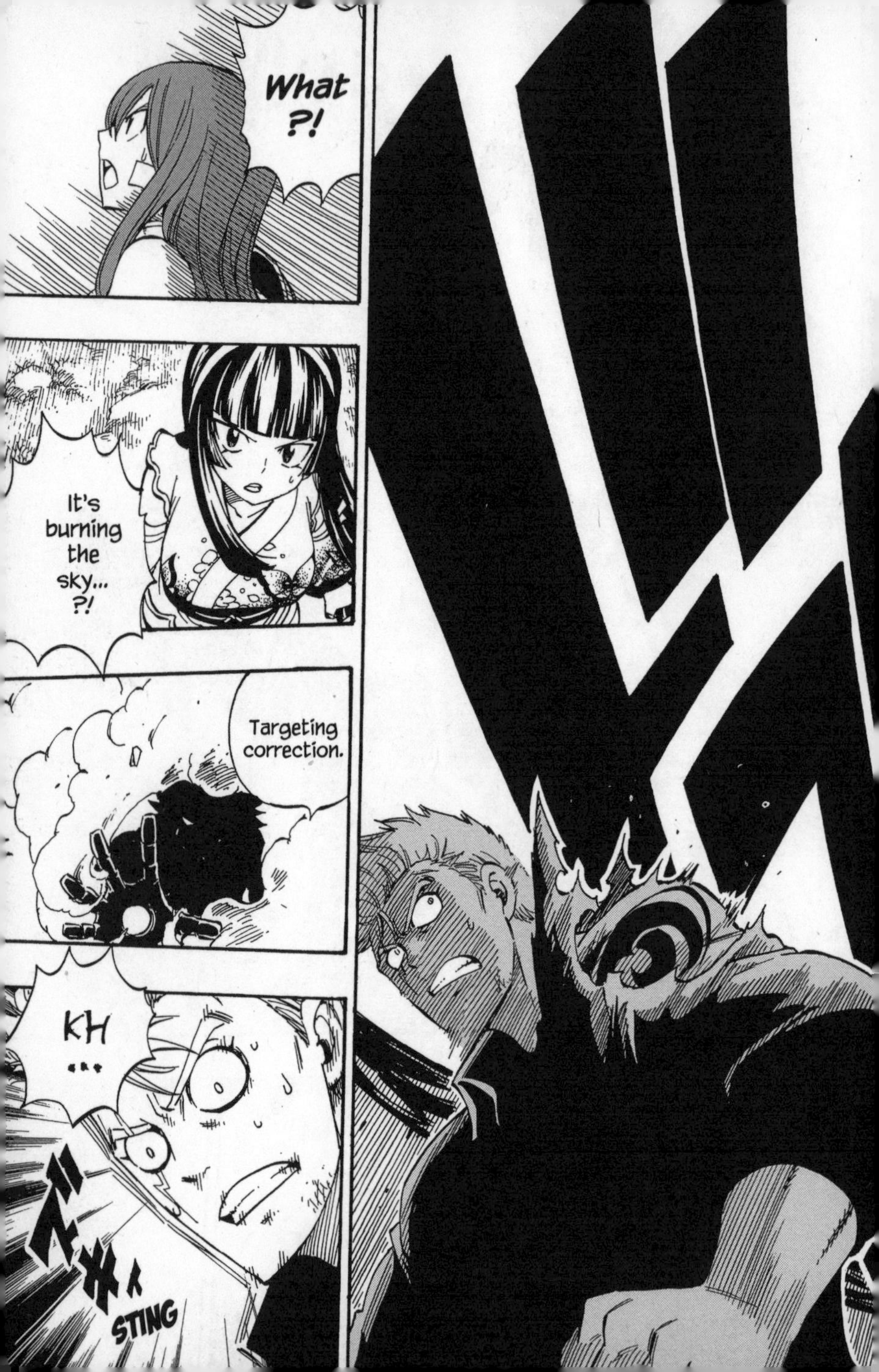
What?!
It's burning the sky...?!
Targeting correction.
KH...
STING

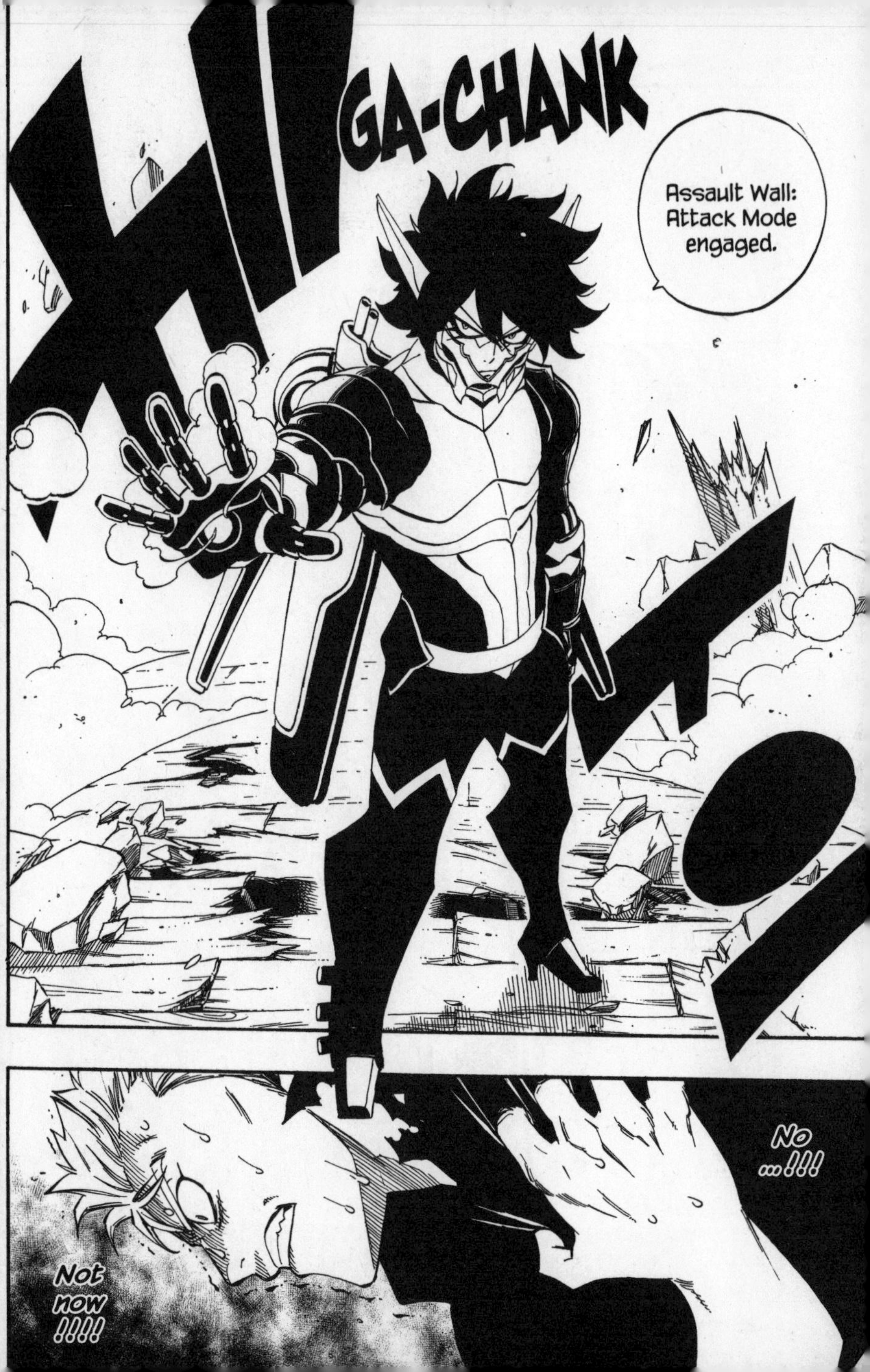
Assault Wall: Attack Mode engaged.
GA-CHANK
No ...!!!
Not now !!!!

FAIRY TAIL

フェアリーテイル

Chapter 473: Red Lightning

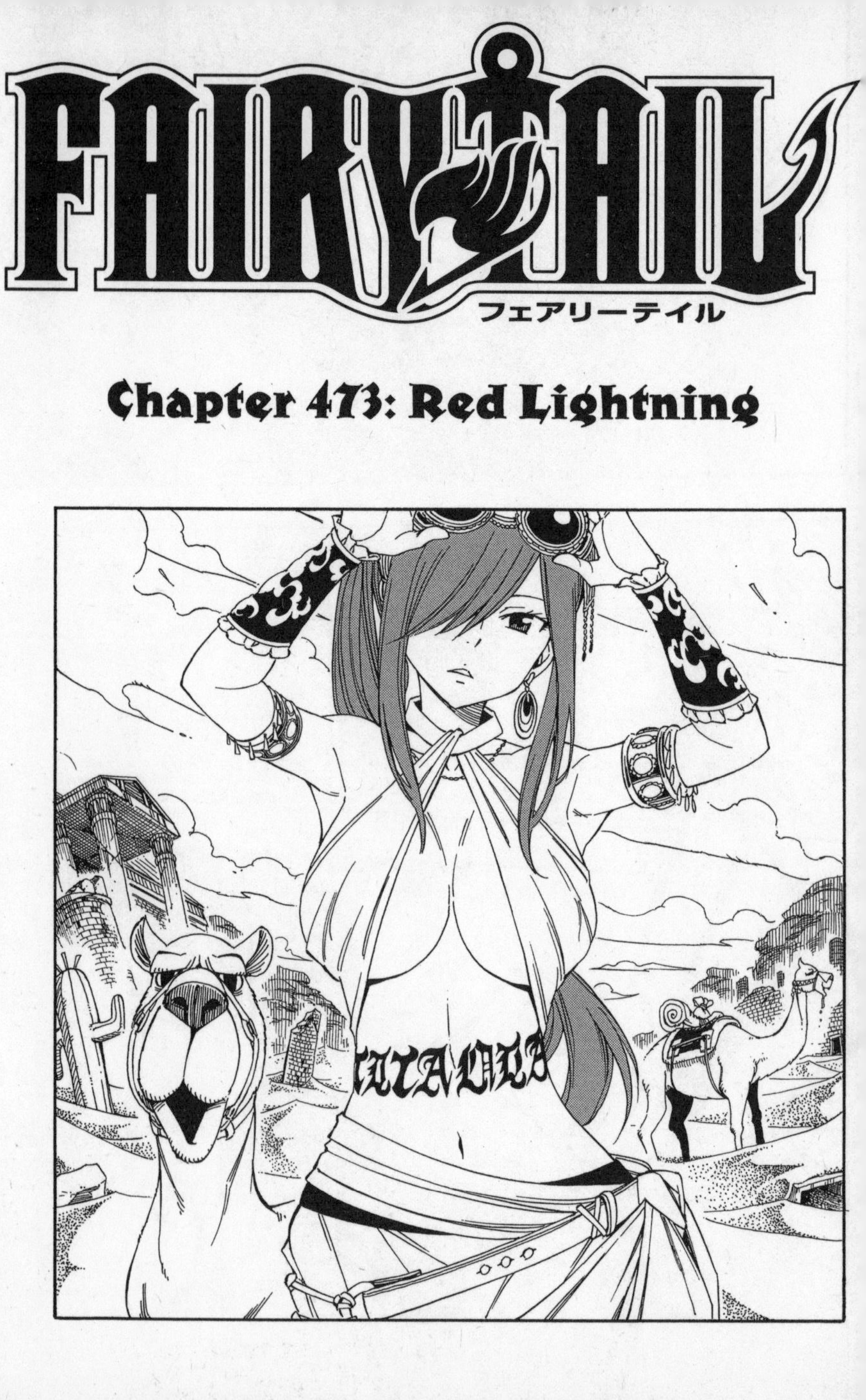

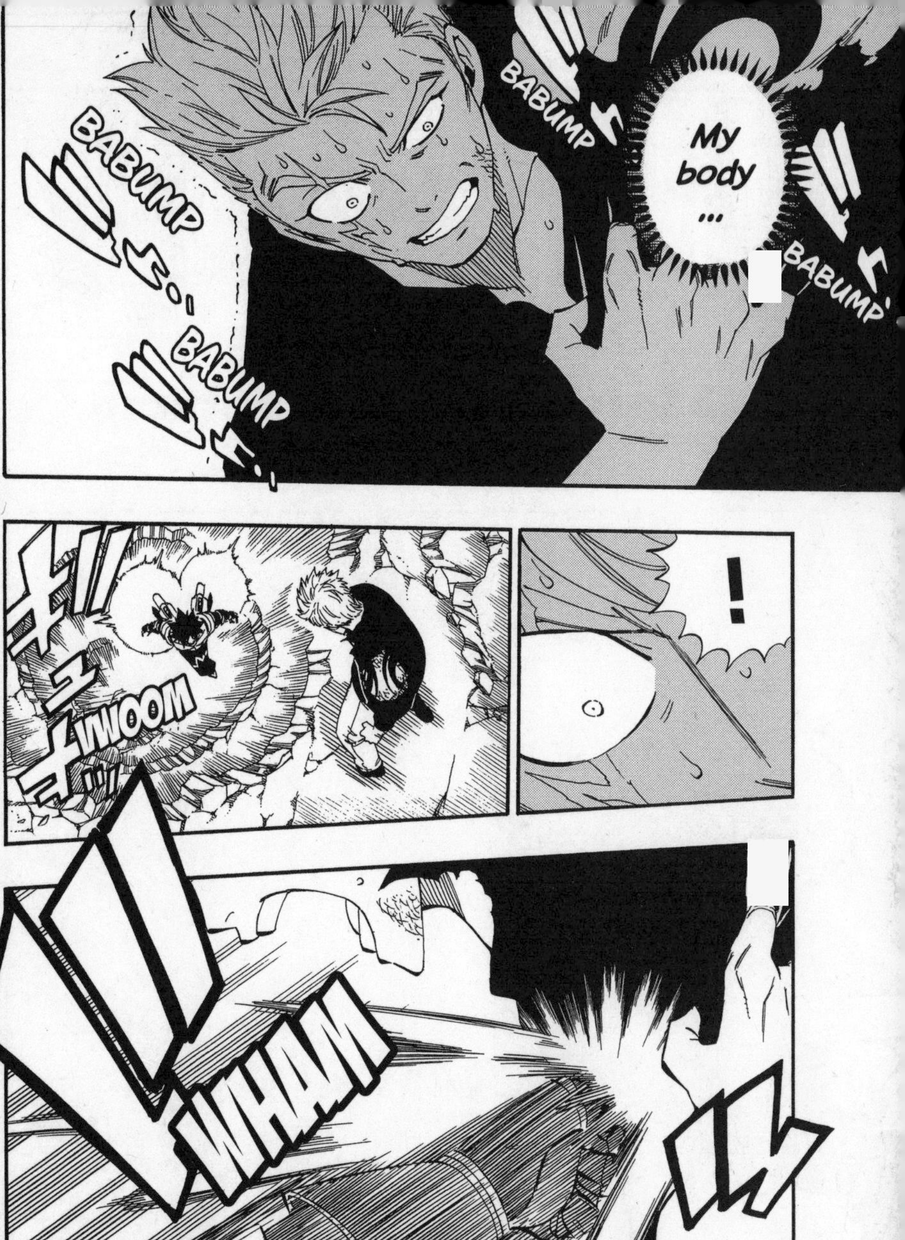
BABUMP
My body ...
BABUMP
BABUMP
BABUMP
!
VWOOM
WHAM

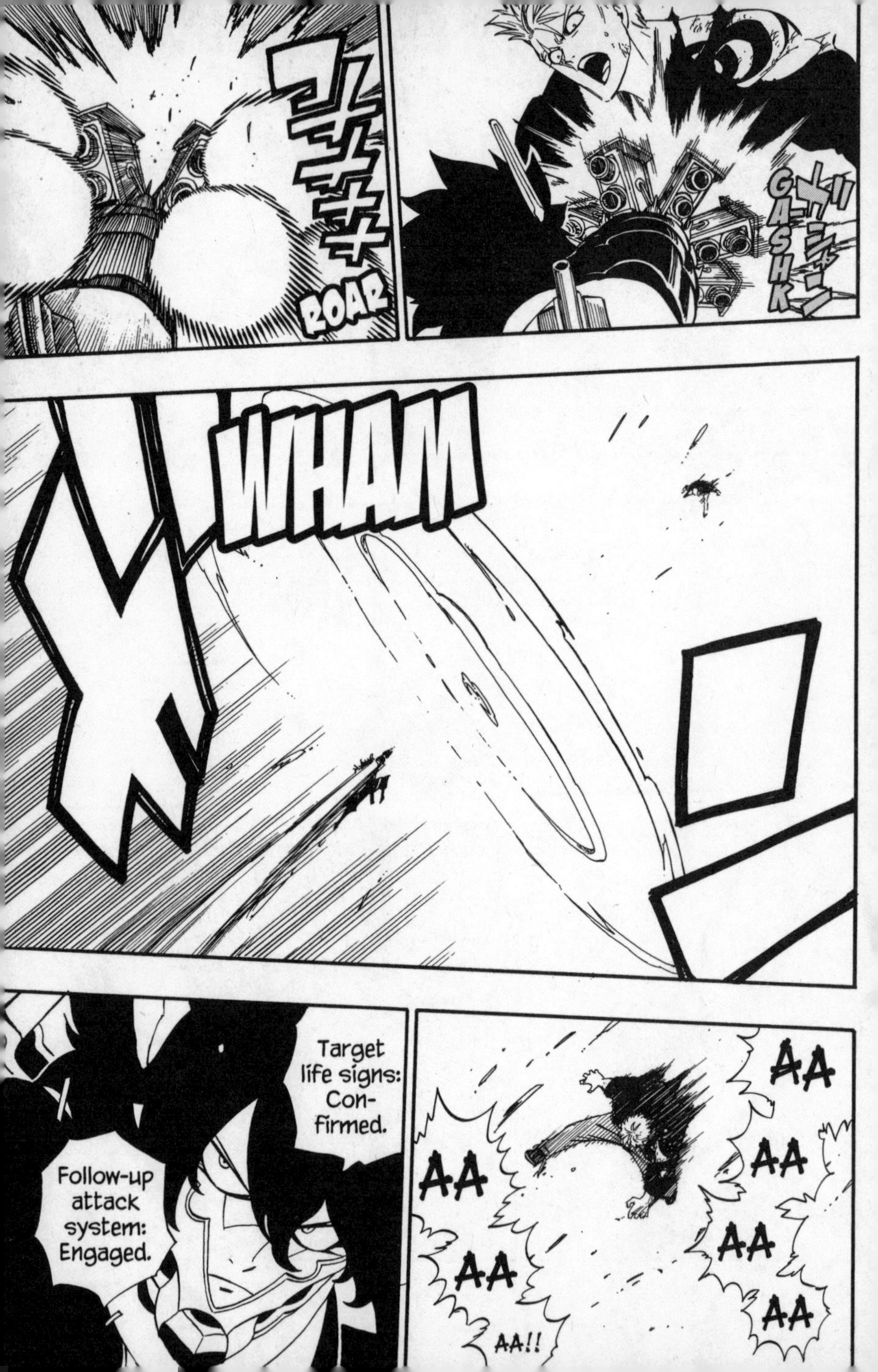
GASHK
ROAR
WHAM
AA
AA
AA
AA
AA
AA!!
Target life signs: Con-firmed.
Follow-up attack system: Engaged.

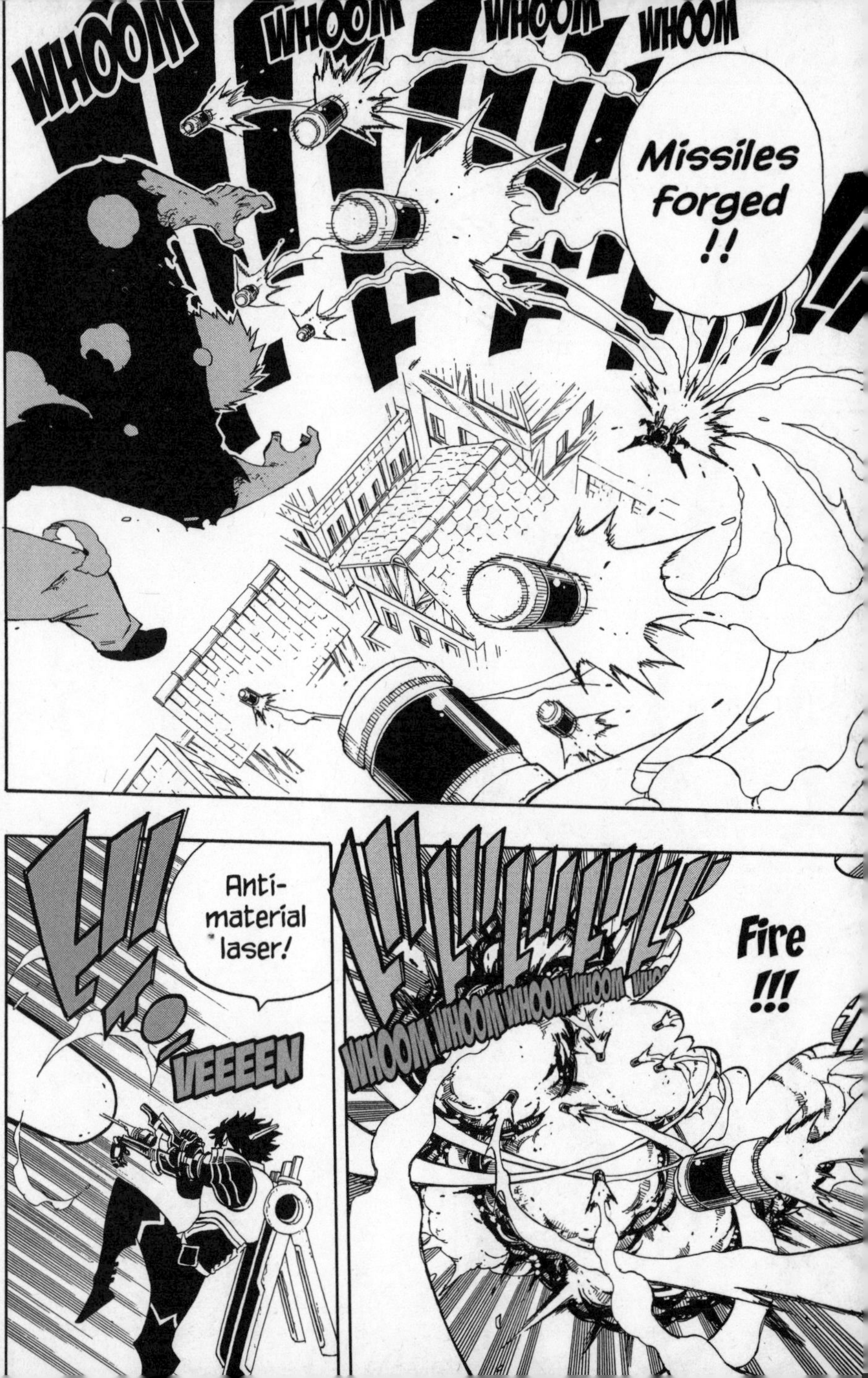
WHOOM
WHOOM
WHOOM
WHOOM
Missiles forged !!
Fire !!!
WHOOM WHOOM WHOOM WHOOM
Anti-material laser!
VEEEEN

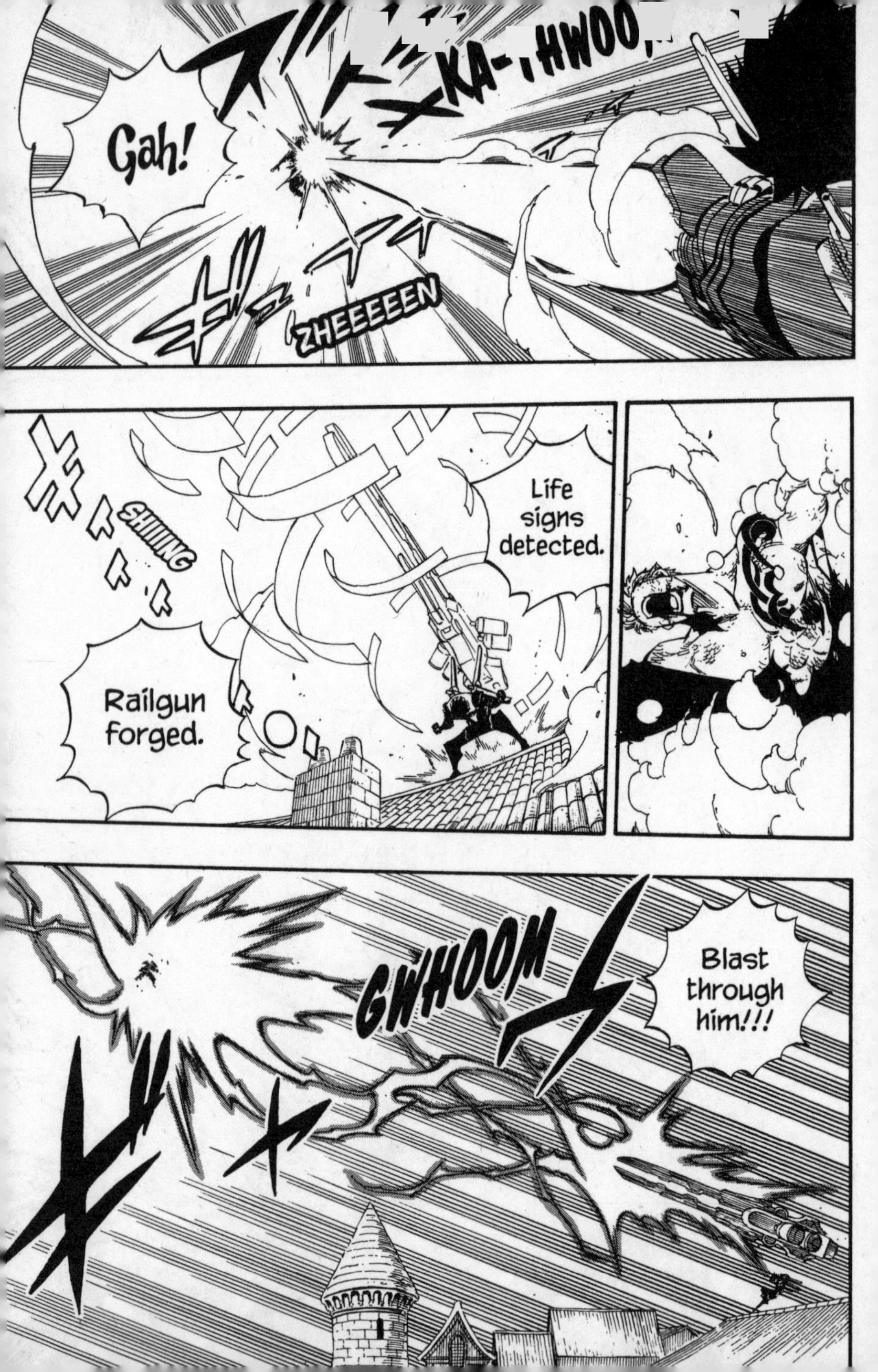
Gah!
ZHEEEEEN
Life signs detected.
SHIIING
Railgun forged.
Blast through him!!!
GWHOOM

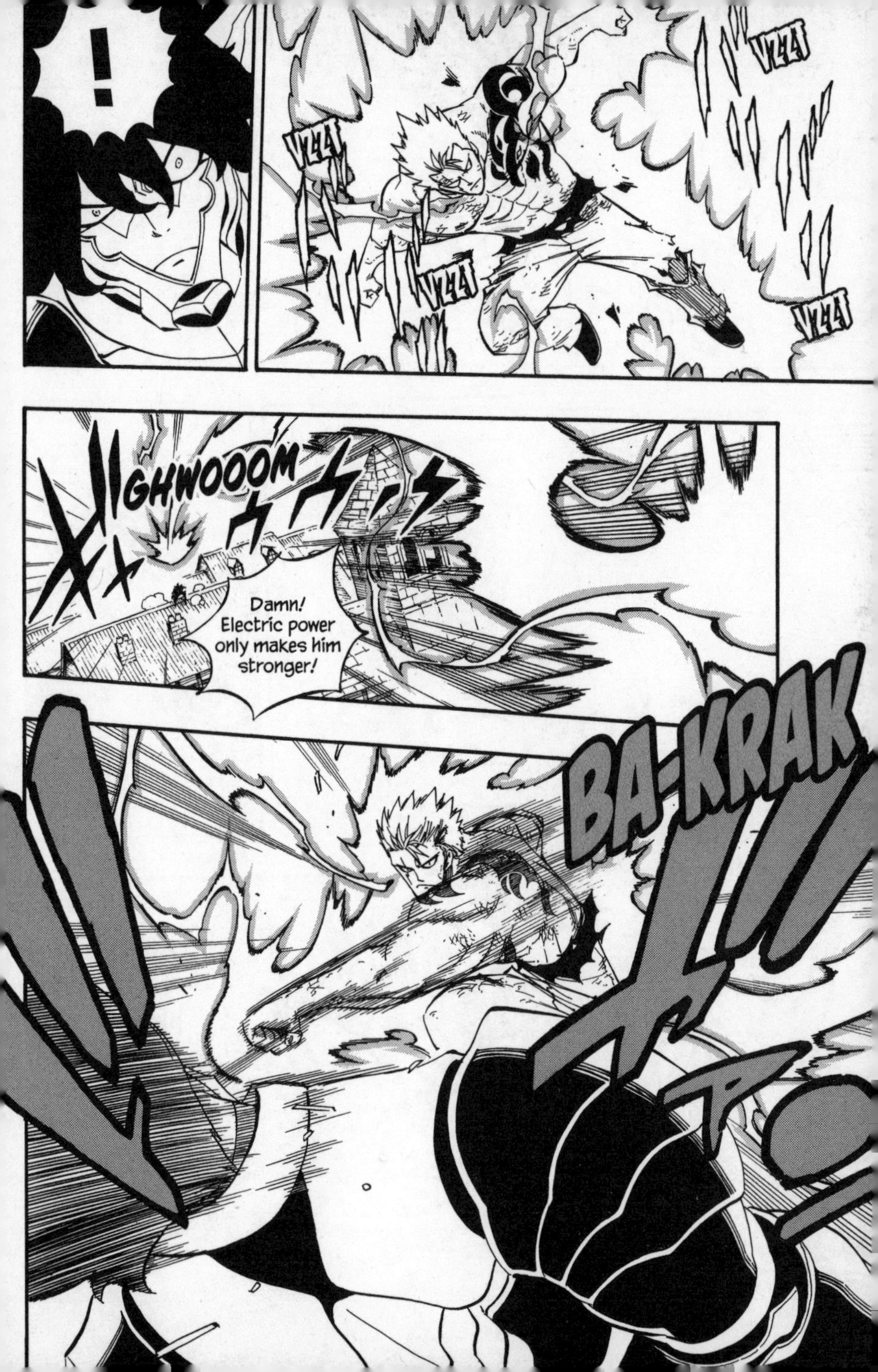
VZZT
VZZT
VZZT
VZZT
!
GHWOOOM
Damn! Electric power only makes him stronger!
BA-KRAK

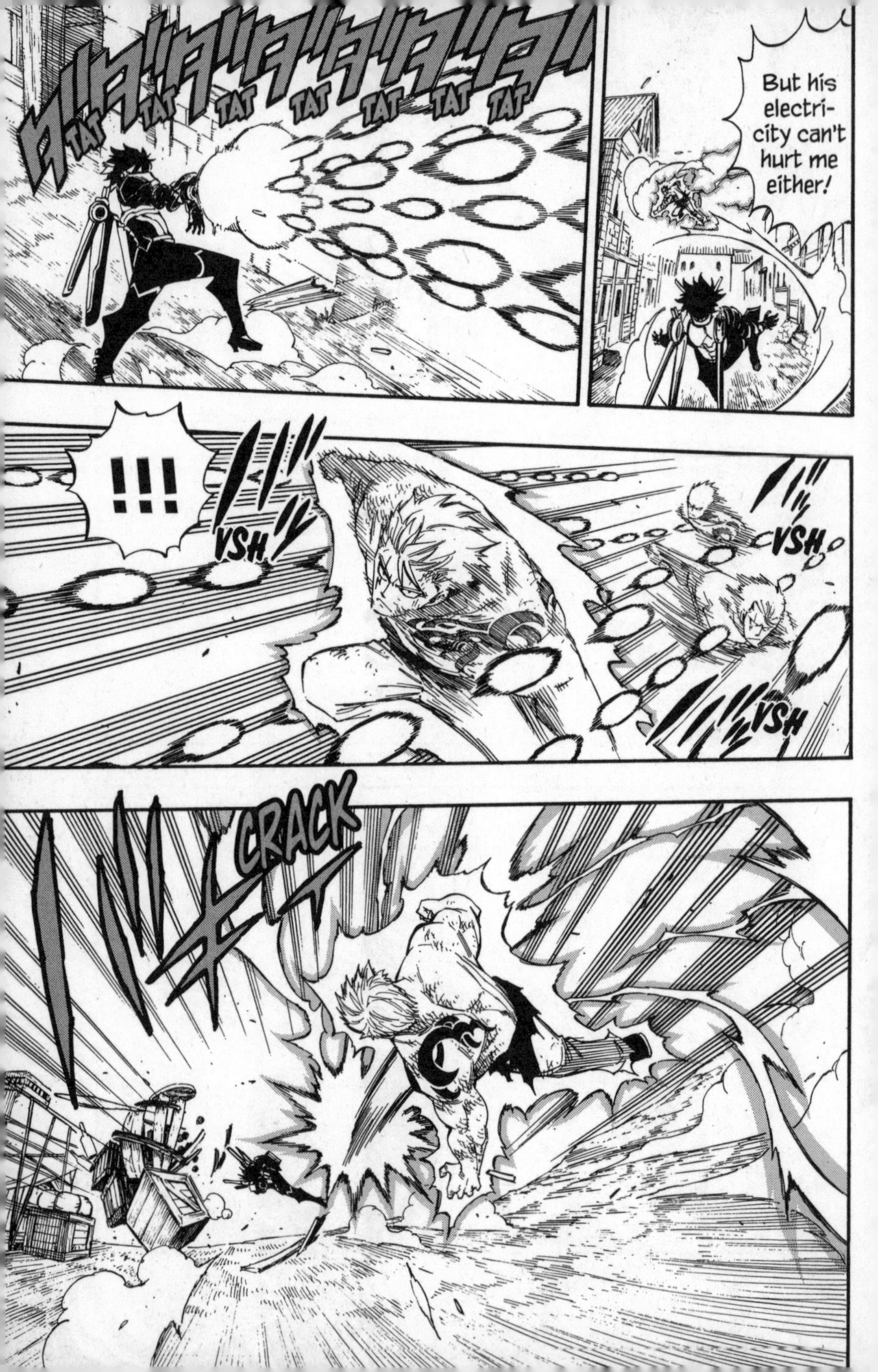
But his electricity can't hurt me either!
TAT TAT TAT TAT TAT TAT TAT
VSH
VSH
!!!
VSH
CRACK

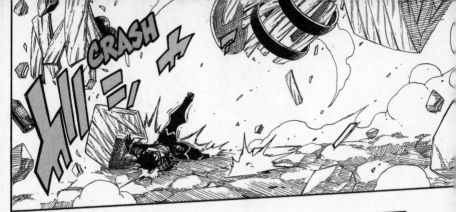

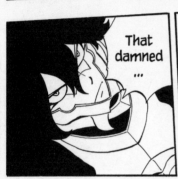

That
damned
...

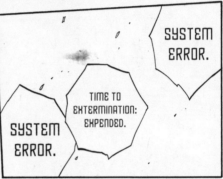

SYSTEM
ERROR.

TIME TO
EXTERMINATION:
EXPENDED.

SYSTEM
ERROR.

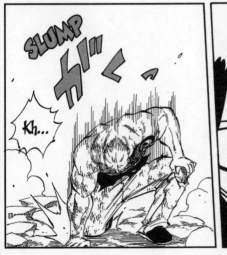

SLUMP

Kh...

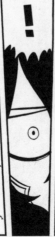

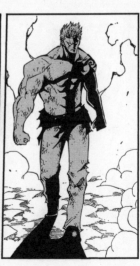

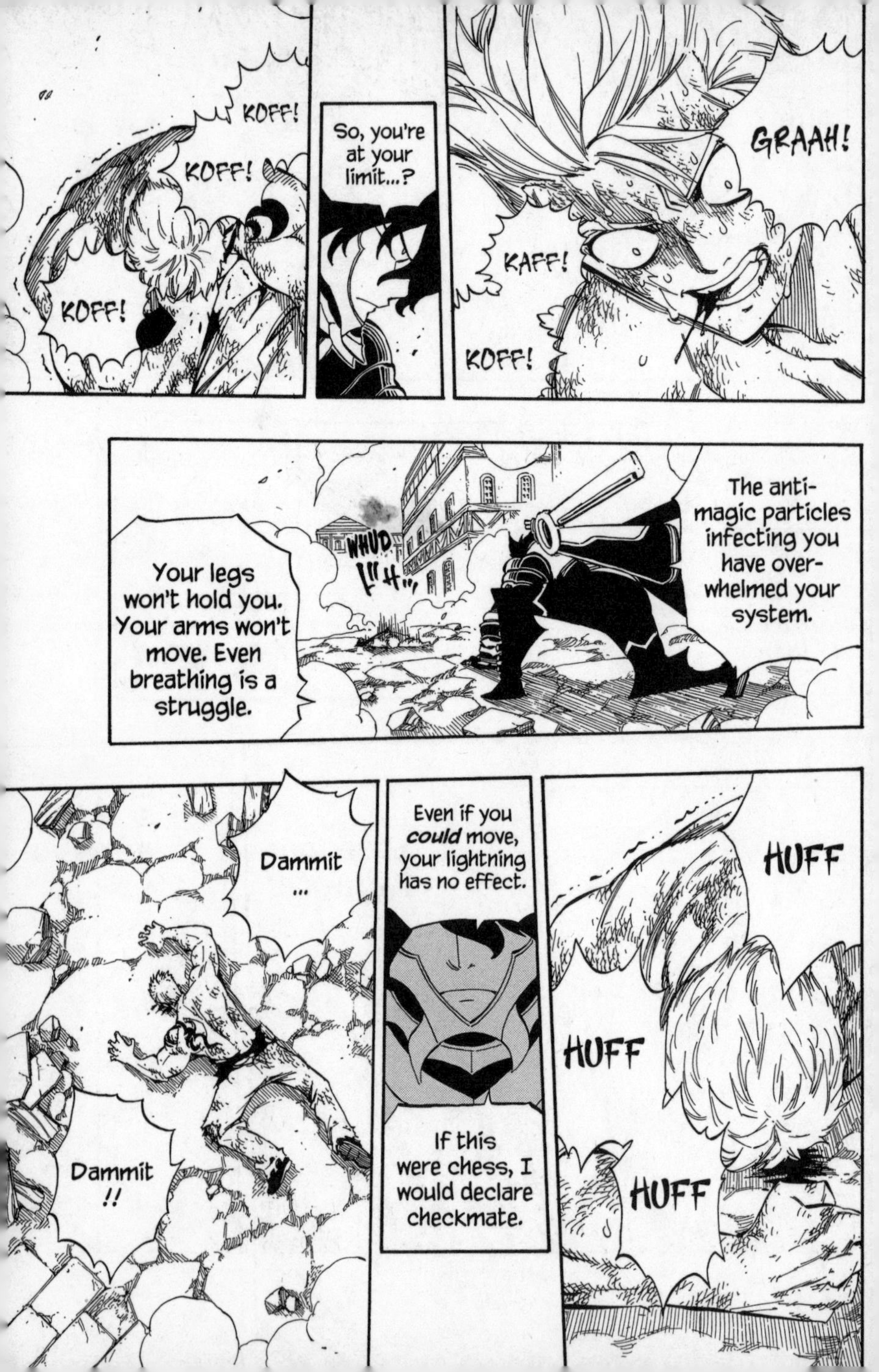
GRAAH!
KAFF!
KOFF!
So, you're at your limit...?
KOFF!
KOFF!
KOFF!
The anti-magic particles infecting you have over-whelmed your system.
WHUD
Your legs won't hold you. Your arms won't move. Even breathing is a struggle.
HUFF
HUFF
HUFF
Even if you *could* move, your lightning has no effect.
If this were chess, I would declare checkmate.
Dammit ...
Dammit !!

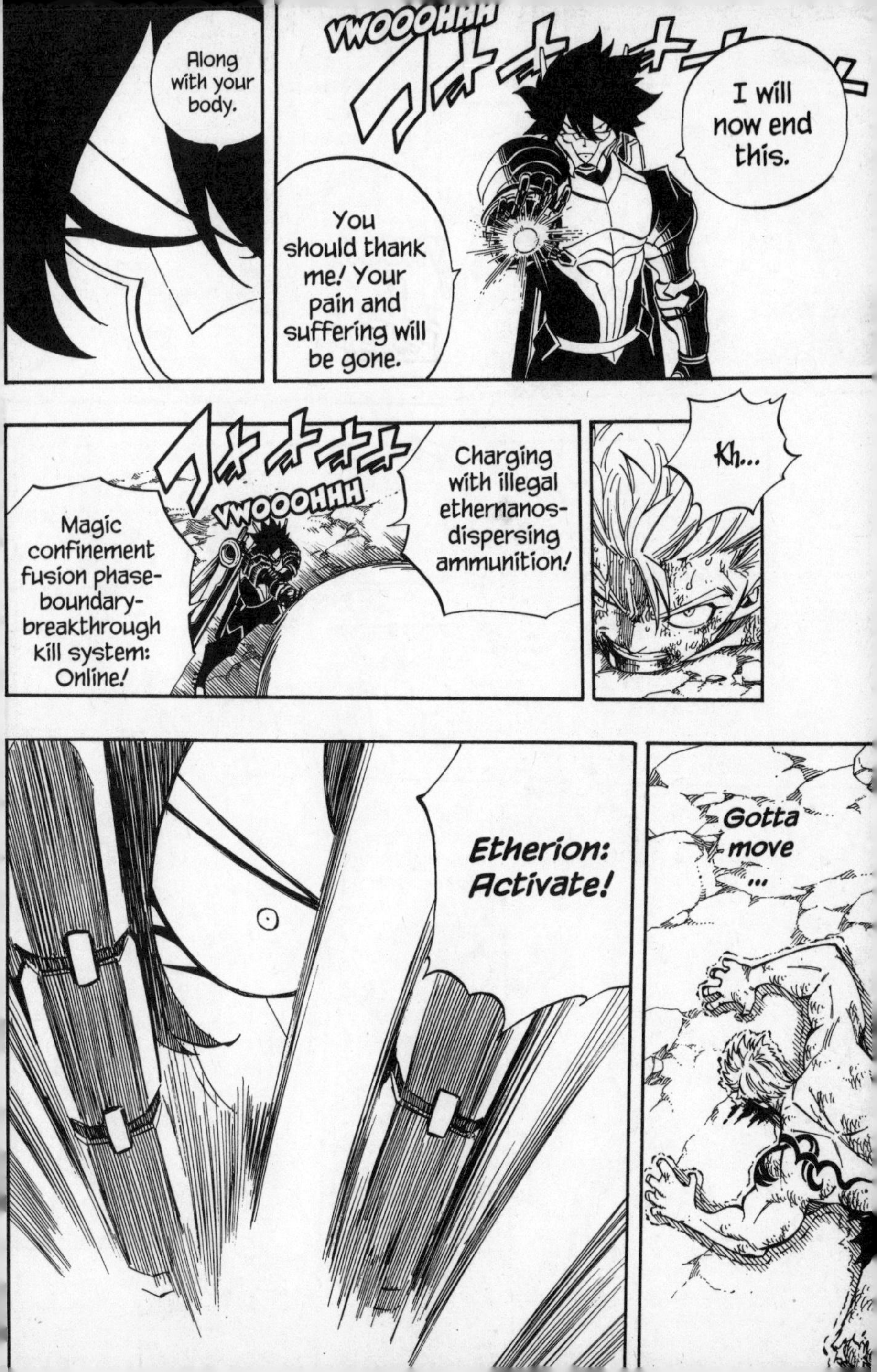
VWOOOHHH
I will now end this.
You should thank me! Your pain and suffering will be gone.
Along with your body.
Kh...
Charging with illegal ethernanos-dispersing ammunition!
VWOOOHHH
Magic confinement fusion phase-boundary-breakthrough kill system: Online!
Gotta move ...
Etherion: Activate!

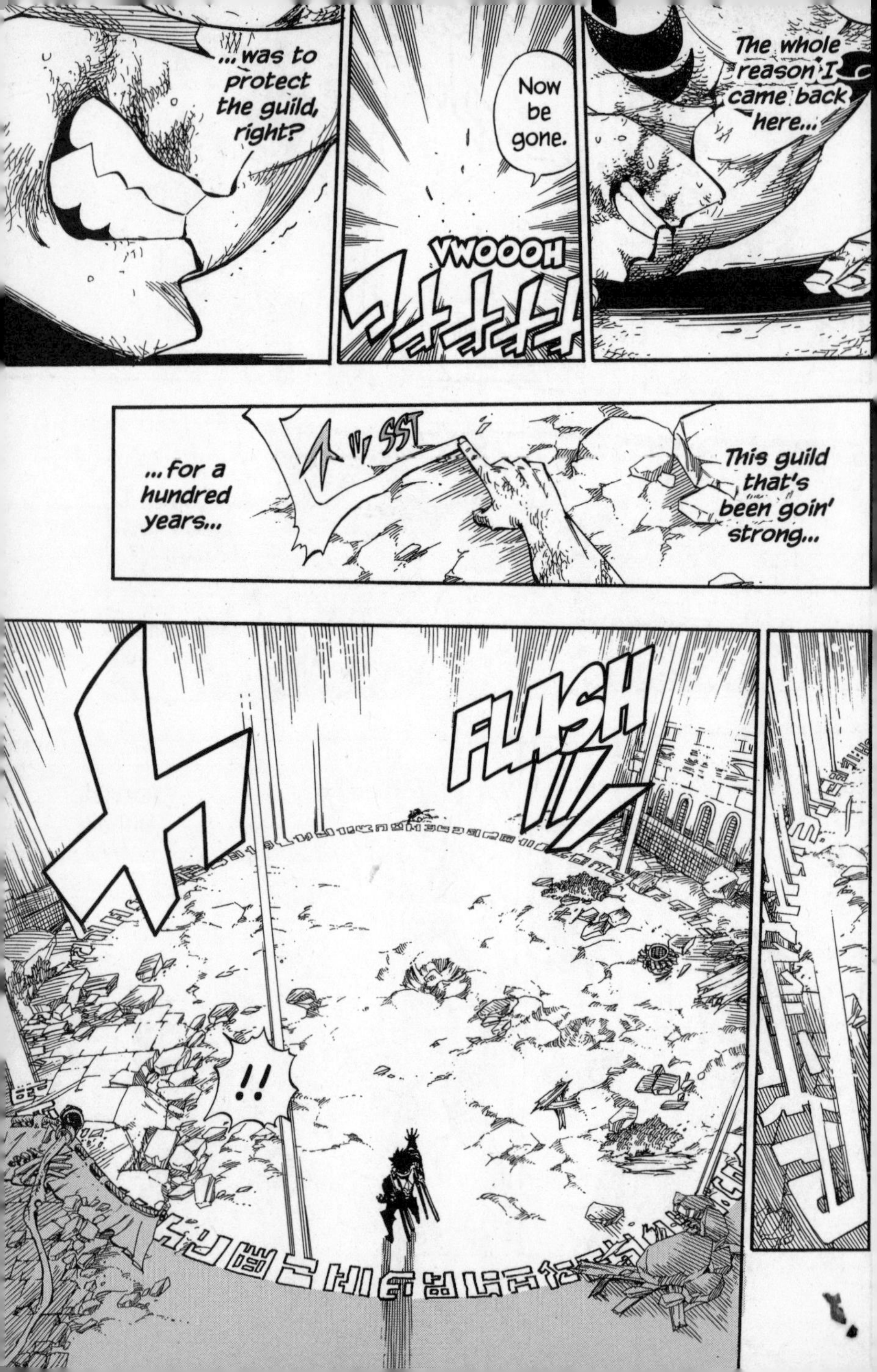
The whole reason I came back here...
Now be gone.
VWOOOH
...was to protect the guild, right?
This guild that's been goin' strong...
SST
...for a hundred years...
FLASH
!!

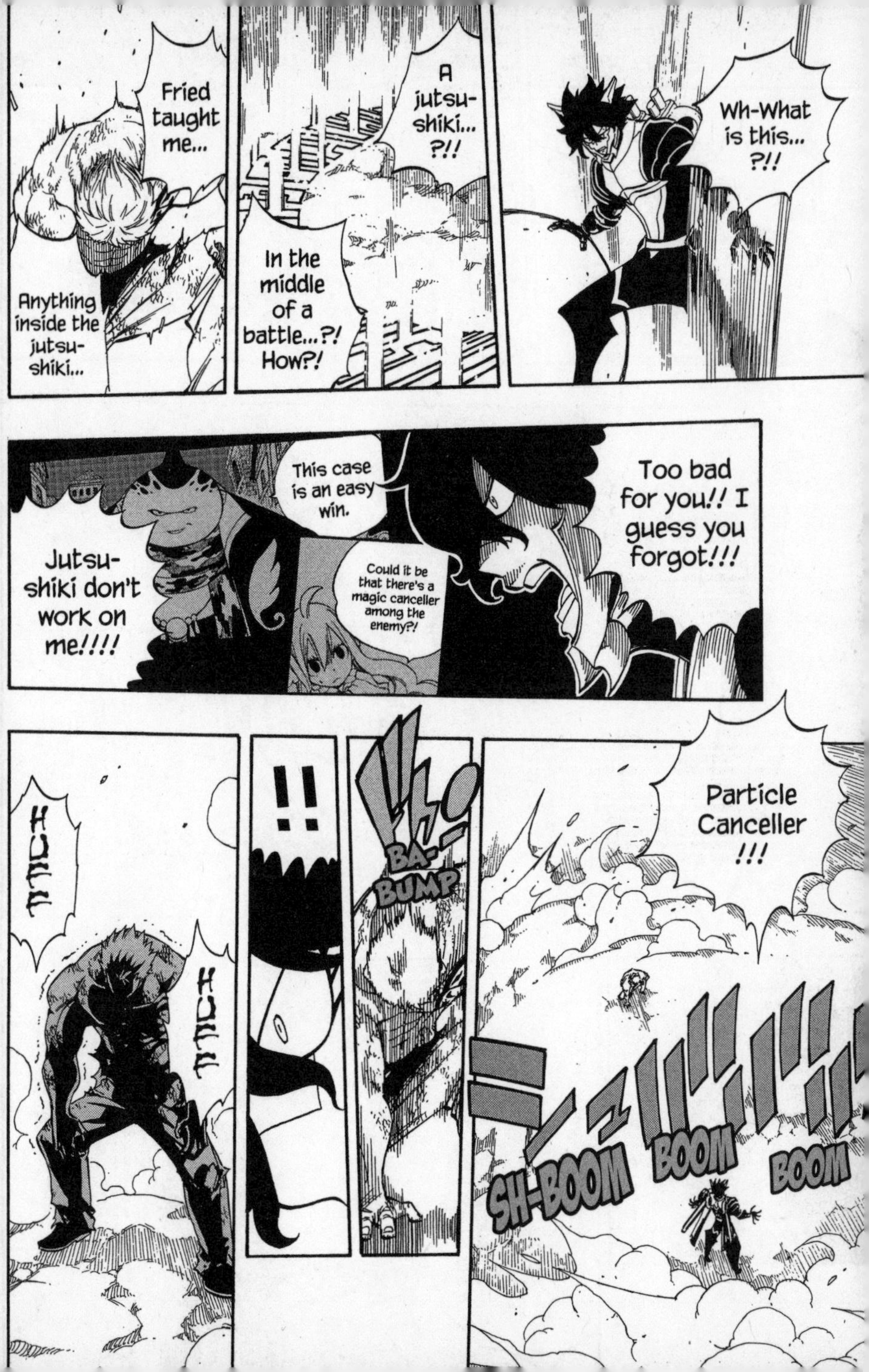
Wh-What is this...?!!
A jutsu-shiki...?!!
In the middle of a battle...?! How?!
Fried taught me...
Anything inside the jutsu-shiki...
Too bad for you!! I guess you forgot!!!
This case is an easy win.
Could it be that there's a magic canceller among the enemy?!
Jutsu-shiki don't work on me!!!!
Particle Canceller!!!
SH-BOOM
BOOM
BOOM
BA-BUMP
!!
HUFF
HUFF

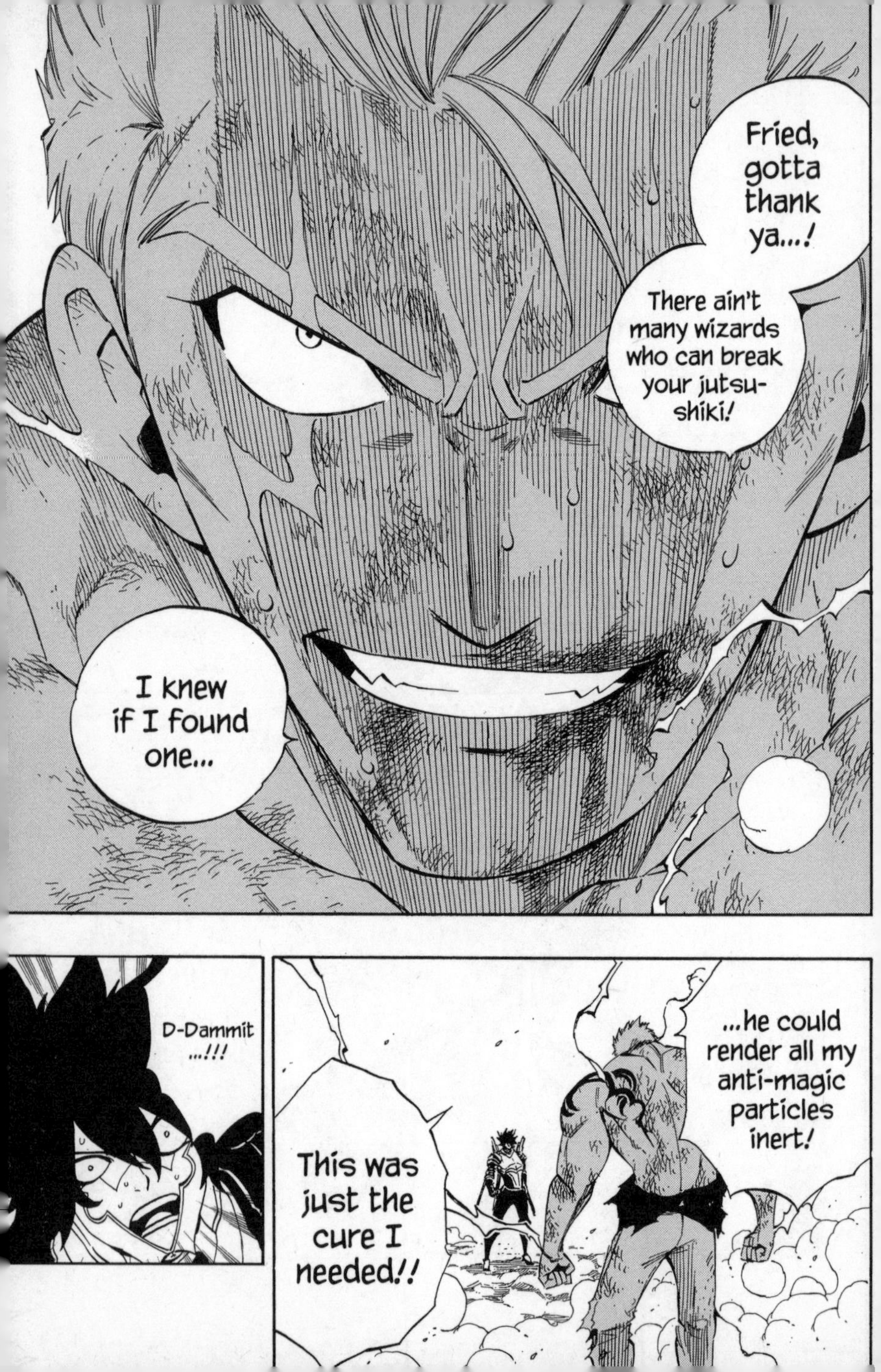
Fried, gotta thank ya...!
There ain't many wizards who can break your jutsu-shiki!
I knew if I found one...
...he could render all my anti-magic particles inert!
This was just the cure I needed!!
D-Dammit ...!!!

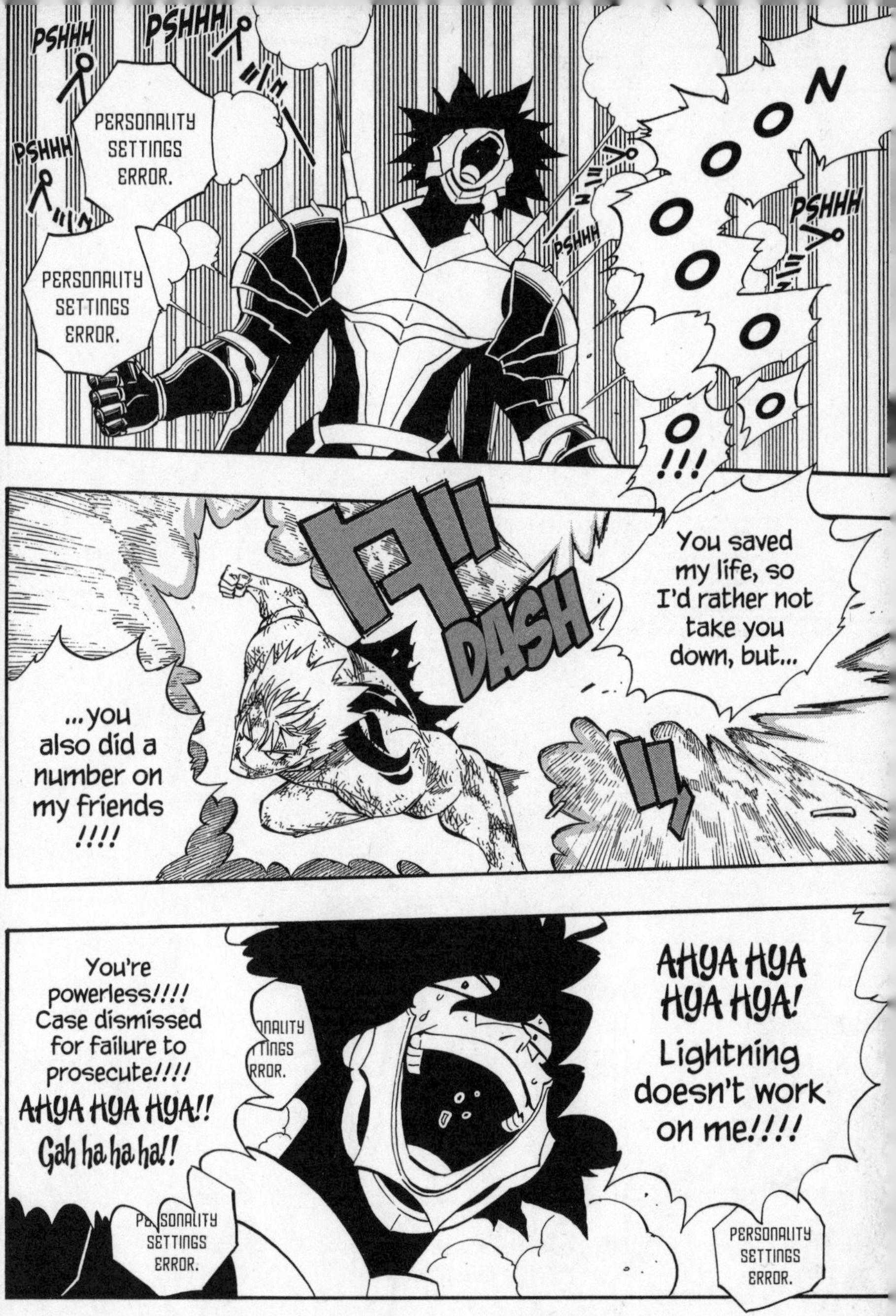
NOOOOOOOOOO!!!
PSHHH
PSHHH
PSHHH
PSHHH
PSHHH
PERSONALITY SETTINGS ERROR.
PERSONALITY SETTINGS ERROR.
You saved my life, so I'd rather not take you down, but...
DASH
...you also did a number on my friends!!!!
AHYA HYA HYA HYA! Lightning doesn't work on me!!!!
PERSONALITY SETTINGS ERROR.
You're powerless!!!! Case dismissed for failure to prosecute!!!!
AHYA HYA HYA!! Gah ha ha ha!!
PERSONALITY SETTINGS ERROR.

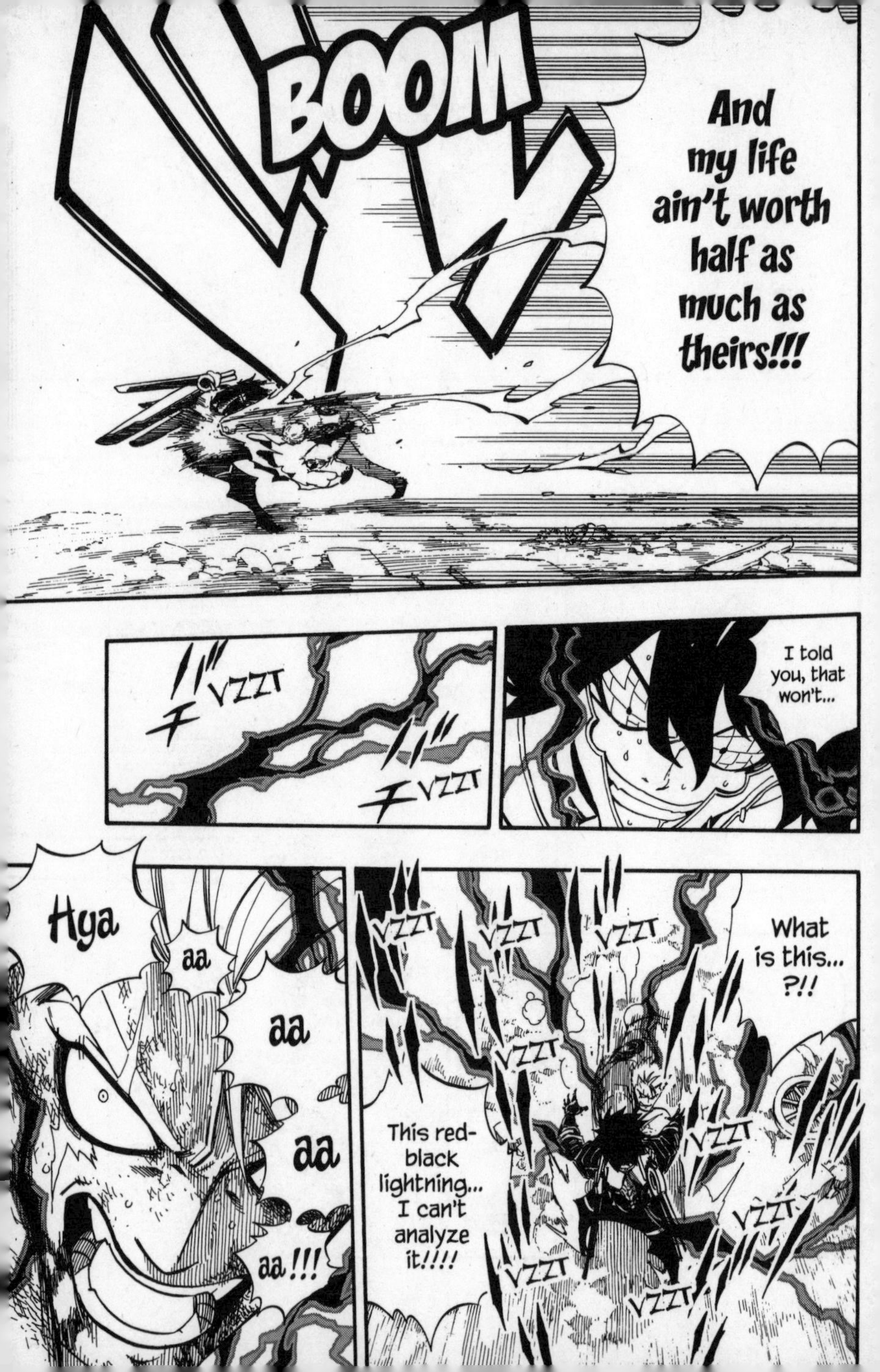
BOOM
And my life ain't worth half as much as theirs!!!
I told you, that won't...
VZZT
VZZT
What is this...?!!
VZZT
VZZT
VZZT
VZZT
VZZT
VZZT
VZZT
VZZT
This red-black lightning... I can't analyze it!!!!
Hya aa aa aa aa!!!

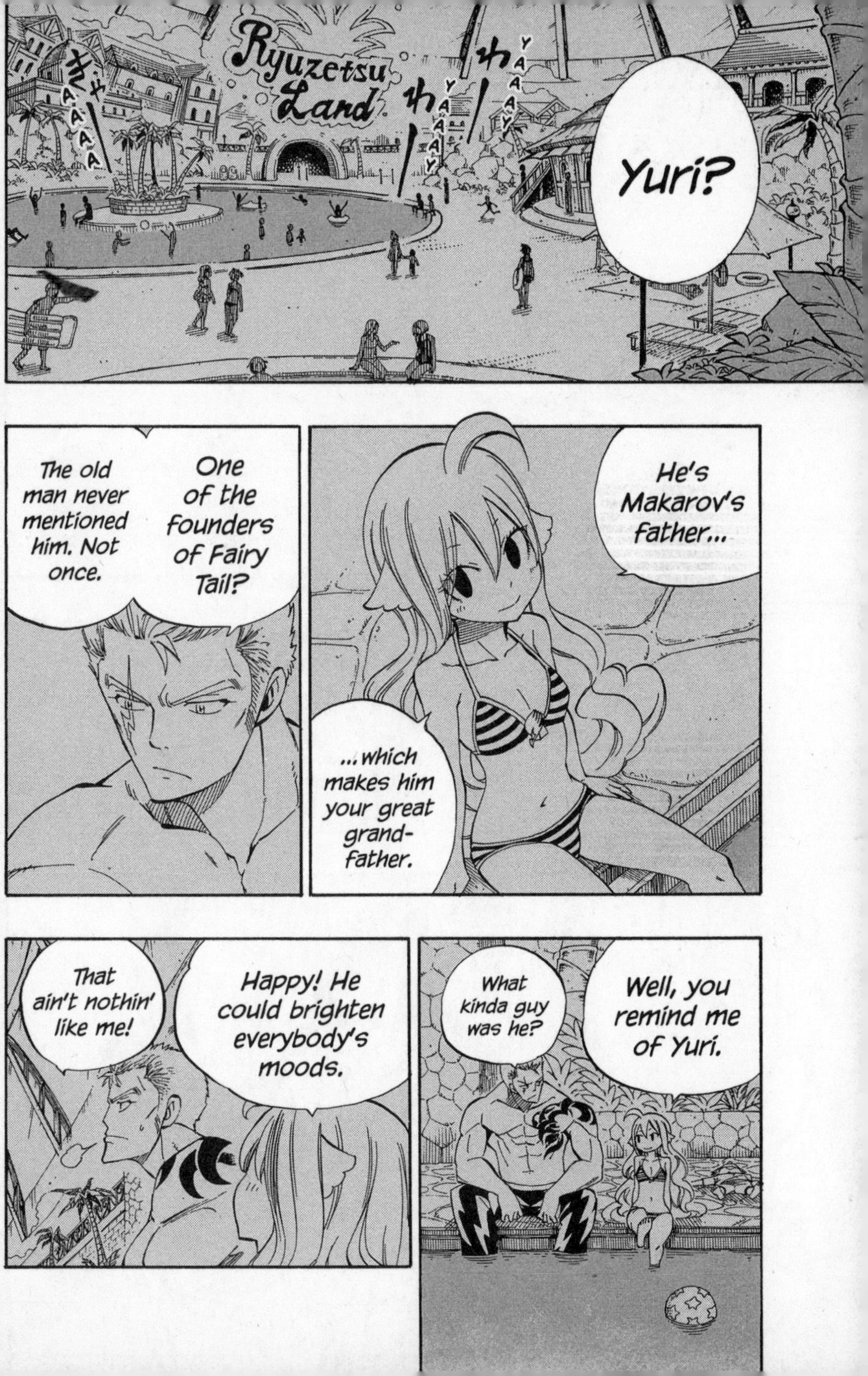
Ryuzetsu Land
YAAAY
Yuri?
He's Makarov's father...
...which makes him your great grand-father.
One of the founders of Fairy Tail?
The old man never mentioned him. Not once.
Well, you remind me of Yuri.
What kinda guy was he?
Happy! He could brighten everybody's moods.
That ain't nothin' like me!

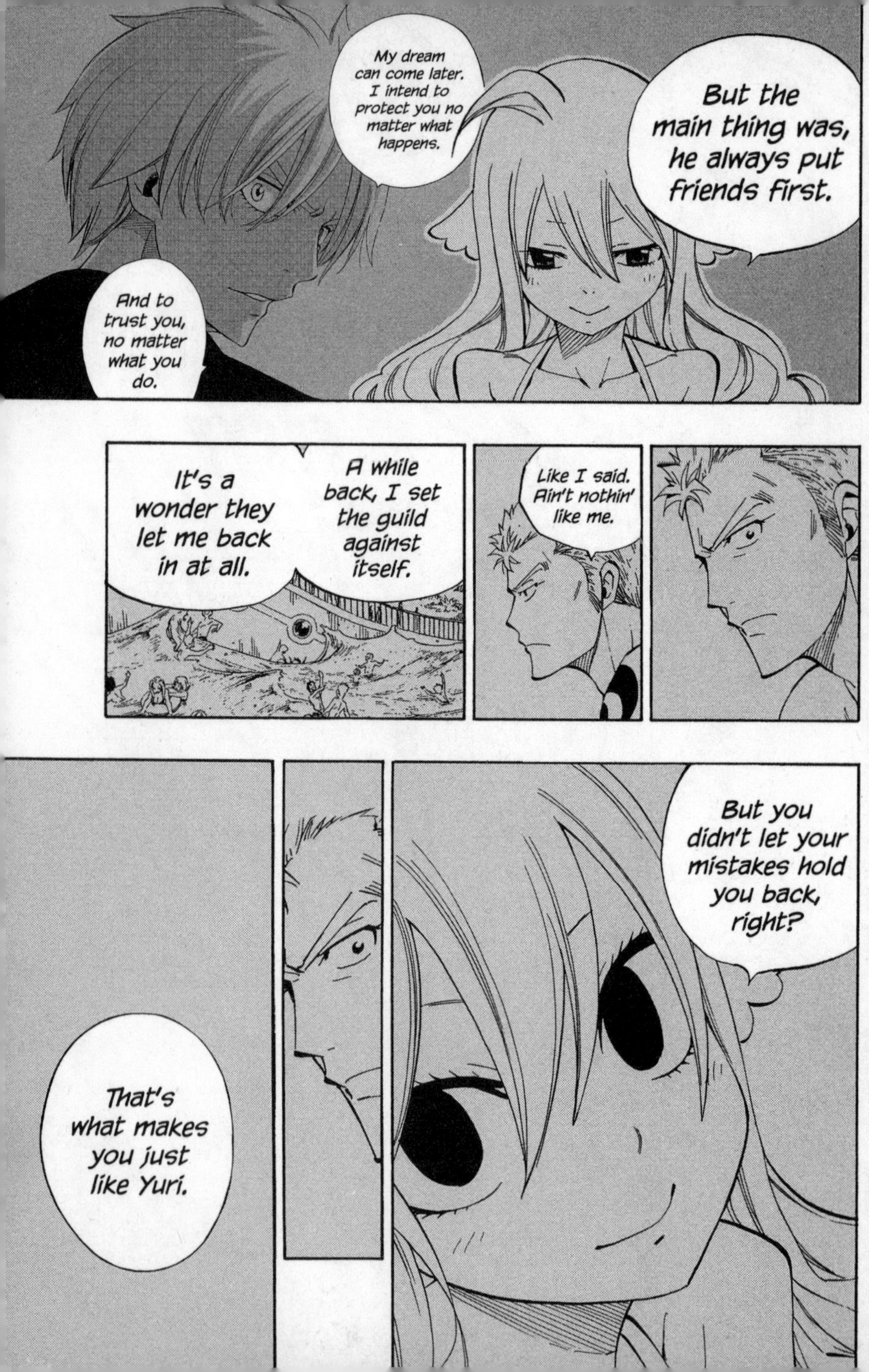
But the main thing was, he always put friends first.
My dream can come later. I intend to protect you no matter what happens.
And to trust you, no matter what you do.
Like I said. Ain't nothin' like me.
A while back, I set the guild against itself.
It's a wonder they let me back in at all.
But you didn't let your mistakes hold you back, right?
That's what makes you just like Yuri.

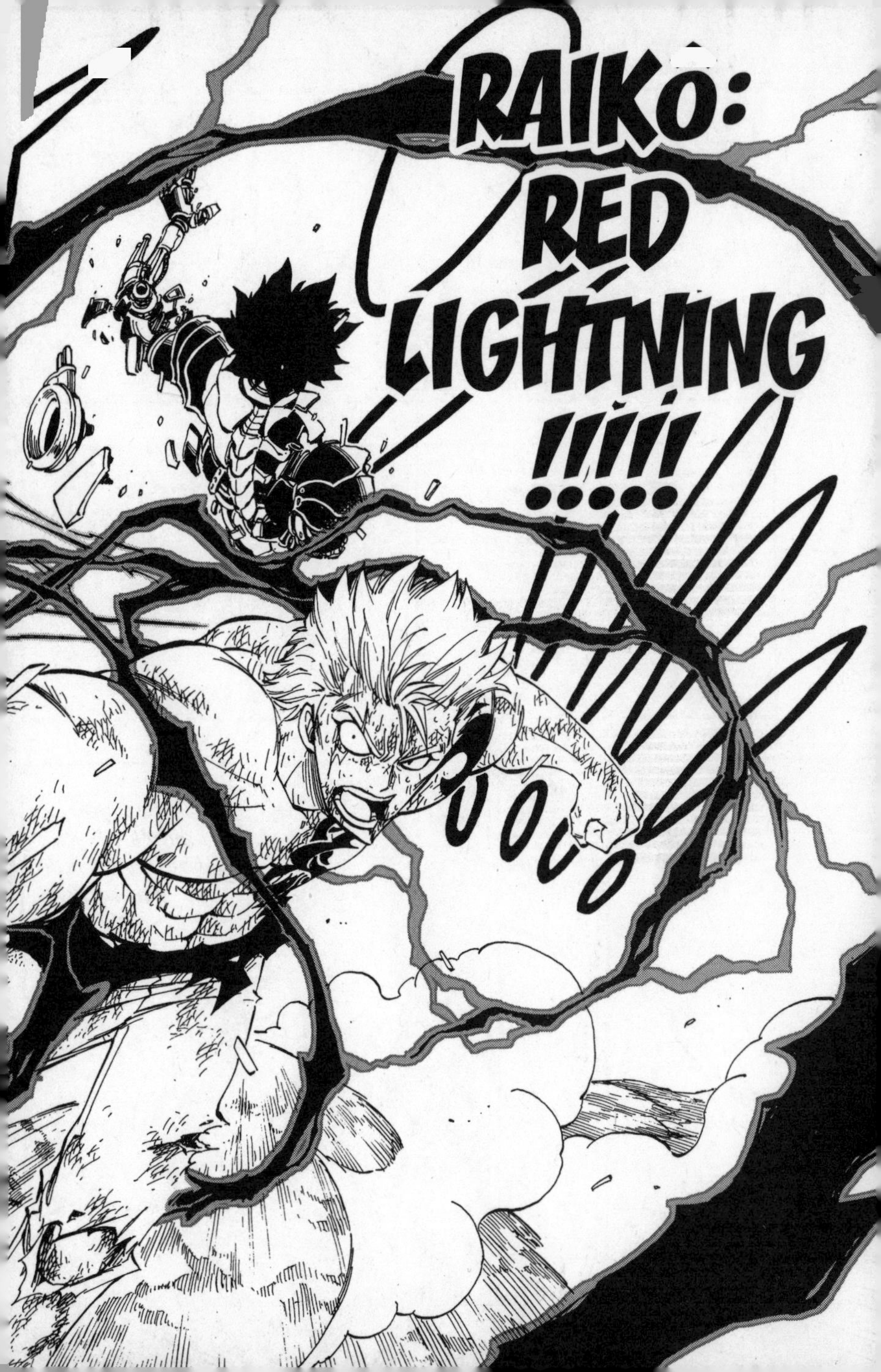
RAIKO: RED LIGHTNING !!!!!!

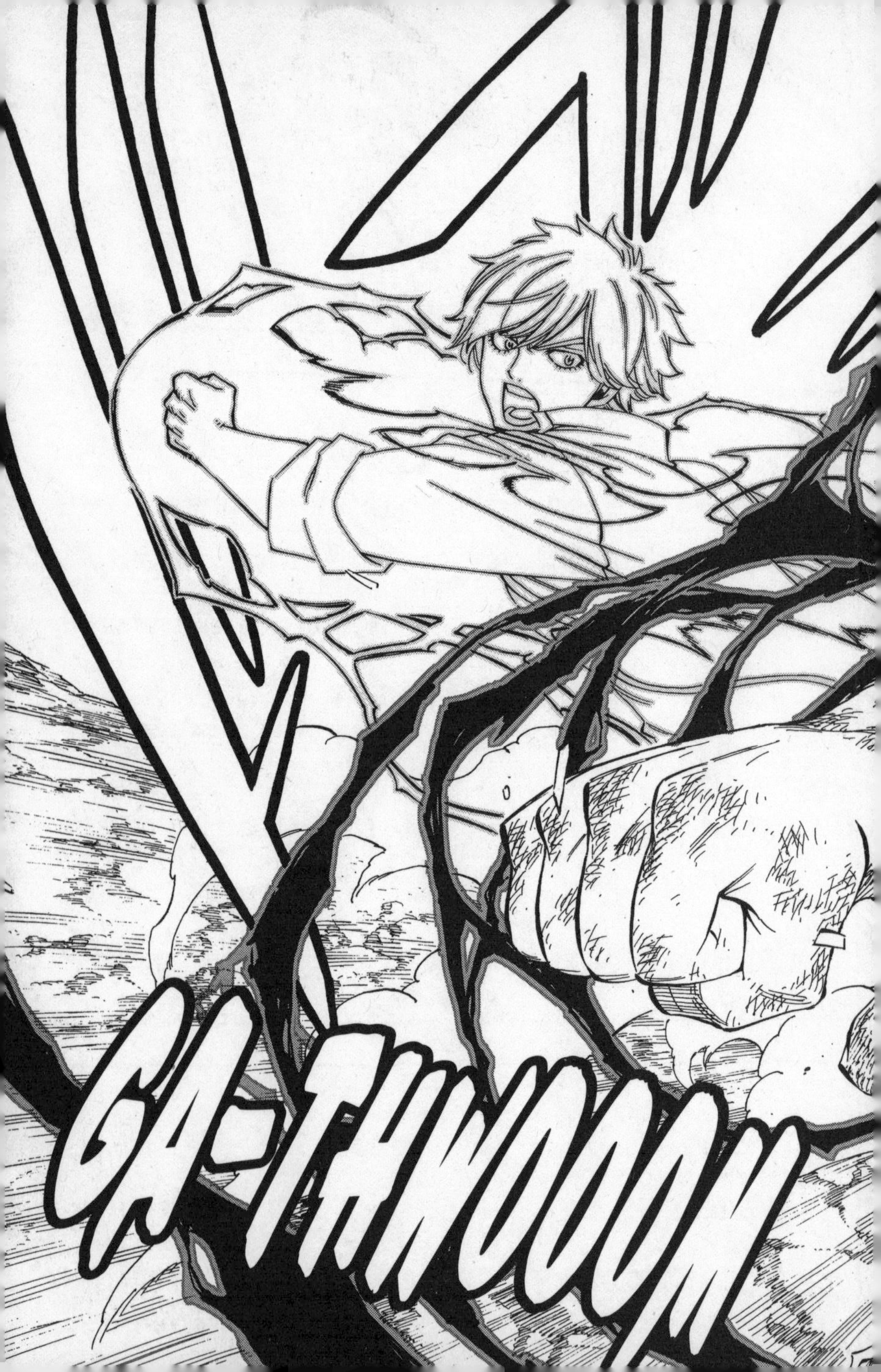
GA-THWOOOM

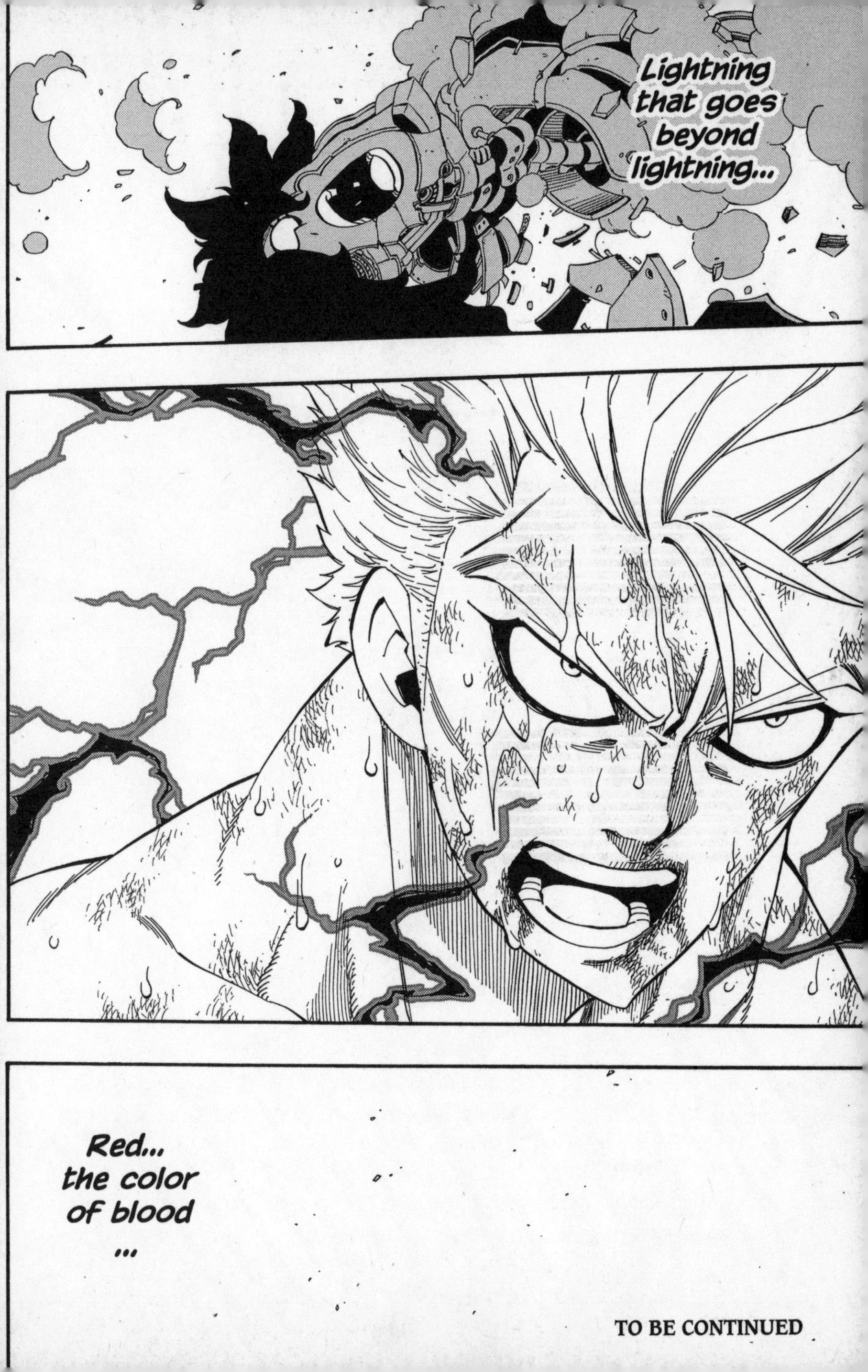
Lightning that goes beyond lightning...
Red... the color of blood ...
TO BE CONTINUED

あとがき

Afterword

When you spend a long time in this industry, it's surprising just how many things there are that I'd like to talk about but just can't. Obviously, I can't talk about what's to come in the story and other company secrets. But there's also upcoming release info, and details of the product, collaborations with others, and info on the anime. Aside from that, I also hear some gossip about other manga artists or editors, and that isn't something I'd pass on to others anyway.

Whenever I'm told not to say something, I never ever say it. But sometimes I think about it from the point of view of the people producing the work and wonder, "Maybe it'd be good timing to announce it soon..." or "I feel like it'd be okay to at least say that part, right?"

If you're wondering why I'm writing this, it's because I've got something I'm bursting to tell people about, but just can't! I know it isn't fair to only touch on it like this, but the final decision is that I can't. But man, do I want to talk about it!

Having this burning urge to say something can seem like it would be stressful, but you'd be surprised to know that that's not really the case. I do my best not to talk about something that has to stay secret, but as time goes on, I have a tendency to forget about the thing that's supposed to be secret! (Laughs) Then, when the item is about to go on sale or when the collaboration is announced, I'm often like, "Oh, yeah, **that**!" And with all things Fairy Tail, there are so many new items going on sale or new collaborations (and I'm really grateful to them all!) that I sometimes just can't keep them all in my head.

Recently, I've even begun to forget the release dates of my own graphic novels, and I end up remembering only because other authors tweet that they have their books coming out on the same day or because fans tweet that they bought the book. Actually, I want to talk about the new graphic novel as soon as I've drawn the cover, and say to everybody, "Here's the cover for the next volume!" But you can only publicly show the cover just before the release date and sometimes, by that point, I'm already coloring the cover for the next volume. So I end up forgetting about the previous one!

FROM HIRO MASHIMA

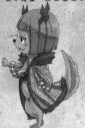

In Japan, this volume, Vol. 55, has both a normal version and a special OAD (original animation DVD) version selling at the same time.

It's been a long time since the last OAD, and we really put a lot of love and effort into it. I hope those who bought the special edition enjoy the anime!

The image above has absolutely nothing to do with the main story, but lately I've just been overwhelmed with how cute Brandish is, so I couldn't help myself! I hope I can get her into the main story even more!

Original Jacket Design: Hisao Ogawa

Translation Notes:

Japanese is a difficult language and translation is often more art than science. For your edification and reading pleasure, here are notes on some of the places where we could have gone in a different direction with our translation of the work, or where a Japanese cultural reference is used.

Page 35, Bloodman
In previous volumes, Bloodman was mistranslated as Bradman. We apologize for any confusion.

Page 45, Tenjin no Boreas
Boreas is the name of the Greek God of the North Wind.

Page 165, Magic Confinement fusion
Magic confinement fusion is a play on the concept of magnetic confinement fusion, a process in which fusion reactions for nuclear fusion-based power generation happen within a magnetic field. For nuclear fusion to happen, it needs to be confined and heated until it becomes plasma. The plasma can be held within a magnetic field as the fusion takes place. In this case, it is magic holding the plasma, or to put it in much simpler terms, Wall is about to generate a whole lot of power.

Page 184, Ryuzetsu Land
There is a plant related to the American "century plant" called "Ryûzetsuran" in Japanese. It's a desert plant that lives for quite a long time (although not a century, as its English name implies)—it can live up to some thirty years. Using Japanese pronunciation, "ran" and "land" sound almost identical, so the name of this water park or spa is a play on the name of the plant

Page 186, Raikô
Raikô is the Japanese word for the compound called mercury fulminate, an explosive that is used these days as a means to trigger other explosives. In the past, it was used to replace flint in muzzle-loading firearms, and later, when they started making ammunition that contained its own gunpowder, mercury fulminate was one of the primers they used to fire the bullets (which was later replaced with more efficient compounds).

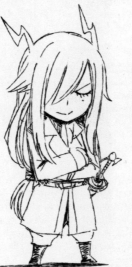

Tsk, tsk.

FAIRY TAIL

フェアリーテイル

55

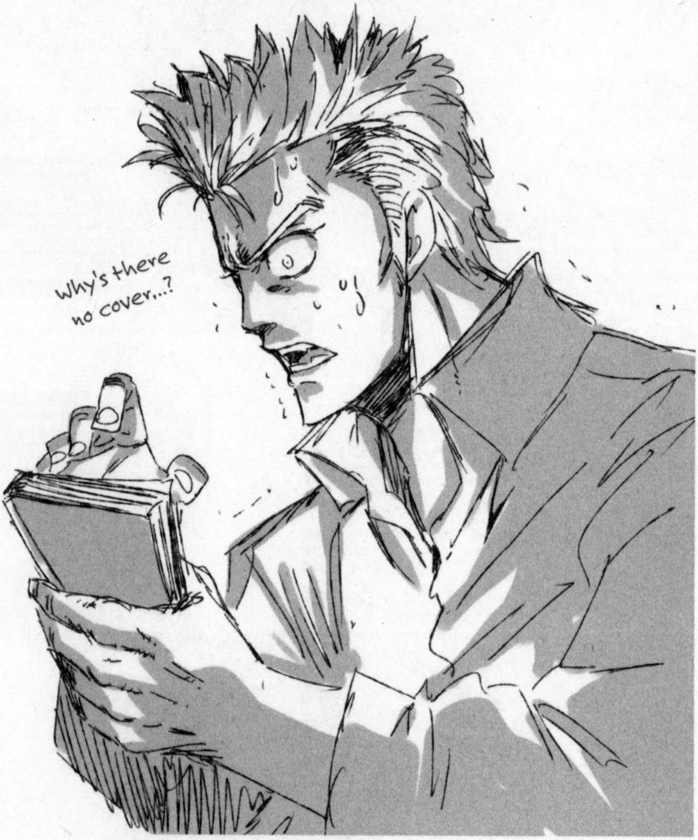
Why's there no cover...?

HIRO 真島ヒロ MASHIMA

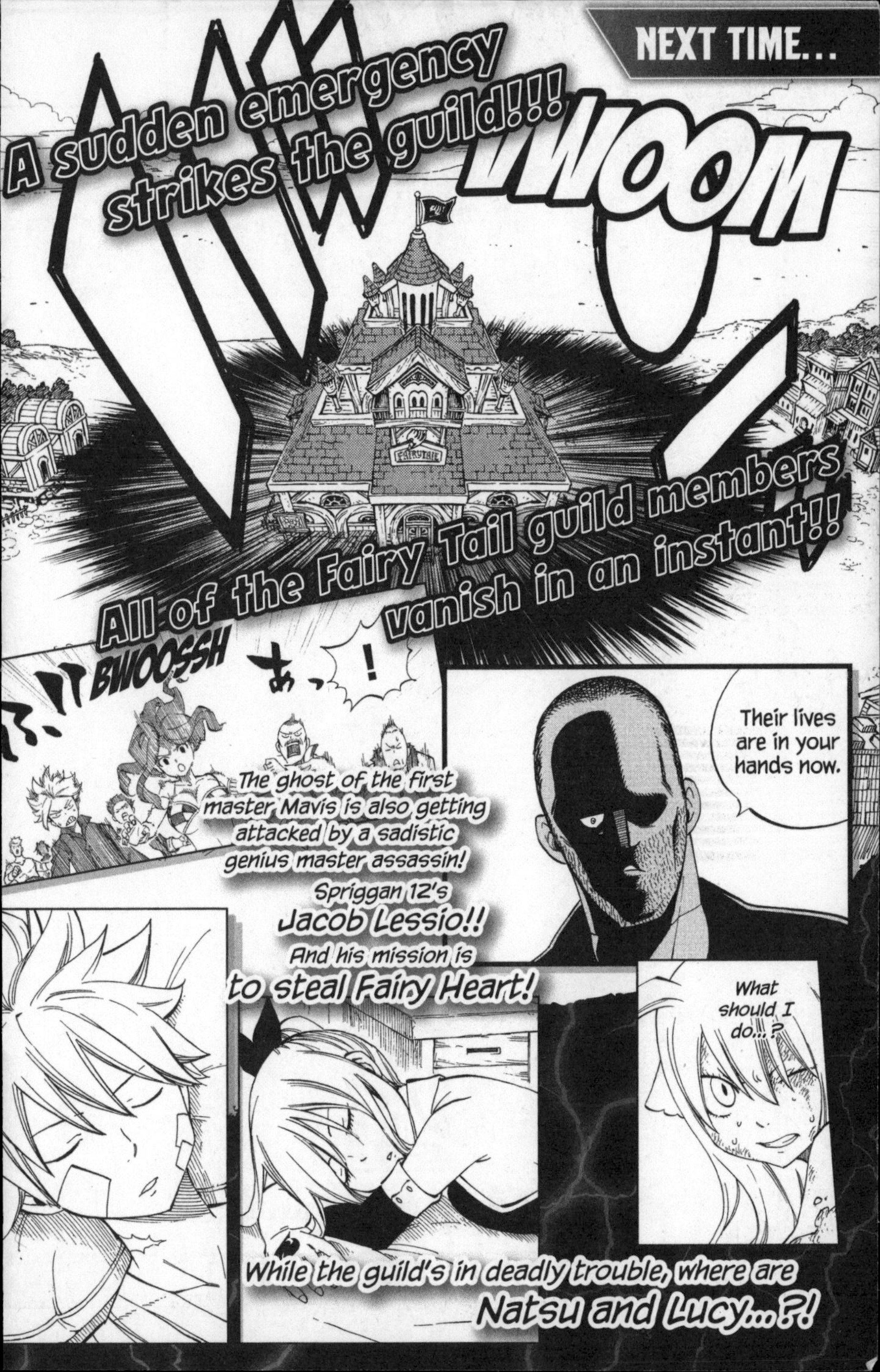
NEXT TIME...
A sudden emergency strikes the guild!!!
VWOOOM
All of the Fairy Tail guild members vanish in an instant!!
Their lives are in your hands now.
BWOOSSH
あっ
!
The ghost of the first master Mavis is also getting attacked by a sadistic genius master assassin!
Spriggan 12's Jacob Lessio!!
And his mission is to steal Fairy Heart!
What should I do...?
While the guild's in deadly trouble, where are Natsu and Lucy...?!

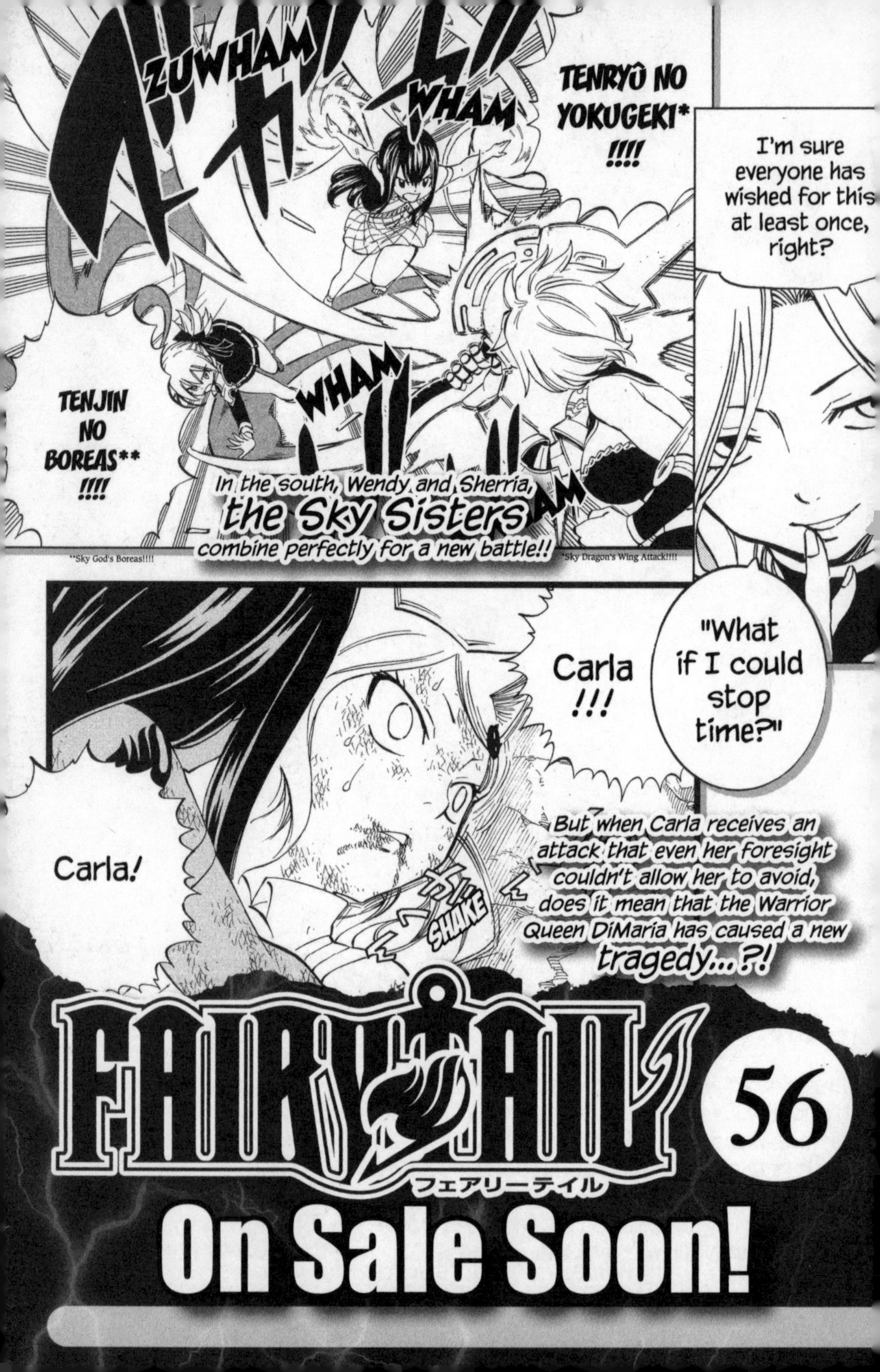
I'm sure everyone has wished for this at least once, right?
"What if I could stop time?"
TENRYÛ NO YOKUGEKI* !!!!
WHAM
ZUWHAM
WHAM
TENJIN NO BOREAS** !!!!
In the south, Wendy and Sherria, the Sky Sisters combine perfectly for a new battle!!
*Sky Dragon's Wing Attack!!!!
**Sky God's Boreas!!!!
Carla !!!
Carla!
SHAKE
But when Carla receives an attack that even her foresight couldn't allow her to avoid, does it mean that the Warrior Queen DiMaria has caused a new tragedy...?!

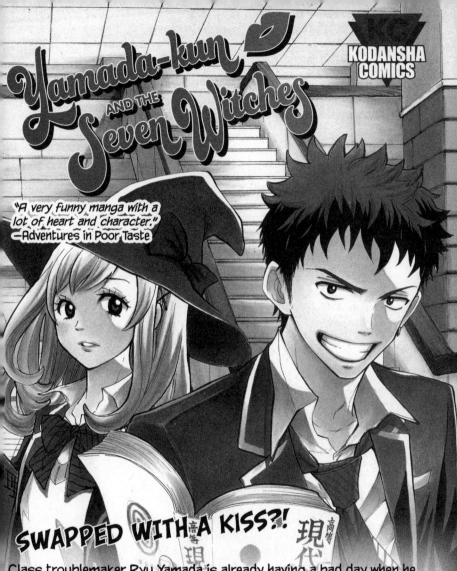

Yamada-kun AND THE Seven Witches

"A very funny manga with a lot of heart and character."
—Adventures in Poor Taste

SWAPPED WITH A KISS?!

Class troublemaker Ryu Yamada is already having a bad day when he stumbles down a staircase along with star student Urara Shiraishi. When he wakes up, he realizes they have switched bodies—and that Ryu has the power to trade places with anyone just by kissing them! Ryu and Urara take full advantage of the situation to improve their lives, but with such an oddly amazing power, just how long will they be able to keep their secret under wraps?

Available now in print and digitally!

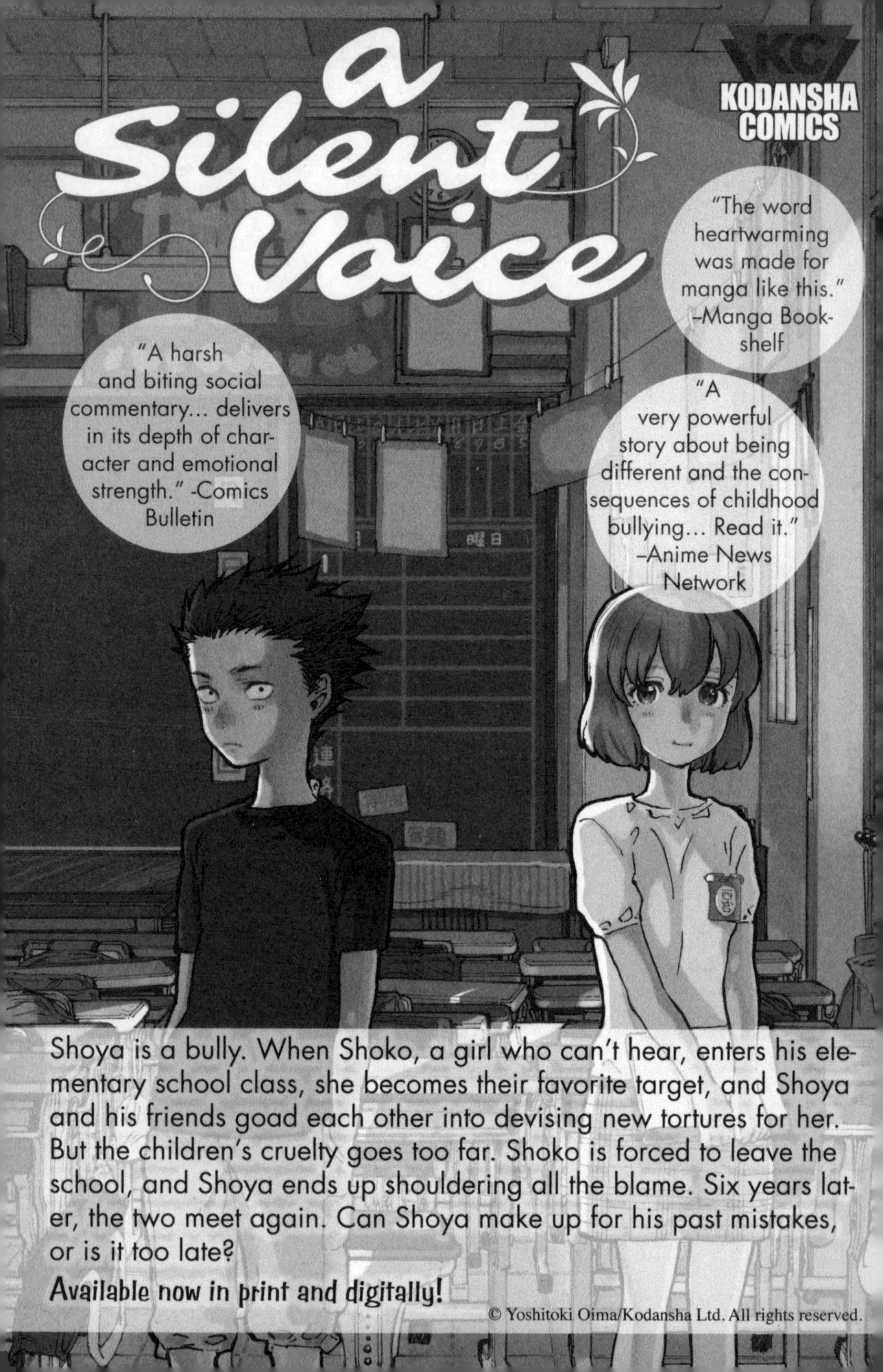
KC
KODANSHA COMICS
a Silent Voice
"A harsh and biting social commentary... delivers in its depth of character and emotional strength." -Comics Bulletin
"The word heartwarming was made for manga like this." –Manga Bookshelf
"A very powerful story about being different and the consequences of childhood bullying... Read it." –Anime News Network
Shoya is a bully. When Shoko, a girl who can't hear, enters his elementary school class, she becomes their favorite target, and Shoya and his friends goad each other into devising new tortures for her. But the children's cruelty goes too far. Shoko is forced to leave the school, and Shoya ends up shouldering all the blame. Six years later, the two meet again. Can Shoya make up for his past mistakes, or is it too late?
Available now in print and digitally!
© Yoshitoki Oima/Kodansha Ltd. All rights reserved.

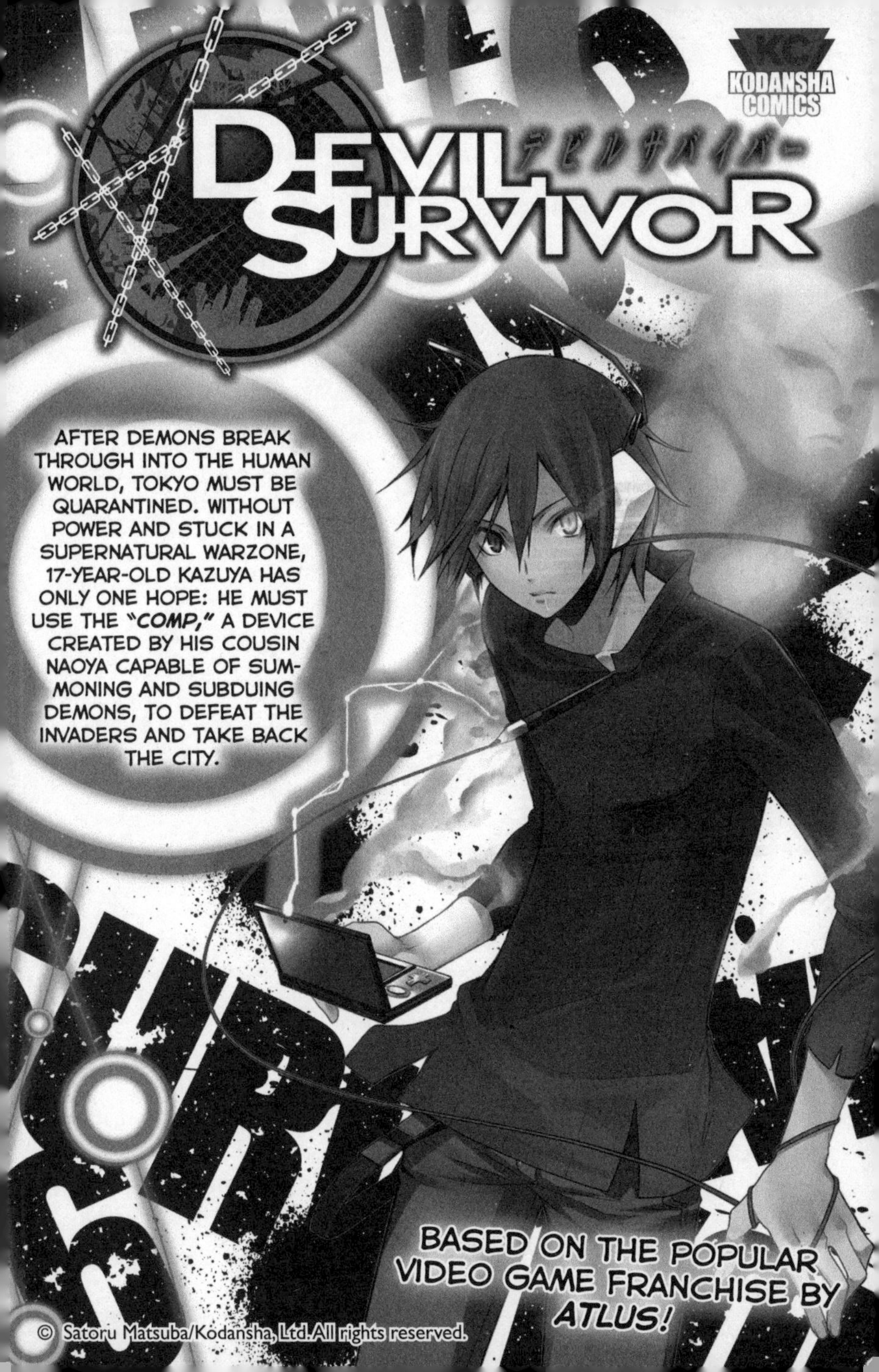
KC
KODANSHA COMICS
DEVIL SURVIVOR
デビルサバイバー
AFTER DEMONS BREAK THROUGH INTO THE HUMAN WORLD, TOKYO MUST BE QUARANTINED. WITHOUT POWER AND STUCK IN A SUPERNATURAL WARZONE, 17-YEAR-OLD KAZUYA HAS ONLY ONE HOPE: HE MUST USE THE "COMP," A DEVICE CREATED BY HIS COUSIN NAOYA CAPABLE OF SUMMONING AND SUBDUING DEMONS, TO DEFEAT THE INVADERS AND TAKE BACK THE CITY.
BASED ON THE POPULAR VIDEO GAME FRANCHISE BY ATLUS!
© Satoru Matsuba/Kodansha, Ltd. All rights reserved.

Fairy Tail volume 55 is a work of fiction. Names, characters, places, and incidents are the products of the author's imagination or are used fictitiously. Any resemblance to actual events, locales, or persons, living or dead, is entirely coincidental.

A Kodansha Comics Trade Paperback Original.

Published in the United States by Kodansha Comics, an imprint of Kodansha USA Publishing, LLC, New York.

Publication rights for this English edition arranged through Kodansha Ltd., Tokyo.

First published in Japan in 2016 by Kodansha Ltd., Tokyo
ISBN 978-1-63236-262-9

Printed in the United States of America.

www.kodanshacomics.com

9 8 7 6 5 4 3 2 1

Translation: William Flanagan
Lettering: AndWorld Design
Editing: Haruko Hashimoto
Kodansha Comics edition cover design by Phil Balsman

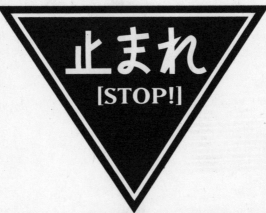

You're going the wrong way!

Manga is a completely different type of reading experience.

To start at the beginning, go to the end!

That's right! Authentic manga is read the traditional Japanese way—from right to left, exactly the opposite of how American books are read. It's easy to follow: Just go to the other end of the book and read each page—and each panel—from right side to left side, starting at the top right. Now you're experiencing manga as it was meant to be!